ENCYCLOPEDIA OF WORLD TERRORISM

VOLUME 1

ENCYCLOPEDIA OF
WORLD TERRORISM

VOLUME
1

Sharpe
Reference

An imprint of M.E. Sharpe, INC.

1997 Library Reference Edition published by Sharpe Reference
Sharpe Reference is an imprint of *M.E. Sharpe*, Inc.

M.E. Sharpe, Inc.
80 Business Park Drive
Armonk, NY 10504

Produced by Brown Partworks Ltd.

Library of Congress Cataloging-in-Publication Data

Encyclopedia of world terrorism / Martha Crenshaw, John Pimlott, editors
p. cm.
Includes bibliographical references and index.
ISBN 1-56324-806-9 (alk. paper)
1. Terrorism. 2. Terrorism—History—20th century.
I. Crenshaw, Martha. II. Pimlott, John.
HV6431.E53 1996
303.6'25'0904—dc20
96-9913
CIP

Printed and bound in the United States.

The paper used in this publication meets the minimum requirements of the
American National Standard for Information Sciences—
Permanence of Paper for Printed Library Materials,
ANSI Z 39.48-1984.

VOLUME 1 CONTENTS

VOLUME 2 CONTENTS

VOLUME 3 CONTENTS

About This Set

Terrorism is a phenomenon that effects many people in the modern world. Terrorists' targeting of innocent victims in order to influence some other group such as a government means that nobody can be totally assured that the shadow of terrorist violence will never darken their lives. However, given that one person's terrorist is another person's freedom fighter, what precisely is *terrorism*? Are covert state-sponsored death squads eliminating political enemies any less terrorists than a revolutionary group assassinating police chiefs? The complex issues of what precisely is *terrorism* must be addressed before the campaigns of modern terrorists can be explored.

Introduction To The ENCYCLOPEDIA OF WORLD TERRORISM

Terrorism – defined as the indiscriminate use of force to achieve political aims – is one of the major problems facing the world as the twentieth century closes. The problem exists on various levels, but can be boiled down to the fact that an individual, acting within a committed terrorist organization, is very difficult to stop when prepared to kill in a random manner.

There have been acts of terror throughout history, but in the late twentieth century, a set of events came together that created a new military target: the civilian who had no link to the front line, nor, indeed, any conscious link to the war-making capacity of a nation. The key period in which this change came about was during World War II. Partly, the civilian was brought into the equation by the racial policies of the German Nazis, who tried to exterminate whole races. German racial policies were mirrored (although at a less extreme level) by Japanese atrocities in the Far East. In both these cases, however, non-combatants, women, and children were killed for reasons that had little or nothing to do with military necessity.

A further aspect of World War II that brought the innocent civilian directly into the firing line was the aerial bombing of population centers. The arguments for bombing German cities and for such acts as the dropping of the atom bombs on Japan have been much rehearsed. There is no doubt, however, that in many raids, the target was the civilian population, in the full knowledge that children too small to speak, never mind express a political opinion, would be killed, the intention being to so intimidate the ordinary people that they would no longer support their country's war effort.

This legacy of the targeting of civilians, and of a war whose horror had surpassed all others in history, was then built upon during the two decades after 1945 by a series of nationalist campaigns against the colonial powers. From Malaya to Algeria and from southern Africa to Cyprus, terrorism became inextricably mixed into guerrilla campaigns across the developing world. For the future, the most menacing campaign was that fought in the 1940s in Palestine by Jewish terrorists against British rulers and the Palestinian Arabs.

The result of these campaigns was that terrorism became an accepted tactic of the insurgent, and has remained so ever since. Insurgencies throughout the developing world, such as in Sri Lanka during the 1990s, made ample use of terror tactics. They have also affected the first world: IRA terrorists in Northern Ireland became one of the world's most successful terrorist groups.

Building on this acceptance of terror, the next wave of terrorism to strike the world came in the late 1960s and 1970s, when Palestinian organizations, trying to overthrow the state of Israel, struck at vulnerable international targets such as airliners. The Palestinian groups became closely associated with various Arab states that supported their aims. The international dimension of terrorism has continued up to the present day, although it has diminished a little since the 1993 Arab-Israeli agreement over the establishment of a Palestinian authority in the Occupied Territories.

At the time that the Palestinian terrorist campaigns were taking off, there was also a wave of revolutionary insurgency using terrorism in many Latin American states, often employing the example of Castro's success in Cuba as a model. These terrorist campaigns were failures, but in many of them, the state used a punitive form of counterterror that also led to many innocent deaths.

Palestinian terrorist groups were also closely associated with European terrorist organizations that wanted to change their society by using terrorist methods. This type of terror has had little success in the developed world, but has been attractive to many groups of malcontents, from those wanting to change society root and branch (such as the Unabomber in the U.S.) to those wishing to affect society's attitude to a single issue like abortion.

The final wave of terrorism that has affected the world is one that has developed in the past 20 years. This is terrorism associated with religious fundamentalism in the Islamic world. It originally took a lead from Iran, where the Ayatollah Khomeini established a revolutionary theocracy in 1979, and has grown to be a severe threat over much of the Middle East, partly because fundamentalist terrorists are often prepared to die during a terrorist act – to act as suicide bombers.

Dealing with these large waves of terrorism – terror connected with World War II, nationalist campaigns to establish new nation states, Palestinian terror against Israel, social revolutionaries in the developed world and Latin America, and religious fundamentalist terrorism – presents four major problems. The first is philosophical. There are few states in the world today that have not, in the past 60 years, been involved in activities in which civilians have been targeted in some kind of terror campaign. Many states have engaged directly in terrorist acts; others have sponsored or aided terrorist groups. It is certainly true that many states would prefer not to have taken steps they considered necessary, but this does not alter the fact that terrorizing the more or less innocent civilian has become a staple of modern warfare.

The second problem is practical. Modern democratic society is extremely vulnerable to terrorism. There are immensely destructive weapons readily available to terrorists, including nerve agents. The networks of modern society – communications vehicles such as aircraft or buses, or urban concentrations of population within business districts and schools – are good targets, while modern methods of transport allow terrorists to move vast distances to strike. Terrorists find the freedom of working within a democracy much easier than trying to work within an autocracy. The restrictions available to autocratic governments mean that they can usually cope with terrorism by instigating a counterterrorist campaign that uses terror itself. Democracies can rarely act in such a manner, however, without damaging the foundations of their very being.

The third problem is political. Terrorists are rarely isolated madmen. Instead, they are usually members of a team that firmly believes in the righteousness of a cause – a cause for which the team is prepared to kill. As long as such causes continue to exist, whether they be the rights of the Kurds to self-determination, or the desire for a fundamentalist Islamic government in Algeria, then the possibility of terrorism of some kind will always be present. And in the modern world, there are many such causes.

The fourth problem lies in the apparent success of terrorism. Jewish Irgun terrorists forced many Palestinian Arabs to flee after the massacre at Deir Yassin in 1948, and made a powerful contribution to the establishment of the state of Israel. Hizb'allah terrorist suicide bombers forced Israeli and international troops from Lebanon in the 1980s. "Ethnic cleansing" moved whole populations in the former Yugoslavia in the 1990s.

The 1993 agreement between Israel and the Palestine Liberation Organization seemed to have reduced world terrorist problems somewhat by easing the situation in the Middle East. Then, in 1996, an outbreak of bombings, in particular a spate of attacks against the U.S., catapulted terrorism to the top of the political agenda. In June, a massive truck bomb went off at an American airbase in Dhahran, in Saudi Arabia, killing 19 U.S. servicemen. A month later, at the Atlanta Olympic Games, a person or persons unknown at the time of writing exploded a bomb in Centennial Park, causing carnage at a concert. Meanwhile, in Europe the Basque separatists of ETA were once again active.

The commitment needed to become a terrorist is usually not taken on lightly. If individuals feel that their cause or their grievance has a chance of being carried through or remedied without terrorism, then they will usually seek the easier, and less dangerous, road. Yet there is no doubt that terrorism is a prominent part of the world today, and will continue to present a very considerable threat for the foreseeable future. ■

JOHN PIMLOTT

THE PROBLEMS OF DEFINING TERRORISM

Terrorism is used to describe different things by different people. As a label for acts of violence, it reflects negatively on those who are labeled as terrorists. In this sense, the term *terrorist* is comparable to other insulting terms in the political vocabulary, such as racist, fascist, or imperialist.

Used carelessly, such terms often lose their original meanings and become part of the rhetoric of insults exchanged between political opponents. If one side in a dispute can characterize the enemy in a negative way, and so win public opinion over to their point of view, they will not hesitate to do so. Hence the saying: "One man's terrorist is another man's freedom fighter."

While the use of a word like *terrorism*, as a means of political insult is now widespread practice, it is highly unsatisfactory from both a moral and a legal point of view. Language ought to be a tool for careful thinking, not an instrument of propaganda. It is important to arrive at a clear definition of terrorism. Only then can we be certain of what is meant by the word, and then design laws to punish the terrorists.

THE ORIGIN OF THE TERM

By looking at the uses of the term *terrorism*, and at the acts of violence attributed to individual terrorists, terrorist groups, and terrorist organizations, it should

---

S U M M A R Y

● From its origins as a specific policy in the French Revolution, the concept of terrorism has gradually changed.

● The problems of distinguishing between a terrorist act and criminal act is complicated by the viewpoint of the observer.

● The clearer the definition of terrorism, the easier it is to legislate against it.

---

be possible to find a precise definition. It is useful to examine the historical origin of the word *terrorism*, before moving on to a clarification of its modern meaning, and to place acts of terrorism in the broader context of political actions and legal practice.

"The purpose of terrorism is to produce terror," dryly noted Vladimir Lenin, the Russian communist leader responsible for the "Red Terror" of 1917-21. Terrorists produce, or aim to produce, terror – extreme fear – among their opponents. Although the word *terror* is of Latin origin (from *terrere*, to frighten), it entered modern Western vocabularies only in the fourteenth century through the French language. The first English usage was recorded in 1528. The basic mechanism of terror was captured in an ancient Chinese proverb: "Kill one, frighten ten thousand."

TERROR – AN INSTRUMENT OF GOVERNMENT

A clearly political meaning was given to the word during the French Revolution. In 1793, France's revolutionary government found itself threatened by aristocratic emigrants who conspired with foreign rulers to invade the country. At the same time, treason at home in support of this reactionary move was suspected. The French legislative, the National Convention – led by a radical faction, the Jacobins, under Maximilien Robespierre – adopted a policy of terror on August 30, 1793, ordering mass executions of suspected traitors.

The newspaper *Courier de l'Égalité* approved: "It is necessary that the terror caused by the guillotine spreads in all of France and brings to justice all the traitors. There is no other means to inspire this terror that will consolidate the Revolution. The Jacobin club has massively adopted this measure – a universal enthusiasm has manifested itself following this order, which will probably mark one of the greatest periods of our history." Originally conceived as a tool to combat subversion by those who supported the former

---

Hulton Getty Picture Collection

Lenin, instigator of the "Red Terror" in Russia, addresses a crowd in 1917.

king and the monarchy, the Terror soon began to make victims of those who had originally been supporters of the revolution and the republic established after the downfall of the monarchy. Former allies of the Jacobins perished in the wave of executions. The moderate "Indulgents" under Georges Danton and the extremist left-wing "Hébertists" both fell victim to Robespierre's campaign. Altogether, at least 300,000 people were arrested during the Terror (August 30, 1793–July 27, 1794). Of these, 17,000 were officially executed, but many other people died in prison, often without a trial.

Those who had originally supported the harsh measures proposed by Robespierre against counter-revolutionaries began to fear for their own lives and conspired to overthrow him. They could not accuse him of *terreur* (terror) because they themselves had earlier declared terror to be a legitimate instrument of government. Therefore, they accused Robespierre of *terrorisme* (terrorism), a word that suggested illegal conduct. For this, Robespierre and his associates were guillotined on July 17 and 28, 1794. The political pendulum had finally swung back and now the agents and partisans of the revolutionary tribunals were termed *terrorists* and thrown into prison.

TERROR AS PROPAGANDA BY THE DEED

The term *terrorism* spread fast throughout Europe, into Russia, and even into India. As it spread, the word changed its meaning. By the late nineteenth century, the term *terrorist*, originally used for those who made unjust mass arrests in the name of the state, became more strongly associated with anti-state violence. The violent French and Russian anarchists of the 1880s and 1890s were the main groups responsible for this shift in meaning.

If the guillotine that beheaded enemies of the revolution had been the symbol of state terror at the end of the eighteenth century, the bomb that exploded in the midst of the political elite became the hallmark of nineteenth-century terrorism. The bomb and the assassin's pistol were used for two purposes. The so-called "exemplary deed" directed at government ministers, parliamentarians, and judicial officers was intended to spread terror among state officials. Such violent acts, especially for the Russian terrorists of the period, were also part of a program to bring about political change. The Russian anarchists' goal was to arouse the masses by acts of violence against targets with a high symbolic value, such as police chiefs or members of the royal family.

Terrorist violence used in this way becomes a means of communication. "Propaganda by the deed" was how nineteenth-century revolutionaries, like the

The guillotine, the main instrument of the Terror of 1793-94, as used by French revolutionaries in Paris.

German John Most, described the value of terrorism as a form of communication. Both aims of terrorist murder were established in the late nineteenth century. They were later picked up by post-1945 terrorist groups and remain in use today.

THE MEANINGS OF TERROR AND TERRORISM
The meaning of the words *terror* and *terrorism* have altered only slightly since the late nineteenth century, but the change is significant. In the 1890 edition of *Webster's International Dictionary*, the word *terror* is defined as "Extreme fear, fear that agitates body and mind, violent dread; fright." As a second meaning Webster's lists "that which excites dread; a cause of extreme fear." Today, *Webster's New Twentieth Century Dictionary* covers essentially the same meanings, listing: "1. intense fear; 2. a person or thing that causes intense fear;" but has the important

additions: "3. a period characterized by political executions, as during the French Revolution; 4. a program of terrorism or a party, group, etc. resorting to this."

For *terrorism*, the modern *Webster's* dictionary offers the following: "1. a terrorizing; use of terror and violence to intimidate, subjugate, etc. especially as a political weapon or policy; 2. intimidation and subjugation so produced." There is some dispute among scholars of the precise meaning of adding the suffix -*ism* to the word *terror* to produce the word *terrorism*. The -*ism* suffix is sometimes added to a word to refer to the theoretical level of a political doctrine. Familiar examples of this include the conversion of *liberal* to *liberalism* and *social* to *socialism*. A more practical use of the suffix is where it refers to a manner of acting or an attitude, such as when *fanatic* becomes *fanaticism*. Both meanings have been applied to the word terrorism. While a few experts attribute a doctrinal quality to terrorism, far more define it as a manner of acting or as a method of action.

However, the historical root of the -*ism* suffix in *terrorism* refers to neither of these two possibilities. It originated in the excessive abuse of violence under the Terror of the French Revolution. Because there have been numerous other reigns of terror since the French Revolution, the term *terror* has become increasingly detached from this specific historical period (1793-94). It has become a generic term applied to regimes that rule by a fear caused by unjust mass arrests and arbitrary trials and executions in which the guilt of the individual matters less than the political intimidation of the populace.

THE PSYCHOLOGY OF TERRORISM
The basic purpose of terrorism is to produce terror in a target audience. A civilian population at large may be targeted, or police officers or government officials may be targeted to deter them from carrying out their duties. It is important, therefore, to look at the psychological dimension of terror. However, remarkably little of the literature on terrorism has paid much attention to terror as a state of mind. Only in the more recent literature on hostages has the experience of being terrorized received some attention.

When terrorists are able to organize a series of acts of violence into a campaign of terror, they manage to maximize fear. Repeated acts of violence make the question "Will I be next?" loom large in the minds of target audiences. The suicide-bomber attacks in Israel

THE PROBLEMS OF DEFINING TERRORISM

Rex Features/Roger Lewis

A Hamas suicide squad, photographed in a secret hideout in the Gaza Strip in 1993.

carried out by the Palestinian Hamas group in 1996 provoked exactly this response among Israelis. When the targeted population is in near-panic and confusion, the desired psychological impact has been reached.

Depending on the setting of terrorist acts, prospective victims may be shocked by numbing fear – as in a hostage situation when the deadline for an ultimatum approaches. Alternatively, those who have witnessed a shooting or bombing may panic and flee at the mere hint of a terrorist attack, to avoid becoming a victim.

NATURAL ANXIETY VERSUS TERRORISM

The fear created by terrorist acts is not the same as the chronic anxiety caused by natural disasters. Natural disasters strike with little warning, and have random effects. A pervasive atmosphere of anxiety can exist in the minds of those who live in the shadow of a volcano, near an earthquake fault, or beside a dam. But such natural terror is likely to be less intense than human-made terror, although both are responses to situations in which survival is in doubt.

More terrifying than natural terror are wartime or criminal acts, such as mass bombings or armed robbery. Here, however, terror is to some extent an unintended by-product of violence. Only when violence is used to intimidate a wider audience than those immediately affected can we speak of terrorism in its pure form.

The victim of a terrorist attack is not necessarily the same thing as the target. The choice of the victim may be almost random. A police officer may be gunned down unaware of the political situation the terrorists are fighting, while a colleague who holds anti-terrorist views is ignored. A government building administering social security payments may be bombed because it is easy to park a truck outside it in the street, even though no law enforcement activity takes place within.

These victims are chosen to reach a wider target audience that identifies in one way or another with the victim. For a single killing to have a widespread effect,

Popperfoto

Rubble in the World Trade Center after the bomb blast of February 27, 1993, which killed five people.

terrorist violence has to be attention-grabbing or in some way extraordinary. This impact can be created in a number of ways. The victim may be a particularly famous or prominent person. The method of attack may involve an unusual form of criminal ingenuity. The location of the attack may be important, or involve a maximum number of observers, such as during the Munich Olympic Games of 1972, or the 1996 Olympic Games in Atlanta. The number of potential victims may be very large, as in the case of the thousands of people affected by the 1993 World Trade Center bombing in New York. Finally, the ruthlessness of the act may be particularly striking, as was the Oklahoma bombing, which killed 15 children.

In classic terrorist assassinations – as opposed to purely criminal ones – there is a distinct difference between the target and victim. The actual victim of the violence is not the real target of this violence.

Individuals, consciously or unconsciously, often identify themselves with people who are prominent in the press or on TV. This identification may be made on the basis of shared opinions, or more superficially because of good looks or an attractive manner. In the popular imagination, these people become symbols. When these symbols are hurt, the people who hold them dear share the hurt. The symbol may be a charismatic leader who embodies the aspirations of the followers, such as the Reverend Martin Luther King, Jr. If the leader is killed, the followers are deprived of their object of identification. They experience a variety of feelings, ranging from grief and powerlessness to outrage and terror.

However, the symbolic victim does not have to be a prominent person. A terrorist attack on a building or religious ceremony, such as the Vietcong assault on the U.S. embassy in Saigon during the 1968 Tet offensive, can have even stronger effects. The identification felt by the larger audience is normally directed toward the victims. This is especially the case if the victims were in an everyday situation, such as riding on a bus. It may prompt members of the audience to think "it could have been me or my child."

The aftermath of a bomb attack on Czar Alexander II's personal train near Moscow, December 1879.

However, if the victim is perceived as a guilty person or organization – perhaps a dictator or an army of occupation – the attack is likely to produce feelings of relief among those who have suffered because of the victim. Some people might then identify with the terrorists themselves, seeing them as heroic martyrs who risk their lives to confront an evil force. Terrorism not only produces terror in an opponent, but it can also produce enthusiasm in the opposite camp, as is indicated in the quote from the *Courier de l'Égalité* earlier. This also brings us back to the saying that "one man's terrorist is another man's freedom fighter." Basques whose desire for national autonomy was denied by Spanish dictator Francisco Franco supported nationalist terrorists.

JUDGING THE TERRORISTS

People judge terrorism by making a comparison either with crimes or with warfare. Those who use comparisons with criminal acts regard terrorism as illegal. Police, for example, are authorized by law to arrest and imprison a person, but a terrorist group abducting someone and holding him or her to ransom has no such approval. The effect in both cases, however, is to deprive a person of his or her liberty. Using a comparison with warfare, on the other hand, draws on the famous statement by the Prussian officer, Karl von Clausewitz: "War is a continuation of politics by other means." A political activist who turns to terrorist violence in a struggle against an oppressive regime becomes a "freedom fighter" in a war for liberty.

However, these frameworks used by ordinary people tend to become blurred by politicians and scholars of political violence. All too often people make their choice between the war model and the crime model, not on logical grounds, but based on their own opinions of the ethnic or political dispute. For instance, a person from the same ethnic group as the government may share the view that the terrorists are criminals, while a person from the ethnic group of the terrorists may instinctively think of them as soldiers at war.

Such contrasting psychological standards do not work well in moral and intellectual terms when judging acts of violence. The reactions of the opposing extremes do not make for calm discussion. There is little or no common ground to offer room for negotiation. In a community divided by acts of terror, such as Northern Ireland, the fact remains that acts of violence are aimed at only one section of society.

FOUR VIEWS OF TERRORISM

The objectivity of any discussion of terrorism is limited by the relationship of the participants to terrorist acts. It is possible to distinguish four different groups who take a view of terrorism.

1. *Academics* attempt to take an entirely objective view. Ideally, universities offer an intellectual forum in which scholars can discuss terrorism without either being attacked by terrorists or being suspected of sympathizing with terrorists.

2. *Governments*, in contrast, are frequent victims of terrorist activity. The official view of terrorism presented by press secretaries whose statements are

colored by the knowledge that those they represent may become involved in fighting terrorism.

3. The *public* may change its opinion dramatically in response to a single incident. In open societies, its view is articulated and influenced through the media.

4. The views of the *terrorists and their sympathizers* reflect the beliefs of people who think they live under a repressive government.

Each of these four groups has a valid view.

THE ACADEMIC VIEW

When scholars look at terrorism, the distance they can keep from the conflict should allow them a more objective perspective. Academics should pursue an intellectual, but not a moral, neutrality between terrorists and victims for the purpose of investigation. The academic culture of curiosity, skepticism, and methodical inquiry can lead to a more independent, non-partisan assessment than is usually possible elsewhere.

Scholars from various universities have come close to agreement on a definition of terrorism. In 1984, an analysis was made of more than 100 existing definitions. A new one was drawn up and circulated. The comments and criticisms made on this were used to amend it until 81 percent of scholars approached could partially, or even fully, agree on it.

The resulting academic definition of terrorism was finalized in 1988. "Terrorism is an anxiety-inspiring method of repeated violent action, employed by (semi-) clandestine individual, group, or state actors, for idiosyncratic, criminal, or political reasons, whereby – in contrast to assassination – the direct targets of violence are not the main targets. The immediate human victims of violence are generally chosen randomly (targets of opportunity) or selectively (representative or symbolic targets) from a target population, and serve as message generators. Threat and violence-based communication processes between terrorist (organization), (imperiled) victims, and main targets are used to manipulate the main target (audience(s)), turning it into a target of terror, a target of demands, or a target of attention, depending on whether intimidation, coercion, or propaganda is primarily sought."

Although the definition is rather long and clumsy, the core elements are now generally accepted. Brian Jenkins, one of the pioneers of empirical research on terrorism, noted in 1992 that "a rough consensus on the meaning of terrorism is emerging without any international agreement on the precise definition." However, this consensus is more obvious among academics than among politicians and civil servants.

THE OFFICIAL VIEW

A precise but lengthy definition such as the one developed by scholars is not likely to be used by governments. Government officials tend to be clearer and harsher in their views, being actively engaged in countering terrorist activity – and being victims of it.

The British government was one of the first to attempt to draw up a legal definition that distinguishes a terrorist act from a criminal act. In 1974, the United Kingdom government concluded that: "For the purposes of the legislation, terrorism is the use of violence for political ends, and includes any use of violence for the purpose of putting the public, or any section of the public, in fear." This British definition is extremely broad and could be interpreted to include conventional war as well as limited nuclear strikes.

The 1975 European TREVI definition (named after a fountain in Rome near which European ministers of justice and the interior deliberated on terrorism) has been modeled on the British definition, except that it excludes war: "Terrorism is defined as the use, or the threatened use, by a cohesive group of persons of violence (short of warfare) to effect political aims."

The European Convention to Combat Terrorism (1977) did not use any definition of terrorism. It simply listed a number of crimes that would make those committing them liable to extradition from one country to another. However, this avoidance of the problem was no solution – as various controversies concerning extradition have made clear ever since.

In 1985, the West German Office for the Protection of the Constitution stated: "Terrorism is the enduringly conducted struggle for political goals, which are intended to be achieved by means of assaults on the life and property of other persons, especially by means of severe crimes as detailed in article 129a, section 1 of the penal code (murder, homicide, extortionist kidnapping, arson, setting off a blast by explosives) or by means of other acts of violence, which serve as preparation of such criminal acts."

The United States government has never issued a formal definition, but its government agencies have proposed unofficial definitions. The Central Intelligence Agency (CIA) was one of the first, in 1976, with this definition of international terrorism: "The threat or use of violence for political purposes when (1) such action is intended to influence the attitudes and behavior of a target group wider than its immediate victims, and (2) its ramifications transcend national boundaries (as a result, for example, of the nationality or foreign ties of its perpetrators, its locale, the identity of its institutional or human victims, its declared objectives or the mechanics of its resolution)."

Over the years, the wording of CIA definitions has fluctuated. In 1980, for instance, terrorism was defined as: "The threat or use of violence for political purposes by individuals or groups, whether acting for, or in opposition to, established governmental authority, when such actions are intended to shock or intimidate a large group wider than the immediate victims."

In 1983, the United States Army used this definition of terrorism: "The calculated use of violence or the threat of violence to attain goals political or ideological in nature. This is done through intimidation, coercion, or instilling fear."

Also in 1983, the Federal Bureau of Investigation (FBI) used this wording: "Terrorism is defined as the unlawful use of force or violence against persons or property to intimidate or coerce a government, the civilian population, or any segment thereof, in furtherance of political and social objectives."

However, the most influential American definition has turned out to be the one proposed by the U.S. Department of State in 1984. Terrorism was defined as: "Premeditated, politically motivated violence perpetrated against noncombatant targets by subnational groups or clandestine agents, usually intended to influence an audience."

One element that kept recurring in U.S. government debates on defining terrorism was whether or not attacks on U.S. military personnel could be labeled terrorist. On October 23, 1983, 241 American Marines died in their barracks in Beirut, Lebanon, when a suicide bomber in a truck crashed through the base's security perimeter. Was this terrorism or was the label *terrorism* to be reserved for attacks against noncombatant civilians?

The U.S. Department of State solved this dilemma by interpreting the term noncombatants to "include, in addition to civilians, military personnel who at the time of the incident are unarmed and/or not on duty." It also considers "as acts of terrorism attacks on military installations or on armed military personnel when a state of military hostilities does not exist at the site, such as bombings against U.S. bases in Europe, the Philippines, or elsewhere."

The many U.S. definitions show that the official discourse varies as circumstances change. At the same time, they share a large common ground.

THE PUBLIC VIEW

The image of terrorism in the media is different from those already examined. A survey among 20 editors of news agencies, television and radio stations, and the press, mostly from Western Europe, provided the following responses.

Answers to the question: "What kind of (political) violence does your medium commonly label terrorism?"

Type of Violence	Percentage of editors using label "terrorism"
Hostage-Taking	80%
Assassination	75%
Indiscriminate Bombing	75%
Kidnapping	70%
Hijacking for Coercive Bargaining	70%
Urban Guerrilla Warfare	65%
Sabotage	60%
Torture	45%
Hijacking for Escape	35%

The answers show agreement in labeling some but not other acts of violence as terrorism. While the European Convention for the Suppression of Terrorism assumes that all hijackings are acts of terrorism, editors make a distinction between a hijacking for escape and one for coercive bargaining. In this particular case, the majority of editors appear closer to the experience of the victims than do the drafters of the European Convention.

Hijacking. Imagine the situation in which an aircraft is hijacked and the hijacker asks the pilot to fly to a different country to that of the original flight destination. In this instance, the passengers will probably feel less terrorized than when the hijacker demands the liberation of 700 prisoners by a country that may not even be the home base of the airliner. In the first case, the pilot can, by altering course, escape the threat of violence. In the second case, the attitude or behavior of the pilot and crew does not matter, only the behavior of the government being blackmailed. In the second example, the term terrorist is more appropriate, the random victims cannot affect the outcome by compliance to demands.

Kidnapping. In the same way, a kidnapping can be either a terrorist act or a crime. When, out of personal greed, a kidnapper asks for money in exchange for an abducted millionaire, the situation is clearly criminal. The crime becomes terrorism when political concessions are asked from a government in return for the victim, as was the case with the German industrialist Hans-Martin Schleyer, who was abducted by the Red Army Faction in 1977.

Political murder. A similar distinction can be made when it comes to murders of politicians or civil service workers. Criminal political assassinations kill an opponent whose policies are different from those of the murderer. The aim of the murder is simply to remove a rival from the scene. The assassination of President Abraham Lincoln is an example of this kind of murder. A terrorist political assassination, on the other hand, involves more parties than the killer and victim. There is the perpetrator, who may act alone or as part of a conspiracy. Then there is the victim of the attack. Finally, there is the target audience at whom the terrorist message or demand delivered by the killing is aimed.

There is a difference, in all political terrorism, between the target of violence and the target of terror. The target of violence is the person who is attacked; the target of terror is the larger audience, whom the terrorist hopes to influence. In a terrorist murder, one victim can be easily substituted for another because the effect on the wider audience is what really counts.

Those who study terrorism distinguish between a criminal and a terrorist assassination by labeling the first "individuated" political murder and the second "de-individuated" political murder. In the case of individuated murder, the victim is chosen as an individual, usually one who knows the opponents and the potential threat before being killed. In the case of de-individuated murder, the victim is chosen because of the post he or she holds, and is often unaware of being a target. The attack is completely unexpected.

This unexpectedness is also the deeper reason why terrorism terrorizes. It does so because the victims are caught by surprise; they are generally victimized arbitrarily and without apparent provocation.

Suddenly, they and those around them are struck with terror. In this form, terror becomes a state of mind.

Terrorism intentionally produces a state of extreme anxiety among possible targets of attack, who fear becoming a victim of arbitrary violence. Terrorists exploit this emotional reaction to manipulate the wider target audience.

THE TERRORISTS' VIEW

Those involved in terrorism and those who support terrorists have a very different viewpoint from all other observers. While in the late nineteenth century many Russian anarchist and socialist bomb-throwers did not shrink from being labeled terrorists, this is not the case with contemporary terrorists and their sympathizers. They are aware of the stigma of being called terrorists and so try to avoid the label.

During a conference on terrorism organized in Leiden, in the Netherlands in 1989, graffiti was painted by a group calling themselves the "Revolutionary Commando Marinus van de Lubbe." The group was named after a Dutch Communist convicted by the Nazis of a terrorist arson attack on the German parliament in the 1930s, a crime of which he was almost certainly innocent. The Revolutionary Commando sent a letter to the local newspaper expressing solidarity with what they claimed were oppressed people in, among other places, Palestine, Ireland, Central America, and Kurdistan. They wrote: "It is clear that so-called terrorism is the logical and just resistance of the people against state terrorism, capitalism, racism, sexism, and imperialism."

Apologists for terrorism often attempt to counter moral objections by comparing their own violence with real or alleged examples of violence by their opponents. By making such a comparison, terrorists and their supporters try to place their aims and actions on the same moral level as their government enemies.

Terrorist groups also use propaganda to achieve the moral high ground in the public's view. They hope that the public or foreign governments might then put pressure on the government or organization they are fighting. To do this, they attempt to justify both themselves and their actions at the same time as putting blame on their opponents.

In World War II, the German occupation forces labeled all members of resistance groups as "terrorists"; the latter, however, thought of themselves as patriots and freedom fighters. The attempt to justify

Yugoslav partisans, labeled terrorists by German forces occupying their country in World War II.

acts whose moral standing is doubtful is part and parcel of the terrorist campaign. The father of modern state terror, Maximilien Robespierre, justified his brutal actions in his February 1794 declaration: "Terror is nothing else than immediate justice, severe, inflexible; it is therefore an outflow of virtue, it is not so much a specific principle as a consequence of the general principle of democracy applied to the most pressing needs of the motherland."

Nearly 100 years later, in 1879, the Russian terrorist underground organization, the People's Will, described terrorism in rather more instrumental terms: "Terrorist activity consists of the destruction of the most harmful persons in the government, the protection of the People's Will from spies, and the punishment of official lawlessness and violence in all the more prominent and important cases where it is manifested. The aim of such activity is to break down the prestige of government, to furnish continuous proof of the possibility of pursuing a contest with the government, to raise in that way the revolutionary spirit in the people and, finally, to form a body suited and accustomed to warfare."

Both of these definitions – by terrorists themselves – emphasize their ultimate aims rather than their tactics. Generally, terrorists try to avoid a discussion of their tactics because this would help label them as criminals; they much prefer a discussion that places their struggle in a framework of a war for political ends. When the language describing terrorism used concentrates on crime, it raises questions of legitimacy very different from when the terminology of war is used to describe terrorism.

TERRORISM AS A WAR CRIME

Which definition of terrorism is correct? Generally, a good definition of a difficult subject is one with which most people can agree. Many people will object to a broad definition – such as "terrorism is violence for political purposes" – for the simple reason that it turns most practitioners of violence into terrorists. In contrast, a lengthy academic definition may be too detailed to be of much practical use. An agreed-upon definition could help governments cooperating to stamp out international terrorism, by establishing a universal standard that would reduce differences between national codes of law. Such a legal definition already exists for other controversial acts, such as war crimes, and there is broad international agreement about what actions should be considered war crimes.

A look at how this agreement developed on what defines a war crime may help set up a model for international collaboration against terrorists.

Included among the acts considered war crimes are attacks on persons taking no active part in hostilities. This also includes members of the armed forces who have surrendered. This protection of the noncombatant stands at the core of international humanitarian law as codified in the Hague Regulations and Geneva Conventions. The rules of war prohibit not only the use of violence against captives but also hostage-taking and most of the other acts committed by terrorists.

Terrorists have, in fact, elevated practices that are considered crimes in war situations to the level of routine tactics. They do not engage in open combat, as do soldiers. Instead, they prefer to strike against the unarmed. Injury to the defenseless is not an accidental side-effect but a deliberate strategy of terrorists.

Categorizing acts of terrorism as war crimes is also appropriate in the sense that terrorists consider themselves as being at war with their opponents. What makes them different from soldiers, however, is that terrorists do not carry their arms openly nor discriminate between armed adversaries and noncombatants. Because terrorists are not fighting by the rules of war, they are, for all practical purposes, war criminals. Like war crimes, acts of terrorism distinguish themselves from conventional warfare, and to some extent from guerrilla warfare, through the disregard of principles of humanity contained in the accepted rules of war.

THE BEST DEFINITION OF TERRORISM

If the international community could agree upon a legal definition of acts of terrorism as *"peacetime equivalents of war crimes,"* a more uniform treatment of terrorists would become possible. A narrow definition of terrorism, placing it on a par with war crimes, excludes some forms of violence and coercion, such as certain types of attacks on the military and destruction of property, which are currently labeled terrorism by some governments. However, this type of narrow and precise definition of terrorism is likely to find broader acceptance than one that includes a wider variety of violent protest.

Lesser forms of political violence, such as vandalizing an opponent's home, are already outlawed by national legislation. Terrorist offenses could be considered international crimes, requiring special treatment. If a definition were accepted that stressed the tactics and not the ends, nobody would be able to confuse terrorists and freedom fighters.

Freedom fighters who adhere to the rules of warfare should be treated like soldiers. Those freedom fighters who target civilians, on the other hand, should be dealt with as war criminals. The same categorization applies to those soldiers acting on behalf of a government. A desirable cause does not excuse acts of violence against unarmed civilians and neutral bystanders.

By placing narrowly defined acts of terrorism in the same category as war crimes, confusion over whether violence is criminal or political will be minimized. Where national authorities are unable or unwilling to deal with such acts, these could be dealt with, as in the case of war crimes, by a special international penal court with power over terrorist offenses as well as other crimes against humanity.

Alex P. Schmid

SEE ALSO:

TERROR IN THE FRENCH REVOLUTION 1789-1815; RUSSIAN ANARCHIST TERROR; FRENCH ANARCHIST TERROR; TERROR IN THE RUSSIAN CIVIL WAR; WORLD WAR II RESISTANCE IN YUGOSLAVIA AND TERRORISM; THEORIES OF TERROR IN URBAN INSURRECTIONS; CATEGORIES OF TERROR; ASSASSINATION; SUICIDE BOMBING; THE BLACK SEPTEMBER ORGANIZATION; TERROR IN LEBANON 1980-1987; THE WORLD TRADE CENTER BOMBING; THE OKLAHOMA CITY BOMBING AND THE MILITIAS; BRITISH COUNTERTERROR METHODS AFTER DECOLONIZATION; THE AMERICAN RESPONSE TO TERRORISM; INTERNATIONAL COOPERATION AGAINST TERRORISM; THE MEDIA AND INTERNATIONAL TERRORISM.

FURTHER READING

- Fattah, E. A. *Terrorist Activities and Terrorist Targets: A Tentative Typology.* New York: Pergamon Press, 1981.
- Groth, A. "A Typology of Revolution." In *Revolution and Political Change*, edited by C. E. Welch and M. B. Taintor. Belmont, CA: Duxbury Press, 1972.
- Rubin, A. P. "Terrorism and the Law of War." *Denver Journal of International Law and Politics* 17, nos. 2-3 (Spring 1983): 219-235.
- United States Department of State. *Patterns of Global Terrorism, 1994.* Washington, DC: Office of the Coordinator for Counterterrorism, April 1995.

THE HISTORICAL BACKGROUND

A Serbian terrorist assassinates Austro-Hungarian Archduke Franz Ferdinand at Sarajevo, June 28, 1914.

THE HISTORICAL BACKGROUND:
Introduction

Terrorism is not a modern invention. It has been a recurring theme in the story of humankind. Terrorism of some kind became a standard course of action in many historical cultures. Where one side believed that the threat of violence might intimidate a foe into submission, it usually did not hesitate to use such threats. The definition of *terrorism* in some of these historical cases is necessarily broad, but in order to set modern terrorism in context, it is necessary to look at how it reflects a broad sweep of human behavior. Terrorism in the ancient world often did not demonstrate all the aspects that go to make up the phenomenon of modern terrorism. Many examples from ancient and medieval history of what, broadly defined, might be termed terrorism, relate more to the use of terror as an instrument of policy.

Historical sources as old as the Bible record many instances of terror being used to achieve an objective. The book of Joshua states that the Israelites "utterly destroyed all that was in the city [Jericho], both man and woman, young and old, and ox, and sheep, and ass, with the edge of the sword." This massacre of a city after it had fallen to an army after a long siege was typical of warfare of this time, and for centuries to come. If a besieged town continued to resist attempts to capture it, the attackers, after successfully overcoming it, would put all its inhabitants to the sword. This slaughter served specifically to frighten neighboring peoples into early submission when their turn came to be under attack.

Another theme that stands out strongly in looking at the history of terrorism up to 1945 is the extent to which terror became easier to use when the group being attacked was something separate – either in terms of race, ideology, or religion. Being able to demonize, or even to dehumanize, their enemies makes it easier for the group using terror to inflict horrors on them. For example, a whole race could be described as "savages" for having customs such as scalping dead or wounded enemies. This label of alleged savagery is then used to justify conduct toward them that is in itself equally savage.

Colonial Europeans used such arguments to justify their brutal suppression of indigenous resistance. Demonization and dehumanization of enemies reached new levels during the Nazis' "Final Solution" – their slaughter of over six million Jews and other allegedly "asocial" groups.

The development of technology in the 2,000 years up to 1945 undoubtedly has made the implementation of terror on a massive scale more achievable. Those perpetrators of terror often hold the general principle that the greater the number of victims, the greater the degree of terror created. As long as individuals had to execute victims personally with sword or gun, then the extent of the slaughter was limited. Of course, the numbers of people a plundering army could kill in a few days was still considerable. In the 1576 "Spanish Fury" at Antwerp, in the Netherlands, during the War of Dutch independence, Spanish troops sacked the captured town, killing 7,000 people in 11 frenzied days.

During World War II, the Nazis became frustrated with the slowness with which the *Einsatzgruppen*, the murder squads slaughtering Jews in the Soviet Union, were accomplishing their murderous task. The development of the gas chambers at extermination camps was a huge leap forward for the heinous process of mass slaughter. Some 2,000 Holocaust victims could be killed in the gas chambers in just 15 minutes using the poison Zyklon-B. Potentially, several tens of thousands of victims could be killed each day. The process of annihilation had reached new levels because of technological advances.

Technological progress has coincided with a general increase in the power of the state. The radicals in the French Revolution may have declared terror "the order of the day," and executed "suspects." But the impact of these examples of state terror were paltry compared with the dreadful results of Nazi control of Europe, or of Stalin's Great Purge in the Soviet Union. The degree of organization and bureaucratization within a state's terror program reached new heights under these reigns of terror, setting the scene for the terrorism we know today. ■

Terror in History to 1939

The word *terrorism* was coined in the guillotine days of the French Revolution, but the practice is much older. Terrorism stretches back in time to the bloody assassinations of the ancient Greeks and Romans and to barbaric customs such as suspending people over fires for not paying their taxes. Few parts of the world have escaped the brutalities and the climate of fear that terrorism creates. Among many examples, there were religious murder cults in the Middle East, massacres during the American Indian resistance, and Stalin's purges in Russia, when some 20 million people died at his hands to make sure that those still alive were cowed into submission.

CHAPTER ONE

TERROR IN HISTORY TO 1939:
Introduction

It is easy, in our concern about terrorism today, to lose sight of the historical perspectives on the subject that enable us to piece together a proper analysis of terror, and, therefore, to work out strategies for coping with it. The examples chosen in this chapter demonstrate different aspects of terror over a period of more than 2,000 years. These case-studies also show how terror can come from the state, from those resisting the state, from the excesses of warfare, from small dedicated ideological groups, and from clashes between different societies or views of society.

Examples of terror used by the state range from Imperial Rome to Stalin's purges in the Soviet Union. Both these examples demonstrate how a ruling class can be cowed by terrorist methods and forced to acquiesce in a dictatorship. The most famous introduction of terror by a state was that of the Committee of Public Safety in 1794. Under pressure from a European-wide coalition and having to deal with a series of revolts within France, the revolutionaries decided that they would terrorize their own population into obedience. The results were undeniably successful: the French armies defeated their enemies both on the frontiers and also within France.

This state terror has in turn produced theories that justify use of any means – including terror – to resist tyrants. Such ideas, ("tyrannicide"), were put forward in Ancient Greece and in the later Roman republic, the most famous example being the assassination of Julius Caesar. Some 1,800 years later the Russian anarchist terrorists cited ideas of tyrannicide in their attempts to murder the Czar.

Fear and terror are a necessary part of warfare. The knowledge that you are likely to die if you undertake a particular course of action – whether it be advancing across a fire-swept plain or climbing a scaling ladder to a fortress – is at the very heart of military science. However, to this can be added the aspect of deliberately threatening civilians. An obvious example of terror against civilians was in medieval siege warfare. Here, there were commonly understood rules about how long fortified places could resist before the inhabitants risked massacre. Similarly, the Mongols made it clear to their enemies that they would exact a savage vengeance if there was any resistance at all. During World War I, however, German threats against civilians in the territories they had occupied were more covert, an approach perhaps influenced by German policies toward subject populations in their colonies.

Much modern terrorism is carried out by small groups with a particular ideology or aim that they wish to force upon others. Again, there are examples of this throughout history. During the Middle Ages, the sect known as the Assassins in the Middle East, representing a particular schism within Islam, used selective assassination of enemy leaders as a weapon. The anarchists of the late nineteenth century also used terror for their ends. Such methods were again adopted by various nationalist groups in the early twentieth century, such as the Serbs who assassinated the Archduke Ferdinand in Sarajevo in 1914.

The use of terror policies may have taken most lives, however, in conflicts between different societies, or different views of society. Where two societies clashed, especially where they were at different levels of technological development, then terror was common. A typical example was in North America, where terror was used by both sides in the wars between the European settlers and the Indian tribes. The tide of European colonization across the world during the eighteenth and nineteenth centuries also saw the use of widespread terror. Massacre was used to terrify and subdue whole populations, and in retaliation by those being conquered.

But if different societies used terror against one another, so too did members of the same society who professed different views. These differences could be ideological, as in the Paris Commune, or in the civil war that broke out in the aftermath of the Russian revolution. In both cases, left-wing radicals fought reactionary conservative forces. Perhaps the most awful examples of this kind of terror took place where religious or racial differences were latched onto by the state. The brutal state-inspired Turkish treatment of Christian Armenians during World War I was an episode that prefigured the Nazi Holocaust. ■

TERROR IN ANCIENT GREECE AND THE ROMAN REPUBLIC

There are several famous instances of political assassination, a form of terror, occurring in the classical world. The methods varied according to the circumstances. In Ancient Greece, assassination and tyrannicide were among the methods employed during struggles between rival factions in city states.

GREEK MURDERS

In Ancient Greece, a tyrant was specifically a ruler who had taken power by force, although some had full popular support. Such was the case with the brothers Hipparchus and Hippias, who became rulers of Athens in 527 B.C. on the death of their father, Pisistratus. However, other aristocrats resented their power and looked for a pretext to bring them down. When Hipparchus sexually assaulted the sister of Harmodius, the vengeful brother and his friend Aristogeiton murdered Hipparchus during a festival procession in 510 B.C.

This left Hippias as sole ruler, and so his enemies brought rivalry with a foreign state into play to further their ends. Conflict frequently broke out between the city states of ancient Greece. None was so bitter and protracted as that between Athens and Sparta. Pisistratus had expelled the powerful Alcmaeonidae family from Athens, who now saw their chance to gain control. They bribed the Spartans to send an army against Athens. Hippias surrendered and was exiled in 509 B.C. The significance Athens attached to the overthrow of these tyrants was indicated by the erection of statues to Harmodius and Aristogeiton in city market places, an honor never previously accorded to anyone. Popularity with the common people counted for nothing in aristocratic power struggles.

ASSASSINATIONS IN ROME

The republic of Rome was born out of such conflicts between aristocrats. A similar pride was held in the ejection of the Etruscan kings in the sixth century B.C. Yet evidence exists that Rome was on friendly terms with Etruria, a region situated northwest of Rome across the Tiber river, and the kings, such as Tarquin I, had their supporters among Romans. Nevertheless, Tarquin was assassinated by supporters of his successor, Servius Tullius. Servius, in turn, met his death in a coup led by his son-in-law Tarquin II, whose overthrow by aristocrats ushered in the republic in 509 B.C.

The constitution of the Roman Republic was designed to avoid this kind of bloodletting. The city was ruled by two consuls, who were elected annually and could not hold office in successive years. Consuls were elected from the ruling body, the Senate, meaning that power rested with a collective body instead of with an individual. Political assassination was generally viewed as a waste of time since officeholders would be gone in a year.

The Senate at this time comprised a small group of noble families, while a panel of tribunes looked after the interests of the masses. The Senate viewed anyone with popular support as a dangerous threat to their power. Two such individuals were the Gracchi brothers – Tiberius who became tribune in 133 B.C., and Gaius, who held office for two terms from 123-122 B.C. They both instigated programs of land reform to help the poor. Both were seen to be usurping the Senate's

KEY FACTS

● Philip II of Macedon, father of Alexander the Great, was assassinated in 336 B.C. Alexander's own involvement has never been ruled out.

● Two acts of terror altered the course of Roman history: the murder of the last king, Tarquin II, in 509 B.C., and the assassination of Julius Caesar in 44 B.C.

Mary Evans Picture Library

Julius Caesar falls in the Senate House in Rome in 44 B.C., knifed by senators opposing his rule.

power by appealing to the masses and were murdered.

Julius Caesar, however, was assassinated because he did not represent the people. He came to power via military prowess, at a time when Rome governed most of the Mediterranean basin. His victories in war enabled him to join two other politicians, the wealthy Crassus and the soldier Pompey. They formed the Triumvirate, or body of three men. Using the power of patronage, they controlled elections in the republic. After Crassus' death in 53 B.C. civil war broke out between Caesar and Pompey. It ended in Pompey's assassination in Egypt.

When Caesar returned to Rome, he became dictator, an ancient republican office offered to a general in times of national emergency. He defeated Pompey's sons in battle and, in late 45 B.C., was offered life dictatorship. Even his supporters saw this as a threat to the republic. On March 15, 44 B.C., a conspiracy of senators

assassinated him. Caesar's appointment as dictator ended the republic. The establishment of Roman rule under an emperor was a direct result of his death.

Paul Szuscikiewicz

SEE ALSO:

TERROR IN THE ROMAN EMPIRE; THE ASSASSINS: A TERROR CULT; RUSSIAN ANARCHIST TERROR.

F U R T H E R   R E A D I N G

- Finley, M. I. *Politics in the Ancient World.* New York: Cambridge University Press, 1983.
- Grant, Michael. *Myths of the Greeks and Romans.* New York: New American Library, 1995.
- Kraut, Richard, ed. *The Cambridge Companion to Plato.* New York: Cambridge University Press, 1992.
- Meier, Christian. *Caesar: A Biography.* New York: Basic Books, 1996.

TERROR IN THE ROMAN EMPIRE

We know that terror was an accepted instrument of government and war in the Roman empire because contemporary writers make clear reference to it. The Roman historian Tacitus says this of his father-in-law Agricola, governor of Roman Britain: "When he had sufficiently terrorized [the British], by showing mercy he displayed the attractions of peace." The Ancient Britons saw the Romans this way too. Tacitus reports chieftain Calgacus encouraging his warriors before the battle of Mons Graupius in A.D. 83 by saying: "When [the Romans] make a desolation, they call it peace."

The Romans waged war to acquire land or quell rebellions. Most of their enemies, particularly in the west, were individual tribes. Many did not have professional armies which the Romans could face in a pitched battle, and there was usually no key city or center whose capture would end the war or put down the insurrection. Fighting could be protracted and unnecessarily tie up much-needed legions, and so the Romans employed terror to settle matters quickly.

WARTIME TERROR TACTICS

Tacitus, writing about a German campaign in A.D. 16, records a Roman general's orders to his troops to be "resolute in killing and taking no prisoners; nothing but the extermination of the race would end the war." Against hostile populations, the pattern was invariable. There was devastation, which involved burning

Augustus, emperor of Rome from 27 B.C. to A.D. 14.

Woodfin Camp & Associates

KEY FACTS

● After a successful siege, the Roman army often slaughtered entire populations, as in Jerusalem in A.D. 70.

● In the bitter civil war after the assassination of Julius Caesar in 44 B.C., 2,130 political rivals died.

● The Roman criminal code was particularly harsh on slaves and the poor. By law, the testimony of slaves was acceptable only under torture.

E. T. Archive

villages, destroying or carrying off crops, slaughtering animals, and killing or enslaving the population. This is shown vividly on Trajan's Column in Rome, which carries scenes in relief of campaigning in Dacia (modern Romania) by the Emperor Trajan.

This scene, from Trajan's Column in Rome, commemorates the Dacian campaigns of A.D. 101-106. It depicts the savagery of the fighting and the cruel subjugation of the vanquished Dacians.

MASS SLAUGHTER IN SIEGES

In the battle zone, non-combatants – people considered unfit to fight – normally moved to a place of comparative safety. But in siege warfare, everyone was a combatant. Stubborn resistance might also lead to the extermination of a tribe. This was the fate of the Salassi, an Alpine people whom the Emperor Augustus ordered to be killed or sold into slavery.

But it was not simply blood-lust on the part of the Romans which fueled this savagery. Those terrorized always had the option of accepting their terms for surrender. These were rarely punitive. Hostages were taken, usually eminent leaders or their families, to ensure continued cooperation. But Rome was savage in dealing with rebellion.

The siege of Jerusalem in A.D. 70 was a result of the Jews rebelling. Their religious beliefs clashed with Roman emperor worship, making it peculiarly difficult for Jews to accept Roman rule. The Romans gave their usual choice to the Jews: terms if they gave in, terror if they refused. By way of encouragement, the Roman general crucified some captives outside the walls of the city, and sent others to offer terms. First, he cut off their hands, to make clear they were genuine prisoners. Rome's determination to extinguish all traces of rebellion explains the effort expended at the siege of

Masada, in A.D. 73, which ended the Jewish War. Many Jewish rebels had retreated to this impregnable hill stronghold. Roman soldiers took months to build a ramp to reach up to the fortress walls. But with defeat – and the fate meted out to the defiant – inevitable, the 1,000 Jews inside committed mass suicide.

The Romans put down the revolt of populations in newly conquered territory with the utmost brutality. In A.D. 60-61, Boudicca of the Iceni tribe in what is now eastern England led her warriors in revolt against 20 years of harsh Roman subjugation. An alleged 70,000 Britons were massacred for being Roman or friendly to Rome. Boudicca was defeated by the Roman garrison.

CRUSHING REVOLTS IN ROME

The authorities treated rebellion in Rome itself with equal harshness. Wealthy Romans administered the empire. They derived their fortunes largely from farms using slave labor. In 73 B.C., as many as 120,000 slaves, led by Spartacus, rose up against their masters and roamed Italy for two years. When Crassus put down the rebellion in 71 B.C., he crucified some 6,000 slaves along the Appian Way, the main road from Rome to southern Italy. The crosses stretched the 100 miles to Capua.

Roman rulers also used terror against movements which they considered might present a threat to the stability of the empire. The fourth-century emperor Diocletian had thousands of Christians hunted down, tortured, and publicly martyred in ever-increasing degrees of gruesomeness.

TORTURE OF ROMANS

Rome used terror as a means of enforcing discipline in the army. The practice of decimation, the selection by lot and putting to death of one-tenth of a body of soldiers who had shown cowardice in the field, was rare under the empire, as was the execution of individuals. But lesser punishments – floggings and mutilations, for example – were available and used.

Terror was also a feature of the Roman criminal code. When Pedanius Secundus, a leading citizen, was murdered by one of his slaves in A.D. 61, the murderer was one of 400 slaves executed for the crime. The other 399 were slaughtered in accordance with a law that require all the slaves in a household to be punished for killing their master.

In Roman law, slaves and the poor could be scourged, sent to the mines, thrown to wild beasts in the arena, or crucified. This was part of a legal code that sought to preserve the interests of the propertied classes by intimidating the poor and the enslaved.

However, terror was most obviously applied in conflicts within the ruling class of the Roman empire. This was nothing new. The general Sulla took power in 82 B.C., when Rome was still a republic, and purged 2,690 enemies, who were hunted down and executed without trial.

During the first century A.D., Roman emperors such as Tiberius, Nero, and Domitian found many victims among the political elite. They used vague accusations of treason to counter the possibility of conspiracies against their rule. The fears of the emperors were genuine. Four of the first 12 were assassinated by conspiracies of senators and officers of the imperial guard. The best protection against such attempts was the existence of an adult successor, provided he was loyal. There was nothing to be gained from assassinating emperors if they had already named as heir someone old enough to step straight into their shoes.

It is notable that dangers of assassination did not seem to come from the external enemies of Rome. Access to the emperor, or to a general, was not easy, but in any case assassination would not benefit them greatly. The fate of Rome was not dependent on one individual. Examples are difficult to find even of successful or attempted assassinations by outsiders of subordinate figures, some of whom were much hated.

Assassination was the Roman empire's closest parallel to modern terrorism. Terror was an instrument of policy that the Romans were willing to adopt when it suited their aims.

Paul Szuscikiewicz

SEE ALSO:

TERROR IN ANCIENT GREECE AND THE ROMAN REPUBLIC; JUSTINIAN II'S REIGN OF TERROR; TERROR IN MEDIEVAL WARFARE; MEDIEVAL SIEGE WARFARE AS TERROR.

FURTHER READING

- Bunson, Matthew. *Encyclopedia of the Roman Empire*. New York: Facts on File Publications, 1992.
- Grant, Michael. *The Fall of the Roman Empire*. New York: Macmillan, 1990.
- Scarre, Chris. *Chronicle of the Roman Emperors: The Reign-by Reign Record of the Rulers of Imperial Rome*. New York: Thames & Hudson, 1995.

JUSTINIAN II'S REIGN OF TERROR

During the third century A.D., the Roman empire entered into a lengthy crisis that only ended during the reign of Justinian I (525-565). By this time, the empire was no longer pagan, or centered in Rome, or across the whole Mediterranean basin. It had become a Christian empire whose ruler lived in Constantinople (modern Istanbul) and reigned over parts of Italy and the eastern Mediterranean. This successor state was known as the Byzantine empire, although its people still called themselves Romans.

Terror was a feature of the political strife among the ruling elite of the Byzantine empire just as in Roman times. For example, Byzantine emperors were just as liable to be victims of conspiracy. The penalties for those guilty of treason, though, could be far more savage.

RECKLESS YOUTH

One emperor who was both victim and perpetrator of terror is Justinian II. He was just 16 years old when he ascended to the throne in 685. One writer described him as "a bold, reckless, callous, and selfish young man, with a firm determination to assert his own individuality and have his own way – he was, in short, of the stuff of which tyrants are made." Yet his intelligence and resourcefulness cannot be underestimated.

Whether it was extravagant building projects, legal reform, or wars of reconquest, Justinian II was always trying to surpass the accomplishments of Justinian I, his great-great-grandfather. In part, he succeeded – but it came at a price. Justinian II was an unpopular sovereign. To pay for his excesses, he burdened his subjects with heavy taxation, which was in fact extortion carried out by ruthless officials. The population became disillusioned. By the year 695, Leontius, a general of repute, had enlisted a group of supporters which included the Patriarch Callinicus, head of the Orthodox Church in Constantinople. They marched on the palace and put Justinian in chains; he was spared execution only because of his father's friendship with Leontius. Instead, Justinian's nose was cut off and his tongue slit, earning him the nickname Rhinotmetus, or "cut-nose." He was paraded around the Hippodrome and exiled to the outer reaches of the empire in the Crimean town of Cherson. This humiliation was too much for him to bear and he swore vengeance.

Determined to seek revenge, Justinian set sail with a group of followers for the kingdom of the Bulgars, then enemy of the Byzantines, hoping to enlisting support for a plan to capture Constantinople. As the story goes, a terrible storm threatened to sink Justinian's ship. One of his men implored him to repent his anger and swear to God that he would spare his enemies in return for a safe journey and the restoration of his throne. On the contrary, Justinian declared: "If I spare a single one of them, may I be drowned this instant." The storm subsided. The Bulgar king gave his support, and in 705 he helped Justinian to besiege Constantinople.

Meanwhile, a usurper named Tiberius had removed Leontius from power. While the Bulgar army remained outside the city gates, Justinian slipped inside and recaptured the royal palace. Encouraged by what he had interpreted as a sign of God's will, he became more ruthless than ever. He captured Leontius and Tiberius, paraded them at the Hippodrome, and, placing one foot on each of their necks, watched the chariot races for more than an hour. Then he ordered their decapitation. The patriarch who had crowned them was blinded and exiled.

REIGN OF REVENGE

Thereafter followed a six-year reign of revenge and terror. Justinian put to death most of the empire's best army officers. The terror became so widespread, it

---

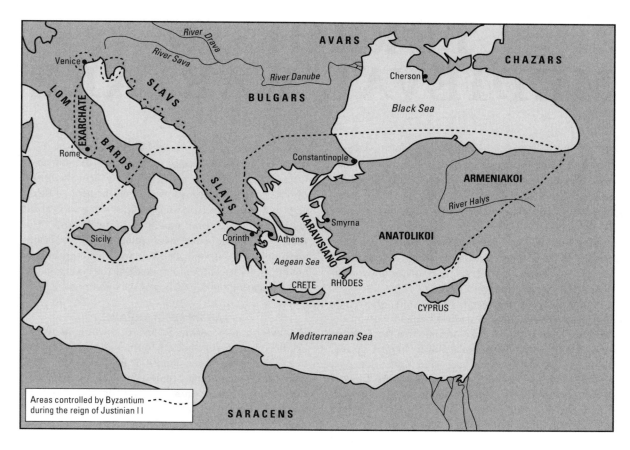

Areas controlled by Byzantium - - - - -
during the reign of Justinian II

The Byzantine empire at the end of the seventh century A.D.

moved one observer to write of Justinian that "as often as he wiped the drops of rheum from his [cut-nose] rhinotmetus, almost as often did he order another one of those who opposed him to be slain."

His desire for revenge was strongest against the Chersonites, who had insulted him during his exile. Justinian ordered Stephen the Savage to terrorize them with the order: "All are guilty and all must perish." Although the slowness of his attack allowed the majority to flee, Justinian's minister still took his toll. He roasted alive seven principal citizens, drowned 20, and sent 42 in chains to the emperor to meet their doom.

Still Justinian was thirsty for vengeance and sent another expedition to Cherson under the patrician officer Bardanes. This time, however, the Chersonites were prepared for the attack and overpowered the emperor's troops. Justinian's soldiers were threatened with death unless they swore their allegiance to Bardanes, who was crowned as Emperor Philippicus in 711. Philippicus sailed to Constantinople where Justinian II, devoid of allies, was overthrown and executed. For the terrified Byzantine populace, it came not a moment too soon.

Paul Szuscikiewicz

SEE ALSO:

TERROR IN THE ROMAN EMPIRE; TERROR IN MEDIEVAL WARFARE; THE ASSASSINS: A TERROR CULT.

FURTHER READING

- Norwich, John Julius. *Byzantium: The Apogee.* New York: Knopf, 1991.
- Ostrogorsky, G. *History of the Byzantine State,* rev. ed. New Brunswick, NJ: Rutgers University Press, 1969.
- Vasiliev, A. A. *History of the Byzantine Empire.* 2 Vols. Madison, WI: University of Wisconsin Press, 1984.

TERROR IN MEDIEVAL WARFARE

"All the common people were put to the sword, and all the priests of the Lord God, with those who served them, were murdered where they stood at the church altars. When they had killed every living soul…the troops burned the whole city, with all the churches and every single building, leaving there nothing but the bare earth." These words, from The History of the Franks, written by Gregory (c. 538-94) bishop of Tours, describe taking the town of Comminges in southwestern France.

The besiegers captured Gundovald, the city's commander, by tricking him into leaving the town. His captors, Count Ullo and Boso, led him to a steep ravine where: "Ullo pushed Gundovald over and, as he fell, the Count shouted: 'There goes your pretender, who pretends that he is the son of one king and the brother of another.' He thrust his lance at Gundovald and tried to transfix him. The rings of Gundovald's [chain-mail suit] withstood the lance and he was not wounded. He picked himself up and tried to scramble to the top of the cliff. Boso threw a rock at him and hit him full in the head. Gundovald fell and as he fell he died. The mob surrounded him and prodded him with their spears. They tied his feet together with a rope and dragged him through the whole army encampment. They pulled out his hair and his beard. Then they left his body unburied on the spot where he had met his death."

KEY FACTS

● Such was the value of ransoming captives that, in 1217 at a battle in Lincoln, England, only one knight died on the winning side and two on the losing side. Around 400 were taken prisoner.

● When captured in 1356, John II of France paid the Black Prince, son of Edward III of England, three million gold coins in ransom.

● A medieval army could never muster more than 100,000 troops, compared with 360,000 during the Roman empire and France's 300,000 in 1710.

These excerpts from a medieval history show how terror was used in warfare to intimidate the defeated. Its use in the early part of the Middle Ages, from the fifth to eleventh centuries, was a continuation of those methods characteristic of warfare since organized human societies first emerged in prehistory. The homes of the defeated were pillaged and prisoners were sold into slavery. Leaders who fell into enemy hands could expect a quick death if they were lucky, and a lingering one by torture if they were not.

RULES OF WARFARE

However, a new attitude toward warfare began to develop during this period, influenced by Christian theology. During the second half of the Middle Ages, from the eleventh to sixteenth centuries, the commanders of armies more often than not accepted the discipline of these new rules and customs. An important idea was that the use of force was permissible only as part of a process of obtaining justice. Armies should help extend peace on earth by refraining from acts of violence on certain days of the week, such as Sunday, and in places like churches, hospices, and markets.

There were also attempts to control the use of weapons. In 1139, the Church's Lateran Council banned the use of the crossbow in wars between Christians; its use was restricted to wars against pagans and infidels. French heretical mercenaries, however, known as Brabançons, who had broken away from the king's control, continued to use it. Indeed, it was a Brabançon captain who accounted for taking the life of the English king Richard I ("the Lionheart") with a crossbow bolt at the siege of Gaillon.

Christian ethics were not the sole influence on this process. The concept of subjecting warfare to rules also developed out of the conditions of medieval warfare. Commanders feared risking their armies in battles, and regarded sieges as difficult, dangerous, and lengthy operations. To maintain an army in the field for more than a few weeks was a major problem. So medieval campaigns tended to be plundering

Edward the "Black Prince" commanded the English in their victory over the French at Poitiers in 1356.

Mary Evans Picture Library

scale was common for many years to come in the campaigns led by Edward the "Black Prince."

Warfare with rules also protected the rulers of medieval society. Knights were more valuable to the enemy alive than dead, since such a prisoner could be ransomed. The chance of a poorer knight or a common soldier making a fortune from ransoming a valuable captive was an important incentive for their going to war. In the battle of Bremule in 1119, out of 900 knights, only three were killed.

However, other groups who took their place on the medieval battlefield did not receive the same protection. Those among the poorer classes who appeared in the ranks of the defeated army were slaughtered. In the battle of Cassel in 1328, at least half of the Flemish city militias were annihilated.

Peasant uprisings habitually resulted in wholesale killing. The later Middle Ages were marked by a long succession of city and peasant rebellions – a notable example being the Peasants' Revolt in England in 1381. In this, peasants from the eastern and southeastern counties of England protested at the new poll tax that had been imposed on them in addition to their traditional duties to their feudal overlords. The peasants received guarantees of reforms, but once they had dispersed back to their homes the local nobility beat some and murdered others. The promises that King Richard II had made were ignored.

The extent to which limits on terror were accepted depended crucially on the social group to which one belonged. In this sense, terror remained a tool used to enforce and maintain the social order of the medieval world, even if attempts were made to restrain it in armed conflict between the ruling elite.

Paul Szuscikiewicz

expeditions. Their aim was to force the enemy to sue for peace by ravaging their land. This inevitably resulted in prolonged conflict, as the Hundred Years' War (1337-1453) between England and France illustrates. The king of England, Edward III, believed he had a claim to be king of France, and he asserted it. The war dragged on into the reigns of his grandson and his grandson's three successors. The countryside of France and the southern coast of England suffered badly, and their populations generally lived in a state of terror. In one four-week campaign in the autumn of 1339, Edward III reportedly sacked 2,117 villages and castles in the north of France. Devastation on such a

SEE ALSO:
MEDIEVAL SIEGE WARFARE AS TERROR.

F U R T H E R   R E A D I N G

- Allmand, Christopher. *The Hundred Years War: England and France at War, 1300-c.1450*. New York: Cambridge University Press, 1988.
- Riley-Smith, Jonathan. *The Crusades: A Short History*. New Haven, CT: Yale University Press, 1990.
- Wedgwood, C. V. *The Thirty Years War*. New York: Routledge, Chapman, & Hall, 1990.

THE ASSASSINS: A TERROR CULT

The Assassins were a fanatical and murderous Muslim sect active in the Middle East from the eleventh century to the thirteenth century. They were members of the Ismaili branch of Shia Islam, the principal branch of which, the Twelver branch, is the official religion of modern Iran. The Ismailis seized power in Egypt in the tenth century and founded the Fatimid dynasty. At the end of the eleventh century, a schism occurred in the Fatimid leadership. The Ismaili missionaries living in Iran supported Nizar in the ensuing power struggle, and became known as the Nizari Ismailis. When Nizar was defeated, the leader of the Nizari Ismailis in Iran, Hasan-i Sabbah, seized the castle of Alamut in the Alburz mountains south of the Caspian Sea. There he dedicated himself to spreading Ismaili Islam throughout the Middle East and formed a devoted group of terrorists, to help him in his quest. These became known as the Assassins.

SUDDEN DEATH BY THE DAGGER

The Nizaris were generally fairly few in number. As a result, they could not meet their enemies in pitched battle with any hope of success. Instead, they developed an approach to warfare that has made them infamous. The sect would send a single member, or a small group, to kill their enemy's leader, almost always with a dagger. The Nizaris saw themselves as emissaries of god, and carrying "his" message was a divine act. They used the sacredness of their mission to justify the murder of anyone who opposed their attempts to convert people to their form of Islam.

Murdering enemy leaders proved effective in reducing the power and influence of the sect's foes. The Nizaris' rivals were more inclined to sacrifice large numbers of troops in battle rather than run the personal risk of sudden, violent death at the hands of a dagger-wielding fanatic. Apologists for the Nizaris have suggested that their ruthless use of terror was a merciful, economical way to achieve their goals without causing unnecessary bloodshed.

FIRST TO DIE

The Nizaris claimed their first victim in 1092, when they sent a lone killer to murder Nizam al-Mulk, the Turkish sultan's chief minister. Butahir Arrani disguised himself as a holy man to get close to the minister. As Nizam was carried from his tent in a litter, Butahir plunged a knife into his chest. The murderer had no chance of escape, and the minister's guards killed him instantly. One of Nizam's sons, Fakhri, also died at the hands of a Nizari. Fakhri's killer was disguised as a beggar.

It may have been the seemingly fanatical courage of the Nizaris, together with the fact that a Nizari rarely made any attempt to escape after committing a murder, that gave rise to the belief that they acted under the influence of drugs. The story goes that the Nizaris drugged the member who was about to undertake a mission and carried him into a beautiful garden, leading him to believe that it was paradise. They then drugged the chosen killer again. When he woke up, they told him to go and carry out his mission.

The Nizaris encouraged the killer to believe that he would be allowed back into paradise on his return, and that if he were killed during the execution of his mission, he would reach paradise even more quickly. However, most modern scholars think that stories of drug-taking are probably untrue, suggesting that they were invented to discredit the sect. After all, a drug-befuddled emissary would hardly be an effective killer.

KEY FACTS

● Simply using the threat of assassination was often enough for the Assassins to cow their potential enemies into submission.

● Sabbah was so devout that he even had one of his sons executed after he was accused of drunkenness.

● An Assassin once killed a religious enemy as he knelt at prayer in a mosque – even though the victim's bodyguard was standing behind him.

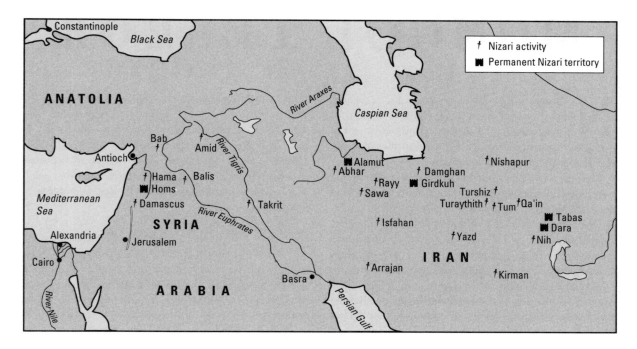

The Muslim sect usually known as the Assassins terrorized the Middle East from the eleventh century to the mid-thirteenth century.

Nevertheless, it was certainly the widespread stories of drug-taking that earned the Nizari Assassins their name. Hashish was allegedly their most widely used narcotic. Thus, the sect became known as *hashishiyya*, *hashishiyyin*, or *hashishin* in Arabic. The Christian Crusaders in Syria picked up these names and carried them back to Europe in the form of *assassin*. The word then became common in many European languages. Its use as a term for political and other murderers survived through the ages. But its Arabic derivation was forgotten until the early nineteenth century.

RELIEF AT THE ASSASSINS' DOWNFALL

The Assassins' contemporaries in the Muslim world regarded the sect with near-universal horror and disgust. This may have been in part because of the Assassins' unusual approach to warfare. But it can be more properly explained in terms of orthodox Muslim abhorrence toward the Assassins' beliefs. At one point, the religious views of the sect involved abandoning strict adherence to Islamic law.

As a result, when the second wave of Mongol conquests reached Iran and Syria in the middle of the thirteenth century, the orthodox Muslim world was delighted with the invaders' determination to wipe out the Assassins. The latter were rumored to have sent a group to assassinate the Great Khan. But they met a more terrible force. Contemporary Muslims felt that the Mongols, despite the general horrors they inflicted, performed a valuable service in obliterating the Assassins. Many had considered the sect a real threat to stability in the Muslim world.

David Morgan

SEE ALSO:

MONGOL TERROR; RELIGIOUS EXTREMISM; ASSASSINATION; TERRORISM AND REVOLUTION IN IRAN.

F U R T H E R   R E A D I N G

- Daftary, Farhad. *The Isma'ilis: Their History and Doctrines.* New York: Cambridge University Press, 1990.
- Daftary, Farhad. *The Assassin Legends: Myths of the Isma'ilis.* New York: St. Martin's Press, 1994.
- Lewis, Bernard. *The Assassins: A Radical Sect in Islam.* New York: Oxford University Press, 1987.

MONGOL TERROR

No conquests in history claimed more civilian lives, nor spread greater terror to a larger part of the world, than those accomplished by the Mongol empire under Genghis Khan. For the Mongols, terror was simply a weapon of war.

Born in the 1160s, Genghis spent until 1206 uniting the various nomadic tribes of Mongolia under his own supreme rule. He then spent the rest of his life directing his armies in a series of military conquests. By the time of his death in 1227, he had achieved astonishing successes in China, Central Asia, and the Middle East. Military expansion continued under the rule of his four sons and a grandson for a further half-century. The Mongol empire reached its greatest extent around the year 1280, when it covered a continuous stretch of territory from Korea to Hungary.

This unparalleled military achievement owed much to organization, strategy, and tactics. Among the various characteristics of the Mongol approach to warfare, the use of terror held a prominent place.

OTHERS DIE BUT NOT THE MONGOLS

Mongol men were hardened soldiers from adolescence. They were not, however, enthusiastic about dying unnecessarily in battle. They were always anxious to avoid Mongol casualties as much as possible, so to ensure that any dying was done by others, the Mongols used terror. When they besieged a city, they made it clear that if surrender was immediate, they would spare its residents, though not necessarily their homes or possessions. But resistance meant no mercy. According to contemporary sources, the Mongols would often put to death the entire population of a city. They killed countless thousands, but usually as quickly as possible, without needless cruelty. The Mongols seem to have regarded such massacres as a military necessity, not as a form of sadistic enjoyment.

The rationale behind such savagery was perfectly clear: it was designed to reduce future Mongol casualties. If a city resisted, and Mongol soldiers were consequently killed, the rest of the army would exterminate the city's residents. Word would quickly spread that it was wise to surrender to the Mongols when summoned to do so. In this way other cities would surrender rather than fight, and Mongol casualties would be avoided.

TERROR TACTICS

The policy of giving citizens the choice of surrender or death amounted to state terrorism on a grand scale. Its effect may be gauged by examining the death toll provided by contemporary writers when the Mongols massacred a city. The Persian historian Juzjani gives a typical example. After the Mongol capture of Herat (now in western Afghanistan) in 1221, Juzjani claims, the victors slaughtered a total of 2.4 million people. When Merv fell in the same year, even more people are said to have died.

These figures should not be taken as reliable statistics. Judging by the physical size of the city, it would have been impossible for Herat to have contained more than a tenth of the number of people stated. Also, the Mongols would have found great practical difficulties in killing so many people in one place in a short space of time. The alleged death toll at Herat and Merv alone was almost as high as the number of Jews killed during all the years of the Holocaust – when the Nazis had available to them all the destructive resources of twentieth-century technology.

What the figures do show, however, is the psychological effect of the ferocity of the Mongol campaigns. Those who suffered Mongol attacks could conceive of nothing so appalling: hence the impossible figures.

KEY FACTS

● Genghis Khan aimed at nothing less than conquest of the world.

● If the Mongols killed a city's inhabitants, they generally let craftsmen live. These would then be marched to Mongolia to work for the khan (ruler).

● In 1281, the Mongols launched a naval attack on Japan, but the fleet was destroyed by a storm. In Japanese, this storm was called *kamikaze*, the name later given to Japanese suicide pilots of World War II.

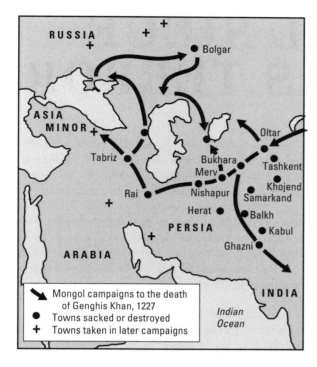

By 1206, Genghis Khan had united the nomadic tribes of Mongolia. He began an 80-year campaign of conquest, continued by his sons and a grandson.

When the Mongols invaded Russia in 1237, they surprised and terrified the entire population by attacking in winter. The invaders' hardy ponies used the frozen rivers as vast, snow-free roads. In a few weeks, the Mongols stormed and captured every Russian city, burning Kiev to the ground. It would be two centuries before the Russians regained their freedom.

CONQUEST OF CHINA

In China, the Mongols were equally skillful at the use of terror. For centuries the nomadic Mongols had raided the Chinese, but Genghis Khan was intent on conquest. In 1211, the Mongols broke through the Great Wall to attack the Chin empire, which covered northern China. The Mongol army succeeded in partially subjugating it. After crushing the Chin armies, Genghis captured Peking in 1215, massacring the population. Like a true nomad, Genghis had only contempt for peasant farmers and measured his wealth in livestock. He ordered his men to exterminate the peasants, both by putting them to the sword and by burning their crops to cause starvation. More than 15 million may have died before Genghis Khan's advisers persuaded him that he would be richer if he kept the peasants alive and taxed them.

Genghis then crushed the Muslim states of central Asia before returning to China. In 1234, the Mongols finished off the Chin and then moved on to destroy the Sung empire in 1279. It was during this campaign that the Mongols made great use of Chinese religious beliefs. After the Mongols captured a city, they did not kill the population at once but instead forced it to march along with the Mongol army. When the Mongols encountered a Chinese force they advanced, driving the captured civilians in front of them. Unwilling to kill possible relatives, the opposing army refused to fight.

MESMERIZED BY FEAR

Anecdotes written at the time of the Mongols demonstrate the effectiveness of their terror policy. According to a Persian chronicler, a Mongol came across a fleeing Persian peasant, stopped to kill him, but found he had left his sword in his tent. He therefore instructed the peasant to wait, rode back to fetch his sword, and returned. The peasant, frozen rigid by terror, was still there when the now armed Mongol came back to kill him.

Whether this story is true or not is not the point. That such tales could be told, and believed, shows the effect Mongol terror had. Clearly terror, from the Mongols' point of view, achieved its end of making conquest easier. For the Mongols, terror was good policy in terms of the military casualties it saved them.

David Morgan

SEE ALSO:

THE ASSASSINS: A TERROR CULT; MEDIEVAL SIEGE WARFARE AS TERROR.

FURTHER READING

- Chambers, James. *The Devil's Horsemen.* New York: Atheneum, 1985.
- Marshall, Robert. *Storm from the East: From Genghis Khan to Khubilai Khan.* Berkeley, CA: University of California Press, 1993.
- Morgan, David. *The Mongols.* Cambridge, MA: Blackwell Publishers, 1990.

MEDIEVAL SIEGE WARFARE AS TERROR

One of the outstanding features of the Middle Ages (from about the year 700 to the sack of Constantinople in 1453) was the extensive use of fortifications as a means of protection. Local rulers had thick-walled castles surrounded by wide moats and impenetrable curtain walls put up wherever they felt their land was vulnerable to attack. Walls encircled cities and towns, too, with gates that were shut tight when danger threatened.

Taking refuge in a fortress had advantages over the battlefield. It fell to the attackers to take all the risks, while the defenders repelled all-comers from a position of safety. Besiegers had to resort to other means of weakening the enemy. Terror became an essential weapon in the attackers' armory if they were to avoid a direct assault or a long and costly siege.

The use of terror by attackers took a variety of forms. At Nicaea, Asia Minor, in 1097, Christian Crusaders catapulted the heads of Turkish corpses into the town. At Antioch in 1098, the Franks beheaded Muslim prisoners in front of the gates. But when Frederick Barbarossa had many prisoners hanged and hacked to death at the siege of Crema, northern Italy, in 1160, the defenders retaliated by killing their captives in full sight of the attackers.

KEY FACTS

● When the First Crusade captured Jerusalem in 1099 after a five-week siege, the Christian troops massacred all the inhabitants to purge the holy city and make it entirely Christian.

● In 1105, English King Henry I burned Bayeux after capturing it. The terror this induced caused several other towns to surrender at once.

● When Edward III of England captured Calais, he demanded that the six most important citizens march out with nooses round their necks ready to be hanged. Having thus terrorized the men, he then let them live to show his mercy.

Attackers also ruthlessly exploited bonds of loyalty between a garrison and a captured lord. King John of England frequently threatened to starve to death lords and their relatives unless castles were surrendered at once. This tactic proved to be useful during his suppression of a widespread baronial revolt in 1215-16 and had been used earlier by his predecessors. In 1174, King Henry II of England imprisoned Robert, Earl of Leicester, without food and threatened to starve him until his retainers surrendered their castles.

THE RIGHT OF STORM

Such terror tactics, designed to encourage surrender in order to save attackers' lives, were not as persuasive as the "right of storm" convention. If the defenders of a fortress refused an initial demand to surrender (known as a summons), and were then defeated and the fortress seized, the attackers had the right to take possession of all the property within the fortress. They could also decide whether to kill or spare the occupants.

The right of storm is mentioned as early as the time of the Old Testament, and examples are quoted in the Book of Deuteronomy. The Romans and other imperial powers of the ancient world, such as Greece and Persia, also carried on the tradition.

The object of invoking this right was to let defenders know exactly what they faced if they chose to refuse the initial invitation to surrender. Besiegers reasoned that they had given their enemies every opportunity to save themselves and, if they were forced to attack, then the defenders would have to take the consequences. From the attackers' point of view, there was an element of justice in this and therefore they had the right to devastate or sack the fortress once it was taken. Sacking usually took the form of indiscriminate destruction and murder.

Mercy was at the victorious commander's discretion. Individual nobles might be moved by piety, chivalry, and the desire for ransom to spare women, members of religious orders, and knights of equal

E. T. Archive

A fresco in Moldovita Monastery, Romania, depicting Turks killing Christians during the Siege of Constantinople in 1453.

rank. Victors showed such mercy at Caen, in northern France, in 1346, during the Hundred Years' War between England and France.

But conquerors usually pillaged and killed ordinary citizens without mercy when the right of storm was invoked. In the sack of Lincoln, England, in 1141, the victors killed far more citizens than during the preceding battle between King Stephen and the forces of Mathilda, his rival for the throne. Another feature of the right of storm was that the victors frequently attacked churches for the wealth to be found within them. Churches were normally immune from attack.

By the right of storm, held to be in operation once the besieger had fired his first cannon, all property was forfeit to the victors. If the besieged fortress was a wealthy one, it was not uncommon for the attackers to frustrate a negotiated peace that might cheat them of booty. For many commanders and common soldiers alike, plunder was the chief motive for waging war.

Sometimes, however, financial gain was not the main reason for sacking captured fortresses. The attackers carefully calculated some acts of terror based on the right of storm. In 1191, the Muslim garrison of Acre, now in modern Israel, surrendered on terms after a siege of nearly three years. King

Richard I of England ("the Lionheart") executed about 2,700 of the garrison when their leader Saladin failed to ratify the agreement.

The extent to which the right of storm was implemented varied considerably. In the eleventh and twelfth centuries, death threats to a garrison were common preliminaries to siege. Yet attackers rarely carried them out. The majority of garrisons negotiated acceptable terms according to the convention of the "law of surrender," whereby the defenders agreed to surrender unless relieved after a set number of days.

It was rare for rulers to refuse pleas to surrender. But they often refused mercy when the adversaries were retainers who had broken their oath of loyalty. Richard I insisted on unconditional surrender by the garrison of Nottingham in 1194, who had aligned themselves with his treacherous brother John and plotted against him. Richard hanged several rebel serjeants in front of the city walls to show the severity with which he would treat the defenders if surrender was not rapid.

Under the right of storm, warlords could in theory do what they liked with vanquished defenders of a fortress. In practice, vengeance was often limited by notions of chivalry and the desire to avoid precedents which might later endanger their own lives. Sacks were bloodiest in wars against the infidel, heretics, or rebels, who were not judged to be of equal status.

The terror that the right of storm inspired often had a bearing on the outcome of negotiations. In the wars of the Spanish Netherlands in the seventeenth century, the Dutch general Justinus readily surrendered the town of Breda to the Spanish under Spinola. He was aware of the terrible precedent of the "Spanish Fury" of 1576 when Spanish troops sacked Antwerp, leaving 7,000 dead after 11 days of savage pillaging.

Antony B. Shaw

SEE ALSO:

TERROR IN MEDIEVAL WARFARE; MONGOL TERROR.

FURTHER READING

- Bradbury, Jim. *The Medieval Siege*. Rochester, NY: Boydell and Brewer, 1992.
- Seymour, William. *Great Sieges of History*. McLean, VA: Brassey's Inc., 1991.
- Watson, Bruce. *Sieges: A Comparative Study*. Westport, CT: Greenwood Press, 1993.

TERROR AND AMERICAN INDIAN RESISTANCE

Contact between settlers and the Indian peoples of North America was dominated by violence. It dated from the earliest days of European settlement in the mid-sixteenth century, when the Spanish came in search of gold. Initial curiosity rapidly gave way to bloody confrontation as the American Indians realized that the newcomers were intent upon exploitation and conquest. Their resistance was hampered by the failure of the different tribes to unite against the settlers. In spite of this, the American Indians did not relinquish their ancestral lands without a long and bitter struggle during which both sides deliberately used terror.

The first clashes between Indians and settlers began when Spanish conquistadors went north from lands already conquered in South and Central America. They were intent on plundering raids in the southeast and southwest of what is now the United States. The violence rooted in that era continued for 350 years, climaxing with the war on the open plains in the late nineteenth century. It ended in 1890 when 150 Sioux died at the hands of the U.S. Seventh Cavalry at Wounded Knee in the South Dakota Badlands.

Throughout the centuries of colonization, acts of cruelty and betrayal by one side triggered retaliatory terror from the other. Tension between the English settlers of Virginia and the local Powhatan Confederacy, for example, erupted in massacres in 1622 and 1644. The two bloodbaths claimed the lives of some 850 men, women, and children among the settlers. The survivors exacted an equally savage retribution in a bitter conflict, not only killing Indians, but also destroying their villages and crops.

RECIPROCAL TERROR

Relations between settlers and American Indians in New England also degenerated into a pattern of reciprocal terror. At first, the English fugitives from religious persecution and the Indians had the common goal of making a living from the land. As the settlements became successful, however, and the settlers wanted more land, disputes arose between the two peoples. The tone was set by the vicious Pequot War of 1637. Massachusetts and Connecticut were alarmed by the militancy of the Pequot Indians and resolved to teach the tribe a lesson. A colonial force surprised the Pequots in their village on the Mystic River. In the ensuing slaughter, the New Englanders butchered every Pequot, including women and children, who came within range of their muskets or swords. The savagery of the attack, combined with the deliberate policy of destruction that followed, exterminated the Pequots and shocked the survivors' Indian allies, the Mohegan and Narragansett tribes.

Throughout the American Indian resistance wars the innocent suffered. In 1782, for example, at Gnadenhutten, Ohio, militiamen massacred 90 peaceful Delaware Indian converts to the Moravian faith. The incident was not forgotten. When Indians routed the Pennsylvania militia at Sandusky, Ohio, later that year, they roasted to death captured commander Colonel Crawford in reprisal.

As the frontier moved west in the next century, the familiar pattern of massacre and retaliation continued.

KEY FACTS

● European contact at first benefited tribes as they acquired horses, sheep, metal, and other European goods, but terror quickly followed.

● During the Colonial wars, 1689-1760, the French and British used Indian allies to terrorize civilian populations.

● By 1875, the U.S. government had forced most Indians to live on reservations.

Peter Newark's Western Americana

Sioux dead are buried following a bloody massacre by the U.S. Army at Wounded Knee, December 29, 1890.

In 1864, at Sand Creek, Colorado, state militia killed and mutilated some 150 Cheyenne of both sexes and all ages. Chief Black Kettle survived that massacre, only to die four years later when General Custer's troops killed another 100 Cheyenne on the Washita River in western Oklahoma. Both incidents heralded reigns of terror for frontier settlers as enraged Indian warriors sought revenge.

Warfare with American Indians was brutal and inglorious by "Old World" standards. Through generations of conflict, both sides waged war with a ruthlessness summed up in the following remark by the Civil War veteran General Sheridan: "The only good Indians I ever saw were dead." Captives could face prolonged torture, while Indians and whites alike employed scalping. Combats frequently ended in massacres rather than simple defeats. For example, when the Sioux leader Red Cloud ambushed Captain Fetterman near Fort Phil Kearny in 1866, he killed all 80 men under the captain's command. Over 200 troops were killed along with Custer in his attack on an Indian encampment at Little Big Horn a decade later. The mutilation of the dead outraged the whites.

GUERRILLA WARFARE

Conventional European methods of warfare were ill-suited to frontier conflicts. The American Indians' aptitude for guerrilla warfare often put Europeans at a disadvantage. The Eastern Woodlands Indians used

guns with surprising accuracy. And in the west, horses attained from the Spaniards transformed the tribes of the Great Plains into devastating mounted raiders. Because of their preference for evasive tactics, American Indians were difficult to defeat in pitched battle. In addition, the whites relied on cumbersome wagon trains for supplies. Only when commanders discarded these in favor of pack horses were they able to pursue their elusive foes. These techniques permitted destructive campaigns to deny American Indians food and shelter. For example, in 1761, a lightly equipped Anglo-American punitive expedition broke Cherokee resistance by burning 15 tribal villages.

Europeans also knew that an effective tactic was to exploit the enmity already existing between some tribes and encourage them to fight each other. General Crook employed American Indian allies from Oregon to Arizona during his campaigns of the 1860s to 1880s. After Custer's disaster at Little Big Horn, it was the Pawnee and the Crow, sworn enemies of the Sioux, who guided the avenging U.S. Army. And when the Apache leader Geronimo was forced to surrender in 1886, it was enemies among his own people who tracked him down.

Both American Indians and settlers used deliberate acts of terror in an effort to intimidate the opposition and preserve two very different ways of life. Despite centuries of bloody and determined resistance by native peoples in defense of their lands and culture, the superior numbers and industrial resources of the encroaching settlers meant that the conflict could have only one outcome.

Steve Brumwell

SEE ALSO:

TERROR IN COLONIAL CONQUESTS.

FURTHER READING

- Utley, Robert M. *The Indian Frontier of the American West, 1846-1890*. Albuquerque, NM: University of New Mexico Press, 1984.
- Waldman, C. *Encyclopedia of Native American Tribes*. New York: Facts on File Publications, 1988.
- Washburn, W. E. "History of Indian-White Relations." In the *Handbook of North American Indians*, Vol. 4. Washington, DC: Smithsonian Institution Press, 1988.

TERROR IN THE FRENCH REVOLUTION 1789-1815

Terror as a tactic to frighten a population into subjugation is forever associated with the period known as the Reign of Terror during the French Revolution. Between February and April 1793, following the execution of the deposed Bourbon king, Louis XVI, the machinery of terror was fashioned into an efficient political instrument by revolutionary leader Maximilien Robespierre. During his rule, countless thousands of French citizens died. The term *terror* thus entered the vocabulary of Western politics.

The Terror, as it became known, is particularly associated with the Reign of Terror conducted by the Committee of Public Safety (the Committee) of the National Convention (the Convention) in 1793-94. But the Terror is also used to describe the whole period of so-called Revolutionary Government from the overthrow of the Bourbon monarch Louis XVI in 1792, to the inauguration of the regime of the Directory (1795-99).

Before 1792, terror was used to describe policies of intimidation and repression of political enemies, if necessary through unlawful acts of violence. But it was largely under the Committee that such policies became official state policy.

The fall from power and execution of Robespierre in July 1794 produced a reaction against state endorsement of terror. Yet many of the repressive and violent policies that had been associated with the height of the Terror continued to be used spasmodically through successive regimes that governed France – the Directory (1795-99), the Consulate (1799-1804), and the First Empire (1804-15). The same period also saw the emergence of what came to be known as the White Terror – violence, reprisals, and assassinations by enemies of the revolutionary regimes.

THE CONTEXT OF FEAR

The political atmosphere in Paris, and at certain times throughout much of France, during the period from 1789 to 1795 was one of fear: of plots, of famine, and of invasion. The language of revolutionaries, and by their reactionary enemies, was deliberately violent and threatening.

The politicians in Paris had few historical parallels on which they could draw; they had no way of guessing what the future would hold. What they did know was that violence and threats of violence had saved the revolution and impelled it forward at key points. In the summer of 1789, for example, when the king was preparing a coup against the radicals in the parliament (the Estates General), the Paris crowd, as the members of the revolution came to be known, altered the political landscape by their assault on the Bastille prison. After the storming, the crowd massacred the garrison and paraded the governor's head on a pike.

The more radical politicians came increasingly to rely on the support of the politicized Paris crowd, especially after the beginning of the war with Austria and Prussia in 1792. The war introduced violence more directly into the political process. As the professional

---

KEY FACTS

● The term *terror* has become synonymous with the Reign of Terror of 1793-94 under the Committees of Public Safety and General Security.

● In just two months, June and July 1794, the revolutionary courts in Paris sent 1,515 people to the guillotine. Many were innocent of any crime.

● Between 1794 and 1802, royalist murder gangs roamed southern France, spreading terror to those who had been involved in the Revolution. Over 10,000 people are thought to have been killed.

● In the southern French city of Lyon, in June 1794, over 700 people were sentenced to death. The guillotine could not cope, so the victims were marched to a square and mown down by cannon.

MASSACRES A PARIS LES 2, 3, 4, 5 ET 6 SEPTEMBRE 1792

D'après une estampe allemande conservée à la Bibliothèque nationale. — A gauche, le couvent des Carmes où fut égorgé l'archevêque d'Arles qui offrait son sang pour apaiser les meurtriers; à droite, est figurée la prison de l'Abbaye; au fond, le Temple; et, sur une terrasse, Louis XVI et Marie-Antoinette à laquelle un forcené présente la tête de la princesse de Lamballe au bout d'une pique. A cette vue, la reine s'évanouit. — Le 2 septembre, au bruit du tocsin ordonné par Danton, la tuerie commence, elle dure six jours et cinq nuits. On compte 1,368 meurtres (Mortimer-Ternaux, *Histoire de la Terreur*, III, p. 548); et, « parmi les morts, deux cent cinquante prêtres, trois évêques ou archevêques, des officiers généraux, des magistrats, un ancien ministre, une princesse du sang, un nègre, des femmes du peuple, des gamins, des forçats, de vieux pauvres. » (Taine, *La Révolution*, II, p. 307.)

reactionary armies invaded France in 1792, their commander, the duke of Brunswick, issued a manifesto threatening "exemplary and memorable vengeance" against Paris if the king should be harmed. The response of the Paris crowd was to storm the royal palace (massacring its defenders, the king's Swiss Guard) in August 1792, an action that led to the deposition and execution of the king. The next month saw more violence in the "September Massacres," when the inmates of jails were murdered by terrified crowds fearing a reactionary uprising in Paris.

By June 1793, the dominant politicians in Paris were the so-called "Montagnards" – radicals who had benefited from the violence of the people of Paris and for whom compromise was impossible. They found themselves fighting for a war not only against most of their European neighbors, but against enemies within France. Their extreme policies alienated opinion over much of the country, including important cities such as Lyon and Bordeaux, and whole sections of the countryside, especially in the west.

In a situation of internal and external crisis, and under pressure from the revolutionaries, who were

A pro-royalist contemporary print of the September Massacres of 1792 in Paris, in which the people's resentment at generations of repression exploded into murderous riots, which left some 1,300 people dead.

worried about rising food prices, the Montagnard politicians declared terror to be the "the order of the day" on September 5, 1793.

THE REIGN OF TERROR

The range of policies implemented under the Reign of Terror included a surveillance of people and opinions, and the expulsion or imprisonment of political enemies, including fellow republicans such as the Girondins, as well as of counterrevolutionaries and royalists. The Montagnards enacted harsh repressive legislation against the rebels, together with laws confiscating the lands and wealth of the nobles and the clergy who had emigrated.

The Terror saw the introduction of policies aimed at securing broad popular support. Notable here was the policy of the Maximum – state price-fixing and other economic measures. The Montagnards also introduced radical educational reforms, abolished slavery, and attempted to create a system of state pensions and support (what would now be called a welfare state), and made plans for land redistribution.

During the time when the Terror was official state policy, France was governed by the Committee, which was set up in April 1793, and consisted of 12 members of the Convention, to which it reported. The members of the Committee never changed when it was at the height of its powers between July 1793 and July 1794. Robespierre was its principal spokesman on policy matters. A number of initiatives, notably the move to establish a new state religion, the Cult of the Supreme Being, were largely his idea. Not all the members shared his political views. Louis de Saint-Just and Bertrand Barère were Robespierre's closest Montagnard allies, but Jean Nicolat Billaud-Varenne and Jean Marie Collot-d'Herbois had strong links with Parisian extremists and were more radical than Robespierre himself.

The Committee controlled every aspect of government but some members were responsible for implementing particular policies. Lazare Carnot and Jean Bon Saint André, for example, were effectively war and navy ministers, respectively.

THE APPARATUS OF DEATH

Although the Committee had wide-ranging powers, it was not in sole control of the Terror in France. State security, political policing, and counterespionage were in the hands of the 12-strong Committee of General Security, which reported to the Committee of Public Safety but acted independently at times. The Paris Revolutionary Tribunal tried counterrevolutionary offenses and was under their joint control.

Key organizers and revolutionary activists in the provinces, the "representatives on mission," were deputies from the Convention sent out to maintain central authority in the country at large. They worked closely with local administrative bodies, political clubs, surveillance committees, and local paramilitary forces. These representatives could also act independently, although they were supposed to work closely with the Committee. Representatives in provinces affected by civil war carried out the most horrific examples of terror. The suppression of revolts in Marseille and Toulon was accompanied by a policy of shooting hundreds of prisoners, under the orders of

the Representative Fréron. At Lyon, revolutionaries retook the city and executed over 2,000 "enemies of the people;" while at Nantes, Representative Jean Baptiste Carrier had thousands of prisoners loaded into boats that were scuttled in the Loire river. News of such events, especially of the mass drownings (*noyades*), led the Committee to recall all of the more violent representatives in the spring of 1794.

THE AFTERMATH

The Reign of Terror was marked by mass political mobilization. France's army swelled to over a million out of a total population of 28 million, while membership of political clubs may have exceeded even this.

The repressive effects of the Terror were considerable. The Revolutionary Tribunal executed fewer than 3,000 people in Paris. But deaths in revolutionary jails throughout the country totaled 12,000 out of the 500,000 imprisoned as political suspects at this time.

Deaths were particularly high in the main areas of civil war, notably in the west around the Vendée department, and the Rhône valley, particularly in Lyon. These areas, together with Paris, accounted for 90 percent of known deaths. Recent research suggests that the previously accepted total of 30,000-40,000 deaths throughout the Reign of Terror, spectacularly underestimates the extent of population losses in the Vendée alone. Revolutionary forces implemented policies of razing everything to the ground to reduce counterrevolutionary peasant royalism. Total deaths in the west over the 1790s as a whole, including deaths of revolutionaries caused by the Vendée rebels and deaths from semi-famine conditions in certain years, may well have reached 200,000.

Contrary to a well-established myth, the vast majority of victims of the Terror were not aristocrats. Nobles accounted for only 20 percent of those executed in Paris, only 10 percent of individuals executed by other revolutionary courts, and an even smaller number of those executed in civil war conditions.

TERROR AFTER ROBESPIERRE

The need for terror ceased in 1794, when revolutionary forces had contained civil insurrection within France and victories against the anti-French coalition in Europe had transformed the military situation. Some members of the Committee, including Robespierre, wanted to continue a policy of national regeneration. The Committee members used state terror to establish

Hulton Getty Picture Collection

GeoffRoy sc.

Maximilien Robespierre: the French Revolution's great "incorruptible" or its most brutal dictator?

a "Republic of Virtue" and also to step up repression, even though threats to the Republic were receding. The Paris Revolutionary Tribunal executed more individuals in June and July 1794 than in all its previous period of existence. Robespierre himself kept a small book in which he would write the name of anyone who opposed him in debate, terrorizing enemies into silence. Eventually, a conspiracy of deputies from both left and right brought about the coup d'état of Thermidor on July 27, 1794, which toppled Robespierre and his allies.

VIGILANTES AND COUNTERTERROR

After the removal of Robespierre's faction, the Convention gradually removed the most striking features of the Reign of Terror. It curbed the wide powers of the Committee and recalled the representatives on mission. It dissolved the popular societies, abolished the Maximum, and freed hundreds of political prisoners.

The Convention was replaced by the Directory in 1795. The regime was no longer provisional and, with the military situation fairly secure, there seemed no need for the emergency measures of the Terror. But

the fall of Robespierre unleashed a White Terror – vigilante attacks on and assassination of ex-terrorists by disgruntled victims of the Terror.

White Terror was pronounced in the south of France, where royalist murder gangs such as the Company of Jehu and the Company of the Sun operated. It was also common in the west of France, where rural bandits operated in the Vendée and Brittany, home of royalist peasant rebels called Chouans. After Napoleon came to power in 1799, he set up special courts to break the resistance of the peasant rebels.

NAPOLEON AND ASSASSINATION

Napoleon added one extra string to the bow of state terror pioneered in the French Revolution: state-led assassination of political enemies. The Committee had distanced itself from the popular lynchings enacted by the crowd of Paris during the September Massacres and assassination as state policy. Napoleon, however, may have used this policy in 1804 to kidnap and execute the duc d'Enghien, grandson of France's most active counterrevolutionary, the prince of Condé, and a relative of the exiled king Louis XVIII.

Although historians have not proved Napoleon's personal involvement in the assassination, this act compromised his reputation in Europe. Subsequent commentators, however, have inseparably linked the Terror in the French Revolution not with Napoleon, but with the era of the Committee under Robespierre.

Colin Jones

SEE ALSO:

THE PARIS COMMUNE: STATE TERROR; FRENCH ANARCHIST TERROR; THEORIES OF TERROR IN URBAN INSURRECTIONS.

F U R T H E R   R E A D I N G

- Doyle, W. *The Oxford History of the French Revolution.* New York: Oxford University Press, 1989.
- Furet, F., and M. Ozouf, eds. *A Critical Dictionary of the French Revolution.* Cambridge, MA: Belknap Press, 1989.
- Jordan, D. *The Revolutionary Career of Maximilien Robespierre.* New York: Free Press, 1989.
- Schama, Simon. *Citizens: A Chronicle of the French Revolution.* New York: Knopf, 1991.

THE PARIS COMMUNE: STATE TERROR

In the late nineteenth century, terror as an instrument of government was a distant memory for the people of France. But in 1871, nearly 80 years after Robespierre's infamous Reign of Terror, violence returned to the streets of Paris.

Like the Terror of 1793-94, the violence that occurred in Paris from March to May 1871 was the result of war. During the Terror, however, the violence was a matter of national emergency. In 1871, the violence occurred because of bitterness at the humiliating defeat in the Franco-Prussian War.

In an attempt to resolve the political and social turmoil into which France fell after the defeat, the government called national elections. Provincial France as a whole voted for the Monarchists, not because they particularly wanted a king but because the Monarchists were the only political group who stood for peace. But Paris voted for Republican factions, and the citizens of the poorer districts believed they could lead a radical national revolution.

KEY FACTS

● In 1871, after the crushing defeat of France by Prussia, the left-wing working classes of Paris rebelled against the new French government.

● The Parisian rebels began systematically terrorizing other sections of society. They executed hundreds of their enemies without formal trial.

● Government troops used terrorism as they recaptured Paris. The soldiers set up execution squads in the Père Lachaise cemetery and in the Luxembourg Gardens. These squads shot at least 25,000 residents of working class areas.

● The radicals of Paris led four revolutions between 1789 and 1871, but, after the crushing of the Commune, there was no further uprising until 1968.

The new parliament, the National Assembly, sat in Versailles, outside Paris, while the government set up its offices in the capital. The head of the government, Adophe Thiers, immediately set about establishing his authority against open armed opposition from the Paris National Guard. He sent army units into the city to seize the rebel weapons and, around Montmartre, soldiers confronted a crowd of national guards and civilians. Shots fired from the crowd hit two generals.

The situation soon became very ugly, and the government withdrew to Versailles. For a week, Paris had no administration at all. Parisian officials held city elections. On March 28, 1871, before a crowd estimated by some at 100,000, the officials proclaimed the Commune of Paris. Civil war began five days later.

CHAOS LEADS TO TERROR

Authority in France disintegrated, and a cycle of violence, terror, and reprisal filled the vacuum. Communication between the various parties collapsed. The government was out of touch with the realities of opinion in Paris; while the population of Paris was ignorant of government attitudes. Neither was there any communication or understanding between the moderate provinces and radical Paris.

Nobody knew who was in control. Thiers had his government, but the Monarchist-dominated Assembly effectively set up another, known as the Committee of Fifteen. Similarly, the army in Versailles had no commander until April. The situation in Paris was even worse. Five political bodies could have claimed to be the city government.

In such chaos, violence ran unchecked. The first stage was a few on-the-spot executions by the army at Versailles. Perhaps two dozen Parisians were shot in April. But the rumor in Paris was that government forces had executed 50, 100, or even as many as 200 people. The damage was done. Pressure for reprisals

---

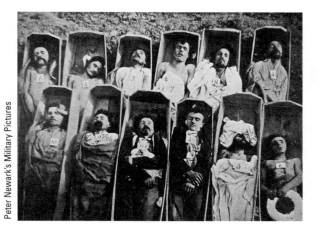

Peter Newark's Military Pictures

Corpses of Communard rebels executed by French troops are displayed to terrorize other resisters.

built up in the Paris press and in the poor eastern districts of the capital.

This led the Council of the Commune to pass a "Law of Hostages," allowing them to seize and execute government figures, although few of the councillors wanted it put into action. There was, however, a small group at the Préfecture of Police who did want to pursue the idea. Their aged hero, Auguste Blanqui, was notorious for conspiring against every French regime since 1815 and was once more in prison. The group was directed by Raoul Rigault, a talented organizer in his early twenties, who set up his own Committee of General Security. In effect, this was a government within a government.

On his own initiative, Rigault ordered the arrest of a number of Republicans, who received no protection from the Monarchist-dominated Assembly. Rigault also arrested various priests and, after trumping up evidence of a plot, the Archbishop of Paris, Georges Darboy. Using the "Law of Hostages" as a pretext, Rigault's Committee tried to obtain from the Versailles government a pledge to stop the summary executions and an exchange of their prisoners for Blanqui.

Secret letters were exchanged between the archbishop in Mazas prison and Thiers in Versailles. They achieved nothing. The negotiators contacted diplomats from other European countries, but none wanted to get involved. Finally, U.S. Ambassador Washburne, who had kept his embassy open, offered his services.

While Washburne was fruitlessly negotiating in Versailles, the Commune's council adopted a proce-dure for formally determining which of its prisoners were to be designated hostages. On April 26, Rigault had himself nominated as public prosecutor, giving him direct responsibility for this matter. The prisoners' prospects began to look bleak.

Only one formal trial actually took place. Commune officials declared 12 men from Montmartre "hostages," and then adjourned the session. The Commune authorities never reconvened the court because, two days afterward, on Sunday, May 21, 50,000 Versailles troops advanced, virtually unopposed, into western Paris. In the evening the street battles for central and eastern Paris began. The Versailles army committed atrocities on a massive scale almost at once. Among the victims was Raoul Rigault. Washburne, in the meantime, had failed to persuade the government at Versailles even to consider an exchange of Darboy for Blanqui.

The execution of the 12 hostages from Montmartre was carried out by supporters of the Commune (Communards), all of whom had lost relatives in the fighting. There were more than 100 volunteers for the first execution squad. Archbishop Darboy was among the first to be shot.

By May 28, the army had captured the city. The Assembly took control of government, and the brief terror of 1871 ended with the demise of the Commune. The hostage-taking of the Communards had had little effect on events, save to inflame the feeling of the Versailles troops. However, the atrocities committed by the Versailles troops could be said to have been a very efficient use of terror.

Paris had been the driving force behind revolution in 1789-94, in 1830, in 1848–50, and again in 1871. Yet in 1871, the conservative provinces took their revenge and crushed the left-wing capital.

Gregor Dallas

SEE ALSO:
TERROR IN THE FRENCH REVOLUTION 1789-1815.

FURTHER READING

- Christiansen, Rupert. *Paris Babylon: The Story of the Paris Commune.* New York: Viking Penguin, 1995.
- Gibson, W. *Paris during the Commune.* Brooklyn, NY: M. S. G. Haskell House, 1974.
- Tombs, R. *The War against Paris, 1871.* New York: Cambridge University Press, 1981.

TERROR IN COLONIAL CONQUESTS

The establishment of European empires over much of the world from the eighteenth century onward involved the widescale use of terror. Fundamentally, this was because the conquerors considered the conquered to be inferior, and were able to justify using terror by pointing to the "barbarous" practices of their victims. This use of terror was evident from the early period of Spanish conquest in the Americas in the sixteenth century. It accelerated, however, during the period after 1850, when European technological superiority became more evident.

During this period, several European powers, including Great Britain, France, Belgium, Portugal, and Germany, secured lands in Asia and Africa, while the Japanese had designs on East Asia. In most cases, colonial rulers thought and behaved as if subject peoples were inferior. In the nineteenth century, many aboriginal peoples in Australia and the Americas were hunted down and killed or forced into reservations simply because they got in the way of European settlers.

"SAVAGE WARS"

Wars by Europeans against Africans or Asians were termed "savage wars"; as compared to the "civilized wars" between Europeans. The terms came into being because many native societies had no concept of either surrender or a distinction between combatants and civilians. Brutality, massacre, and torture were frequent occurrences even before Europeans arrived.

Colonial armies often had access to more modern weapons than their enemies. So colonial conquest inflicted unprecedented violence on many societies in Africa and Asia. Brutal methods were employed, including burning villages and crops, and murdering civilians and prisoners. Terror tactics subdued hostile civilian populations. During the Dutch pacification of Borneo in the 1850s, a Dutch official told the military not to listen to the "voice of humanity"; while a French officer fighting in Madagascar in the late 1890s reported that "the punishment was terrible; we burned all rebel villages and cut off all rebel heads."

In nearly all colonial wars the imperial states recruited local allies whom they did not restrain on the battlefield. The French advancing into Chad in 1898 used terror to force people to become bearers. In East Africa during World War I, all the colonial powers used threats and violence to secure bearers, of whom about 100,000 died. Bearers sometimes included women and children, as in the Ashanti campaigns in Africa during 1873-74 and 1895-96.

Resistance to colonial rule was often put down with great brutality, as during the Indian Mutiny of 1857 and the Morant Bay rebellion in Jamaica in 1865. In many cases, colonial rulers used their military and judicial powers to exact revenge and to demonstrate their coercive power. The many people who died in anti-colonial revolts in Asia and Africa demonstrate the harsh means and tactics used to crush resistance.

Colonial powers responded to resistance to their authority with severe punishments. Africans were dynamited in caves in the 1896-97 Rhodesian risings against British rule. The British also put down the Zulu rising of 1906 in Natal, southern Africa, with great ferocity. In India, British soldiers killed 400 protesters at Amritsar in 1919. The Herero tribes resisting the Germans in South West Africa were driven into the desert to die. In the 1905-06 Maji Maji rising in Tanganyika (part of modern Tanzania) against the

KEY FACTS

● Colonial powers often used terror policies in order to suppress resistance by natives to their conquests and continued exercise of authority.

● Europeans in Tasmania persecuted Aborigines ruthlessly. The natives became extinct less than a century after the first European settlement.

● Some local peoples fought back. The Zulus wiped out a British army of 1,500 men in 1879. The Ethiopians defeated an Italian army at Adowa in 1896 and remained independent until 1936.

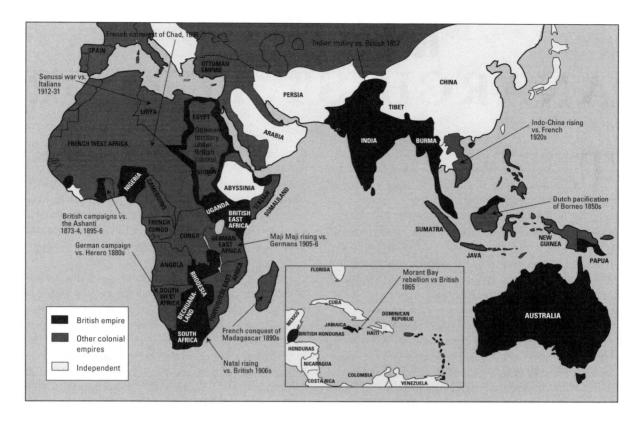

A map of colonial empires in 1898 showing clashes between colonialists and indigenous peoples.

Germans, as many as 100,000 people died. The French killed 60,000-100,000 people during the 1947 revolt in Madagascar. The occasional protests by humanitarians in Europe had little effect; they were too distant, too few, and too late.

TWENTIETH-CENTURY HORROR

Colonial conquest and pacification continued into the twentieth century. Terror policies were extensively used by the authoritarian regimes of Italy and Japan in the 1930s. Both powers used the latest machines and means of war against less technologically advanced peoples. In 1931, the Italians brutally crushed Senussi resistance to their rule in Libya. In the mid-1930s, they attacked Abyssinia (modern Ethiopia) with tanks, aircraft, bombs, and gas. They murdered civilian hostages in an attempt to break Abyssinian resistance.

Japanese attacks on China in 1937 led to mass murder, as in the killing of 100,000 people during the "Rape of Nanking." Similarly brutal methods were used by the Japanese military in many parts of Southeast Asia from 1942 to 1945. With such figures in mind, it is hardly surprising that terrorism in colonial struggles has been so bloody.

Antony B. Shaw

SEE ALSO:

THE AMRITSAR MASSACRE; JAPANESE TERROR IN THE FAR EAST; JAPANESE TERRORIZATION OF PRISONERS; TERRORISM IN COLONIAL INDIA 1900-1947.

FURTHER READING

• Olson, James. E. et al., eds. *Historical Dictionary of the British Empire*. Westport, CT: Greenwood Press, 1995.
• Porter, A. N. *European Imperialism*. Atlantic Highlands, NJ: Humanities Press International, 1995.
• Smith, Woodruff D. *European Imperialism in the Nineteenth and Twentieth Centuries*. Chicago: Nelson-Hall, 1982.

RUSSIAN ANARCHIST TERROR

The frequent use of the word *anarchism* does not conceal the fact that it is not a precise term. This imprecision is due to the wide variety of political and social theories included under this heading. In the aftermath of the French Revolution, anarchism became synonymous with chaos, revolutionary terror, and politically motivated murder. By the late nineteenth century, assassination plots were the trademark of several political movements that based their actions on anarchist writings.

NO NEED FOR GOVERNMENT

Anarchism generally describes a principle or theory of life and conduct in which society exists without a government. Harmony is obtained not by submission to law or by obedience to an established authority, but by free agreement between the various groups of society. The key principle is voluntarism – the free association of free individuals. This principle may include voluntary revolutionary activity. This is based on belief in the existence of a dormant, revolutionary popular energy. Anarchists have contended that this energy could be unleashed by propaganda or by terror, the so-called propaganda of action.

The idea of the propaganda of action was particularly common in nineteenth-century Russian anarchism. Unlike in Western Europe, anarchist theories did not take root in Russia until the middle of the century. Their full development is particularly associated with one charismatic figure, Mikhail Bakunin. Like so many Russian anarchists, Bakunin was born of an aristocratic family and served briefly as an officer in the Imperial Guard. In 1835, he resigned his commission, disgusted by the oppressive character of Czarist autocracy.

Under the influence of the writings of the German philosopher G. W. F. Hegel and the French anarchist Pierre J. Proudhon, Bakunin developed his own brand of anarchism. For most of his life Bakunin lived abroad. For his participation in the 1848-49 revolution in Germany, however, Bakunin was handed over to the Russian authorities. In 1855, he was banished to eastern Siberia, from where he escaped to the United States and then to Britain in 1861. He spent the rest of his life in exile, mostly in Switzerland.

FREEING THE ENSLAVED MASSES

Bakunin's revolutionary anarchism was extremely frank and comprehensive in its destructiveness. He rejected all ideal systems, in whatever shape or name, from the idea of God downward, and every form of external authority, be it monarchic or parliamentary. According to Bakunin, each form of authority enslaves a large majority of the people. To free the enslaved majority, he argued, existing society had to be overturned. For this purpose, Bakunin developed a revolutionary system that had to be pursued without scruples of morality, religion, or private feelings.

Although Bakunin spent most of his politically active life outside Russia, his periodic expressions of a belief in a revolt by the oppressed Russian peasants found ready admirers there. Bakunin's most important remaining link with Russia was through Sergei Nechayev. In 1869, after meeting Bakunin in Switzerland a year earlier, Nechayev set up a revolutionary organization in Moscow, the Narodnaya Rasprava (the People's Reckoning). Though suppressed by the government in the same year, parts

---

K E Y   F A C T S

● The anarchist movement in Russia began with a group of 44 people and never rose above 500, out of a population of nearly 100 million.

● In January 1878, the mass trial of 193 anarchists prompted the movement's first terrorist act, the shooting of the St. Petersburg police chief.

● After the arrests of key activists in 1881 and 1882, the anarchist party fell under the influence of left-wing radicals, including Alexander Ulyanov, brother of the future Bolshevik leader, Lenin.

Hulton Getty Picture Collection

Czar Alexander II is killed by a bomb planted by the terrorist group, the People's Will, on March 1, 1881.

of the organization survived, to be replaced in 1873 by a mass movement known as Back to the People. The movement derived its name from a pamphlet written by Alexander Herzen entitled *Narod* (To the People).

Herzen's pamphlet, an appeal to Russia's youth, made a strong impact in student circles. Its title gave a name to the revolutionary movement which began to develop in 1870s known as the Narodniki (Populists). Their activities were initially confined to propaganda – their main aim was to preach a vague revolutionary message to the rural masses. Despite these propagandist efforts to stir up the peasants against the injustices of the Czarist regime, the masses remained inert. As followers of Bakunin, however, Populists continued to believe that the peasants were instinctive rebels who would rise up once they were told that their strength lay in their vast numbers.

FROM WORDS TO VIOLENCE

Disillusioned with the negligible effect of their radical propaganda on the people, the most determined and political radicals were driven toward terrorism. The shift indicated their increasing isolation from the object of their liberation movement, the rural masses.

In the fall of 1879, this minority took the name of Narodnaya Volya (the People's Will). It was a secret organization which comprised 30 members; it was dedicated to fighting the Czarist regime using systematic terror in the hope of kindling the revolutionary energy of the peasants. On its founding, the executive committee of the organization passed a death sentence

on Czar Alexander II. The assassination of the Czar was now the group's prime objective. The People's Will was the first terrorist group in Russian history and a model for later groups. The very existence of this group resulted in terrorist violence becoming a recognized means of opposition.

The People's Will was as secretive as it was elitist. Indeed, the organization's name was a misnomer. The people had become an abstract concept with no equivalent in the real world. It was, however, on behalf of the people that the People's Will assumed the authority to speak. The organization's objective was to assassinate government officials and, ultimately, the Czar himself. This, it was hoped, would help to undermine the regime and break down the mystique surrounding rulers.

ASSASSINATING THE CZAR

The terrorist campaign launched by the People's Will caught the government unprepared. Still, three times the organization failed in its attempts to assassinate the Czar. These failures led to a considerable thinning of the membership of the People's Will.

The police arrested the guiding figures of the group, including A. D. Mikhailov. Sofya Perovskaya now carried on the activities of the dwindling organization. It was Perovskaya who achieved the group's main objective, by organizing the assassination of the Czar. On March 1, 1881, Alexander II fell victim to a terrorist bomb. But the assassination did not produce the desired political results: the peasantry did not rise; moderate urban public opinion was horrified; and the radical cause lost support. Anarchist terrorism, exemplified by the Populists, had run its course.

Thomas G. Otte

SEE ALSO:

FRENCH ANARCHIST TERROR; THEORIES OF TERROR IN URBAN INSURRECTIONS.

F U R T H E R   R E A D I N G

- Avrich, Paul. *Anarchist Portraits*. Princeton, NJ: Princeton University Press, 1990.
- Avrich, Paul. *The Russian Anarchists*. Westport, CT: Greenwood Press, 1980.
- Joll, James. *The Anarchists*. Cambridge, MA: Harvard University Press, 1980.

FRENCH ANARCHIST TERROR

Anarchism in the late nineteenth century is popularly associated with terrorist violence by sinister conspirators. Bombs in public places and attempted murders of individuals by anarchists became increasingly widespread in Europe and the United States from the 1880s to the 1900s. These attacks claimed their most prominent victims through the assassinations of politicians or members of royal families, including Canovas del Castillo, prime minister of Spain, in 1892; the Empress Elizabeth of Austria in 1898; King Umberto of Italy in 1900; and President McKinley in 1901.

The practice of terrorism was intended to be propaganda by the deed, but it was only one aspect of anarchism at a particular period. The nature of anarchist theory excluded large-scale political movements geared to fighting in the public arena to conquer state power. There were widespread claims in the press that a Black International of anarchists was orchestrating the violence, but although the tactic had been approved at international anarchist meetings in 1880 and 1881, such decisions did not lead to concerted action by anarchists.

The reality was one of scattered small groups or isolated individuals who shared some measure of common ideology and in some cases shared readership of the same books or periodicals. International contacts between anarchists were made largely on an individual level when activists moved from one country to another, often as exiles.

The question was how to promote the move from capitalism under state authority to an anarchistic form of social organization. This implied either gradual change through teaching and example, or else some form of revolution, or a combination of the two. However, even those who believed in revolution did not necessarily think in terms of armed overthrow by systematic violence. The revolutionary general strike was one example of a non-violent anarchist weapon.

ANARCHIST TERRORISM

The idea of using terrorism as a weapon of propaganda had begun to take root in anarchist circles during the 1870s. The meeting of Russians Sergei Nechayev and Mikhail Bakunin in Geneva in 1869 led to collaborative production of a number of pamphlets expounding the notion of terrorism. The successful assassination of Czar Alexander II in 1881 also played its part in spreading the attraction of acts of violence against persons and/or property seen as symbols of the established social order.

Meanwhile, in Italy, Errico Malatesta, Carlo Cafiero, and others had fomented attempts at insurrection intended to stir the oppressed classes to spontaneous revolt. These actions were abortive and extremely limited in scope. Nevertheless, they contributed to the spread of ideas concerning propaganda by the deed. This term meant, in effect, seeking to carry out exemplary acts of violence against symbolic targets to raise the awareness among the oppressed and to spread fear among the oppressors.

The fact that the perpetrators of terrorist acts were often caught and subjected to execution or long prison sentences created martyrs. At first, this only served to encourage recruitment. Furthermore, the trials of suspected anarchists also provided a pulpit in the courtroom where they could proclaim their views.

K E Y   F A C T S

● Anarchist terrorism began in France in the early 1880s and was largely abandoned by 1895.

● Léon-Jules Léauthier's stabbing of a Serb diplomat in a Paris café in November 1893 shocked French society. Cafés were widely used as friendly meeting places and the attack did much to lose public support for the anarchists.

● In August 1894, the French authorities put 30 French anarchists on trial in Paris. The public objected to the atmosphere of the show trial, and the jury acquitted 27 of the defendants.

June 24, 1894: French president Sadi-Carnot is assassinated in Lyon by the anarchist Santo Caserio.

Hulton Getty Picture Collection

In France, with its revolutionary tradition still alive despite the bloody suppression of the Paris Commune of 1871, anarchist theorists preached propaganda by the deed in the 1880s. Yet there were few significant acts of terrorism in France during that period and some of those that were attributed to anarchists may not have been their work. By the early 1890s, some theorists were becoming increasingly wary of terrorism and favored more patient means of spreading the word. But by then a number of anarchists, inspired at least in part by the writings of revolt, were turning to acts of terrorism.

ASSASSINATION ATTEMPTS

The peak of anarchist outrages in France occurred in 1892-94, with 11 significant bombings and many lesser incidents. The most notorious of the bombings were those committed by Emile Henry, François-Claudius Ravachol (two attempts to blow up judicial officers), and Auguste Vaillant (a bomb hurled down on parliamentarians in the Chamber of Deputies). Sometimes the weapon of attack was the knife or the gun, as when Charles Gallo fired off shots in the Paris stock exchange in 1886, and when Santo Caserio stabbed President Sadi-Carnot to death on June 24, 1894, on a public street.

The motives of the attacker were often complicated by personal desperation or by criminality. Nevertheless, their shared aim was to destabilize bourgeois society, avenging the suffering of the oppressed and that of earlier, martyred terrorists. Their hope was to serve as pointers toward revolution so that the working masses would in turn rise up.

These outrages gave the authorities the pretext they wanted for taking determined action. In the spring of 1894, there were over 100 anarchists in custody in French prisons waiting for trial on some charge or other. Doubts now hung over the value of propaganda by the deed.

Nevertheless, anarchist commentators tended not to condemn the terrorists outright. They had to acknowledge the extent to which terrorism attracted massive publicity. Although terrorist attacks were the object of frenzied denunciations in the mainstream press, anarchism also profited from these acts. This was especially true in avant-garde circles, where anarchism gained a following for a time. Furthermore, there was some unwillingness among the public to endorse wholesale repression of the movement.

After 1894, anarchist terrorism largely ceased in France. Instead, propaganda was carried out through writing, education, and the development of anarcho-syndicates. Increasingly, the anarchists influenced French labor unions through Syndicalism. Syndicalism preached an anarchic society composed of individuals linked into unions by class or trade and freely cooperating without a state apparatus. The Syndicalist movement was behind the strikes of 1909, but was swept away by the patriotic mobilization of 1914. The last expression of anarchism had failed.

Chris Flood

SEE ALSO:

RUSSIAN ANARCHIST TERROR; THEORIES OF TERROR IN URBAN INSURRECTIONS.

FURTHER READING

- Avrich, Paul. *Anarchist Portraits*. Princeton, NJ: Princeton University Press, 1990.
- Joll, James. *The Anarchists*. Cambridge, MA: Harvard University Press, 1980.
- Sonn, Richard D. *Anarchism*. New York: Twayne Macmillan, 1992.

TERROR'S USE IN MACEDONIA 1893-1934

In the Balkans, almost 40 percent of the historic region of Macedonia now belongs to the Republic of Macedonia. The rest is shared between Bulgaria and Greece. Between the fourteenth century and early twentieth centuries, Macedonia lay within the Ottoman Turkish empire and was administratively divided into three provinces.

The population, numbered at 2.5 million according to the Turkish census of 1904, was divided by nationality. The largest group comprised Orthodox Christian Slav-speakers. Most of these defined themselves as Bulgarians and spoke a language closely akin to Bulgarian. There were also large numbers of Albanians, Serbs, Greeks, Muslim Slavs, Vlachs, and Turks. The economy was mainly rural.

RIPE FOR REVOLUTION

In the nineteenth century, the Ottoman empire in Europe was disintegrating. Greece, Serbia, Romania, and Bulgaria became independent states. Macedonia remained within the empire, where its population was subject to heavy tax and the arbitrary rule of local administrators. But Turkish rule in the Macedonian provinces was largely confined to the main cities and communication routes. The weakness of Turkish authority in the countryside made possible the emergence of a revolutionary organization – with terrorism at its core.

"FREEDOM OR DEATH"

The Internal Macedonian Revolutionary Organization (IMRO) was founded in 1893 in Thessaloniki, although it was only so named in 1906. At its start, IMRO committed itself to "freedom or death," and to ridding Macedonian territory of Turkish rule.

Nevertheless, IMRO was divided as to its other goals. Some members wanted to create an autonomous Macedonian state as the focus of a Balkan federation of Christian Slavonic peoples. Others saw the liberation of Macedonia as the forerunner of annexation by Bulgaria. IMRO was followed in 1895 by the establishment of an "external" counterpart, based in Bulgaria and known as the Supremacists. This group supported the aim of Macedonia's inclusion in the Bulgarian state.

Although IMRO claimed its support was strongest among the peasantry, its members came mostly from the intellectual and professional classes. IMRO was based upon a network of cells, grouped within a hierarchy of local and regional committees, and headed by a central committee. Warbands, or *chetas*, usually consisting of 15-20 men, operated largely independently of this framework.

THE MOST EFFECTIVE TERROR TACTICS

The principal tactic of IMRO was to commit spectacular terrorist acts in order to draw the attention of the great powers to the plight of the Macedonians. IMRO also wanted to force reprisals that would attract the peasantry to become members of IMRO.

Internal records, however, show disputes between those who favored a general insurrection and those who recommended terrorist acts. After 1897, members of IMRO engaged in sporadic violence, including the murder of Turkish border guards and Ottoman sympa-

---

KEY FACTS

● In 1902, the Ottoman authorities amassed over 300,000 troops in Macedonia in response to the Supremacist revolt. Albanian and Ottoman irregulars supported the authorities, intimidating the local population by raping and murdering villagers.

● A revolutionary organization (later known as IMRO) rose up the next year, 1903, burning haystacks, destroying bridges and telegraph lines, occupying strategic centres, and intimidating village headmen.

● In 1993 the Yugoslav republic of Macedonia declared itself independent, leading to disputes with Greece and Serbia.

In the late nineteenth century, Macedonia was divided among three provinces of the Ottoman empire in the central Balkans.

thizers. Since membership dues secured very little money, IMRO's *comitadji* or "committee-men" had to raise money through extortion, kidnapping, and protection rackets.

GOVERNMENT RESPONSE

The Ottoman authorities responded to IMRO's activities with mass arrests and the destruction of villages of supposed sympathizers. IMRO was also involved in running battles with members of the Bulgaria-based Supremacists and with pro-Serbian and pro-Greek guerrilla units operating in Macedonia. They were ill-equipped to keep a revolutionary movement going and support among the local population was never particularly strong. In 1903, IMRO could scarcely muster 40,000 activists.

In 1902, the Macedonian Supremacists had launched a revolt in Macedonia, which was rapidly suppressed. Fearful in case its own networks were

uncovered in the crackdown, IMRO launched its own uprising in August 1903. This was known as the St. Elijah's Day (Illinden) Uprising, and was followed some days later by the Resurrection Day (Preobrazhenski) Rising in the region of Adrianople, which bordered Macedonia. Neither rebellion gathered much support among the peasantry. By mid-September, the revolt was largely over, although the Ottoman authorities were forced to promise that they would make reforms.

THE DEMISE OF THE ORGANIZATION

After the failure of the Illinden-Preobrazhenski Uprisings, IMRO's influence waned. Macedonia never achieved independence, but was partitioned among neighboring Serbia, Bulgaria, and Greece after the Balkan Wars of 1912-13 and World War I. Between 1918 and 1939, IMRO engaged in terrorist actions to liberate those parts of Macedonia that had been incorporated into Yugoslavia in 1919, and to set up an effective state-within-a-state at Petrich on the Bulgarian-Yugoslav border. IMRO also mounted terror attacks against the Bulgarian government and in 1923 were involved in the assassination of the Bulgarian prime minister. In 1934, a new Bulgarian government, installed in the wake of a military coup, effectively broke up IMRO.

With the collapse of communism in Yugoslavia, IMRO reformed in Macedonia in 1990. But it was now a nationalist political party, not a terrorist organization.

Martyn Rady

SEE ALSO:

WORLD WAR II RESISTANCE IN YUGOSLAVIA AND TERRORISM; TERROR IN THE FORMER YUGOSLAVIA.

FURTHER READING

- Jelavich, Charles, and Barbara Jelavich. *The Establishment of the National Balkan States, 1804-1920.* Seattle, WA: University of Washington Press, 1986.
- Perry, Duncan. *The Politics of Terror: The Macedonian Revolutionary Movements, 1893-1903.* Durham, NC: University of North Carolina Press, 1988.
- Pribichevich, Stoyan. *Macedonia: Its People and History.* University Park, PA: Penn State University Press, 1982.

ASSASSINATION AT SARAJEVO 1914

Few cases of terrorist murder had such momentous consequences as the assassination of Archduke Franz Ferdinand, the heir to the Habsburg throne and future ruler of the multi-ethnic Austro-Hungarian empire. The event triggered a chain reaction among the powers of Europe, resulting in the outbreak of World War I (1914-18). At the war's end, the monarchies of Eastern and Central Europe were swept away; the political map of Europe was redrawn; and the seeds of World War II were sown.

It was hardly surprising that the Archduke Franz Ferdinand should be a target for extremist nationalist groups in the Balkans. The withdrawl of the Ottoman empire from the Balkans in the course of the nineteenth century left a power vacuum which Austria-Hungary and its rival power in the region, Russia, were keen to fill. Austria annexed Bosnia in 1908, causing great resentment among parts of the population who had hoped for some measure of independence from foreign powers. Serbia, the largest most powerful Balkan state and enjoying the backing of Austria's rival, Russia, was also bitterly opposed to the move. Bosnia, then as now, had a large population of Serbs, giving Serbia a reason to lay claim to the land. There was no hope of the Serbian government taking on the fading, but still mighty, Austrian empire. But extreme nationalists began to form secret underground societies whose aim was to destabilize the region using terrorist tactics.

THE BLACK HAND

One such group was the conspiratorial organization Ujedinjenje Ili Smrt ("Union or Death"), better known as Crna Ruka or the Black Hand, which had been created in May 1911 by a group of Serbian army officers angered by the cautious stance of Serbian prime minister Nikola Pasic. The Black Hand was a secret society which supported a number of terrorist groups in Macedonia and Bosnia, although it was never clear whether the Black Hand wanted a united Slav state ("Yugoslavia") or simply a Greater Serbia.

By late 1911, the Black Hand was under the energetic leadership of Colonel Dragutin Dimitrijevic, former head of Serb intelligence. He had come to political prominence because of his leading role in the assassination of King Alexander of Serbia in 1903. That murder had ended the pro-Austrian Obrenovic dynasty and brought to power the pro-Russian, Serb nationalist Petar Karadjordjevic. This accounted for Serbian opposition to Austria's taking power in Bosnia-Herzegovina five years afterward.

The Black Hand, under the control of Dimitrijevic, intensified its terrorist connections, concentrating on Austrian targets in Bosnia such as government buildings. Among its contacts in that province were Trifko Grabez, Nedeljko Cabrinovic, and a 19-year-old student called Gavrilo Princip. These three wanted a spectacular outrage that would shake Austria's resolve to keep troublesome Bosnia within its empire. As early as summer 1913, they were conspiring with four other sympathizers, Mehmed Mehmedbasic, Danilo Ilic, Cvetco Popovic, and Vasa Cubrilovic, to plan the assassination of Archduke Franz Ferdinand.

KEY FACTS

● Resentment of Austrian rule in Bosnia was concentrated among the middle classes, the majority population was largely indifferent.

● June 28, 1914, the day of the assassination, was the 525th anniversary of the destruction of the medieval Serb empire at the battle of Kosovo – a highly symbolic date for Serbs.

● Serb support of the terrorists led directly to the Austro-Bulgarian conquest of Serbia in 1915.

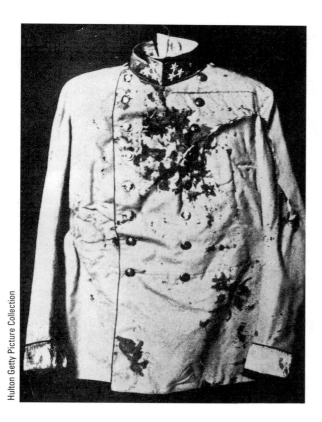

The blood-stained coat of Archduke Franz Ferdinand, assassinated by Gavrilo Princip in 1914.

In late spring 1914, Cabrinovic, Grabez, and Princip were brought out of Bosnia to the Serbian capital Belgrade for weapons training by the Black Hand. In May, they were smuggled back into Bosnia by secret service officers under the command of Dimitrijevic. Determined to further the cause of Serb nationalism and encouraged by the support of Dimitrijevic, they and their four co-conspirators went ahead with their plan to kill Franz Ferdinand.

PISTOL SHOTS

The archduke had repeatedly been advised against making a long-planned visit to Sarajevo, the capital of Bosnia-Herzegovina, because of the explosive situation in the province, but he insisted on going. He finally decided to make the visit on June 28, 1914. For Serbia and the Serbs living in Bosnia, this date marked a day of national mourning to commemorate the crushing defeat of the medieval Serb empire by the Turks at the

battle of Kosovo in 1389. For the heir to the throne of Bosnia's oppressors to parade in its streets on that very day was regarded as provocative.

Habsburg intelligence had been carefully monitoring the situation in Bosnia and had little doubt that the archduke was in danger from Serb nationalists. Despite repeated warnings not to go, Franz Ferdinand rejected all advice and went to Sarajevo with his wife Sophie, duchess of Hohenburg.

The plan was to drive through the streets to an official reception given by the mayor at the town hall. Possibly by way of protest, the Bosnians did not make the security arrangements that were usual for visiting royalty. No soldiers lined the route, and no extra police were put on duty, even though the procession of the archducal couple through the town would attract a large crowd of onlookers.

Hidden in the crowd, and positioned at different places along the route, were the seven conspirators. Their first attempt on the archduke's life was a grenade attack on his open car. Eyewitnesses claim the archduke picked up the bomb and hurled it behind him, where it exploded, injuring the occupants of the following car.

Incredibly, the procession was not halted. Instead, the route was changed, but the driver of the first vehicle continued to drive along the original route, until his mistake was pointed out and he slowed down to change direction. Gavrilo Princip saw his chance. He broke through the thin line of police officers posted in front of the crowd, pulled out a Browning automatic pistol, and shot the archduke and his wife at point-blank range. The duchess died instantly, and Franz Ferdinand expired ten minutes later, at 11:30 A.M.

AUSTRIA RETALIATES

The Austrian authorities quickly rounded up and arrested all of the conspirators. Their link with Serbia was soon established but their association with Dimitrijevic and other high-ranking officials in the Serbian government only emerged after 1918. At the time, the Austrian government only had strong suspicions that Serbia was involved. Such suspicions were strengthened when Serbia failed to launch an immediate inquiry into the role played by the Black Hand organization in the assassination plot.

Austria was more or less forced into making an appropriate response to the outrage, for it was a direct challenge to its authority in Bosnia. To do nothing might encourage Serbia to annex Bosnia itself. This in

Franz Ferdinand, moments from death, rides with scant security through troubled Sarejevo.

Hulton Getty Picture Collection

turn might precipitate a wave of independence movements in other parts of the creaking empire, and hasten its disintegration.

Ironically, although Franz Ferdinand was unpopular at court in the Austrian capital Vienna, he had been a moderating influence for peace within the government. Hence, his death was an event of considerable importance. After this, nothing shielded the aging Emperor Franz Joseph and foreign minister Count Leopold Berchtold from the demands of the more warlike members of the government and the army. The latter's chief of staff, Field Marshal Franz Freiherr Conrad von Hötzendorf, in particular, had long demanded a military action against the increasingly hostile and pro-Russian Serbian state.

HURTLING TOWARD WAR

Any punitive action against Serbia, however, would involve great risks. If Russia, the self-appointed protector of the Serbs, opposed such action, Austria-Hungary either had to back down or risk all-out war with Serbia and Russia. As a result, Austria sought the support of her ally Germany, and duly obtained firm backing for a swift military retaliation against Serbia.

On July 23, the Habsburg government presented Belgrade with a 48-hour ultimatum, including what they knew to be unacceptable conditions. Failing acceptance, the Austro-Hungarian ambassador to Serbia was instructed to sever diplomatic relations with Belgrade.

Serbia retaliated by mobilizing its troops on July 25, and events escalated at an alarming rate. On July 28, Austria-Hungary declared war on Serbia, and the next day its navy began to bombard Belgrade. Two days afterward, Russia mobilized 1.2 million troops. Germany, fearing an imminent Russian attack on its ally Austria, demanded the immediate cessation of Russia's mobilization preparations. This demand, together with the Austrian bombardment of Belgrade, convinced the Russians that the two powers had intended war from the start.

On August 1, Germany declared war on Russia. France, committed by a treaty of alliance to come to Russia's aid, placed its army on a war footing but did not declare war on Germany. On August 3, however, the German government declared war on France, and marched into Belgium. As Belgian neutrality was guaranteed by Britain in a treaty dating back to 1839, Britain joined the war on the side of France and Russia, and declared war on Germany on August 4.

All the great powers of Europe were now at war. World War I had begun, just five weeks after a terrorist attack intended to make Austria-Hungary consider pulling out of Bosnia.

Thomas G. Otte

SEE ALSO:

TERROR'S USE IN MACEDONIA 1893-1934; TERROR IN WORLD WAR I.

FURTHER READING

- Gilbert, Martin. *The First World War: A Complete History.* New York: Henry Holt, 1994.
- Joll, James. *Origins of the First World War.* White Plains, NY: Longman Publishing Group, 1991.
- Joyce, C. Patrick. *Sarajevo Shots: Studies in the Immediate Origin of World War I.* Brooklyn, NY: Revisionist Press, 1979.
- Williamson, Samuel R., Jr. *Austria-Hungary and the Coming of the First World War.* New York: St. Martin's Press, 1991.

TERROR IN WORLD WAR I

The horrors of World War I were not confined to the battlefields. The armies of the Central Powers – Germany and Austria-Hungary – both used terror tactics against civilians.

An important part of the strategy of the German army, which invaded Belgium and France in 1914, was a set of policies known as *Schrecklichkeit* ("dreadfulness" or "frightfulness".) German forces had already used such an approach in colonial warfare. In German South West Africa between 1904 and 1906, for example, the Germans used particularly callous methods to crush the revolts of the Herero and Hottentot peoples who lived in the colony. Thousands of men, women, and children were murdered. They were shot, hanged, or forced out into the desert to die of starvation. The final death toll – amounting, in the case of the Herero people, to 80-85 percent of the population – amounted to genocide.

The greatest fear of the German forces during the invasion of France was of the *francs-tireurs* (sharpshooters), partisans (guerrillas) who operated in the rear of the invading army. During the invasion of France in 1871, some 25 percent of German forces were employed in guarding such rear areas. From the start of World War I, the Germans pursued a policy of brutal reprisals against civilians in Belgium and France in response to partisan activity. If there were German casualties, civilians were rounded up and shot, often in far greater numbers than the German soldiers killed. This policy was intended to act as a deterrent to civilians, warning them not to resist the German occupation or undertake resistance activities.

METHODS OF BRUTALITY

Hostage-taking was another method used to keep the local populations in line. Both male and female civilian hostages, usually the most prominent citizens, were taken by the German forces as a matter of course. The Germans did not have any scruples about executing such hostages in retaliation for partisan activity. Even priests, who were regarded by the Germans as ringleaders of partisan activity, were taken. Six are known to have been executed in the Belgian town of Warsage.

The threat to kill the hostages was sometimes enough to subdue local populations, but often their capture was only a pretext to remove leaders who might organize resistance. In Belgium, around 150 hostages were killed at Aerschot, and 612, including a baby, at Dinant. When the town of Tamines was sacked, over 380 civilians were shot outside the church.

CRUSHING RESISTANCE

Belgian resistance to the advance of the German army undoubtedly led to a hardening of attitudes within the German military. Worse, the Belgian army's destruction of key points, such as bridges, in an attempt to delay the enemy advance was interpreted by the Germans – made nervous by memories of the 1870-71 war – as the work of partisans. Incidents in which parties of Germans accidentally shot at each other (what would now be called "friendly fire" incidents) were also regarded as the work of partisans. While there was some partisan activity in Belgium, it was

---

KEY FACTS

● At the start of World War I, the German advance into Belgium and France in the autumn of 1914 was marked by the adoption of a terror policy of *Schrecklichkeit* (dreadfulness).

● In March 1917, the Germans withdrew to a more defensible position, the Siegfried Stellung, known to the Allies as the Hindenburg Line. The German army evacuated 125,000 French inhabitants to camps in German-held territory. The Germans destroyed bridges, roads, railroads, and buildings. They chopped down fruit trees, polluted wells, and laid ingenious booby traps.

● Turkey used deliberate terror in World War I, directed against its ethnic minorities to prevent their taking advantage of war chaos to rise up.

Peter Newark's Military Pictures

The passenger liner Lusitania *is sunk by a German submarine on May 7, 1915, with the loss of 1,400 lives.*

nowhere near the scale the Germans believed. Life for civilians in German-occupied France and Belgium was hard. The Belgian birth rate declined and the death rate rose sharply. The German army dragged hundreds of thousands of civilians from their homes to be used as forced labor in Germany's mines and factories. About 120,000 Belgians and 100,000 French workers were deported to Germany during the occupation.

OUTRAGE AT ATROCITIES

German terror tactics may have subdued the terrified citizens in occupied territories, but they were counterproductive in the effect they had on the civilian population of Germany's enemies, particularly Britain. Stories of atrocities against women and children, brought back by returning soldiers, were a gift to recruiting sergeants.

The initial rush of volunteers had begun to dry up as tales of horror in the trenches filtered back home. Clever propaganda posters showing "the Hun" impaling babies on bayonets brought outraged citizens flocking to join up. Furthermore, any qualms the civilian populations of the Entente Powers – France,

Britain, Russia – might have had about the legalities of declaring war were swept away and replaced by a conviction that they were fighting a just war against unspeakable evil. Meanwhile, the Germans excelled in their capacity for outrage when they burned the Belgian medieval university town of Louvain on August 26, 1914. On the previous night, nervous German troops had opened fire, probably as a response to an unexpected noise in the dark, but the Germans claimed Belgian snipers had been at work. The complete destruction of the town, and especially the famous library with its irreplaceable collections, greatly shocked the world.

Similar actions were carried out in France. The village of Nomeny, in the north-eastern province of Lorraine, for example, was destroyed by the Germans on August 20, 1914. Fifty civilians died in the inferno.

The Germans justified their policy of *Schrecklichkeit* on the grounds that Belgium, as a neutral power, had broken international law by their resistance. The Germans saw the hand of the Belgian government and local authorities in the organization of what they termed "illegal resistance." The commander of the German Third Army, General von Hausen, justified the destruction of Dinant by claiming that it was the fault of the Belgian authorities, because they had "approved this perfidious street fighting contrary to international law."

The German military's view of the illegality of Belgian resistance was plainly hypocritical. By invading Belgium, Germany knew that it was breaking an international treaty that it had signed in 1839 along with Britain, Russia, France, and Austria. This treaty declared that Belgium was an "independent and perpetually neutral state." But, because Germany's plans for the invasion of France, made in the decade preceding 1914, depended on its troops' being able to go through Belgium, such legal niceties as Belgian neutrality had been brushed aside in favor of the strategic considerations.

Another German strategy that might be construed as the use of terror tactics against civilians was the move toward unrestricted submarine warfare. In the early part of the war, submarines were instructed to attack only enemy shipping, and to give a warning beforehand so that the ship's personnel could be evacuated first. Soon, however, the order was given that any shipping entering enemy waters was at risk. The sinking of the passenger liner *Lusitania* in May 1915, with the loss of 1,400 lives, was a tragic consequence of this policy.

EASTERN FRONT TERROR

The pattern of German behavior in France and Belgium during World War I was also repeated on the Eastern Front. Here, Germany, together with its Central Power ally, the Austro-Hungarian empire, fought against France's ally Russia.

Early in August 1914, the Germans indiscriminately shelled the town of Kalisz in Prussian Poland in retaliation for shots fired at German troops by suspected partisans. During the following year, the Central Powers captured much of Poland from the Russians, and the Germans stripped Poland of factory machinery and raw materials.

The Austro-Hungarian forces also had a similar, if less dramatic, policy of economic asset stripping. These forces also retaliated savagely against any Poles and Ukrainians accused of collaborating with the enemy when the Russians successfully advanced into eastern Galicia. Such use of terror, however, was not the sole prerogative of the Central Powers: the Russians also carried out acts of terror during their retreat from Poland during 1914.

THE AUSTRIANS IN SERBIA

The Austrians carried out a form of *Schrecklichkeit* during their abortive invasion of Serbia in 1914. The Serbs proved to be a tough and resourceful enemy, and Austro-Hungarian failures on the battlefield resulted in the punishment of Serb civilians. Many became the victims of reprisals, such as the mass execution of Serb women at Macva in August 1914. According to a *Report on Atrocities Committed by the Austro-Hungarian Army*, there were many examples of the rape, torture, and murder of females.

In Serbia and elsewhere, Austrian troops committed atrocities against enemy civilians, possibly out of sheer frustration. The Austro-Hungarian empire went into the war against Serbia believing that it would win an easy victory. The reality was a war of attrition that drained its resources and hastened its downfall.

The Central Powers' use of terror in World War I prefigured the behavior of the Nazi German occupying armies. German counterinsurgency in World War II, particularly in Poland and the Soviet Union, fitted into a pattern of response that stretched back beyond the conflict of 1914-18 to the conflict with *franc-tireurs* in the Franco-Prussian War of 1870-71.

W. B. Brabiner

SEE ALSO:

TERROR IN COLONIAL CONQUESTS; TERROR IN THE GERMAN OCCUPATION OF THE EAST; GERMAN TERROR IN FRANCE AND ITALY; TERROR IN THE FORMER YUGOSLAVIA.

FURTHER READING

- Cull, N. J. *Selling War: The British Propaganda Campaign against American Neutrality in World War I*. New York: Oxford University Press, 1995.
- Gilbert, Martin. *Atlas of World War I*. New York: Oxford University Press, 1995.
- Gilbert, Martin. *The First World War: A Complete History*. New York: Henry Holt, 1994.
- Marshall, S. L. A. *The American Heritage History of World War I*. Boston, MA: Houghton Mifflin, 1985.

TERROR IN IRELAND 1916-1923

When World War I broke out in 1914, Ireland was a largely Catholic nation (albeit with an important Protestant majority in the northern province of Ulster) and an unwilling part of the British empire. The case for independence was overwhelmingly popular within Ireland, while even the Parliament at Westminster seemed to have accepted the justice of the Irish Nationalist cause by agreeing to a Home Rule Bill. The bill, however, never took effect – its provisions were suspended as soon as war broke out.

THE EASTER RISING

The issue may have been shelved in Britain, but not in Ireland. Despairing of a political solution, nationalists in Ireland, the Irish Volunteers, rebelled on Easter Monday, April 24, 1916. After taking key buildings in the capital Dublin, they declared an Irish Republic, with Commandant Padraig Pearse as president. The British sent in troops, fought pitched battles all over the city center, and sent gunboats up the River Liffey to shell rebel strongholds. It was all over in a week.

The Easter Rising was doomed by bad luck, lack of popular support, and the failure of the efforts of rebel retired British diplomat Sir Roger Casement to secure German aid. Pearse was executed on May 12, with six others including one James Connolly, who had to be wheeled from his hospital bed to meet the firing squad. Casement was tried for high treason and hanged in London. The British executed 16 rebels for an insurrection that caused 794 civilian and 521 military casualties. The British had responded with excessive brutality, making the rebels into martyrs, the Easter Rising into a legend, and further alienating the Irish.

BIRTH OF THE IRISH REPUBLICAN ARMY

After the failure of the Easter Rising, some nationalists realized that a new strategy was needed. A new type of resistance began to take shape. The Irish Volunteers were reorganized into the Irish Republican Army (IRA) and prepared for a guerrilla war.

The nationalists also formed a political party named Sinn Féin (Ourselves Alone), which ran candidates in elections to the British House of Commons in 1918. They won all the Irish seats except those in the northern province of Ulster. The Protestant majority there supported the Ulster Unionist Party, which insisted that Ulster be excluded from any deals on Home Rule.

While the Sinn Féin Members of Parliament (MPs) argued their case publicly, the IRA practiced terrorist methods designed to frustrate the British authorities and to make the policing of Ireland much more difficult and costly. There were rural guerrilla attacks on troops and police, and serious rioting in the cities, incited by secret IRA brigades. Terrorist activity was coordinated by Michael Collins, a former civil servant turned gifted, ruthless guerrilla fighter.

Unlike Pearse and the Irish Volunteers of 1916, Collins enjoyed mass popular support. The nationalists were confident enough in 1919 to form an unofficial Irish parliament, which included the 25 Sinn Féin MPs who had refused to take their seats in the House of

KEY FACTS

● When Irish nationalists rose up in the Easter Rising in 1916, the British were outraged at rebellion while the United Kingdom was in the throes of World War I. Their sense of indignation fueled the force with which they put down the rebellion.

● The 1921 treaty leaving Ulster under British control did not satisfy hard-line members of the IRA. In April 1922, opposers to the treaty seized the Four Courts, a large building in the Irish capital, Dublin, and barricaded themselves in. The Irish government had to drive them out.

The civil war in Ireland in April 1922: the two sides clashed in the Battle for the Four Courts in Dublin.

Peter Newark's Historical Pictures

Commons. Their president was Eamon de Valera, a Sinn Féin MP jailed in 1918, when British forces rounded up 500 Sinn Féin supporters after IRA attacks.

BLACK AND TANS

The British responded to IRA attacks with counterterror, most notably with the arrival in Ireland, on March 26, 1920, of 800 jobless disbanded soldiers, known as the Black and Tans from the color of their uniform. The Black and Tans' use of violence against the ordinary Irish people was excessive. This and other methods of suppression were met by a Sinn Féin arson campaign. On the fourth anniversary of the Easter Rising 120 police stations and 22 tax offices were burnt.

Acts of terror on both sides reached fever pitch during 1920. The IRA routinely murdered police and troops, and bombed public buildings such as Cork City town hall on October 9. The British fought city rioters with the utmost ferocity and threw hundreds into jail. Many of the prisoners went on hunger strikes. Some, like Cork mayor Tomas MacSwiney, died in prison and

became instant martyrs. By December, the British had 43,000 troops in Ireland and had declared martial law.

Matters were getting out of hand when a political initiative put forward by British prime minister David Lloyd George a year earlier resulted in the Government of Ireland Act of 1920. This offered limited self-government to the loyalists in the North and nationalists in the rest of Ireland. The Ulster Protestants accepted London's offer. In the rest of Ireland, nationalists dedicated to an all-Ireland republic fought on.

The British became bogged down in a guerrilla war with the IRA and so, in December 1921, Lloyd George offered a treaty that created an Irish Free State, excluding six of the eight Ulster counties. A majority of nationalists accepted this offer. But nationalists who wanted nothing less than a united free Ireland, including Eamon de Valera, refused to sign. He resigned as president, and became a leader of the rebels. Michael Collins became head of government. The differences between government and nationalist supporters erupted into civil war in 1922.

Running battles were fought to control whole towns and cities. Government property and personnel became legitimate targets for IRA bombs and bullets, one of which killed Michael Collins on August 22. In 1923 de Valera gave up the struggle and formed a new political party, but the IRA went underground.

The legacies of the IRA's early struggles – the role of martyrs, symbols, spies, money, and smuggled arms; the blend of politics, terror, and propaganda; the appeal to legitimacy, the military techniques and tactics – have become hallmarks of modern terrorism worldwide.

John Bowyer Bell

SEE ALSO:

IRA: ORIGINS AND TERROR TO 1976; NATIONALIST TERROR IN NORTHERN IRELAND 1976-1996; COUNTERTERROR IN THE BRITISH EMPIRE BEFORE 1945.

F U R T H E R   R E A D I N G

- Bell, John Bowyer. *The Gun in Politics: An Analysis of Irish Violence.* New Brunswick, NJ: Transaction Publishers, 1991.
- Foster, Roy F. *Modern Ireland, 1600-1972.* New York: Viking Penguin, 1990.
- Ward, Alan J. *The Easter Rising.* Wheeling, IL: Harlan Davidson, 1980.

THE AMRITSAR MASSACRE

By 1919, British rule in India had lasted nearly 200 years. It was first founded on trade through the East India Company in the early eighteenth century. The colonial administration, which became known as the Raj, was at its height in the late nineteenth century. Its success was due to the effective combination of organization – a few hundred civil servants ran a country of 300 million people – and military control. Indian rebellion against British rule was put down with ruthless ferocity. The Indian Mutiny of 1857, which began when Sikh soldiers refused to bite ammunition that had been oiled in pig fat, was just one example.

One of the most brutal suppressions of a public demonstration came when Britain's imperial power was beginning to wane. By the early twentieth century, there were increasing calls for independence in India. One famous leader was Mohandas Gandhi, known as the Mahatma, or wise man. During World War I, Britain had seemed to favor constitutional reforms. In 1918-19, however, the British delayed the promised reforms and introduced instead the draconian Rowlatt Act. Far from loosening the bonds of colonial rule, this measure extended into peacetime security regulations introduced during the war. The Act caused widespread discontent throughout the whole of India. In the state of Punjab, Gandhi organized a strike for March 30, 1919, and a second on April 6, 1919. This action fanned the belief among British officials that an outbreak of rebellion in the region was imminent. As a result, several known agitators were arrested in the Sikh holy city of Amritsar.

TERROR IN AMRITSAR

News of the arrests caused a mob of 30,000 Indians to run riot in the city on April 10. They destroyed the railway station and rampaged through the European quarter, killing three people. The civil police sent for British army reinforcements from the garrison at Lahore, which were placed under the command of Brigadier-General R. H. Dyer on April 11, 1919. After a series of arrests by the civil police, there was peace throughout the city on April 12.

But Dyer marched the British and Indian troops around the town's outer wall in a show of strength. He issued a proclamation that banned all movement in and out of the city by the local inhabitants and imposed an 8 p.m. curfew. The proclamation also forbade public meetings, stating that "any processions or gathering of four men will be looked upon as an unlawful assembly and dispersed by force if necessary." Despite the declaration, various acts of sabotage occurred during the next day, April 13. These actions convinced Dyer that revolutionaries were plotting a full-scale insurrection.

News then reached the general that an unauthorized mass meeting was to take place at 4:30 p.m. that day in the Jallianwalla Bagh. The latter was a large enclosed piece of wasteland near the Sikh Golden Temple. Dyer hurriedly led 90 Gurkha and Indian Baluchi troops supported by two armored cars to disperse the illegal meeting. However, without giving any prior warning to the crowd to disperse or face the consequences, Dyer ordered his troops to open fire. As the crowd of 20,000 unarmed men, women and

---

K E Y   F A C T S

● Three days before the Amritsar massacre, General Dyer had flogged any Indian who refused to crawl at a point in the road where someone had attacked a white woman.

● At the enquiry into the massacre, Dyer stated that he would have used the machine guns on his armored cars if he could have done so, and that his intention was to cause terror. "I thought I would be doing a jolly lot of good," he said.

● The majority of the British community living in the Punjab initially hailed Dyer as the "savior of India." They believed that he had averted another Indian rebellion.

Brigadier-General Dyer ordered his troops to open fire on unarmed demonstrators, killing 380 people.

children ran about in panic, the troops continued firing, discharging over 1,650 rounds of ammunition. Within ten minutes, 380 people were dead and 1,200 wounded, according to official estimates. Dyer only withdrew his forces when their ammunition was nearly exhausted. The dead and wounded were left where they fell.

THE REPERCUSSIONS

The Amritsar incident was a deliberate act of terror, calculated to frighten people involved in other disturbances taking place throughout Punjab. It had the desired effect. The riots very quickly subsided and the British managed to restore order in the state. Dyer's actions at Amritsar were endorsed by Punjab's lieutenant governor, Sir Michael O'Dwyer.

However, as news of the shooting and the number of casualties spread in Britain and India, it provoked outrage in the press and led to a debate in the British parliament. A committee of enquiry was appointed to investigate the incident. Controversy regarding Dyer's actions focused on his intentions and the background against which his actions took place. He clearly believed that by issuing his proclamation, martial law was in effect and therefore he was justified in using whatever force he thought necessary to restore order. The committee did not agree. It concluded that Dyer was not suppressing a rebellion, but was merely dispersing an unlawful assembly.

Dyer was censured for acting "out of a mistaken concept of his duty" by not giving advance warning of firing and continuing after the crowd had begun to disperse. He was relieved of his command and sent back to Britain in disgrace, despite continued strong public support and efforts made by O'Dwyer to clear both their names.

Amritsar was a turning point for Anglo-Indian relations. The political damage done to the Raj by the massacre was incalculable. The Amritsar incident alienated Indian public opinion, and poisoned relations with nationalist leaders, who were now united in their belief that Britain was indifferent to their political aspirations. The moral basis of British rule was undermined. The Jallianwalla Bagh became a memorial and a rallying call for resistance to British rule. Indeed, in March 1940, the Jallianwalla Bagh claimed its last casualty when O'Dwyer was assassinated in London by Udam Singh in an act of direct revenge for the massacre.

Tim Moreman

SEE ALSO:

TERROR IN COLONIAL CONQUESTS; TERRORISM IN COLONIAL INDIA 1900-1947.

F U R T H E R   R E A D I N G

- Fein, Helen. *Imperial Crime and Punishment at Jallianwalla Bagh and British Judgment.* Honolulu: University of Hawaii Press, 1977.
- Sarkar, Sumit. *Modern India,1885-1947.* New York: St. Martin's Press, 1989.
- Shepherd, C. *Crisis of Empire: British Reactions to Amritsar.* Cambridge, MA: Harvard University Press, 1992.
- Wolpert, Stanley. *A New History of India.* New York: Oxford University Press, 1993.

Topham Picture Library

TERROR IN THE RUSSIAN CIVIL WAR

On August 31, 1918, the Bolshevik prime minister of Soviet Russia, Vladimir Lenin, was shot and gravely wounded in a terrorist assassination attempt at a Moscow factory. Combined with the killing, on the same day, of the head of the Soviet secret police in Petrograd (St. Petersburg) this gave the new regime a sense of extreme vulnerability, both to external and internal enemies.

SOCIALIST FATHERLAND IN DANGER

On September 5, 1918, the Bolshevik government made a declaration of Red Terror – consciously imitating the Jacobin Terror in revolutionary France. The Bolsheviks took hostages and sent enemies to concentration camps. They punished conspiracy against Soviet rule by anti-Bolshevik former Czarist officers, or Whites, with immediate death. In Petrograd (St. Petersburg) alone, they executed 900 hostages. Many victims were senior officials of the imperial government. The focus was not on individual guilt but on class membership, and the aim was to terrorize. Such terrorism was a central feature of the Russian Civil War (1917-21), although the Red Terror decree only gave a formal basis to existing practices.

In the autumn of 1918, the Bolsheviks faced a perilous situation. They had negotiated Russia's way out of World War I, but German and Austrian armies were still deep in Russia. Also, the peace had alienated both Russia's former external allies and the Socialist Revolutionaries. The consequences included the uprising of the Czechoslovak Legion and the emergence of an anti-Bolshevik front east of Moscow. A Socialist Revolutionary uprising took place in Moscow, while north of Moscow the Socialist Revolutionary terrorist Boris Savinkov organized a revolt. For this reason, in late July 1918, the Bolsheviks passed a decree declaring the "Socialist Fatherland in Danger" and calling for "mass terror" against the bourgeoisie. The July 1918 execution of the Czar and his family, ordered by Moscow, was part of this campaign.

RED TERROR

The Red Terror was not simply counterterror in an emergency. Its roots lay in the class hatred of Bolshevik activists. The pre-revolutionary Bolsheviks, unlike the Socialist Revolutionaries, had rejected terrorist attacks against individual representatives of the czarist regime. But after the revolution, these same Bolsheviks had no doubts about their right to defend the new regime by any means possible. So, in 1918, the Bolshevik leaders, particularly Lenin and Commissar for War Leon Trotsky, turned to terrorism. This was a correct move in terms of Marxist theories of class conflict. The Marxists rejected the idea, held by orthodox lawyers, that all legal systems should be impartial.

For the party's mass of new recruits, the Red Terror was based less on ideas than on centuries of oppression. For Soviet leaders and ordinary party members, terror was an effective tool for creating order in the turmoil that followed the Bolshevik coup of October 1917.

It is significant that the organization that carried out the Bolshevik terror was created early in the regime's history – in December 1917. This organization was the Extraordinary Commission for the Struggle with Counterrevolution and Sabotage (Cheka). Its leader was the fanatical Pole, Feliks Dzerzhinskii. The Revolutionary Tribunal, based on the French Revolutionary example, was also important. It was introduced in November 1917 to hand out instant justice.

KEY FACTS

● The Bolsheviks used terror throughout 1917-21, to destroy opponents and control their own people. The Red Terror employed concentration camps, hostage-taking, and execution without trial.

● Trotsky embraced terrorism to the extent of writing a pamphlet towards the end of 1919, called *Terrorism and Communism*.

Peter Newark's Military Pictures

Bolshevik Commissar for War Leon Trotsky (left) was an unflinching proponent of terror.

By late 1918, large White armies were advancing from southern Russia and Siberia on Moscow. The Bolsheviks had created an army to defend the state against these counterrevolutionaries, but they felt they could not trust it. The Red Terror, therefore, changed its point of focus to the army's front lines. Here it imposed discipline both among the peasant conscripts and among the ex-Czarist officer staffs. Its methods included deploying detachments behind the front line to prevent desertion, making hostages of commanders' families, and employing firing squads.

But the Bolsheviks applied Red Terror even more ruthlessly to their enemies. In 1918-19, they attempted to wipe out the Cossacks in southeastern Russia. And right up to the fall of the last White base area, in 1920 in the Crimea, they often tortured or shot captured officers.

A further, hidden side of Red Terror was directed at the population within Soviet-controlled Russia. The Mensheviks (a rival Marxist faction) and the Socialist Revolutionaries still had some influence among the urban working class and the peasantry. Even without

this influence, workers and peasants were dissatisfied with Bolshevik rule. The collapse of the economy meant that the Bolsheviks could secure food only through brute force – by mass arrests and hostage-taking. The Cheka and other paramilitary bodies kept order through terror. The struggle intensified when frontline fighting ended late in 1920. The Cheka brutally crushed rural disorder and urban unrest at Petrograd (St. Petersburg) and Kronstadt.

WHITE TERROR

The use of terror was not confined to the Bolsheviks. The Socialist Revolutionaries carried out acts of individual terrorism, most notably attempts to kill Lenin. The Whites were merciless with captured Communists, and Red propaganda made much of White Terror. The Whites also used punitive detachments against the peasantry. But White Terror was much less systematic than its Red counterpart, under which an estimated 50,000 to 200,000 people were executed.

The Bolsheviks use of terror proved essential to the survival of their minority regime. In this way, the Red Terror may have changed history by consolidating the Bolshevik grip on power. But the price was high. Terrorism isolated the Bolsheviks from world socialism and set back the prospects of revolution elsewhere.

Evan Mawdsley

SEE ALSO:

TERROR IN THE FRENCH REVOLUTION 1789-1915; THE PARIS COMMUNE: STATE TERROR; RUSSIAN ANARCHIST TERROR; TERROR IN THE FINNISH CIVIL WAR; STALIN'S GREAT TERROR.

┌──┐
F U R T H E R   R E A D I N G

- Brovkin, V. N. *Behind the Front Lines of the Civil War: Political Parties and Social Movement in Russia, 1918-1922.* Princeton, NJ: Princeton University Press, 1994.
- Chamberlain, William H. *The Russian Revolution, Volume II: 1918-1921: From the Civil War to the Consolidation of Power.* Princeton, NJ: Princeton University Press, 1987.
- Leggett, George. *The Cheka: Lenin's Political Police.* New York: Oxford University Press, 1986.
- Mawdsley, Evan. *The Russian Civil War.* New York: Routledge, Chapman & Hall, 1987.
└──┘

TERROR IN THE FINNISH CIVIL WAR

Amid the chaos of the Russian Revolution, on January 4, 1918, Finland received its independence from the Bolshevik leader Vladimir Lenin. It was barely two months since he had taken power, and Lenin had too many pressing problems associated with establishing Bolshevik authority throughout the vast Russian empire to worry about Finnish separatism.

The Bolsheviks were confident that the Finnish socialists would soon take power in the revolutionary atmosphere of the newly independent Finland. There were shortages, strikes, and food riots. Parliamentary government had largely broken down and, on January 28, 1918, left-wing Red Guards, the workers' militia, seized power in the capital, Helsinki. Civil war broke out between the Reds and the government forces.

Unlike much of the revolutionary unrest in Europe following World War I, the Finnish conflict was a full-scale civil war fought on several fronts. The experienced ex-Czarist officer General Mannerheim led the Finnish Government's forces, known as the White Guards, to ultimate victory against the poorly trained and led Finnish Red forces. The small number of ex-Czarist Russian army troops remaining in Finland who did fight for the Red Guards against the Finnish White Guards were ill-disciplined and had poor morale. In encounters between Red and White troops, these forces tended to be more of a liability than an asset.

RED GUARDS TERRORISM

Before the Finnish civil war, the Red Guards had gained a wide reputation for brutality, particularly during the general strike of November 1917. Undoubtedly some used the opportunity for looting and revenge that this unrest presented. The socialist leadership could not control some elements of the Red Guards, and once civil war broke out in Finland the problem became worse. It is clear that during the four-month civil war, the Reds murdered 1,649 people. These killings came in two waves. There were 703 deaths from the war's start until the end of February, 1918, during the establishment of the new independent regime. Killings dropped to 205 in March 1918, but in April in the confusion of the Red defeat, 697 people were killed.

Surprisingly, the obvious targets of class-conflict – the rich, the clergy, and opposition political leaders – went largely unscathed, although the Red Guards executed 184 captured White troops. Aside from this, the Reds treated their prisoners reasonably well. The worst single exception was the Reds, massacre of 30 White troops in Viipuri prison just before the city fell. Overall, the Red Terror was irrational, purposeless, and tragic. It was not authorized by the socialist leaders. It caused internal dissent, undermined the workers' morale, and let the Whites present the Reds, both at home and abroad, as barbaric.

THE WHITE TERROR

On the other hand, the Whites also frequently shot Red prisoners taken in battle. Although Mannerheim had instructed that "in no circumstances may prisoners be shot out of hand," his orders were sometimes ignored. This was particularly the case after the fall of the

---

KEY FACTS

● The Finnish Civil War, fought between the anti-Bolshevik White Guards and Finnish socialists, or Red Guards, lasted just four months, between January 28 and May 18, 1918.

● Though short, the civil war was very bloody. Out of a population of just 3 million, the war accounted for the deaths of close to 30,000 people, or nearly one percent of the population.

● Nearly 12,000 Red prisoners died in White captivity. The Red Terror killed almost 1,700 Whites.

Hulton Getty Picture Collection

Field Marshal Carl Gustav Mannerheim led the White Guards, the Finnish government's forces.

strategic inland city of Tampere. Here, around 200 people who could be identified as Russians were summarily executed, as were 150 Finns. A Swedish observer wrote that "the sight was unimaginably repulsive: a heap of bleeding bodies on the ground." This case of mass murder could not even be justified as an spontaneous act of soldiers seeking vengeance. There had been no Red Terror in Tampere during the period when the town was under their control, nor had any of the White prisoners held by the Reds in the city during the siege been harmed.

When the town of Viipuri fell to the Whites, similar incidents occurred. Again, all Russians found were killed, including a number of bourgeois White sympathizers and the unfortunate odd Pole and Ukrainian. Their monument at Viipuri cemetery reads: "We waited

for you as liberators and you brought us death." But the worst single atrocity committed by the White Guards was the mass killing of 50 workers by machine-gun fire in a ditch after the end of hostilities.

THE SCALE OF THE WHITE TERROR

The number of deaths caused by White Guards' terrorist activity totalled 2,400 by the end of April 1918. But, in the following five weeks, from April 28 to June 1, the figure almost doubled to 4,745. In the peak period of May 5-11 there was an average of 200 killings a day. In total there were at least 8,380 illegal murders of captured Reds, including 58 males under the age of 16 and 364 women. After the defeat of the Reds, the White government set up special courts to provide legal retribution and to halt the unauthorized killing. These special courts convicted 67,000 people of terrorist crimes and passed 555 death sentences, of which 265 were carried out.

The most tragic aspect to the White Terror was that it was largely avoidable. The Finnish military authorities had made little provision for the 80,000 prisoners in their custody. The country was suffering from a famine and feeding Red prisoners was not high on the Whites' priorities. Consequently, 11,783 prisoners died in captivity of malnutrition and disease.

Some 23,000 Finnish Reds died on the battlefield, in prisoner-of-war camps, and by summary execution. Many thousands more were imprisoned. Yet the majority of the Finnish population supported the White Terror. The only possible justifications for the appalling brutality of the Finnish civil war were that it helped ensure continued Finnish independence and led to the establishment of a strong democracy.

M. Christopher Mann

SEE ALSO:

TERROR IN THE RUSSIAN CIVIL WAR.

FURTHER READING

- Alapuro, R. *State and Revolution in Finland.* Berkeley, CA: University of California Press, 1988.
- Hamalainen, Pekka K. *In Time of Storm: Revolution, Civil War, and the Ethnographic Issue in Finland.* Albany, NY: SUNY Press, 1979.
- Nordstrom, Byron J. *Dictionary of Scandinavian History.* Westport, CT: Greenwood Press, 1986.

THE ARMENIAN MASSACRES

Modern Armenia, situated in Asia Minor east of the Black Sea, is a former member state of the Soviet Union. For centuries, however, it was divided between two empires – the Ottoman empire (modern Turkey) in the west and, in the east, first Persia (modern Iran) until 1828, then Russia.

Generally, the eastern regimes tolerated their Christian Armenian subjects. But the Muslim Ottoman Empire harbored an ongoing ill-feeling toward Armenia which, after 1870, developed into outright persecution. Religious differences were only marginally responsible for this situation. A stronger reason was that the position of all minorities was deteriorating within the weakening Turkish empire as the central power grew suspicious of culturally independent peoples within its sphere.

Within Turkish Armenia itself, Turkish administration amounted to little more than tax-gathering. The Armenians shared much of their land with the Kurds, a nomadic people who still occupy land in Turkey and in what is now northern Iraq. When the Kurds became violent toward the Armenians, the Turkish authorities did not intervene. Indeed, the Turkish authorities actively encouraged the Kurds in acts of atrocity.

By 1890, the Kurds were well organized into military regiments. The Turkish authorities were actively encouraging them to harass the Armenians and to commit acts of violence and murder. Turkish government policy meant that Armenians, particularly those in rural areas, were outside the protection of the law.

An eyewitness account of the situation in 1895 vividly describes the brutal injustices practiced by the Ottoman authorities against their subject people. The evidence of armed extortion, torture, rape, and murder against Armenians because of their religion and nationality is a shocking example of a government employing terrorist tactics to displace an unwanted population. There was a deliberate policy to reduce the number of Armenian people, either by driving them out of their homeland or by killing them.

Many Armenians were fortunate enough to evade persecution and reach the frontier with Russian Armenia, but hundreds of thousands fell victim to what amounted to organized state terrorism. In the autumn of 1895 alone, as many as 200,000 Armenians were massacred, not just in their homeland, but at many locations throughout the Ottoman empire.

THE ARMENIAN REACTION

Acts of state terror provoked a spiral of individual terrorist acts by Armenians as they sought to defend themselves. They murdered government officials and staged spectacular attacks, such as seizing the Imperial Ottoman Bank in Istanbul in August 1896.

In April 1909, the reigning Ottoman sultan was overthrown by the Young Turks, a revolutionary movement that was supported by the army. With the downfall of the despotic Sultan Abdul Hamid II, ethnic minorities were briefly left in peace. However, a key policy of the Young Turks was the creation of a homogeneous state, with a uniform language and culture. Since the Ottoman Empire was multi-ethnic, and the Turks were the ruling nationality, such a policy posed a serious threat to non-Turkish cultures.

Meanwhile, the Ottoman Armenians were making some headway with the new regime and in February 1914 scored some minor diplomatic successes. When Turkey entered World War I in October of that year, there was no immediate hostility toward the

---

KEY FACTS

● In 1894, Turkish troops and Kurds slaughtered thousands of Armenians for not paying their taxes.

● In 1896, when Armenian rebels seized the Ottoman Bank, more than 50,000 Armenians were killed by state-coordinated mobs of Muslim Turks.

● In 1915, the Turkish government deported about 1,750,000 Armenians. Hundreds of thousands died of starvation or exhaustion in the desert, or were executed by Turkish troops.

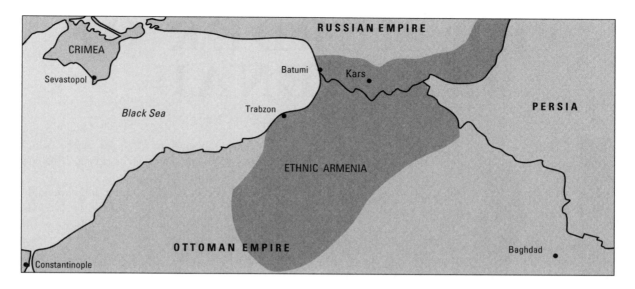

Armenians, even though the Turks could claim they were a security risk because half of Armenia was under enemy Russian control.

By March 1915, the situation had changed. The Young Turks regime began to persecute Armenians. The government defended its actions by citing the disloyalty of a number of Armenians, who had joined volunteer regiments in enemy Russian territory, across the border.

But anti-Armenian measures went far beyond any possible punishment for disloyalty, since most Turkish Armenians remained loyal to their empire. It is more likely that the Young Turks used disloyalty as a pretext to clear out the Armenians. Completely different culturally, Armenians stood in the way of pan-Turkism, an ideology that sought uniformity of language, culture, and religion right across the Turkish empire.

SYSTEMIZED GENOCIDE

The Young Turks now implemented a policy of massive depopulation by genocide, not only in Armenia itself, but of Armenians living all over the empire. They shot Armenians in their homes, or force-marched them hundreds of miles over rough terrain until they died from exhaustion. They penned up many more thousands in open-air concentration camps, where the prisoners eventually died of exhaustion. At one place, Deir-en-Zor, the Young Turks herded thousands of Armenians into caves, which were then sealed. Government guards stopped those people driven over the border into neighboring countries from accepting food and drink offered by charities from neutral

The areas of the 1915 Ottoman and Russian empires populated by ethnic Armenians.

nations. The Turkish explanation for this mass displacement was that the Armenians were being relocated away from the war zone for their own safety. But the explanation was a cover-up. Government telegrams in the Ottoman archive suggest that there was a coordinated plan of extermination. By August 1916, a total of 1.5 million Armenians were reported dead, and more than a million had been deported. This decimation of Armenians at the hands of a fading imperial power constituted one of the most atrocious acts of state terrorism in the twentieth century.

Robert P. Anderson

SEE ALSO:

THE HOLOCAUST; SADDAM HUSSEIN'S TERROR IN KURDISTAN.

F U R T H E R   R E A D I N G

- Hovannisian, Richard G., ed. *The Armenian Genocide: History, Politics, Ethics*. New York: St. Martin's Press, 1992.
- Somakian, M. J. *Empires in Conflict: Armenia and the Great Powers, 1895-1920*. New York: Taurus, 1995.
- Walker, C. *Armenia: The Survival of a Nation*. New York: St. Martin's Press, 1990.

THE MURDER OF RATHENAU

German foreign minister, Walther Rathenau, in 1922, shortly before his murder.

The murder of Walther Rathenau on June 24, 1922 was an act of extreme right-wing terrorism. The assassination had a traumatic effect on the development of democracy in Germany after the country's defeat in World War I, four years earlier.

Rathenau was a businessman who had been in charge of distributing raw materials in World War I. His efforts to increase the efficiency of the German war economy helped Germany sustain the conflict for four years until 1918. After hostilities ended with the signing of the armistice in November of the same year, Rathenau joined the liberal German Democratic Party. He quickly became a prominent politician and gained ministerial office. But he made many enemies among right-wing factions because of his left-wing, social-reforming principles and because he was Jewish.

Rathenau was no less patriotic than his nationalist opponents. In 1921, he resigned his ministerial post in protest against the division of Upper Silesia, which gave territory to Poland, although he accepted the post of foreign minister shortly afterward.

Rathenau came in for abuse from anti-communist and anti-Semitic right-wing nationalists. He incensed his enemies more by signing the Treaty of Rapallo with the Soviet Union in May 1922. The treaty restored diplomatic relations and both countries dropped war reparations claims. Right-wing pamphlets called for his assassination. He was accused of complicity in a Jewish conspiracy against Germany, and of selling out the country's interests as foreign minister.

Such propaganda persuaded three students, Erwin Kern, Hermann Fischer, and Ernst Techow, to murder Rathenau. After serving in the Navy during World War I, they had joined a right-wing paramilitary group then the conspiratorial nationalist group "Organization C." On June 24, 1922, as Rathenau's car left his villa in a Berlin suburb, the assassins pulled their car alongside. Kern fired nine shots and Fischer threw a grenade, killing Rathenau almost instantly. The murderers then fled to the Baltic coast but missed the boat to Sweden. They were caught in a shoot-out in which Kern was killed, Fischer shot himself, and Techow was arrested.

Rathenau's assassination created an enormous sensation and exposed internal unrest in Germany. It was regarded as a rejection of the new constitutional order by growing nationalist factions.

Thomas G. Otte

SEE ALSO:

ASSASSINATION AT SARAJEVO 1914; THE HOLOCAUST.

> **FURTHER READING**
>
> - Felix, David. *Walther Rathenau and the Weimar Republic: The Politics of Reparations*. Baltimore, MD: Johns Hopkins University Press, 1971.
> - Peukert, Detler J. *Weimar Republic*. New York: Hill & Wang, 1993.

Hulton Getty Picture Collection

STALIN'S GREAT TERROR

In 1956, the rulers of the Soviet Union made their first public admission of the existence of a police terror apparatus. They blamed Joseph Stalin, who had died in 1953 after nearly 25 years as absolute ruler. He was not the first to use government terror. Labor camps had appeared after the October Revolution of 1917, when the Bolsheviks came to power under Vladimir Lenin. He used class enemies as forced labor.

In 1922, Stalin became secretary of the Communist party, as the Bolsheviks were now known. When Lenin died in 1924, Stalin became the dominant figure among Bolshevik leaders, and from 1928 was in effect dictator.

Stalin's reign of terror began as an offshoot of an economic policy, his first five-year plan. Designed to make the Soviet Union a modern industrialized economy, the five-year plan requisitioned all land for state use and nationalized all industries. Mass resistance from the peasantry, especially the upper class land-owning "kulaks," led to famine. Thousands of kulaks disappeared into remote labor camps or died under a hail of bullets from Stalin's death squads.

The same techniques were used in industry, when inefficient, ill-disciplined workers failed to meet targets. Failures were blamed on saboteurs or "wreckers." They too were sent to work-camps. Forced labor became a basic part of the Soviet economy, and fear of arrest, torture, and execution by Stalin's police, a way of life.

Stalin made the show trial a hallmark of his terror system. Highly placed dissident officials and groups of lowly workers were arrested and put on public trial. The evidence was rigged and a guilty verdict certain.

Joseph Stalin, who ruled the Soviet Union as effective dictator from 1928 to 1953, unleashed a reign of terror that left millions dead.

Stalin made sure the trials were high profile to stifle opposition and encourage people to work harder.

Stalin first used show trials to do with economic issues. In May 1928, for example, he condemned engineers at the Shakhty mines for failure to meet productivity targets. But Stalin next extended the reign of terror to the Communist party itself, with a series of brutal purges. While purges were not new, previously they had only involved expulsion from the party. The innovation of the 1930s was to criminalize the victims, who could now be sent to one of the many harsh labor camps or even be executed.

KEY FACTS

● Some 25 million farming households were forced to collectivize, dissenters were shot, and famines resulted. About 10 million peasants perished.

● In 1989, a Soviet historian estimated that more than 20 million died as a result of the labor camps, execution, forced collectivization, and famine.

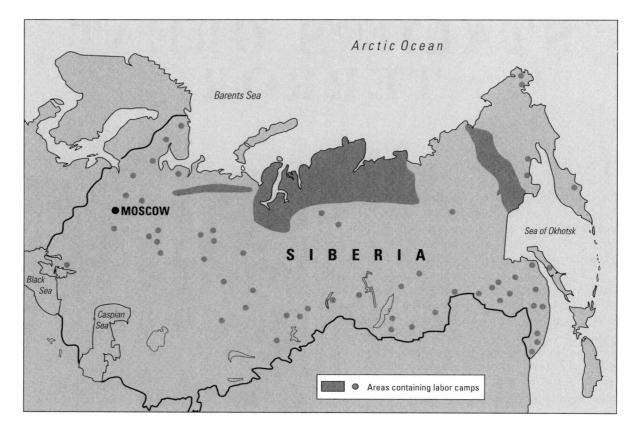

Soviet labor camps were mainly located in the harsh wilderness of Siberia.

State prosecutors conducted show trials at which they forced the accused to "confess" to crimes of disloyalty. Some even asked for death to purify the communist system. By 1938, party membership had fallen from 3,555,000 to 1,920,000. Purged members filled the camps. and terror was used against any threats. Even its perpetrators were not safe. Yagoda and Yezhov, the commissars responsible for the terror, became its victims in 1936-38. In 1937-38, nine-tenths of the army's generals disappeared, seriously weakening the Soviet military.

The number of purge victims is unclear since Soviet government secrecy, together with the many forced labor institutions, prevent accuracy. It is impossible, then, to be sure that the figure of seven million executions, recently quoted in Russian publications, is correct.

More than 18 million people were probably inmates of the camps between 1934 and 1952. By 1952, they included enemies, returning Soviet prisoners of war,

dissident nationalists from newly acquired territories, and those suspected of collaborating with the Nazis.

By the time of Stalin's death in 1953, few Soviet citizens did not know of a "kulak" or a "wrecker" and what had happened to them. Many detainees were released after 1956, but often never came to terms with the psychological effects of their confinement.

Peter Morris

SEE ALSO:

TERROR IN THE RUSSIAN CIVIL WAR; RESISTANCE IN THE EAST AND TERRORISM.

FURTHER READING

- Conquest, Robert. *The Great Terror: A Reassessment.* New York: Oxford University Press, 1990.
- Mandelstam, N. Nadezhda. *Hope Against Hope: A Memoir.* New York: Atheneum, 1978.
- Tucker, Robert C. *Stalin in Power.* New York: Norton, 1990.

Terror During World War II

As if the horrors of the battlefield were not enough, much terrorism occurs on the sidelines of war. World War II saw examples of the worst atrocities of all time. Many acts of violence were sanctioned by governments, others were the work of frenzied individuals. The war was characterized by a degree of savagery in Axis occupation policy never before witnessed. Even the norms of warfare were barbarized by the bitter, often ideologically inspired, fighting. The line between combatants and civilians blurred as few could escape the effects of all-out slaughter and torture.

TERROR DURING WORLD WAR II:
Introduction

In 1939, Nazi Germany's aggressive foreign policy eventually forced the Allies to make a stand over the German invasion of Poland. In this way World War II in Europe began, fought between the Allies – Britain, France, the Soviet Union (from June 1941) and the United States (from December 1941) and the European Axis – Germany, Italy and their satellites. The war fought by Japan, the other Axis power, with China, from 1933, escalated by 1940-41 to a conflict in the Pacific ocean with the western Allies, and not with the Soviet Union until 1945. World War II became the greatest conflict in history. The societies and economies of the combatant nations were mobilized to a greater extent than ever before. The conflict was also portrayed as a total battle between the forces of democracy and the evil of right-wing, racist extremism. Consequently, this conflict witnessed the emergence of total war. Given the scale of effort being directed toward prosecuting the war, the stakes involved in the conflict rose correspondingly. Consequently, the war could only be settled by a total victory of one side over the other. Hence, the notion of the total surrender of the enemy was implemented. There were three contributory developments that influenced this emergence of total war: the savagery of Axis occupation policies, the barbarization of the norms of warfare, and the particular odiousness of the racist policies of the Nazis, and their genocide of the Jews and the Slavs in Eastern Europe.

During the war there was an unprecedented savagery in Axis occupation policies. Throughout history, military forces had used terror to facilitate their conquests and to subdue resistance to their authority. Equally, terror had been used to help with the economic exploitation of conquered territories, as in the colonial conquests of the late nineteenth and early twentieth centuries. However, in the age of total war, these methods were greatly intensified and systematized. The Axis deliberately plundered occupied economies on a hitherto unknown scale. Moreover, the Axis crushed Resistance acts with the utmost savagery and the deliberate use of terror. The Axis adopted the policy of brutal reprisals against innocent hostages, usually notable community figures, in response to Resistance activity. The key principle to this policy was asymmetry: the reprisal was always many times – often ten or one hundred times – worse than the original Resistance act that had inspired it.

Another key development in World War II was the barbarization of warfare. This was both related to, and influenced in turn, the savage occupation policies and the emergence of total war. All the Axis powers, as well as the Soviets, mistreated prisoners of war. Moreover, in the brutal partisan conflicts occurring behind the front, many innocent civilians were killed.

The savagery of Axis occupation policies, and the barbarization of warfare were also two components in the process toward the emergence of total war. One aspect of this process was the debate over aerial warfare. In 1939 there was an aversion, particularly by the Allies, to adopting indiscriminate terror bombing of civilian areas to break the morale of the enemy. Yet the Germans initiated terror bombing, and by 1944 the British in particular were prepared to resort to these methods as the most effective way of prosecuting the war. The ultimate example of this process was America's decision to drop the atomic bomb on Japan in August 1945. During World War II, therefore, there emerged one of the preconditions of the later phenomenon of modern terrorism; that there was no such things as innocent civilians, that all members of an enemy society were legitimate targets. This development, when coupled with the nationalism erupting in the Imperial colonies in the aftermath of the war, led to the campaigns of decolonization of the 1950s.

After victory in 1945, the Allies tried the Axis leaders as war criminals. This was an attempt to impose justice on those who had callously used terror for their own ends. The issues were complicated, however: the dropping of the atomic bomb, for instance, was the ultimate in terror bombing. Such ambiguities again haunt the quest for justice underway in the war crimes trials being held in 1996 regarding the conflicts in Rwanda and the former Yugoslavia. ■

TERROR IN THE GERMAN OCCUPATION OF THE EAST

One of the major instruments of terror in the Third Reich was the German army. Critical historians base this damning assertion not on its front-line combat role, but rather on its sinister activities in the rear areas. One myth, created after 1945, was that the German army had been engaged in a "normal war" against enemy soldiers; any brutal action behind the front was a direct response to partisans (civilian forces organized to drive out occupying troops) who had taken the first step in abandoning the accepted rules of warfare. The brutal treatment of civilian populations in the rear areas cannot, however, be separated from Nazi racial policy. The army was the instrument by which the Nazi regime spread ideologically motivated murder and terror all over Europe.

Terrorist policies were particularly evident in the vast areas of the Soviet Union, which remained under military occupation during 1941-44. Popular views of the conflict attribute the mass killings, especially of the Jews, to Nazi special agencies such as the party's paramilitary arm (the SS) and the Security Service (SD). However, the army was deeply implicated in this systematic and deliberate policy of extermination. Plans to conduct a genocidal war against the Soviets had been drawn up by the German High Command several months before the attack on the Soviet Union in June 1941. Military planners intended to pursue a "hunger-strategy" that would condemn millions of Russians to death through starvation.

To implement its plans, the army introduced new martial laws. They encouraged German soldiers to abandon rules of warfare regarding captured enemy troops and the rights of civilians. Such cruel terror policies were an essential aspect of the initial successful advance of the German army into Russia. Such policies were not, as apologists argue, a forced response to the later problems of military stalemate or the increased Soviet partisan menace in the rear areas.

DEATH IN NAZI CAPTIVITY

As many as 3.3 million of the 5.7 million Soviet Red Army prisoners of war who had surrendered to the German armed forces died in captivity. To accord with the Nazi Commissar Order, all Soviet political officers and Jews were singled out immediately for liquidation. Hundreds of thousands of other Red Army prisoners died after deliberate mistreatment, particularly of starvation, exposure to cold, exhaustion, and beatings.

Official plans for the economic exploitation of the occupied territories in the east did not just encourage terrorization of the entire civilian population. Systematic terror was even included in the army's mandate. The army was ordered to live off the land, which necessitated the plunder of the already impoverished local inhabitants. The army's commands were also to remove by force vast quantities of food and raw materials, as well as slave-labor, for shipment back to the Reich. Russian peasants responded initially to these seizures with grim resignation rather than active resistance. Yet, despite the absence of any concerted opposition, the German army, under the guise of the necessity of war, took the severest measures against anyone who withheld their total cooperation.

KEY FACTS

● As a reprisal for the murder of Reinhard Heydrich, the Nazi protector of Bohemia-Moravia, the Czech village of Lidice was destroyed. The men were shot, the women imprisoned in concentration camps, and the children sent to be brought up in German families. In all, 1,300 civilians were killed.

● Following the Commissar Order, the German army executed on the spot some 60,000 Russian soldiers after they were captured.

Novosti

A Red Army partisan hanged by the Germans as a deterrent to other guerrilla activity.

The army also took an active part in implementing the Holocaust. Army units not only assisted the SS and the Security Service (SD) in rounding up Soviet Jews for transportation to the extermination camps, but often undertook large-scale summary executions of Soviet Jews behind the front line. This was terror motivated by ideology rather than by any clear military purpose, even though the pretense was made that the Jews helped the Soviets.

Terror by the German army was most graphically illustrated in the area where racially motivated extermination of the Jewish population blurred with perceived threats to rear-area security. New martial laws let the army execute individuals merely suspected of lending assistance to "bandits," and also allowed for "collective reprisal measures." Numerous villages were razed to the ground, with the inhabitants expelled or murdered, and hostage-taking and execution occurred on a horrific scale. Army commanders recommended the shooting of all suspicious persons, including women, children, and the elderly. Tens of thousands of villages were destroyed and hardly a single Russian family in the occupied area remained untouched by some act of savagery. The number of civilians eradicated is thought to have exceeded 1.4 million. By contrast, German losses in anti-partisan actions were usually small, and sometimes as low as six percent of those of the "enemy."

PROVOCATION BY THE PARTISANS

A main objective of the Soviet partisans was to provoke the German forces into reprisal actions. Terror against Russians in the German-appointed local administration eroded any tendency on the part of the population to coexist with the occupiers. The Russian civilians found themselves beaten between the hammer of the German army and the anvil of the partisan movement. They usually sided with whomever was strongest at a given time. A small number of German officers realized that indiscriminate terror was counter-productive since it drove the locals into the hands of the partisans. Yet, despite these reservations, the level of violence continued to escalate. The impulse for terror was increasingly based on ideology rather than military pragmatism.

The barbarous acts committed by the army were much more than a simple litany of crimes that developed ad hoc in an attempt to pacify the rear areas. The war of terror fought by the German army should be regarded as an integral component of the Nazis' racially determined extermination policies.

Theo J. Schulte

SEE ALSO:

GERMAN TERROR IN FRANCE AND ITALY; TERROR AND THE NAZI BARBARIZATION OF WARFARE.

F U R T H E R   R E A D I N G

- Bartov, Omer. *Hitler's Army: Soldiers, Nazis, and War in the Third Reich.* New York: Oxford University Press, 1991.
- Hirschfeld, G., ed. *The Policies of Genocide: Jews and Soviet Prisoners of War in Nazi Germany.* Boston, MA: Allen & Unwin, 1986.
- Schulte, Theo J. *The German Army and Nazi Policies in Occupied Russia.* New York: Berg, 1989.

ROMANIAN TERROR IN TRANSNISTRIA

The experience of Romania in World War II demonstrates how devastating the use of terror tactics can be when applied even for a short period. But it also shows that other methods can be more effective in pacifying a conquered population.

During the 1930s, pro- and anti-German factions battled to control Romania. The fascist, anti-Semitic Iron Guard movement advocated terrorism to overthrow the state and assassinated two prime ministers. In September 1940, the Iron Guard and General Ion Antonescu jointly came to power in Romania in a German-sponsored coalition. Their government continued to have Nazi support after the German occupation of Romania from October 7, 1940. The four months in which the Iron Guard shared government were marked by the murder of hundreds of political opponents and Jews. The Iron Guard's reign of terror ended in their failed January 1941 attempt to seize sole power. The ensuing riots and massacres were so damaging to Romania's internal stability that Hitler let Antonescu suppress his one-time Fascist allies.

THE DOOM OF THE JEWS

From 1942, Antonescu eased Romania's policy toward the Jews, and those living in central Romania were the biggest Jewish community in Axis Europe to survive the war largely intact. Despite the relative good fortune of these Jews, Romania was still responsible for the second-largest number of Jewish deaths in Axis Europe. The eastern provinces of Bukovina and Bessarabia (now in modern Moldova, a former member state of the Soviet Union, situated on Romania's eastern border) fell under the control of the Soviet Union following the latter's invasion of June 28, 1940. At the outbreak of war between the Soviet Union and Germany in June 1941, German and Romanian forces reclaimed these provinces. The Romanians now treated the Jews of Bessarabia and Bukovina as enemy aliens, whereas previously the Jews had lived relatively safety as Romanian nationals. The Romanian army and Germany's Einsatzgruppe D, one of the four groups ordered to destroy Soviet Jews, conducted mass killings as they advanced through the province. At least 13,000 Jews were killed within three months.

Later in 1941, the remaining Bessarabian and Bukovinan Jews were driven into Transnistria, a province in Soviet Ukraine, just over Romania's southeastern border. Transnistria's vast territory, covering 15,600 square miles between the Dniester and Bug rivers, was now occupied by Romanian troops. Here, some 17,000 Jews died from starvation and fatigue on the long march east and another 67,000 later perished in makeshift concentration camps, largely from typhus. Only 52,000 Jews survived this attempted genocide. General Antonescu repatriated them in 1943.

Transnistria bore the brunt of Romanian revenge after the Romanian Fourth Army suffered huge casualties against Soviet forces in the fight for Odessa, Transnistria's capital, on October 16, 1941. Romanian troops immediately began to take hostages and hang suspected collaborators and spies from streetlights. Six days later, a bomb destroyed the Romanian headquarters in Odessa, killing the general commanding the garrison and 51 of his staff. Although probably preset by the retreating Red Army, the Romanians blamed local partisans for the bomb. The Romanian army, again assisted by the Germans of Einsatzgruppe D, responded by massacring up to 19,000 Odessan

---

KEY FACTS

● Romanian troops arrested 3,500 local Jews on July 29, 1941. The day before, a Romanian soldier of the 14th Infantry Division reported that he had seen a Jew in the town of Iasi signalling to Soviet aircraft. They executed most Jews in the first of several mass killings that took place over the following months.

● From 1942, Romanian ruler General Antonescu relaxed the policy of persecuting Jews – but not before his troops had killed over 100,000 of them.

Wartime Romania: most victims of atrocities were Jews from the provinces of Bessarabia and Bukovina or the occupied Ukrainian territory of Transnistria.

civilians, mostly Jews. The remaining Transnistrian Jews were herded into concentration camps where tens of thousands died over the savage winter of 1941-42. It is impossible to establish accurate figures for Jewish deaths attributable to the Romanians. They undoubtedly totalled at least 110,000, and possibly twice that number.

ANTI-PARTISAN POLICY

Transnistria had a wartime population of 2.25 million, of which 80 percent were Ukrainians. In 1942-43, the Romanian garrison there averaged 100,000 troops. The Romanians set reprisal ratios of 200 communists to be executed for every officer killed by partisans, and 100 for every soldier. But after late 1941, however, the Romanians did not implement such terror tactics. Some 90 percent of executions in Transnistria were in the first few weeks of the occupation.

The Red Army had left behind groups of activists in Odessa to serve as partisans under the direct orders of Stalin himself. From late 1941, the Romanians introduced the efficient Special Intelligence Service to counter them. This agency had frequent success against partisans in Odessa using intelligence, infiltrators, and informants. But the Service could not eliminate those partisans using the 125 miles of uncharted catacombs beneath the city. The Romanians tried blocking many of the 160 known entrances, and a number of partisans were starved to death. According to Soviet reports, the Romanians also tried to saturate the catacombs with tear gas, and later used poison gas, but this failed because the complex was too large. Even so, the catacomb partisans were reduced to a low of about 35 people in late 1942. Although their numbers grew into hundreds by 1944, they had little impact beyond providing an example of legendary endurance. The few small Soviet partisan bands in the interior of Transnistria had equally little success.

Romanian security policy in 1942-43 was very effective in keeping Transnistria passive without resorting to the ruthless terrorist measures used elsewhere with less success by the more powerful Germans. Indeed, refugees tried to flee from German to Romanian jurisdiction. Romanian policies in Transnistria resulted in the best food, health, and education provisions in Axis-occupied eastern Europe. The Romanians allowed religious and cultural revivals, released Transnistrian prisoners of war, and amnestied many local communists.

Such leniency eased Transnistrian hostility toward Romanian occupation after the initial terror of 1941. The moderation also undermined Soviet attempts to recruit partisans. Even when the withdrawing Romanians looted Transnistria in March 1944, the local partisans could not mobilize civilian support.

Despite his relative restraint in subjugating civilians in occupied Transnistria, Antonescu, his interior minister, and his governor of Transnistria, were all executed for war crimes on June 1, 1946.

Bertrande Roberts

SEE ALSO:

TERROR IN THE GERMAN OCCUPATION OF THE EAST; RESISTANCE IN THE EAST AND TERRORISM; TERROR AND THE WAFFEN SS.

FURTHER READING

- Axworthy, Mark, Cornel Scafes, and Cristian Craciunoiu. *Third Axis, Fourth Ally.* New York: Sterling, 1995.
- Butnaru, I. C. *The Silent Holocaust: Romania and its Jews.* New York: Greenwood Press, 1992.
- Schulte, Theo J. *The German Army and Nazi Policies in Occupied Russia.* New York: Berg, 1989.

GERMAN TERROR IN FRANCE AND ITALY

By the fall of 1941, much of Europe was under German occupation. Hitler's *Blitzkrieg* ("lightning war") policy had paid off and his armies had thundered over the continent, pushing all before them. Just as swift, however, was the need to make the newly occupied territories secure and to eliminate the resistance that would inevitably follow from the conquered civilian populations.

The German authorities had had nearly a decade of practice in suppressing opposition. A quarter of a million of their own people had been sent to concentration camps after Hitler had come to power. It was unlikely that foreign nationals would be treated any better. Nazi occupation policies in France from 1940 and Italy from 1943 were extremely harsh. Deliberate and systematic methods of terror were used to deter civilians from resisting Nazi authority and to crush this resistance as soon as it arose.

FRANCE, 1940-44

After France capitulated in 1940, Germany established its own military administration in the north and west of the country. In the south, a substitute French government was installed in the spa town of Vichy. This regime was compelled to collaborate with the Germans. The head of state was the aged World War I hero Marshal Pétain, but the effective ruler was Pierre Laval, who had twice briefly served as prime minister in the 1930s and as foreign minister in 1934–36.

German occupation policy was to maintain a stable and peaceful France, so that the country's economic resources could be exploited fully to support the German war machine. But both the German regime and its puppet Vichy government rigorously pursued a policy of subduing the civilian population by terror. Attacks on German installations and personnel were met with summary reprisals in the form of random executions and hostage-taking.

In addition, as early as October 1940, German racial ideology had also become a reason for persecuting French civilians. The Germans in northern France and the Vichy government progressively enacted anti-Semitic legislation. Laval's regime even blamed the Jews for the fall of France. In August 1942, the Germans and the Vichy government had begun to round up and deport Jews from both the occupied and unoccupied regions. One third of France's Jewish population ended up in German concentration camps, where most subsequently perished.

The German invasion of the Soviet Union on June 22, 1941, transformed Nazi occupation policy in France. It led to the recruitment of a French volunteer regiment for service in the East and the drafting of French civilians for forced labor in German factories. This was because the increasing German losses on the Eastern Front during 1942 meant more German nationals were conscripted to fight, leaving a shortage of workers at home. Unsurprisingly, this sparked off a wave of protests.

The French Resistance, by now a nationwide network of regional cells, capitalized on the situation and organized strikes, as in the province of Haute Savoie in early November 1942. The resistance also carried out attacks on German personnel. The Germans responded by strengthening the presence of

---

KEY FACTS

● On June 10, 1944, in response to Resistance support for the D-Day invasion of Normandy, the SS Nazi militia murdered 642 civilians in the village of Oradour-sur-Glane.

● In March 1944, in the Ardeatine caves outside Rome, 335 Italian prisoners were executed as a reprisal for the killing of 32 SS officers.

Popperfoto

Police indicate finger marks on a wall left by manacled prisoners of the Gestapo.

the Nazi party militia (SS) and the Security Service in the occupied north under the command of Brigadier Karl Oberg.

VICHY OCCUPIED

On November 11, 1942, German forces occupied Vichy France, as a direct response to the Allied landings in French North Africa (Operation Torch). Although now under direct occupation by the Germans, the Vichy authorities attempted to resist increased German control of French internal security by reducing the need for German intervention. To do this, the Vichy government needed to combat the resistance, so in January 1943, it set up its own paramilitary force, known as the Milice.

The Milice quickly gained a reputation for brutality. The force was hated and feared more for this than for its obvious collaboration with the Germans, because it was terrorizing its own people. The German occupiers also replied to intensified resistance with brutality. German troops shot civilian hostages in retaliation for resistance attacks. At the same time, captured partisans were routinely tortured and killed.

By the spring of 1944, it was clear that German terror tactics were having little effect in curbing the activities of the French Resistance. The campaign was partly misdirected because of the Nazi obsession with the Jews, who were seized as hostages or executed whether they were active in the resistance or not. Prior to the D-Day invasion of Normandy (June 6, 1944), partisans attacked French communications in order to assist the Allies in isolating the region. After D-Day, the resistance sabotaged movements of German reinforcements and supplies to the front. Inevitably, the Germans responded with ferocious reprisals.

With Allied troops now on French soil, the clashes between the Milice and the resistance in the south became more bitter and savage. And during July 1944, when the resistance encouraged a general uprising in the southwest, the German security forces mounted a final, coordinated, anti-partisan operation.

However, the progress of the Allied advance from Normandy and, from August, from the south of France, forced the Germans to abandon the interior of the country rapidly. The final act of the German occupation was the forcible removal of the Vichy government to Germany in September 1944.

ITALY, 1943-45

Mussolini's fascist Italy had entered World War II in summer 1940 as Germany's ally in order to benefit from German successes in the war. But military disasters in North Africa and on the Eastern Front meant that by 1943 the war was unpopular in all sections of Italian society. In September, after the Allied invasion of Sicily, Mussolini was deposed and a new government under Marshal Badoglio signed an armistice with the Allies.

The Germans had been expecting this development and immediately occupied Italy. German forces took Rome after a brief fight, occupied Italy as far south as Naples, and disarmed the Italian military. German troops executed several thousand Italian officers who had ordered their troops to resist. Meanwhile, Allied forces landed on the southern Italian mainland and began fighting their way north.

German occupation policy was to reestablish a fascist republic – the Italian Social Republic – at Salo on Lake Garda in northern Italy. The republic was led by Mussolini, who had been sprung from prison by German commandos in early September. The German military strategy in Italy was mainly defensive, aiming to slow down the progress north of the Allies and inflict heavy casualties.

The Germans raised, trained, and equipped a small new Italian National Republican Army loyal to Mussolini, while the Italians themselves raised their own National Republican Guard for internal security operations. At the same time, Hitler annexed the South Tirol in northern Italy, which had a large ethnic German population. General Karl Wolff was appointed head of internal security and anti-partisan operations there, crushing opposition with hand-picked men from the SS.

Along with the occupying forces came Hitler's racial policy. For the first time in modern Italy, Jews were at risk. Although they were a small minority, Italian Jews were loyal, even to the fascists. But after the Nazi occupation, widespread anti-Semitic riots broke out in September 1943. Jews from the northern Italian cities were rounded up and deported, first to the Fossoli di Carpi concentration camp in the South Tirol and later to a host of similar camps throughout northern Italy, where thousands perished.

ANTI-COMMUNIST OPERATIONS

The strongest opposition to Nazi rule in Italy came from communists, who were concentrated in the urbanized north. During the spring of 1944, the resistance from communist partisans intensified, especially in the Italian Alps. Germany's response was to strengthen its security forces. However, German troops were in short supply, for they were now having to defend German occupied territories on the Eastern and Western Fronts from imminent invasion.

Instead, an array of anti-communist Cossacks, Turks, and sympathizers from the Baltic States (Estonia, Latvia, and Lithuania) arrived for occupation duties. General Wolff increasingly relied on Mussolini's forces to fight the communist partisans. The security forces routinely murdered hostages in retaliation for partisan attacks. One act of reprisal followed a bomb attack that killed 33 German police officers. Italian priests, Jews, women, and two 14-year-old boys were arrested and shot in Rome by the Gestapo.

The formation of a united front among the various guerrilla groups in mid-1944 prompted Mussolini to reform the infamous fascist Blackshirt militia, known as the Armata Milizia, to fight the partisans. The Blackshirts' response to the resistance's assassinations, bombings, and ambushes was a deliberate campaign of terror. They destroyed many towns and villages, deported thousands of people to concentration camps, and carried out summary mass executions of the male population.

Yet even this orchestrated terror failed to suppress partisan activity. As the Allies advanced on northern Italy during the fall of 1944, resistance activity intensified. The partisans escalated their activities from sabotage, bombings, and individual assassinations to more ambitious, larger-scale military operations designed to wipe out Axis forces and liberate entire Italian communities from fascist control.

Despite constant, vigorous, and murderous Axis anti-partisan sweeps, large swathes of northern Italy were under partisan control by spring 1945. In April, the partisans launched a general insurrection that liberated Genoa, Milan, and Turin. They now threatened to sever German communications as Axis forces attempted a general withdrawal through the Alpine passes and Germany beyond. This action helped force the German command to a separate surrender of the Axis forces in Italy to the Allies on May 2, 1945, six days before Germany's formal capitulation.

Russell A. Hart

SEE ALSO:

TERROR IN WORLD WAR I; TERROR IN THE GERMAN OCCUPATION OF THE EAST; GERMAN TERROR IN NORWAY; TERROR'S USE BY THE FRENCH RESISTANCE; WWII RESISTANCE IN YUGOSLAVIA AND TERRORISM; TERROR AND THE WAFFEN SS.

F U R T H E R   R E A D I N G

- Gordon, B. *Collaborationism in France During the Second World War*. Ithaca, NY: Cornell University Press, 1980.
- Puzzo, D. *The Partisans and the War in Italy*. New York: P. Lang, 1992.
- Zuccotti, S. *The Italians and the Holocaust: Persecution, Rescue, and Survival*. New York: Basic Books, 1987.

GERMAN TERROR IN NORWAY

The Germans invaded Norway on April 9, 1940. In a brilliant yet costly two-month campaign, the German armed forces (Wehrmacht) decisively beat the unprepared Norwegian forces and their equally disorganized British and French allies. King Haakon VII and his government fled to London, and the Germans were left in control of a dazed population. The invaders were eagerly welcomed by Vidkun Quisling, whose name remains synonymous with the word *traitor*. He headed the previously unimportant Nazi-style Nasjonal Samling (National Union) and proclaimed himself head of government.

QUISLING AND COLLABORATION

It suited the Germans to have such a willing collaborator as Quisling. They needed a stable base in Norway from which to mount attacks upon Britain. In addition, the country was rich in mineral resources, especially coal, which were vital to the German war economy.

There was also the ideological factor. As Norwegian historian Olav Riste wrote, the Norwegians had the "dubious honor of being regarded [by the Nazis] as a kindred folk – a wayward Nordic tribe that should be led into the Greater German Reich through persuasion." When Nazi attempts at persuasion failed, Reichskommissar Josef Terboven, chief German official in Norway, resorted to more traditional Nazi terror methods.

KEY FACTS

● The Germans operated a brutal reprisal policy to deter resistance acts. In late 1942, in Trondheim, west-central Norway, the Nazis executed ten prominent civilians as "atonement" for sabotage.

● After British agents attacked German facilities near Bergen, in southern Norway, on January 25, 1943, the Nazis arrested 200 Norwegian civilians and deported them to concentration camps.

In the first year of German occupation, there was little resistance in Norway. However, Quisling soon alienated the Norwegian people by attempting to intimidate a society unused to political violence. He believed that the active demonstration of his Nasjonal Samling party's power would stimulate fear and respect. A campaign of street violence by party workers was organized and, in the schools, teachers and school administrators were beaten up.

The Norwegian people staged large-scale protests in Oslo in December 1940. Quisling's attempt at the Nazification of the Norwegian education system was also deeply resented by the people. The German navy complained that such actions were destabilizing the country and threatening the security of their bases. But Reichskommissar Terboven could not allow the authority of the Nasjonal Samling to be flouted. He decided to stage a demonstration of German power.

GERMAN REPRESSION

In September 1941, Terboven observed that: "I have without success placed myself at the beck and call of the Norwegians. I will now force them to their knees." Thus, when the Norwegian Federation of Trade Unions declared a strike in Oslo on September 8, 1941, Terboven saw his chance and declared a state of emergency. The Nazi party's paramilitary force, the Schutz Staffeln (SS), and the Nazi secret police, (Gestapo), rounded up 300 resistance workers and trade unionists, two of whom were executed.

The rounding up and execution of Norwegians was the first use of systematic terror by the Germans in Norway and it served as a warning to the population that Terboven was willing to use terror. One of his officials, Dr. Alfred Huhnhäser, noted that if Terboven had in the beginning been inclined to treat the Norwegians well in order to win them over, as was Hitler's wish, then he changed his mind "from the time of the state of emergency and began a reign of terror."

Terboven decided to help Quisling with the Nazification of education by arresting 1,300 male

Mary Evans Picture Collection

"The truth about the Swastika" – this caption, in a Norwegian resistance propaganda photograph depicting Germans rounding up suspects, emphasizes the repressive terror of the Nazi occupation.

teachers, of whom 500 were sent as forced labor to the extremely harsh conditions of the Arctic. And when the Norwegian police refused to round up laborers for Quisling's 1943 Work Effort, Terboven had the police leader Gunnar Eilifsen executed and 1,300 officers deported to a concentration camp in Poland.

THE CONSEQUENCES OF RESISTANCE

The German response to resistance, either by British agents or the Norwegian resistance, was even more brutal. In April 1942, British agents killed two Gestapo men at Tælevåg, near Bergen. The Nazis obliterated the village, interned every inhabitant, shot 18 hostages, and deported all the males to the Sachsenhausen concentration camp, where 76 of them died. Such a brutal reprisal had the desired effect on the Norwegian people. It caused great local resentment against the resistance and led the Norwegian government-in-exile to demand of their British ally "No more Tælevåg!"

On October 5, 1942, British agents, aided by the local Norwegian resistance, attacked the iron ore mines at Fosdalen. In retaliation, the Germans executed 35 local villagers without trial. When the Norwegian police chief Karl Marthinsen was killed on February 8, 1945, 30 hostages were shot in reprisal.

The public reaction forced the resistance to stop killing Nasjonal Samling members. But one month later, the resistance warned that continued use of terror would lead to an escalation of defiance. By this time, the Germans knew the war was lost and retribution imminent. They executed no more hostages.

PERSECUTING NORWEGIAN JEWS

Quisling was a fervent anti-Semite, and the Nasjonal Samling actively aided the Nazis' round-up of Norwegian Jews late in 1942. The Norwegian resistance managed to spirit 925 to Sweden, but 759 were deported, most of them to the Auschwitz death camp, where only 25 survived.

Compared with the extreme brutality of German rule in Eastern Europe, the suffering in Norway was not extensive, largely because of the high status of Norway in Nazi racial theories. But although both Terboven and Quisling were prepared to use ruthless measures when necessary, the use of terror to intimidate the population was a failure. It merely united the Norwegians against him. The German repression met with some success, however, causing temporary suspensions of resistance activity.

M. Christopher Mann

SEE ALSO:

TERROR IN WORLD WAR I; TERROR IN THE GERMAN OCCUPATION OF THE EAST; GERMAN TERROR IN FRANCE AND ITALY; TERROR'S USE BY THE FRENCH RESISTANCE; THE HOLOCAUST.

FURTHER READING

- Hayes, Paul M. *Quisling: The Career and Political Ideas of Vidkun Quisling, 1887-1945*. Bloomington, IN: Indiana University Press, 1972.
- Petrow, Richard. *The Bitter Years: The Invasion and Occupation of Denmark and Norway, April 1940- May 1945*. New York: Morrow Quill, 1979.
- Vigness, Paul C. *The German Occupation of Norway*. New York: Vantage, 1970.

RESISTANCE IN THE EAST AND TERRORISM

On June 22, 1941, Nazi Germany invaded the Soviet Union in a war designed to eliminate the "Jewish Bolshevik enemy," and Soviet Communism. Hitler aimed to subjugate the "subhuman" Slavs, which included most western Soviet citizens, and to win vast territories as new settlements for Germany. At first, German troops were welcomed in many areas as liberators from communist rule, but they soon met increasing popular resistance as the brutality of Nazi occupation policies became apparent. But German terror was only half of an increasingly dreadful picture. Soviet terror quickly formed the other. For example, at the outbreak of war, Soviet dictator Joseph Stalin ordered the immediate execution of political prisoners and suspected spies.

Next, the Soviet secret police, the NKVD, and the regional committees of the Soviet Communist Party received orders to set up a resistance network in areas occupied by the Germans. On July 3, 1941, in his first wartime broadcast, Stalin announced that a "people's war" involving a vast partisan movement would be waged against the Germans with the the aim of producing "intolerable conditions for the invaders."

The partisan movement, which unleashed a savage internal war in German-occupied Soviet territory, grew slowly. No preparation had been made for partisan warfare in the Soviet Union before 1941. The first partisan groups consisted mainly of NKVD sabotage groups plus Red Army soldiers cut off in the rear by the advancing Germans. Weapons were extremely scarce and this severely hampered any expansion. The main activities were sporadic raids on German headquarters or small German garrisons.

A large-scale partisan movement only appeared in late 1942. After this, the partisans were regularly reinforced by Red Army troops who parachuted behind German lines. Neither the German army in its anti-partisan operations nor the Soviet partisans paid any heed to the accepted laws governing war conduct, and neither showed any concern for the local population. Both sides used widespread terror against peaceful populations in a savage struggle that cost more than 1 million lives.

The communist partisans gathered intelligence, infiltrated German military staffs as interpreters or clerks, organized sabotage, and assassinated German officers. Soviet terrorist actions were often calculated provocations designed to stimulate ferocious German reprisals, making coexistence between the population and the German occupiers virtually impossible. In one Soviet village, for instance, the Germans shot over 300 local Russians in revenge after partisans killed three German officers. Similarly, in March 1942, the Germans discovered that villagers near Bobruisk, White Russia, to the east of Poland, were aiding the partisans. The Nazis launched a terror reprisal, burning down villages and killing 3,500 peasants to warn others not to cooperate with the partisans.

Soviet partisans, however, also used terror against their own population. The partisans assassinated collaborators or attacked their families. Partisans also attacked German camps holding captured Soviet soldiers, presumably to discourage surrender at the front or to swell the ranks of partisan units with escaped prisoners. The partisans also terrorized Russians who worked for the German administration as mayors or policemen. In areas under their control, partisans put up Red Flags, symbols of communist sympathies, which they attached to hidden mines. The mines blew up any anti-Soviet sympathizers attempting to remove the flags.

KEY FACTS

● During the 1941-45 Soviet-German conflict, Stalin established large numbers of partisan detachments to carry on a brutal terror struggle against Nazism behind enemy lines.

● The Nazis also used terror tactics to defeat the Soviet partisans. In a March 1942, operation in the Crimea, on the Black Sea, the Germans killed not only 153 partisans, but also 1,800 innocent peasants, to warn others not to aid the partisans.

Novosti

While the partisans brought a degree of Soviet rule back to the occupied areas, for the local population they simply replaced Nazi terror with their own Red terror.

Partisans also used terror within their own ranks. The death penalty was the basis of discipline within partisan units, and executions were used deliberately as a means of intimidation and coercion.

TAKING THE PARTISAN WAR ABROAD

Up to 1944, Soviet partisans had also carried on within the Soviet Union a bitter war of extermination against anti-Soviet organizations and nationalist political groups such as those in the Ukraine. In 1944, after the advancing Red Army had liberated all Soviet territory, the partisan movement changed. Stalin ordered the partisans to advance across the Soviet frontier to begin a "revolutionary struggle" in Soviet-occupied eastern Europe, which would introduce a Stalinist political system. The partisans infiltrated behind German lines and advanced ahead of the Red Army into Poland. These communist bands both provoked German reprisals against the local population and also killed members of the anti-Soviet Polish resistance.

With the Red Army closing on Czechoslovakia in the spring of 1944, the partisans decided to "assist" the Czechoslovaks by sending ten Soviet-trained partisan groups into Slovakia. In reality, these partisans were preparing the way for Soviet domination of Slovakia. During the last months of the war, the partisan struggle against German occupation of Slovakia became a bitter struggle between communist and anti-communist

Soviet Partisans in Vitebsk, White Russia (east of Poland), take an oath of allegiance to the struggle of the Great Patriotic War against Nazism.

elements. The Soviet partisans deliberately used terror tactics to destroy their non-communist opponents.

The Soviet struggle against German occupation cost more than 1 millions lives and was characterized by universal use of terror. By 1944-45, these tacticsbecame part of the competitions between communists and nationalists for control of eastern Europe.

John Erickson

SEE ALSO:

TERROR IN THE GERMAN OCCUPATION OF THE EAST; WWII RESISTANCE IN YUGOSLAVIA AND TERRORISM; TERROR AND THE NAZI BARBARIZATION OF WARFARE; TERROR AND THE SOVIET BARBARIZATION OF WARFARE.

F U R T H E R   R E A D I N G

- Dallin, Alexander. *German Rule in Russia, 1941-1945.* New York: St. Martin's Press, 1981.
- Linz, S. J. ed. *The Impact of World War II on the Soviet Union.* Totowa, NJ: Rowman and Allanheld, 1990.
- Lukas, R. C. *Forgotten Holocaust: The Poles Under German Occupation, 1939-1944.* New York: Hippocrene Books, 1990.

TERROR'S USE BY THE FRENCH RESISTANCE

The Resistance in France consisted of a network of groups acting against the German occupation of 1940-44. Resistance activity was not substantial or widespread at first but, as the Allies slowly gained military dominance over the Germans in 1943-44, the Resistance became invaluable to preparations for the invasion of Europe.

Resistance fighters were routinely called terrorists by the Germans, but only some of their activities fit that description in any way. Espionage and helping shot-down airmen return to Allied territory were important Resistance activities, but those engaged in them usually tried to avoid violent incidents that might lead to detection. However, other resisters carried out sabotage, assassination, and other "terrorist" attacks on the Germans and their French collaborators.

VICHY AND THE FREE FRENCH

After defeating France in May–June 1940, the Germans did not overrun the whole country but chose instead to divide it into two zones. The Germans occupied the northern one and left the southern part to be controlled by a French puppet government based in the town of Vichy. The Vichy government was led by Marshal Philippe Pétain, one of France's heroes of World War I. Pétain's government was regarded by most French people, in 1940 at least, as the legitimate government of France. The Germans occupied the whole of France from November 1942, when the Allies liberated the French colonies in North Africa. After this, with the Allies clearly winning the war, Resistance activities increased and Pétain's position declined.

Some Frenchmen denied Vichy's authority from the start. Charles de Gaulle, the most junior general in the French army (Pétain was the most senior), escaped to Britain, announced the existence of "Free France," and, with a few followers, urged all French people to fight on. Pétain condemned de Gaulle as a traitor but de Gaulle was supported by the British and, from mid-1943, by the Americans, although he had many disagreements with both. By the time of the Allied invasion in 1944, de Gaulle and the Free French had become the major focus of the French Resistance.

THE ROLE OF THE COMMUNISTS

The French Communist Party had been banned by the French government early in the war. However, from June 1940 until the Nazis invaded the Soviet Union a year later (while the Nazi–Soviet Pact of 1939 was still operative) the communists were tolerated by the Germans and, obedient to Moscow, they did not resist the German occupation. Like communists elsewhere, however, the French communists' history of clandestine political operations and their influence in labor unions gave them a leading role in the Resistance when the party line turned against the Nazis after the June 1941 German invasion of the Soviet Union. The main communist organizations involved in the Resistance were the National Front and its military wing, the Francs-Tireurs et Partisans. From late 1943, the communists, too, reluctantly accepted de Gaulle's authority as leader of the French forces in exile.

Various British organizations were involved in helping develop the Resistance. MI6 (the British spy

---

KEY FACTS

● The Resistance was a loose network of groups determined to fight the German occupation of northern France and the collaborators at Vichy.

● The Resistance used terror tactics, particularly assassination, against the German occupation forces and their Vichy collaborators. They also used terror against rival resistance groups and to discipline members of their own organization.

Hulton Getty Picture Collection

service) and MI9 (the department responsible for escape lines) did important work, but in terms of "terrorist" activity the most significant department was the Special Operations Executive (SOE), whose role was to stir up armed rebellion against the Germans. In 1944, the British sent special forces' teams, consisting mainly of Special Air Service personnel, to France to lead and direct local uprisings. As British contact with the Resistance was already well established when the United States entered the war (and because the U.S. Government's political relations with de Gaulle were very poor), the American role in assisting the French Resistance was less substantial than Britain's. However, the U.S. Office of Strategic Services (OSS), the forerunner of the modern CIA, joined the SOE and other British agencies in their activities.

Resistance in France began with small, separate groups of like-minded people starting to work against

French Resistance members capture a wounded German soldier near Montneyan in September 1944.

the Germans. These groups had a vast range of personal and political motives, and enormously varied backgrounds, training, and aptitude for resistance work. By 1944, these ineffective and disparate groups had joined a single organization with substantial training, access to large quantities of arms and explosives, and the capability of carrying out a wide range of tasks in response to orders from Allied commanders.

Arms and explosives came, apart from small amounts purloined from the Germans, from the Allies. In the course of the war, Britain and the U.S. sent 500,000 weapons to the Resistance. SOE transported 700 agents in and out of France and distributed thousands of copies of pamphlets on guerrilla warfare and bomb-making to provide further training. Orders were received by secret radio operators and coded messages were included in British BBC broadcasts.

The work of unifying the various separate groups in France was led by Jean Moulin, a former civil servant dismissed by the Germans for refusing to carry out punitive measures they had ordered. By the time the Allies invaded France in June 1944, all important Resistance groups were part of a formal military structure known as the French Forces of the Interior.

ASSASSINATION AND SABOTAGE

Assassination was a favorite Resistance tactic. One example is the August 1941 murder on the Paris subway of a German naval official, Alphonse Moser, by communist Resistance member Pierre Félix Georges. Another example is the October 1941 killing of Colonel Holtz, the German town commandant at Nantes.

Most victims of assassination were Germans, but some 5,000 were French collaborators. A notable example occurred in December 1942, when Bonnier de la Chapelle, a supporter of de Gaulle, assassinated Admiral Jean Darlan, deputy to President Pétain, in Algiers. The Resistance also carried out reprisals against sections of its own organization, executing many Francs-Tireurs as "bandits." Resistance members justified their behavior on the grounds that this was a fight for survival against a brutal occupying power.

Resistance members considered themselves "freedom fighters," but the Germans looked upon them as "terrorists" unprotected by the laws of war. The Nazis responded to Resistance terror with terror of their own. Assassinations resulted in a gruesome spiral of reprisal and counter-reprisal. Within a few days of the Holtz killing, for example, the Germans had taken some 600 hostages and shot over 100.

Sabotage was an even more important Resistance role, bringing a steady drain of German casualties. These actions were very effective – on the night of June 5-6, 1944, as Allied forces approached the Normandy beaches, Resistance groups cut railroad tracks in 950 places throughout France. This was in addition to many other sabotage tasks and direct attacks on German forces at the same time. The June 1944 murder by SS troops of 642 villagers from Oradour-sur-Glane was the most notorious German atrocity carried out as revenge for resistance attacks.

Besides the German secret police and security organizations, those engaged in the brutal struggle against the Resistance included various Vichy police forces and other collaborationist groups, notably the 45,000-strong paramilitary Milice Française.

As well as carrying out sabotage and other small-scale operations, Resistance leaders hoped to organize insurrections to liberate large areas of the country in conjunction with the invading Allied armies. In 1943, therefore, resistance groups collaborated to organize a secret army known as the Maquis. Maquis uprisings took place in several rural areas, particularly in southern France, in the weeks following the Allied landings in Normandy. Although they certainly hampered the Germans, the lightly equipped Maquis were no match for the German army in a stand-up fight.

THE RESULTS OF RESISTANCE

It is hard to judge how effective were Resistance activities. The Resistance became most effective and gained most recruits after the Germans had lost the war. The Resistance alone could not have defeated the Germans but the Allied efforts to develop it, and the German ones to defeat it, suggest that it was effective.

After the war, some 300,000 French people received official veterans' status, and another 170,000 were recognized as Resistance volunteers. About 100,000 had lost their lives in Resistance-related activities. Some two million people, or around 10 percent of the adult population participated in some manner in resisting the German occupation, but at lesser risk.

Steve Weiss

SEE ALSO:

GERMAN TERROR IN FRANCE AND ITALY; GERMAN TERROR IN NORWAY; RESISTANCE IN THE EAST AND TERRORISM; WWII RESISTANCE IN YUGOSLAVIA AND TERRORISM; TERROR AND THE WAFFFEN SS; WORLD WAR II WAR CRIMES TRIALS.

FURTHER READING

- Funk, Arthur. *Hidden Ally*. New York: Greenwood Press, 1992.
- Kedward, H. Roderick. *In Search of the Maquis*. New York: Oxford University Press, 1993.
- Morris, Allan. *Collaboration and Resistance Reviewed*. New York: St. Martin's Press, 1992.
- Novick, Peter. *The Resistance versus Vichy*. New York: Columbia University Press, 1968.

WWII RESISTANCE IN YUGOSLAVIA AND TERRORISM

The fighting on Yugoslav territory during World War II was partly a war of liberation against the Axis powers (Germany, Italy, and Bulgaria), partly a civil war, and partly a revolution. This complex conflict involved three main groups among the Yugoslavs, a number of smaller groups, and the Axis occupation forces. The use of terror to cow opponents was, at some stage, used by almost all the participants.

Yugoslavia was the name given to a union of Balkan lands – Serbia, Bosnia-Herzegovina, Croatia, Slovenia, Montenegro, and Macedonia – set up in 1918 after World War I when the Austro-Hungarian Empire was broken up. It was never a truly united country, due to the many different cultures, religions, and languages of the member countries. There were always political conflicts over territories within Yugoslavia. The central clash was between Serbs, who saw the whole territory as theirs, and others, especially Croats, who sought their own states.

When war broke out in 1939, therefore, and the country faced German invasion, all manner of separatist groups saw their chance to break free from the union. At first, Hitler guaranteed Yugoslavia's borders but only when the government signed a pro-Axis pact. When a popular uprising finally deposed the government in protest over this alliance, Germany invaded on April 6, 1941. After a ten-day campaign of occupation, Yugoslavia was dismembered. Parts were given to Germany's allies Italy and Bulgaria, while some areas came under direct Nazi occupation.

A Serbian Protectorate was also created under German domination. This was run by General Milan Nedic, who assisted in the Nazi extermination of Jews and others in the region. An independent state of Croatia was established, which incorporated Croatia, and most of Bosnia-Herzegovina, but not the coastal region of Dalmatia. Croatia itself was divided between German and Italian zones of influence.

RESISTANCE ACTIVITIES

The three main Yugoslav military-political movements were the communist-led partisans, the Serb royalist Chetniks and the Croatian nationalist Ustasha movement. In addition, there were various other militia-style forces in different parts of the country engaged in resistance activities against the Germans, as well as Albanian and Macedonian nationalist movements. This complex set of conflicts within a war resulted in the death of around one million Yugoslavs. The majority of these are thought to have been killed by other Yugoslavs in a brutal conflict in which terror was the order of the day.

Initial resistance to the German occupation, in the form of spontaneous revolts, first occurred in Serbia and Montenegro. Serbian attacks were led primarily by the Chetniks, who were groups of former royal army officers operating from the mountains in central Serbia following the flight of the royal government to Britain. Their leader, Colonel Draza Mihailovic, was later appointed Minister of Defense by this royal government-in-exile. Communist partisans in Montenegro, encouraged by the strength of local feeling, also began attacking German occupation forces – in spite of

---

KEY FACTS

● After Yugoslavia was conquered by the German armed forces in 1941, a multifaceted resistance war and civil war broke out.

● Tito's communist partisans and Mihailovic's royalist Chetniks both fought one another as well as the Axis occupation forces. The latter were supported by the Ustasha, the Croatian fascist regime established by the Nazis, which carried out a brutal campaign of terror against Serbs.

Novosti

orders from the leader of the partisans in the Serbian capital Belgrade, Josip Broz, better known as Tito, who believed the time was not right.

A band of Tito's communist partisans sheltering in woods in an attempt to avoid the German forces that were making a sweep of the area.

REPRISAL KILLINGS

The reaction of the occupation forces to resistance activity was fierce. In Montenegro, the Italians drafted reserves from Albania and used Albanian auxiliary troops to terrorize communities. As a result, most resistance fighters returned home to protect their families. In Serbia, the Germans ordered that 100 Yugoslavs would be executed for every German killed in resistance attacks. This attempt to suppress rebellion by highly disproportionate reprisal killings occurred partly because the Germans were short of manpower for occupation duties in the Balkans. Only four relatively weak divisions were stationed on Yugoslav territory during the war. These were supplemented by a further two divisions for specific anti-partisan offensives.

During the first months of the war in Yugoslavia, the Chetnik leader Mihailovic made contact with partisan chief Tito, although each faction continued to act independently. From September to November 1941, meetings took place to organize a common resistance front. However, the negotiations fizzled out by the end of 1941. The Chetnik leader decided to adopt a waiting policy until he could join an Allied invasion of Yugoslavia; Tito, in contrast, ordered his partisans to undertake a series of uprisings. The positions adopted by these leaders reflected their different objectives. Mihailovic limited Chetnik resistance because he feared that Nazi reprisals would destroy the social structure of the old, royalist Yugoslavia. But Tito maximized his partisan offensives because he wanted to destroy the old order and replace it with a communist republic.

Whatever their political agenda, the partisans gained popular support for three reasons. First, they were prepared to fight the occupying forces. Second, they were a genuinely multi-ethnic group – Tito was a Croat, but the majority of partisans were Serbs. Third, they stood whole-heartedly for a new regime that seemed to offer hope for the future – something the Chetniks, associated with the discredited monarchy, could not do. The strength of this idealism was one reason the Allies ultimately supported the partisans.

The partisan campaign of resistance by terror deliberately provoked German reprisal killings. This was a complete change of plan from earlier in 1941, when Tito had tried to halt communist resistance activity in Montenegro and Slovenia. Tito had a threefold aim: to resist the Axis powers, to conduct a revolution and seize power, and to install a communist regime.

As the only resistance movement whose membership came from many national groups, the partisans could establish a regional government wherever they were based. However, they were not always successful in maintaining control. By the winter of 1941, the partisans were forced to retreat from the republic they had established around the town of Uzice in southern Serbia. They were finally able to establish themselves in western Bosnia during 1942.

The partisans were able to consolidate their position in western Bosnia because their active campaign of resistance attracted strong support from the inhabitants of that area and in the adjacent Dalmatian hinterland. In particular, this support was strong because local Serbs, who made up three-quarters of the total partisan strength at this time, were anxious to join a movement which offered resistance to the Ustasha-ruled Croatian state. If the savage German reprisal campaign had been good for partisan recruitment in southern Serbia, the Ustasha's campaign of terror against the Serbs performed the same function in Croatia and Bosnia.

CROATIAN NATIONALISM

The Ustasha movement, once an illegal Croatian terrorist group led by Ante Pavelic, had been based in Italy and now was installed in power in Croatia following the Axis conquest. Initially the Ustasha was popular in parts of Croatia, but its attraction faded in many places as its rule took effect. The Ustasha government began a program to kill one-third of the Orthodox Serb population, to expel another third, and to convert the final third to Roman Catholicism. The attempt to implement this program included the use of massacre and mutilation as instruments of terror. Slitting throats, gouging

eyes, castrating and skinning people alive were methods used, especially in the areas on either side of the border between Croatia and western Bosnia. Concentration camps were also established at this time. The main camp, Jasenovac, doubled as a death camp where tens of thousands of Serbs, Jews, anti-fascist Croats, and others perished. The reactions of the Serbian population to this Ustasha terror campaign were an important factor in the growth of the partisan movement.

As an ultimate Allied victory became likely, the main focus of the war in Yugoslavia was more on the defeat of opposing internal factions. The partisans sought to defeat both the Ustasha and the Chetniks while, after 1941, the main focus of Chetnik activity was to prevent a communist takeover when the Germans left. Chetniks were also involved in the massacre of thousands of Slav Muslims in Bosnia – an act that prefigured the "ethnic cleansing" of the war in the 1990s. Chetniks collaborated first with the Italians, until the latter surrendered in September 1943, and then with the Germans. Partisan contact with the Nazis was limited to one failed attempt to agree to a truce in 1943 to allow the partisans to concentrate on the Chetniks.

The terror was to continue after the war. The communists killed tens of thousands of people who had collaborated or had fought with the Ustasha, the Chetniks, the Albanian nationalists, or the militia forces. Those executed included several thousand Yugoslavs repatriated by British forces in Austria. There is no doubt that the horrors of World War II and its aftermath left bitter memories that would resurface when Yugoslavia broke up 50 years later.

James Gow

SEE ALSO:

TERROR IN GERMAN OCCUPATION OF THE EAST; RESISTANCE IN THE EAST AND TERRORISM; TERROR'S USE BY THE FRENCH RESISTANCE.

FURTHER READING

- Djilas, Milovan. *Wartime*. New York, Harcourt Brace Jovanovich, 1980.
- Lindsay, F. *Beacons in the Night*. Stanford. CA: Stanford University Press, 1993.
- Vucinich, W. S. *Contemporary Yugoslavia: Twenty Years of Socialist Experiment*. Berkeley, CA: University of California Press, 1969.

THE HOLOCAUST

Between 1933 and 1945, the Nazi regime in Germany implemented policies of increasing persecution against the Jewish people. The maltreatment began with legal restrictions, arrests, and beatings. The Nazis' vicious mistreatment of Jews escalated until the regime, in 1941-42, commenced the deliberate, systematic murder of six and a half million people. Most of the Nazis' victims were Jews, although other "asocials" – Gypsies, homosexuals, the handicapped and mentally ill, and Soviet prisoners – were also included. Historians term this genocide, or the deliberate attempt to destroy a racial group, the Holocaust. The Nazis referred to it as the "Final Solution" to the Jewish Question. Although anti-Semitism, or hatred and persecution of Jews, had occurred for centuries in Europe, the sheer scale and utter brutality of the Holocaust was unique. Throughout history, humans have probably never sunk any lower in terms of organized, large-scale barbarism and savagery.

Nazi anti-Semitism was based on Nazi leader Adolf Hitler's personal loathing of Jews. Key Nazi beliefs were social darwinism, racialism and anti-Semitism, and German military expansion. In the Nazi interpretation of social darwinism, life was a bitter struggle for survival among the world's races. The Nazis ranked these races according to racial "superiority," with the Aryans (Germans and Nordic peoples) at the top.

After the Nazis' 1933 seizure of power in Germany, they passed laws that both forced the Jews out of public life and turned them into second-class citizens. Nazi paramilitary groups also subjected the Jews to increasing violence. Nazi prewar persecution peaked in the brutal Nazi *Kristalnacht* (Crystal night) pogrom, or attack on Jews, of November 9-10, 1938. During the pogrom, 30,000 Jews were arrested, and Nazi attackers looted 7,000 Jewish businesses and killed 91 Jews.

World War II broke out in September 1939, after the German invasion of Poland and the declarations of war by France and Great Britain. Nazi persecution then spread to include all Jews in German-occupied Europe. From mid-1941, Nazi cruelties against Jews further intensified. The German invasion of the Soviet Union on June 22, 1941, had the purpose of racial annihilation. The Nazis entrusted four task forces, or *Einsatzgruppen*, with the execution of Soviet Jews and Bolshevik officials. From mid-1941 until late 1942, these forces, aided by German and Axis (German-allied) army units, killed 1 million Jews and communists in Axis-occupied Soviet territory. Throughout the East, the Schutz Staffeln (SS), the Nazis' elite paramilitary force, shot and killed groups of Jews, after forcing them to dig ditches and kneel in front of them.

In late 1941, the Nazis began planning to deport all Europe's Jews by rail to six extermination camps set up, or to be set up, in Poland, including Auschwitz. While there were appallingly brutal concentration camps in Germany, such as Bergen-Belsen and Dachau, these did not have large gas chambers and did not exist primarily to slaughter thousands of Jews, as did the extermination camps. This extermination plan was finalized at the January 20, 1942, Wannsee Conference. The SS, under the direction of Adolf Eichmann, their expert on Jewish affairs, took control of the Holocaust.

ORGANIZED TERROR AND DEHUMANIZATION

The Holocaust was made even more terrible by the amount of organization and regimentation involved. Nazi officials organized train timetables and monitored figures for deaths as if these were routine industrial matters, rather than the murder of millions of human beings. One tool employed in the task of killing Jews was the Nazis' deliberate use of terror.

The Nazis used systematic terror during their extermination of Europe's Jews for three main purposes: first, to dehumanize the Jews in the eyes of the Germans and their allies who were charged with carry-

---

KEY FACTS

● During the Holocaust, in their extermination camps, the Nazis killed 6 million Jews, and at least 500,000 Gypsies, homosexuals, mentally and physically handicapped people, and Soviet prisoners.

● The Nazis murdered millions of Jews in the gas chambers constructed at their death camps, in which 2,000 people could be killed every 15 minutes. Their corpses were burned in vast crematoria.

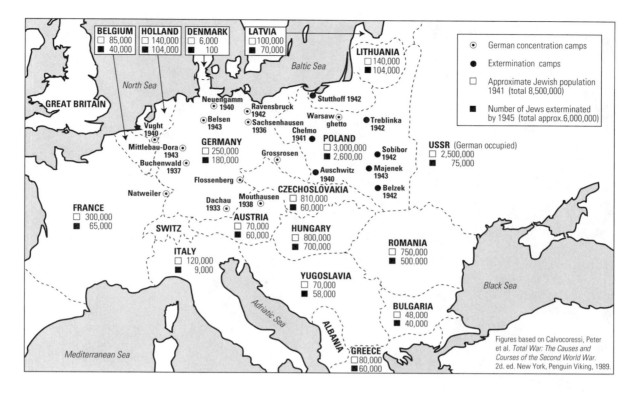

BELGIUM □ 85,000 ■ 40,000	**HOLLAND** □ 140,000 ■ 104,000
DENMARK □ 6,000 ■ 100	**LATVIA** □ 100,000 ■ 70,000

⊙ German concentration camps

● Extermination camps

□ Approximate Jewish population 1941 (total 8,500,000)

■ Number of Jews exterminated by 1945 (total approx.6,000,000)

LITHUANIA □ 140,000 ■ 104,000

Baltic Sea

North Sea

GREAT BRITAIN

Neuengamm ⊙ 1940

Stutthoff 1942

Ravensbruck ⊙ 1942

Belsen ⊙ 1943

Sachsenhausen ⊙ 1936

Warsaw ghetto

Chelmo 1941 ●

Treblinka ● 1942

Vught ⊙ 1940

Mittlebau-Dora ⊙ 1943

GERMANY □ 250,000 ■ 180,000

POLAND □ 3,000,000 ■ 2,600,00

Sobibor ● 1942

USSR (German occupied) □ 2,500,000 ■ 75,000

Buchenwald ⊙ 1937

Grossrosen ⊙

Auschwitz ● 1940

Majenek ● 1943

Flossenberg ⊙

Natweiler ⊙

Dachau 1933 ⊙

Mouthausen 1938 ⊙

CZECHOSLOVAKIA □ 810,000 ■ 60,000

Belzek ● 1942

FRANCE □ 300,000 ■ 65,000

SWITZ

AUSTRIA □ 70,000 ■ 60,000

HUNGARY □ 800,000 ■ 700,000

ROMANIA □ 750,000 ■ 500.000

ITALY □ 120,000 ■ 9,000

YUGOSLAVIA □ 70,000 ■ 58,000

Black Sea

Adriatic Sea

BULGARIA □ 48,000 ■ 40,000

ALBANIA

Mediterranean Sea

GREECE □ 80,000 ■ 60,000

Figures based on Calvocoressi, Peter et al. *Total War: The Causes and Courses of the Second World War.* 2d. ed. New York, Penguin Viking, 1989.

Nazi concentration and extermination camps, and the Jewish population before and after the Holocaust.

ing out the Holocaust; second, to morally corrupt those carrying out the Final Solution; third, to demoralize the victims of the Holocaust to the extent that they would meekly accept the terrible punishment being inflicted on them.

For the Nazis, dehumanizing the Jews was an important factor in achieving the mass slaughter of Europe's Jews. While many of those carrying out the Holocaust were sadistic and brutal Nazis, others were ordinary German policemen. A few of the camp guards found the task of killing Jews psychologically devastating. By 1942, some *Einsatzgruppen* personnel could not carry on killing at the required rate. As a result, some of the Holocaust's appalling brutality sought to make the victims seem like animals rather than human beings in the eyes of their persecutors. Deliberate starvation turned the Holocaust's victims into walking skeletons. With shaven heads and identical uniforms, the thousands of camp prisoners became indistinguishable from one another. This helped ease the death camp guards' work. After the war, a reporter asked a Nazi death camp commandant, "If you were going to kill [the Jews] anyway, what was the point of the humiliation, why the cruelty?" The commandant replied, "To condi-

tion those who actually had to carry out the policies, to make it possible for them to do what they did."

The Nazis also used terror in the Holocaust to corrupt those carrying out the process. Camp authorities encouraged guards to inflict sadistic and casual violence on Jews, as this contributed to the guards' moral degeneration. At Chelmno death camp, Poland, the guards placed bottles on inmates' heads and amused themselves with target practice. At one Polish slave labor camp, the commandant fired randomly at the inmates. Particularly bestial camp officials earned deservedly monstrous nicknames. For example, Dr. Josef Mengele, who carried out heinous medical experiments on Jews, was known by the inmates as "the Angel of Death." In this way, camp guards became anesthetized to the horrors inflicted on the Jews.

Potential Jewish resistance also needed to be minimized. The first step toward this occurred even before the Jews reached the death camps. After 1940, the Nazis forcibly moved Polish Jews into ghettos in

large cities such as Warsaw and Lodz, and compelled them to subsist on starvation rations. Jewish ghetto leaders were then forced to cooperate with the Nazis under threat of far worse reprisals. Jewish administrators allowed the deportation of groups of Jews because the Nazis had threatened to deport the entire ghetto if the right number was not handed over by the ghetto leaders. As a result, the Jewish authorities were unable to resist the destruction of their own race. The threat of massive and brutal reprisals was a powerful instrument in the hands of the utterly ruthless Nazis.

JOURNEY INTO HELL

The SS police used classic terror tactics during the rounding up process. Round ups of Jews were carried out at dawn, and without warning. The deportees were often given only a couple of minutes to collect their belongings. The SS used random violence and excessive noise. All this was designed to confuse, disorient, and frighten the victims into meek acceptance of their

Jewish deportees are rounded up by Nazi police in the Warsaw Ghetto, Poland, after the 1943 uprising.

fate. Resisters were shot dead as a warning to others.

Each day, the Nazis sent deported Jews by rail to the death camps in Poland. These journeys, sometimes lasting three to four days, were a nightmarish experience. The SS forced hundreds of Jews to stand tightly packed in horrendously overcrowded cattle cars. The deportees had no food, virtually no water, and no sanitary facilities. By the time the trains reached the death camps, around one in five people had died from exhaustion, cold, hunger, and dehydration. Many had died where they stood, since there was no room for their bodies to fall to the ground. Consequently, even the physically and psychologically strongest Jews reached the camps greatly weakened. These potential resisters were now far less likely to put up a fight against the terrible treatment awaiting them. On arrival, the weakest survivors, especially the young, old, and infirm, were sent to their deaths in the gas chambers.

The Germans feared mass escapes by death camp inmates because the camps were not heavily guarded: the Germans could not spare many soldiers from the front line. To minimize the threat of escape, the Nazis deliberately kept the Jewish camp inmates weak, hungry, and terrorized. Starvation also made economic sense. The destruction of the Jews was not meant to be an economic burden on Germany. The few inmates caught trying to escape were given terrible public punishments that served as warnings to others. At Maidanek, for example, those attempting to escape were beaten to death in front of the camp's inmates.

Even the Jews sent to work at the labor camps attached to the death camps, such as Birkenau at Auschwitz, were fed only enough to keep them working, but not enough to enable them to actively resist their tormentors. Being selected for slave labor only postponed the inevitable because of the workers' pitiful food rations. The Nazis decided that 500 French Jews from a group deported to Auschwitz on March 27, 1942, were fit to labor at Birkenau. Five months later, only 21 remained – the rest had died from exhaustion or had been gassed after becoming too weak to work.

The labor camp population exploded as the German war economy struggled to produce the armaments needed to make up for the huge losses suffered by the Nazis on the Eastern front. The Nazis continued to deport thousands of relatively fit Jews to replace those who had been literally worked to death.

MINIMIZING RESISTANCE

Pockets of spontaneous Jewish resistance did occur, but were ruthlessly crushed by the Nazis. A train-load of deportees arriving at Sobibor death camp on April 30, 1943, attacked the guards with planks ripped from the sides of the wagon trucks. The SS killed the whole train-load with grenades. In January 1943, the 60,000 Jews remaining in the Warsaw Ghetto refused to be deported and took up arms. In 28 days of fighting, SS troops crushed the revolt with terrible brutality: 20,000 Jews were killed, with less than 100 German casualties. The surviving Jews were sent to the death camps. In August 1943, at Treblinka death camp, Jewish slave laborers disposing of corpses discovered that the Nazis planned to shoot them next. Some 700 Jews tried to escape. The Nazis machine-gunned to death all but 150 of them.

Given that many Jews suspected what was going on in the camps, it may to some seem surprising that large-scale, organized Jewish resistance was rare. But this lack of resistance was due to the crippling effects of the Nazis' bestial treatment and their cruel deceptions. The Nazis alleged that the deportations were resettlements to more pleasant farms in the East. In the Warsaw Ghetto in July 1942, thousands of hungry Jews accepted the German offer of bread and jam if they volunteered for deportation. For many it was to be their last meal.

The Nazis also used threats of execution or deportation to the camps against people aiding Jews. While some Poles were anti-Semitic, a few were sympathetic to the Jews' plight. To prevent these Poles from aiding the Jews, the Germans in Przemsyl, in eastern Poland, announced, on June 27, 1942, that anyone impeding "the deportation of the Jews will be shot." In Belzec camp in 1942, 1,500 Poles were gassed for aiding Jews.

THE NAZIS' LEGACY

The systematic murder of 6 million Jews has important resonances both in the Middle East and worldwide. In the late 1940s, displaced Jews felt that the Holocaust justified their use of terrorism to carve out a homeland in the Middle East, an action that has yet to be resolved peacefully with their neighbors. In worldwide terms, the Nazis' use of terror created a climate in which terrorism later flourished. They helped establish both the methods of terror used, and the principle that innocent people are legitimate victims of terror.

Stephen A. Hart

SEE ALSO:

TERROR IN THE GERMAN OCCUPATION OF THE EAST; ROMANIAN TERROR IN TRANSNISTRIA; TERROR AND THE NAZI BARBARIZATION OF WARFARE; WORLD WAR II WAR CRIMES TRIALS; TERRORISM IN PALESTINE IN 1947.

FURTHER READING

- Browning, Christopher. *Ordinary Men*. New York: Harper Perennial, 1993.
- Dawidowicz, Lucy. *The War against the Jews, 1933-1945*. New York: Holt, Rinehart and Winston, 1975.
- Hilberg, Raul. *The Destruction of the European Jews*. rev. ed. 3 Vols. New York: Holmes and Meier, 1985.
- Yahil, Leni. *The Holocaust: The Fate of European Jewry, 1932-1945*. New York: Oxford University Press, 1990.

JAPANESE TERROR IN THE FAR EAST

At the beginning of World War II in Europe in 1939, much of the Japanese army was based in China, engaged in a campaign of conquest. German victories in Europe opened up possibilities for the takeover of a number of European-held and poorly protected colonies in Southeast Asia and the Pacific. By mid-1942, much of the western Pacific, including most of what is now Indonesia, Malaysia, Singapore, the Philippines, Hong Kong, Thailand, and Burma had fallen to the Japanese. In addition, Japan had ruled Korea since 1910.

As a result, by 1942, the Japanese armed forces were in control of vast areas of the Far East and had to deal with a range of subject populations. Japanese behavior towards these subjects often involved acts of terrorism, which left millions dead. At the same time, the actions of the Japanese occupiers bequeathed a legacy of terror that was important in the nationalist and communist uprisings that convulsed much of the region after 1945.

THE SUBJUGATION OF CHINA

In 1931, the Japanese had entered into a conflict with China that had escalated into full-scale war in 1937. In spite of large areas of the country falling to the invaders, the Chinese Kuomintang government of Chiang Kai-shek refused to capitulate and eventually moved its capital far inland to Chungking. By 1941, the Japanese army was heavily committed in China (with 35 of its 51 divisions stationed there), but was unable to claim a decisive victory. Resistance, from Mao Zedong's communists, among others, led to savage Japanese reprisals. Beatings, arrests, rapes, and killings became commonplace, as the Japanese sought to punish the Chinese for their resistance.

During the initial Japanese conquests in the coastal area, there had been many examples of terror being used to weaken Chinese resistance. The most notorious of these was the 1937 Rape of Nanking. After the capture of the city, Japanese troops went on an orgy of rape, murder, pillage, and destruction in which 200,000 Chinese perished and much of the city was destroyed.

SOUTHEAST ASIA AND THE PACIFIC

The takeover of the former European colonies in 1941 and 1942 was principally seen as an opportunity to remedy Japan's chronic shortage of raw materials such as oil, rubber, and tin. But there was also a strong strain of idealism: many Japanese saw it as their destiny to purify and to cleanse Southeast Asia of alien and corrupting Western influences. They intended to liberate Asians from Western exploitation.

During the initial conquest, then, the Japanese forces enjoyed a certain amount of good will, and many Asians were happy to accept them as liberators. In many industries, and in companies selling cash crops such as rubber, the Japanese were able to offer a real increase in status to junior managers who had always been restricted in their opportunities by whites. This was particularly true in Java, but in the Philippines as well, some people worked happily with the Japanese.

However, good will collapsed under twin forces. First, many Japanese soldiers and sailors saw themselves as part of the purest race in the world. As in the case of the Nazis, with whom the Japanese had formed the Axis pact on September 27, 1940, this sense of racial superiority led many Japanese to feel

---

K E Y   F A C T S

● On some islands the problem of food shortages was temporarily "solved" by the mass execution of civilians by their Japanese occupiers.

● The Japanese killed many forced laborers who were unable to continue working because of sickness, disease, or malnutrition.

● The Japanese spared no one in their brutal reign of terror: Red Cross hospitals, orphanages, and churches were all attacked.

Hulton Getty Picture Collection

Japanese soldiers in China in 1937, prepare to execute – by beheading – two Chinese civilians.

that other racial groups were almost sub-human. This feeling justified the brutal treatment of other Asians. Second, Japanese forces given occupation duties were under great strain. They were required to extract raw materials as rapidly as possible using forced labor, but found themselves under pressure from guerrilla forces and, as the war dragged on, from Allied blockades.

The extensive raw material extraction meant that the people of the occupied territories were generally deprived of their economic base and left with few resources on which to survive. The problem was exacerbated by severe Japanese import restrictions. The people of the occupied territories soon fell victim to starvation and disease.

Racist acts of violence by the Japanese were common among the many atrocities carried out against civilians in Japanese-occupied territories. Torture, humiliation, and summary execution of suspects were day-to-day realities. In February 1942, Japanese soldiers occupying Singapore killed 5,000 ethnic Chinese residents over a two-week period. Tens of thousands of Asian women were forced to become

"comfort women," or prostitutes, for the Japanese military; and Japanese military doctors conducted grotesque medical experiments on live patients, including vivisection and mutilation. At times, some prisoners were even used as live targets for firing squads or for bayonet practice by Japanese soldiers.

TERROR IN DEFEAT

In the latter stages of the war, atrocities increased as isolated Japanese garrisons ran low on provisions. On Andaman Island, off the east coast of India, "useless" civilians were deported to nearby uninhabited islands redundant and left to starve to death. Similarly, Japanese occupation forces came close to exterminating the entire Sulak people, who inhabited a number of islands off north Borneo.

Atrocities also occurred when Japanese troops were forced to withdraw from occupied territories. Japanese troops often engaged in the massacre of civilians and implemented systematic destruction of settlements, utilities, and infrastructure. The worst of these incidents occurred on the eve of the liberation of Manila, in the Philippines, in February 1945, when Japanese soldiers murdered 91,000 Filipinos.

The mortality rates were enormous among Asian civilians in the territories occupied by the Japanese. An estimated 10 million Chinese died in the war with Japan and at least 3 million civilians died during the Japanese occupation of Java.

Russell A. Hart

SEE ALSO:

TERROR IN THE GERMAN OCCUPATION OF THE EAST; GERMAN TERROR IN FRANCE AND ITALY; TERROR AND THE NAZI BARBARIZATION OF WARFARE; JAPANESE TERRORIZATION OF PRISONERS; WORLD WAR II WAR CRIMES TRIALS; THE DEBATE OVER THE ATOM BOMB.

F U R T H E R   R E A D I N G

- Dower, John. *War without Mercy: Race and Power in the Pacific War.* New York: Pantheon, 1986.
- Piccagallo, Philip. *The Japanese on Trial: Allied War Crimes Operations in the East, 1945-1951.* Austin, TX: University of Texas Press, 1979.
- Spector, Ronald H. *Eagle against the Sun: The American War with Japan.* New York: Free Press, 1984.

JAPANESE TERRORIZATION OF PRISONERS

The Japanese armed forces of World War II were extraordinarily effective. Initially, they inflicted a series of defeats on armies that were numerically superior but unable to resist the ability and confidence of the often poorly equipped Japanese units. During the campaign in Malaya, for example, 90,000 British Commonwealth troops surrendered to just 30,000 invaders. The relative morale of the two forces is perhaps best expressed in the contrasting nicknames the troops had for their respective commanders: to his soldiers, the Japanese commander Tomoyuki Yamashita was "the Tiger." The British troops called General Arthur Percival "the Rabbit."

However, Japanese success in combat was linked to a disregard for prisoners and defeated enemies that led to widespread abuses and the use of terror against prisoners of war. There were three main reasons why the Japanese treatment of prisoners of war often plumbed the depths of human behavior, and they were mirror images of the attributes that made Japanese combat forces so formidable.

The first reason was the nature of the warrior code, *Bushido*, which governed the Japanese attitude to war. Every Japanese soldier had it instilled into him that he was a warrior whose duty it was to fight and that warriors do not surrender. The Japanese Field Service Instructions included the instruction: "Never permit yourself to be humiliated by being taken prisoner alive. Do not leave behind a name sullied by dishonor – kill yourself first." This helped create a body of fighting men who were dominant in combat, but it also meant that they had little or no respect for enemies who did surrender. There was thus little or no attempt to mitigate the harsh circumstances in which many prisoners found themselves when captured.

Second, and linked to this warrior ethos, was a very definite feeling of hostility to white prisoners. Many Japanese demonized Westerners as hostile, materialistic, selfish, decadent, and weak. Even today, some Japanese still refer to the 1868 American diplomatic contacts as "the coming of the barbarians." The chance to inflict some kind of revenge on the West for forcing Japan to open its doors to the outside world in the late 19th century helped motivate fighting men. All this led to treatment of prisoners that was not in accord with the 1929 Geneva Convention. In fact, although a signatory to this convention – which set out rules governing the treatment of prisoners of war and of conquered civilians – Japan had never actually ratified the treaty.

The third reason prisoners suffered was that the Japanese army, as a warrior force, had a logistics problem. Supply and organization off the battlefield was its great weakness. As a result, Allied prisoners of war had a poor diet, but so did their captors. The logistics problem was also the reason that the Japanese used Allied prisoners as slave labor.

THE BATAAN DEATH MARCH

The most notorious example of Japanese maltreatment of prisoners of war was the Bataan "death march." Allied resistance on the Philippines ended when about 70,000 soldiers defending the Bataan peninsula surrendered in 1942. They were ordered to undertake a 65-mile trek to detention camps, a trek that claimed the lives of nearly 10,000 prisoners,

---

KEY FACTS

● Between July 1941 and May 1942, Japanese armed forces took control of French Indochina (modern Vietnam, Laos, and Cambodia), Malaya, the Philippines, Borneo, New Guinea, Singapore, Java, and Burma.

● Reports of Japanese atrocities reached the West in early 1944 via liberated prisoners of war.

U.S. troops dig up the remains of prisoners of war who had been burnt alive by their Japanese captors.

mostly Filipinos. Weakened by combat, malnutrition, and disease, the troops were forced to march under constant threat of beatings and clubbings, and without adequate shelter, food, or medicine. Often, prisoners who fell were bayoneted or buried alive. There was little or no attempt to care for the injured, and many of the survivors believed that their captors were happy about the large number of fatalities.

This treatment of recently surrendered enemy troops was not confined to the land war. At sea, from spring 1943, Japanese submarines killed survivors of torpedoed enemy ships. On January 28, 1944, for example, the Japanese battened down the hatches on a sinking U.S. ship, condemning 1,800 men to drown.

TREATMENT IN CAMPS

Even when prisoners were in camps, their guards were not inclined to treat them with respect and were prepared to use terror tactics to cow their charges and make discipline easier. There were many recorded instances of brutal treatment of Allied prisoners, who were decapitated, bayoneted, or incarcerated in cages and exposed to the unremitting tropical sun.

Terror was used as a deterrent to escape, but the worst punishments were inflicted on those escaped prisoners whom the Japanese managed to recapture. Recaptured prisoners were beheaded, or put to the agonies of torture, such as being forced to drink gasoline and then shot in the stomach with incendiary bullets so that they exploded in flames.

However, these brutal punishments accounted for far fewer fatalities than malnutrition, disease, and exhaustion. Most prisoners of war were required to carry out tasks of arduous labor while being kept on a wretched diet. For example, the Japanese believed a railroad was critical for getting supplies to their forces in the north of Burma. Consequently, in 1942, thousands of Allied prisoners were sent to build the Burma–Siam railroad. Allied prisoners and Asian slave laborers worked 14–20 hours a day, seven days a week, with a daily ration of one cup of rice. In all, 16,000 Allies and at least 42,000 Asians died.

Such treatment meant that mortality rates among Allied prisoners in the Pacific theater – 27 percent – were much greater than in Europe, which amounted to only 4 percent. Of the 20,000 American prisoners of war taken after the fall of the Philippines in January 1942, for example, only 8,000 survived the war. But it is important to emphasize that although terror was certainly a significant element in the treatment of Allied prisoners of war, the vast majority of deaths were caused by starvation and inadequate shelter.

Russell A. Hart

SEE ALSO:

TERROR AND THE NAZI BARBARIZATION OF WARFARE; JAPANESE TERROR IN THE FAR EAST; WORLD WAR II WAR CRIMES TRIALS.

FURTHER READING

- Dower, John. *War Without Mercy: Race and Power in the Pacific War*. New York: Pantheon, 1986.
- Russell, Lord. *The Knights of Bushido: The Shocking History of Japanese War Atrocities*. New York: E. P. Dutton & Co., 1958.
- Spector, Ronald H. *Eagle Against the Sun: The American War with Japan*. New York: The Free Press, 1984.

TERROR AND THE NAZI BARBARIZATION OF WARFARE

Both the German armed forces (Wehrmacht) and the Waffen SS (fighting units of the Nazi party's paramilitary organization, the Schutz Staffel) fought on the Eastern Front between 1941 and 1945. They did not confine their use of terror to controlling the population of conquered territories and intimidating enemy forces. The Germans also employed terror tactics among their own soldiers to maintain discipline and discourage faintheartedness at the front.

Commanding officers were willing to clamp down with the utmost severity on any signs of weakness in the ranks and slackness in combat. According to recent estimates, German officers executed at least 20,000 of their own soldiers. The officers imposed such terror partly to force the soldiers to endure the exceptional harshness of the fighting conditions and partly to put Hitler's master plan into practice on the Eastern Front.

Hitler based all his expansionist plans on his ideology of racial mastery. His drive into the Soviet Union was not merely to conquer territory but also to wipe out populations. Punishing any lack of enthusiasm among the German rank and file helped goad soldiers

into suppressing the Soviet population. Then Germany could secure territories gained in battle. Terror also encouraged soldiers to follow the policy of the Nazi regime – systematically to destroy what Hitler considered the "racially inferior" Slavs and Jews, and also other political groups under German control.

The fighting ability of the German armed forces during World War II was impressive. The Germans achieved astonishing early victories, and they still proved tenacious defenders during the final phase of the war, when they were retreating on all fronts in the face of the Allies' overwhelming strength.

The discipline of the German troops was the result of many factors, not just the brutality and terror that controlled them. The soldiers had a strong sense of loyalty to their colleagues, an ideological conviction, a fear of the enemy (especially the Red Army), and a powerful belief in Hitler as the invincible leader of the Third Reich, the new German empire. This combination of hope and fear bound the army together.

CRUELTY TO SOVIET CITIZENS

The ruthless disciplinary system brutalized the troops, but did not regulate how the army treated conquered populations. Officers knowingly overlooked criminal actions against civilians in occupied countries. The Soviets had not signed the Geneva Convention, which governed the rules of warfare. So German officers rarely checked acts of cruelty against Red Army prisoners. Letting the soldiers pass on harsh treatment served the goals of the Third Reich. Its policy had always been that the German army could not fight the Soviet Union according to the conventional rules of war. Eradication was the ultimate objective. Hitler needed troops with the humanity beaten out of them if

---

KEY FACTS

● The SS killed about 700,000 Soviet civilians in the first year of the Soviet-German conflict.

● From mid-August to mid-October 1941, the Germans murdered 18,000 Soviet prisoners of war in Sachsenhausen concentration camp alone. The average was 300 deaths a day.

● An estimated 3.3 million Russian prisoners of war died at the hands of the Nazis.

Novosti

they were to implement his racial policies successfully.

It was not just professional soldiers who carried out acts of extreme cruelty against a defenseless population. Conscript soldiers were equally zealous. This willingness to commit atrocities had its roots in the skillful propaganda the Nazi regime employed to control the attitude of its fighting forces. Years of Nazi indoctrination in school motivated the Hitler Youth. Army training continued to encourage the troops to regard the Soviets as subhuman and worthy only of total eradication. And officers constantly repeated images depicting the Soviet people as agents of the devil to soldiers under their command.

The German army invaded the Soviet Union on June 22, 1941. Its commanders received orders drafted by the High Command of the Land Forces and approved by the Supreme Command of the Armed Forces and Hitler himself. It was now a soldier's duty to execute on sight all Red Army commissars – Communist party officials attached to military units. Soldiers were also to collaborate closely with the *Einsatzgruppen*, or task forces, the death squads composed of men from the SS and the *Sicherheitsdienst* (the Nazi security

Nazi forces carried out summary executions of suspected Soviet partisans as a common terror tactic.

service). This meant treating as partisans all political and racial enemies of Nazism – Jews, Communist party members, and other "inferior races." The German troops were to kill them or hand them over to the SS.

The German High Command's orders did not indicate that conquered populations were to be treated decently. Any legal protection was abandoned as far as Soviet civilians were concerned. No one punished criminal actions against civilians unless they interfered with combat discipline. The "criminal orders," as they have come to be known, had devastating and often fatal consequences for millions of Soviet citizens.

During their occupation, the Nazis laid to waste vast tracts of Soviet territory and burned thousands of villages to the ground. They murdered the inhabitants or transported them to concentration camps where the majority died. The German army commandeered food wherever it went. It so exploited the economy of the occupied territories that famine became common and epidemics rampaged. This brutality grew out of the Nazi desire to conquer *Lebensraum* (living space) in the East for ethnic Germans subsequently to colonize.

CIVILIANS RETALIATE

The slaughter of a country's civilian population after the defeat of its armed forces in battle was nothing new. But the concept of conquered civilians organizing themselves into paramilitary units to resist the occupying forces was relatively recent. The French fought in this way during the Franco-Prussian War of 1870-71, and so did some of Europe's beleaguered citizenry in World War I. The conquering German armies in both these wars had to contend with civilian partisans attacking their rear, as well as with armed forces on the battle front. It was the same when Hitler's armed forces poured into the Soviet Union in 1941.

The scale of partisan resistance roughly matched the level of brutality the German armed forces showed civilians as they pushed deep into Soviet territory. Accordingly, the scale of German reprisals rose to exceed resistance attacks, murders, and assassinations. Both soldiers and generals of the German army were now terrified. The Nazi regime's brutality and its portrayal of the enemy as subhuman had already terrorized the soldiers. But the generals were fearful of having to deal with partisans supported by the enemy population. German generals were thus determined to stamp out Soviet guerrilla warfare by using the deterrents of massive retaliation and collective punishment.

While German terror against the Soviet population led to fierce resistance, German commanders used this partisan activity to justify even harsher reprisals. The war behind the lines in the East soon became a vicious spiral of massacres. The SS suspected any civilians in authority and killed factory managers or farm foremen on the slightest pretext. If the SS suspected a village of aiding the partisans, they took hostages for questioning and torture. On January 22, 1943, near Slonim, in White Russia, east of Poland, the Germans launched a reprisal action after a partisan attack. In addition to killing 1,676 partisans, the Germans murdered 1,510 civilians as alleged sympathizers. Often entire villages and their inhabitants were destroyed in such reprisals. But the secret police and security services could not achieve such devastation alone.

Since the war, historians have found enough evidence to disprove German claims that the armed forces were confined solely to combat. The German army was deeply involved in terrorist and criminal acts against the Soviet population. Documents discovered in the former Soviet Union, along with detailed research in German archives, provide conclusive evidence. The army commanders were willing to collaborate with the SS in bringing about Hitler's Final Solution – the Nazis' murder of 6 million European Jews. But ordinary soldiers also participated directly in mass executions. They assisted the SS in placing large numbers of Jews in ghettos and concentration camps, as well as in deporting them to death camps.

The participation of regular troops in such atrocities was usually passed off as being part of legitimate actions against partisans. But these operations often involved the mass murder of civilians. Many combat units and individual soldiers also acted on their own initiative. They either passively observed or actively took part in executions. This evidence demonstrates that large numbers of soldiers were directly implicated in actions previously blamed only on the Gestapo (Nazi secret police) and the SS death squads.

To conclude, Hitler used the regular German armed forces as a deliberate instrument of terror on the Eastern Front. The army was an essential tool in the implementation of Nazi policies. German troops were terrorized by a brutal disciplinary system and images of the enemy. They, in turn, terrorized the enemy population and massacred prisoners of war.

Bertrande Roberts

SEE ALSO:

TERROR IN THE GERMAN OCCUPATION OF THE EAST; RESISTANCE IN THE EAST AND TERRORISM; THE HOLOCAUST; TERROR AND THE WAFFEN SS; WORLD WAR II WAR CRIMES TRIALS.

FURTHER READING

- Bartov, Omer. *Hitler's Army: Soldiers, Nazis, and War in the Third Reich*. New York: Oxford University Press, 1991.
- Hirschfeld, G., ed. *The Policies of Genocide: Jews and Soviet Prisoners of War in Nazi Germany*. Boston, MA: Allen & Unwin, 1986.
- Klee, E., W. Dressen, and V. Riess, eds. *"The Good Old Days": The Holocaust as Seen by Its Perpetrators and Bystanders*. New York: The Free Press, 1991.

TERROR AND THE SOVIET BARBARIZATION OF WARFARE

The 1941-45 Soviet-German war was waged with unparalleled savagery. Both sides, but particularly the Germans, massacred civilians, and shot, tortured, and starved prisoners of war. Both sides disregarded the Geneva Convention, which set humane conditions for the treatment of battle casualties, prisoners of war, and civilians in the war zone. The Soviets were not signatories to the Convention, so neither side felt obliged to apply its constraints to their treatment of enemy soldiers or civilians.

The German army in the Soviet Union pursued its own reign of terror at the front and in occupied territory. The Red Army experienced not only the brutal fighting but also the terror imposed upon it by Soviet dictator Joseph Stalin and his secret police, the NKVD. Stalin used terror on a massive scale to force Soviet soldiers and civilians to resist the Germans.

After suffering huge losses in the summer of 1941, the Red Army faced the "discipline of the revolver" on Stalin's orders. Fearing his soldiers would desert, Stalin instructed his secret police to shoot "cowards." The NKVD executed both generals and frontline soldiers for failing to halt the German advance. The secret police also branded as traitors Soviet soldiers

taken prisoner. Soldiers attempting to desert faced NKVD machine-gunners deployed as "holding units" behind them. When Soviet soldiers escaped German capture and reached Soviet lines, the NKVD secret police interrogated them as "traitors and spies," and sent most to forced labor camps, the infamous Gulag.

THE PROPAGANDA CAMPAIGN

Two particular factors stimulated the brutal behavior of the Red Army soldier, besides the influences of patriotism and fear of German conquest. The first was the suffering inflicted on Soviet soldiers by the Soviet regime's use of systematic terror. Beatings, imprisonment, and execution were common punishments for even the most minor infraction of army rules. The second stimulus came from Joseph Stalin's summons, in his broadcasts of July 3 and November 6 and 7, 1941, to wage an all-out war of extermination against the Germans. Stalin knew that Hitler's war against him aimed at annihilation, and that the Germans would pitch the bulk of their military might against him.

To meet this threat, a torrent of propaganda rained down on both Soviet soldiers and civilians. Killing Germans was declared a patriotic duty and a sacred obligation to deliver Mother Russia from the invader. Coupled with knowledge of the many atrocities committed by the Germans, this propaganda aroused the Soviet soldier's desire for revenge on the invader.

During the further German advances of mid-1942, Stalin intensified the use of terror, creating Red Army penal battalions. More than 400,000 Soviet soldiers convicted of offenses were forced to fight in these units. These punishment units undertook the most hazardous assignments, some little better than suicide missions. Few armies used penal troops on this scale.

KEY FACTS

● Soviet propaganda – through radio, movies, the press, and Party agitators – instilled hatred for the Germans with slogans like "Let us kill. If you have killed one German, kill another."

● During the battle of Stalingrad in 1942-43, 13,500 Red Army soldiers were shot for disobeying orders or allegedly displaying cowardice.

TRH Pictures

Thousands of captured German soldiers are herded through the streets during a Soviet victory parade before being sent to brutal prisoner of war camps.

In 1943, supervision of the Red Army was taken over by SMERSH. This organization's title was an acronym of the Russian phrase meaning "death to spies," and accurately described its role. Stalin no longer kept the Red Army in line by terror, as both morale and the supply of weapons had improved after the January 1943 Soviet victory at Stalingrad. But SMERSH watched the troops closely to root out "spies." SMERSH abandoned regular military procedures, executing vast numbers of "unreliables" without trial.

After 1943, the Red Army advanced westward. The Germans had moved vast columns of Soviet prisoners west in 1941, many to be killed or to die from neglect. Now the Red Army sent thousands of German prisoners east, many to die in captivity. For both sides, the Eastern Front remained a nightmarish place.

Discipline in Red Army frontline units remained strong. But units assembled from Soviet soldiers liberated from German prisoner-of-war camps, gave them a weapon, and sent them to the front. These troops left behind a trail of rape, murder, and looting, which forced Soviet officers to take drastic action to restore military discipline.

In 1945, collaborators were hanged, while "passive traitors," including forced laborers and prisoners of war, were sent to the Gulag. The barbarization of the battlefield finally engulfed both the conquerors and the conquered.

John Erickson

SEE ALSO:

TERROR IN THE GERMAN OCCUPATION OF THE EAST; RESISTANCE IN THE EAST AND TERRORISM; TERROR AND THE NAZI BARBARIZATION OF WARFARE.

FURTHER READING

- Glantz, D. M. *When Titans Clashed: How the Red Army Stopped Hitler.* Lawrence, KS: University of Kansas Press, 1995.
- Linz, S. J., ed. *The Impact of World War II on the Soviet Union.* Totowa, NJ: Rowman and Littlefield, 1990.
- Ziemke, Earl F. *Stalingrad to Berlin: the German Defeat in the East.* Washington, DC: Center of Military History, U.S. Army, 1968.

TERROR AND THE WAFFEN SS

The Waffen SS was the armed fighting branch of the general Schutz Staffel (SS) – the elite paramilitary organization of the Nazi party. The Waffen SS was deployed alongside the German armed forces (Wehrmacht) as they advanced across Europe during 1939-41. But the Waffen SS was also used both to maintain internal security within the Nazi empire and to carry out the Nazis' genocidal racial policies.

Unlike Wehrmacht troops, who were a mixture of professional soldiers and conscripts, Waffen SS troops were mostly volunteers. And while the ordinary German soldier fought for Hitler and the Fatherland, many Waffen SS men were Nazi fanatics dedicated to the aims of the Nazi party, and, in particular, the eradication of "inferior races." For many Waffen SS soldiers, their struggle was as much ideological as it was military. Consequently, their foe was the entire enemy population. The beliefs and training of SS men blurred the distinctions between combatant and civilian traditionally accepted in international law. This was crucial in the desperate conflict of annihilation to be fought out on the eastern front. Hitler had used terror to subjugate the German population and to eliminate opposition. The Waffen SS merely extended this policy into the frontline.

The Nazis' belief that the so-called Aryan people – Caucasians of non-Jewish descent – were engaged in a racial struggle for survival allowed Nazi propagandists to portray non-Aryan civilians as racial enemies. As the vanguard of an Aryan empire, the Waffen SS viewed itself as an organization above international law. Hence, the Waffen SS was quite ready to use terror as an instrument of policy to achieve its ends.

THE FIRST SS ATROCITIES

The first use of the SS as the Nazis' spearhead force, and the first recorded SS atrocity, occurred during the 1939 Polish campaign. On September 19, an SS private summarily executed 50 Jews. In a strange turn of events, in the light of later developments, the private was actually tried and convicted by a courtmartial, although he was immediately pardoned and never served a day in prison.

After the fall of Poland, forces closely associated with the Waffen SS, the Totenkopf ("Death's Head") concentration camp guard regiments and the Police Division cleansed Poland of "undesirables." These included Jews, communists, gypsies, homosexuals, and intellectuals. Thereafter, SS training units maintained the internal security of the General Government, as the Polish state was now known. In April 1943, for example, some of the 60,000 Jews of the Warsaw Ghetto took up armed resistance to avoid deportation to the Nazis' death camps. SS trainees suppressed the revolt, in which 20,000 Jews perished, while the remainder were sent to the death camps.

The first recorded Waffen SS atrocity against Western Allied troops occurred in 1940. During the German offensive in France, British troops repulsed the attacks of the newly raised SS Totenkopf Division at La Bassée Canal, near Bailleul, close to the Belgian border. This reverse was perceived as a slur on the combat reputation of this elite Nazi force. In retaliation, junior officer Lieutenant Fritz Knochlein killed 100 prisoners from Britain's Royal Norfolk Regiment at Le Paradis farm. Knochlein was neither punished nor was his career adversely affected by the massacre; he even went on to win the Knight's Cross later in the war.

KEY FACTS

● The ideological motivation of the Waffen SS led to contempt for prisoner's rights and a blurring of the distinction between civilians and combatants.

● During the May 1940 German invasion of western Europe, Waffen SS soldiers murdered 85 British prisoners in a barn at Wormhout, near Dunkirk, in northern France.

● An infamous Waffen SS atrocity in western Europe was the murder of 83 American prisoners at Malmédy, Belgium, in December 1944.

TRH Pictures/U.S. Army

The bodies of captured American soldiers shot by the Waffen SS at Malmédy in December 1944 are left to be covered by snow.

During 1940-41, the Waffen SS expanded to five divisions of 20,000 men each, including the raising of the Wiking division. This consisted of western Europeans who were expressly recruited for the Nazi "Crusade against Bolshevism" following Operation Barbarossa, Hitler's invasion of the Soviet Union, on June 22, 1941. Hitler believed that his new German empire, which he expected would last 1,000 years, needed *Lebensraum* (living space) to survive. To achieve this living space, Germany conducted a genocidal war of annihilation (*Vernichtungskrieg*) in the east to destroy communism, subjugate the allegedly racially inferior Slavic peoples, and eliminate eastern Europe's Jews. The Waffen SS was intended to spearhead this struggle, and thus the bulk of Waffen SS atrocities occurred on the Eastern Front.

The Waffen SS provided about one quarter of the personnel for the infamous *Einsatzgruppen*, or task

forces, which carried out special operations (*Sonderbehandlung*) in occupied Soviet territory. During these operations, 500,000 Soviet citizens were exterminated in 1941 alone. At the same time, three SS brigades and Order Police units, under the direct command of Reichsführer SS Heinrich Himmler, ruthlessly imposed Nazi authority over German-occupied Soviet territories. The shooting of prisoners and civilian hostages as well as the complete destruction of towns and villages became commonplace. Barely two weeks into Barbarossa, the Wiking division of the Waffen SS set the tone for subsequent behavior by murdering 600 Jews from Galicia, in southern Poland. As the struggle on the Eastern Front became more desperate and bitter, the scale of atrocities increased. During a spring 1942 German reprisal against partisan attacks, the 1st SS Division, named Leibstandarte, executed 4,000 Soviet prisoners of war.

THE WAFFEN SS ON MANY FRONTS

At the front, Waffen SS units suffered appalling casualties during the bitter fighting of 1941-42. As German prospects of immediate victory dimmed, Hitler ordered the expansion of the Waffen SS and withdrew its formations for rebuilding. In spring 1943, the three senior SS formations, Leibstandarte, Das Reich, and Totenkopf, returned to the Eastern Front grouped in a new SS Corps commanded by General Paul Hausser. The new SS Corps acted as an elite mobile force being rushed from one crisis to another. During Field Marshal Erich von Manstein's spring 1943 counteroffensive, the SS Corps recaptured the city of Kharkov in the Ukraine in an aggressive drive. But during their brief occupation of the city, SS troops murdered an estimated 20,000 Soviet prisoners and civilians.

Waffen SS formations also became locked in a vicious cycle of atrocity and reprisal with Yugoslav partisans in the Balkans. Here, the SS relied heavily on ethnic German (*Volksdeutsch*) and volunteer formations raised from Croatia, Albania, Bosnia, Hungary, and Romania to destroy the partisans. The mix of ethnic and religious hatred fueled this brutality. When Hitler's allies, the Italians, surrendered to the Allies in September 1943, Hitler sent German troops into northern Italy and also unleashed the Waffen SS on them. The SS Leibstandarte Division destroyed the town of Boves and executed most of its inhabitants as part of the general subjugation of the population. The following summer, in 1944, the new 16th SS Division, known as Reichsführer SS, killed 3,000 Italian civilians after British forces defeated the division on the Arno River.

After the Allied invasion of France on June 6, 1944, (D-Day), the Waffen SS used terror tactics as reprisals for military setbacks or resistance attacks. The 12th SS Panzer Division Hitlerjugend, consisting largely of determined 18-year-old Hitler Youth members, was deployed to spearhead the German effort to push the Allies back into the sea on June 7. When the Canadian 3rd Division managed to repulse them, the young Nazi fanatics murdered 64 Canadian prisoners. Thereafter, the two divisions fought a vicious struggle in which no quarter was given by either side.

The invasion also intensified French resistance activity. When the resistance killed one of the SS Das Reich Division's senior commanders on June 10, the division conducted a "cleansing operation," in which 642 people, virtually the entire population of Oradour-sur-Glane, in southwest France, were burned or shot to death, mostly in the village church.

One highly publicized SS combat atrocity occurred during the December 1944 German counteroffensive in the Belgian Ardennes area (the so-called Battle of the Bulge). The spearhead battlegroup of the SS division Leibstandarte, commanded by Joachim Peiper, massacred 83 American prisoners of war near Malmédy.

THE ANNIHILATION OF WARSAW

Some of the worst atrocities committed by the Waffen SS occurred during the Warsaw Uprising of August-September 1944. With most of its troops fighting the Red Army, the Germans employed two unsavory SS brigades, Dirlewanger and Kaminski, named after their infamous commanders. Dirlewanger was a discredited commander, convicted of sex crimes, who had salvaged his career thanks to his close friendship with SS recruitment chief Gottlob Berger. Berger allowed Dirlewanger to raise a penal unit from convicted poachers, political prisoners, and courtmartialled soldiers. The unit was infamous for its lack of discipline. Kaminski was a pro-Nazi White Russian who raised his own private army. When the Soviets recaptured White Russia in 1944, Kaminski retreated westward and the Waffen SS absorbed his so-called army, forming the SS Kaminski Brigade. In Warsaw, these two formations were so undisciplined and their behavior so barbaric that they appalled even hardened Nazis; the two brigades were subsequently withdrawn. Kaminski died soon after in mysterious circumstances,

but Dirlewanger received the coveted Knight's Cross medal for his pacification of Warsaw.

Hitler finally ordered Waffen SS forces to fire on their own countrymen. As the Wehrmacht was pushed back on all fronts in early 1945, SS flying courts summarily executed thousands of German soldiers and civilians for alleged negligence or cowardice.

During the series of trials of war criminals begun at Nuremberg in 1946, the International Military Tribunal indicted the Waffen SS as a criminal organization. It stood accused of the mass murder of Jews and of atrocities committed against prisoners and enemy civilians. The Allies convicted several hundred Waffen SS personnel and many were executed, including Fritz Knochlein for the Le Paradis massacre. Joachim Peiper and 42 other Leibstandarte personnel were condemned to death for the Malmédy massacre, but these sentences were commuted to prison terms. Peiper served only ten years for his crimes, while General Kurt Meyer, whose death sentence for the murder of Canadians in Normandy was also commuted, served only eight years in prison.

Nazi apologists have campaigned vigorously ever since to rehabilitate the Waffen SS. They disassociate the frontline, regular Waffen SS formations from atrocities committed by general SS security and police forces in occupied territory. They also claim that Waffen SS troops were just fighting soldiers like members of the Wehrmacht. But the Waffen SS, like the regular German army, was deeply implicated in the Nazi atrocities that occurred during the war.

Russell A. Hart

SEE ALSO:

TERROR IN THE GERMAN OCCUPATION OF THE EAST; WWII RESISTANCE IN YUGOSLAVIA AND TERRORISM; TERROR AND THE NAZI BARBARIZATION OF WARFARE; WORLD WAR II WAR CRIMES TRIALS.

F U R T H E R   R E A D I N G

- Reitlinger, G. *The SS: Alibi of a Nation, 1922-1945.* Englewood Cliffs, NJ: Prentice Hall, 1981.
- Schulte, Theo J. *The German Army and Nazi Policies in Occupied Russia.* New York: Berg, 1989.
- Stein, George H. *The Waffen SS: Hitler's Elite Guard at War, 1939-1945.* Ithaca, NY: Cornell University Press, 1966.

WORLD WAR II WAR CRIMES TRIALS

At the end of World War II, the victorious Allies were determined to punish the Axis powers for their aggression and use of terror as part of state policy. This resulted in the Nuremberg and Tokyo war crimes trials before the United Nations (U.N.) International War Crimes Tribunal. The tribunal leveled four indictments against Axis defendants: conspiracy to commit aggressive war; crimes against peace; war crimes; and crimes against humanity.

The tribunal had strong legal precedents for indictments of war crimes based on contraventions of the 1907 Hague and 1929 Geneva Conventions (which established rules for wartime treatment of prisoners, the sick, and the wounded). But few precedents existed for the indictments of unlawful aggressive war, which were the cornerstone of the proceedings. The Allied attempt to find precedent for this charge in the provisions of the 1928 Briand–Kellogg Pact, in which the signatories agreed to seek peaceful solutions to international disputes, was not compelling.

THE NUREMBERG TRIALS

The problems of securing convictions on such novel charges were most evident in the Nuremberg trials, where only a single defendant was condemned to death solely on the grounds of conspiring to conduct aggressive war; a further three defendants were acquitted. The emphasis on charges of aggressive war

KEY FACTS

● Of 22 German military and political leaders indicted at Nuremberg, 12 were hanged, 7 were jailed from 10 years to life, and 3 were acquitted.

● The tribunal rejected the commonly offered major defense that only the state, not the individual, could be found guilty of war crimes.

made the tribunal's task of prosecution more complex and ensured that the trials placed less emphasis on crimes against humanity, such as the Holocaust.

Moreover, the tribunals had to wrestle with the problems inherent in victor's justice – the fact that those who had won the war were doing the prosecuting – in particular, the difficulty of corroborating evidence. For example, the Soviet Union blamed the Nazis for the Katyn massacres of Polish soldiers that had in fact been committed by the Soviets in 1940. Another thorny legal issue was whether to prosecute as war crimes the Germans' unrestricted use of submarine warfare and area bombing of civilian population centers, methods which were subsequently adopted by the Allies themselves. Indictments for such "crimes" were noticeably absent at Nuremberg.

THE TOKYO TRIBUNAL

As at Nuremberg, the United States and Great Britain took the lead in prosecuting Japanese war criminals. In January 1946, the International Military Tribunal for the Far East indicted 28 alleged war criminals on 55 counts of crimes against humanity committed between January 1, 1928, and September 2, 1945. The trial took place in Tokyo from June 3, 1946, until November 1948.

Of those initially indicted by the Tokyo tribunal, three died during the trial and 16 were condemned to life imprisonment, largely for waging a war of aggression. Two received shorter prison sentences and seven were condemned to death by hanging for crimes against humanity. Of those sentenced to death, the most infamous were Colonel Itagaki, General Iswane Matsui, Tomoyuki Yamashita, and Hideki Tojo.

The tribunal found Itagaki, minister of war in 1938, guilty of ordering, authorizing, and permitting those in charge of prisoner of war camps and civilian labor camps to violate the laws of war by maltreating prisoners. It found General Matsui responsible for the Rape of

TRH Pictures/ US National Archives

Hideki Tojo makes his deposition against prosecutors at the war crimes trials in Tokyo, January 1948.

Nanking. His troops had massacred 200,000 Chinese civilians and raped thousands of women from December 1937 to February 1938. Tomoyuki Yamashita was found guilty of the Rape of Manila, even though he was nowhere near Manila at the time. The Allies needed a scapegoat, and it has been suggested that he was killed in revenge for his defeat of the British forces in Singapore. The tribunal found that Hideki Tojo, head of the Japanese cabinet from 1941, bore primary responsibility for waging a war of aggression. He was held criminally liable for the mistreatment of prisoners in the Bataan Death March and in the construction of the Burma–Siam railroad in 1942. Most participants claimed military necessity. This defense was undermined by the Hague Convention's judgment that the rules of war took specific account of military necessity.

The Allies had intended the tribunal to be a permanent element of the new U.N. Organization to investigate and adjudicate breaches of international law and the laws of war. But the deepening of the Cold War and the rehabilitation of West Germany and Japan as democratic states saw the lapse of the tribunal. In the

1990s, the international community resurrected the notion of a permanent U.N. International War Crimes Tribunal, in the light of atrocities in Rwanda and Bosnia. Whether there will be a permanent tribunal may depend on the success of the war crimes trials in The Hague concerning atrocities in former Yugoslavia.

Russell A. Hart

SEE ALSO:

TERROR IN THE GERMAN OCCUPATION OF THE EAST; GERMAN TERROR IN FRANCE AND ITALY; GERMAN TERROR IN NORWAY; THE HOLOCAUST; JAPANESE TERROR IN THE FAR EAST; JAPANESE TERRORIZATION OF PRISONERS; TERROR AND THE NAZI BARBARIZATION OF WARFARE; TERROR AND THE WAFFEN SS.

FURTHER READING

- Piccagallo, P. *The Japanese on Trial: Allied War Crimes Operations in the East, 1945-1951.* Austin, TX: University of Texas Press, 1979.
- Smith, B. F. *The Road to Nuremberg.* New York: Basic Books, 1981.
- Taylor, Telford. *The Anatomy of the Nuremberg Trials.* New York: Alfred A. Knopf, 1993.

THE DEBATE OVER AERIAL BOMBING

Since the beginnings of aerial warfare early in the twentieth century, military commanders have been fascinated by the possibility that air attacks could cripple an enemy's economy or terrorize its people. But these ambitions have always led to a debate over the morality of bombing civilians. Attempts were made before World War I to agree to legal restrictions on the use of air power against civilians, but these failed.

World War I saw the first major use of air power against civilian society in the form of bombing now normally described as "strategic." From 1915, German bomber aircraft and Zeppelin airships mounted a few raids on Britain. They were supposedly aiming at targets with obvious military value, such as London's armament factories, but soon found it hard to pinpoint any target smaller than the city as a whole. Nevertheless, they continued bombing, hoping to destroy the intended targets and to damage British civilian morale. The raids did create short-term panic, but the terror was too localized to have a major impact: 1,117 civilians were killed during 643 raids over Britain.

S U M M A R Y

● In World War II, the German air force initiated the development of indiscriminate attacks on civilian targets – "terror" bombing.

● For most of the war, the British RAF carried out indiscriminate "area bombing" attacks on German cities. In 1944-45, American forces similarly devastated Japan's cities. Allied leaders accepted that area bombing would cause major civilian casualties. Critics questioned the morality of the strategy.

● The most notorious events, before the atom bomb attacks, were the fire bombing of Dresden and the attacks on Tokyo early in 1945.

In 1918, the British formed an independent air force, the Royal Air Force (RAF), to defend their cities and to retaliate against Germany, but the war ended before the new RAF had launched more than a handful of raids. The French also conducted a number of raids on Germany.

By the end of World War I, military commanders had only limited experience in using bombers as instruments of terror. Civilian populations, too, had had only a small taste of being on the receiving end of such bombing, and the effects of larger and more sustained assaults could not really be predicted.

BOMBING TO TERRORIZE THE ENEMY

Between the two world wars, the RAF was a new armed service competing with the army and navy for limited defense funds. The RAF made a strong case to Britain's political leaders that it should have an independent role, separate from any land and sea battles, in their plans in any future war. The proposal was to use a strategic bombing offensive to cripple an enemy state. Concentrated attacks on the enemy economy and infrastructure would destroy such targets as factories, rail yards, and oil installations.

The enemy population was not a specific target, but it would be intimidated by the bombing and dismayed by the shortages and the disruption of essential services. Strategic bombing would thus lead to an atmosphere of crisis and collapse. In support of this policy, Lord Trenchard, the RAF's chief of staff from 1919-29, said (without substantial evidence) that the overall psychological effect of such bombing would be 20 times greater than the physical destruction caused.

Trenchard had commanded the Royal Flying Corps during World War I. Two other leaders of air services in World War I also contributed to the development of theories of air power. Brigadier Billy Mitchell had commanded the small U.S. Army air forces during

World War I. In the 1920s, as assistant chief of the Army Air Service, Mitchell strongly argued that the U.S. should establish an independent air force like the RAF. He also believed in the power of aerial bombing and staged a number of unrealistic tests in 1921-23 in which, to "prove" his point, various dilapidated warships were bombed and sunk. Mitchell resigned after quarrels with his superiors, but his ideas remained influential in U.S. aviation circles. However, America's air force (officially named the U.S. Army Air Force – USAAF – during World War II) remained weak until after America entered World War II in 1941.

The other important advocate of bombing was the Italian Giulio Douhet, commander of Italy's first military aviation unit in 1912-15. After World War I, he commanded Italy's Army Aviation Service and wrote extensively on the role and potential of air power. His influential book, *The Command of the Air* (1921), predicted how massed bomber fleets would devastate cities and terrorize populations in a future war, making bombers the decisive factor in determining an outcome.

When Hitler's Germany rearmed during the 1930s, one of the first and most important steps taken was the creation of a powerful air force, the Luftwaffe. In fact, the Luftwaffe concentrated its development of tactics and aircraft on assisting the German army on the battlefield, with strategic bombing of cities seen only as a subsidiary. Despite this, fears of whether British cities and their populations could stand up to enemy bombardment came to dominate British policy-making. Predictions made before 1938 expected up to 750,000 casualties for London during the first three weeks of an air attack. These fears were reinforced by images of German terror bombing in Spain during the Spanish Civil War (especially the bombing of Guernica in 1937), by Italian attacks on Abyssinia (modern Ethiopia) in 1935-36, and by Japanese sorties over China throughout the 1930s.

In this pre-radar era, there was a belief that "the bomber would always get through," whatever fighter defenses were in position. The British response was to build a bomber force as a deterrent against air attack.

LEGAL LIMITATION ON BOMBING

International law concerning bombing remained unchanged in the interwar period. A Hague Conference during 1922-23, considering limitations on aerial warfare, prohibited bombing "for the purpose of terrorizing the civilian population," and stated that bombing was legitimate only when directed at military installations. Legitimate targets also included factories engaged in war production and military communication systems, but these were not to be attacked if it would involve the incidental bombing of adjacent civilian areas. However, the rules were never adopted by any state, mainly because countries were reluctant to accept restrictions that would limit their own war strategies. At the outbreak of World War II, in September 1939, U.S. President Franklin D. Roosevelt appealed to Britain, France, and Germany to refrain from all but strictly military bombing. All three powers accepted the appeal, but also stated that they would ignore this obligation if their opponents reneged on it.

GERMANY BREACHES THE LIMITATION

The first bombing outside a strictly military context was undertaken by Germany on Warsaw after Hitler invaded Poland on September 1, 1939. Raids on the city were planned for the first days of the war, but were cancelled due to bad weather. They actually began on September 24, 1939, when the city was within the zone of fighting on the ground. According to the Germans, being in the battle zone made Warsaw a legitimate target, and military installations were targeted.

The first major German bombing raid of the war in the West came on May 14, 1940. Rotterdam, the major oil terminal and refinery in the Netherlands, was close to the front line and the attack was nominally aimed at military targets. However, the center of the city was destroyed and 980 civilians were killed, although contemporary reports put the death toll at up to 30,000. Germany used the terror imagery of the raid in propaganda aimed at other countries that it was about to invade, in an attempt to weaken resistance.

The British government judged the attack indiscriminate and a breach of the limitations on air attacks agreed to at the start of the war. On May 15, 1940, the RAF was therefore authorized to attack military and industrial targets throughout Germany, on the basis that its navigation and bomb-aiming were sufficiently precise to hit them without causing major civilian casualties. The limited attacks on German shipping carried out in the earlier months of the war had shown that daylight attacks cost the bombers unacceptably high casualties. Consequently, although the RAF's Bomber Command was now free to implement its pre-war strategy of mass attacks on Germany, for now such attacks would have to be carried out by night.

"THE BLITZ" TERRORIZES BRITAIN

Bombing on a large scale was first carried out by Germany against Britain. During the summer of 1940, the Luftwaffe attacked Britain's air defense network as the first stage of Hitler's invasion plan, Operation Sea Lion. On August 24, German aircraft bombed London, triggering in retaliation a British raid on specific targets in Berlin the following night. From this point, Germany persisted in attacks on British cities with the urban population sanctioned as a target. As the German raids were increasingly flown at night to avoid British fighters, they became entirely indiscriminate. The resultant terror bombing campaign was commonly known as "the Blitz" (from *Blitzkrieg* – "lightning war") and lasted until May 1941. During this period of area bombing, the British government estimated that 3,000 civilians were killed a week and 350,000 houses were destroyed. Much of this damage was inflicted during the last two weeks of November 1940, including the notorious bombing of Coventry on the night of November 14, followed by raids on Birmingham, Glasgow, Sheffield, Liverpool, and Southampton. On some nights, more than 400 bombers were sent over to drop hundreds of tons of bombs and incendiaries on British cities, particularly on the ports.

Despite this escalation of hostilities into "total war," this was a much lower level of destruction than had been projected, and it was soon apparent that the civilian population was far more resilient in living with bombing than had been expected. Once people had survived the initial shock, and a system of air raid precautions was functioning smoothly, it was possible to continue with daily life despite severe disruptions.

AREA BOMBING: THE BRITISH RESPONSE

This German campaign can be contrasted with the British Bomber Command's operations during the same period. British aircraft were given very specific industrial targets, but they were forbidden to bomb general urban areas, unlike their German counterparts. Significant results were claimed, but in August 1941, an official investigation, the Butt Report, came up with very different conclusions. Photographs taken from the bombers showed that, on moonlit nights, only a third of bombs fell within five miles of the target. On moonless nights results were far worse. German production remained virtually unaffected.

However, as an invasion of German-occupied Europe remained only a distant possibility, bombing

Britain's Air Chief Marshal Arthur "Bomber" Harris studies a map of possible targets in Germany.

appeared to be the single means of attacking Germany. Bombing attacks were also politically necessary to demonstrate to the Soviet Union (attacked by Germany in June 1941) that Britain was still very much in the war. Britain had, therefore, committed much of her war effort, up to one-third according to some estimates, to the production of heavy bombers.

A new bombing policy accordingly came into effect from February 14, 1942. This stated that attacks "should now be focused on the morale of the enemy civil population and, in particular, of the industrial workers." The new targets were to be residential areas, since they were larger and easier to hit and more flammable than factory sites. Stress was placed on "dehousing" the workers and depressing and terrorizing them to the point where it affected German war production. Killing civilians was supposedly not a deliberate aim of this policy, but it was accepted as an unavoidable consequence. Whether such attacks were morally justified was not an issue for the British

Hulton Getty Picture Collection

The ruins of Hamburg after the Allied bombing raid of July 27-28, 1943; 40,000 Germans died, either as a result of the bombs or from the ensuing firestorm.

leaders; the only concern was for the campaign's effectiveness. German propaganda, however, described the raids as "terror attacks" and cited these as examples of their enemies' "barbarism."

This "area bombing" strategy was vigorously put into effect by Air Chief Marshal Arthur "Bomber" Harris, who led the RAF Bomber Command from late February 1942 until the end of the war. One of the most devastating raids was on Hamburg on the night of July 27–28, 1943. Bombs dropped by 787 aircraft combined with the hot, dry conditions to create a single huge fire which sucked in surrounding oxygen, suffocating large numbers of people. More than 40,000 died, 900,000 lost their homes, and Hamburg lost two months of war production. However, the constantly improving German defenses meant Bomber Command always sustained heavy losses. By the winter of 1943-44, radar developments and other innovations had made bombers as vulnerable by night as by day. For

example, on the night of March 30-31, 1944, 95 British bombers were lost during a raid on Nuremberg, while only 69 Germans were killed.

AMERICAN OPERATIONS

By the time the United States joined the war on December 7, 1941, after the Japanese attacked Pearl Harbor, a massive aircraft building program had begun to create a powerful air force. The leaders of the USAAF believed in daylight precision bombing of military and industrial targets, with the bombers protecting themselves from enemy fighters by their own defensive machine guns. It took some time to build up this force and it was not until the summer of 1943 that the USAAF was able to operate in strength.

The first important tests of its bombing strategy were attacks made on factories at Schweinfurt in central Germany, which made most of Germany's ball-bearings. In theory these were crucial to the German war effort since ball-bearings formed part of every important machine. Although the bombers inflicted significant damage on the factories, the attacks failed because of the horrendous losses that the bomber forces sustained.

Hulton Getty Picture Collection

The ruins of Dresden after the Allies' controversial attack of February 13-14, 1945.

The USAAF found an effective answer to these losses in the P-51D Mustang fighter. It could escort bombers all the way to Germany from bases in eastern England. Through the spring of 1944, these aircraft destroyed the Luftwaffe's fighters, and by the summer, Allied bombers could operate freely during daylight.

Throughout this period and until the end of the war, the USAAF maintained its policy of precision attacks on targets with clear military value. The reality, however, was that weather conditions and the short-comings of the available equipment meant that many raids were no more accurately targeted than those of the RAF and were "area attacks" in all but name.

Both the British and American bomber forces reduced their attacks on targets in Germany during the summer of 1944 to support the Allied invasion of

France, which began on June 6, 1944. Their main targets were roads and railroads, which they attacked as precisely as possible in an effort to avoid French civilian casualties.

THE FINAL STAGES

Germany's Luftwaffe was unable to mount any impor-tant strategic bombing raids after 1941, but German scientists did develop two new terror weapons that were used to attack civilian targets. These were the jet-engined V1 cruise missile and the rocket-powered V2 ballistic missile. Neither type was accurate enough to hit any military target; for the Germans they were seen as retaliation for the equally indiscriminate Allied air attacks. Over 9,000 V1s were launched against Britain from France and Belgium. Roughly 5,000 reached their targets (the V1 flew slowly enough to be intercepted by Allied fighter aircraft or anti-aircraft fire). The super-sonic V2 could not be intercepted. Over 1,000 were fired at targets in Britain, and others at Allied forces in

France and Belgium after these countries had been liberated in 1944.

From September 1944, both the Allied bomber forces resumed major attacks on Germany. Air Marshal Harris maintained his policy of area bombing, while the American leaders, and some senior British officers, argued for attacks to be focused on specific sectors of the German war effort. The Americans accordingly concentrated on precision attacks on Germany's oil industry to dramatic effect.

By the winter of 1944-45, some politicians and religious leaders were beginning to question the morality of continuing with the all-out bombing of Germany. These doubts came to a head with a series of raids carried out by both British and American bombers against Dresden on February 13-15, 1945. At least 30,000 civilian deaths resulted, although figures of more than 100,000 have been claimed. Dresden was said to have had little military value and was certainly crowded with helpless refugees fleeing the advance of the Soviet forces from the east. By this stage, the German war effort was in shambles and doubts about the bombing campaign became secondary as Germany itself was overrun by Allied armies.

STRATEGIC BOMBING AGAINST JAPAN

In the Pacific war, Allied strategic bombing was conducted solely by American forces. They attacked Japan from bases in China and later from the Marianas Islands in the Pacific Ocean south of Japan. They captured the Marianas bases from the Japanese in the summer of 1944, but for months the air attacks on Japan were ineffective.

From March 1945, American forces carried out low-level area bombing raids over Japanese cities. Since many buildings were built of flammable materials, the effect was devastating. In a raid on Tokyo on March 9-10, 1945, at least 87,000 Japanese were killed, more than the death toll after the atomic bomb was dropped on Hiroshima in August 1945. By the end of the war, 66 Japanese cities were more than 40 percent destroyed.

As in Europe, the tactics used were those judged to cause the most damage to the enemy war effort, without regard to the civilian casualties they might involve.

THE EFFECTS OF BOMBING

Strategic bombing in World War II evolved from an initial policy of bombing only military targets in a vicious spiral toward indiscriminate and terror bombing. When they held the upper hand in the early war years, the Axis powers made little effort to avoid civilian casualties and hoped for a terror effect. Having originally attempted more discriminate bombing, the Allies eventually followed a similar policy.

Terror became an aspect of both British and American bombing policy, though rarely the dominant one. The overriding objective was to wreck enemy war efforts. This was achieved to a lesser extent against Germany and to a greater extent against Japan. Both bombing campaigns contributed significantly to the defeat of these states. The bombing policies followed were authorized by British Prime Minister Winston Churchill and U.S. President Franklin D. Roosevelt, the popular leaders of the world's two largest democracies, during the crisis of a total war. The massive scale on which the assault was mounted led to at least a million civilian deaths. This in turn meant the moral basis of the campaign became increasingly dubious until final victory was assured, although not as far as ordinary people were concerned.

By the end of the war, the Allied leaders were well aware of concern about morality. At the post-war war crimes trials of Axis leaders, the Allies did not charge anyone with organizing indiscriminate air attacks, to stop them from citing Allied actions in their defense. Second thoughts about the bombing campaign also had other effects. Of all the campaign medals awarded to British forces for outstanding duty, no medal was ever struck for Bomber Command's veterans.

Stephen Prince

SEE ALSO:

THE DEBATE OVER THE ATOM BOMB; TERROR IN THE KOREAN WAR; TERROR IN THE VIETNAM WAR; COUNTERTERROR IN THE BRITISH EMPIRE BEFORE 1945.

FURTHER READING

- Boog, Horst, ed. *The Conduct of the Air War in the Second World War*. New York: Berg, 1992.
- Howard, Michael, George J. Andreopoulos, and Mark R. Shulman. *The Laws of War*. New Haven, CT: Yale University Press, 1994.
- McIsaac, D., ed. *The United States Strategic Bombing Survey*. New York: Garland, 1976.
- Schaffer, Ronald. *Wings of Judgment*. New York: Oxford University Press, 1985.

THE DEBATE OVER THE ATOM BOMB

On August 6, 1945, the world discovered the terrors of the atomic age. Acting on the orders of U.S. President Harry S. Truman, the United States Army Air Force (USAAF) dropped an atomic bomb on the Japanese city of Hiroshima. This uranium fission weapon – nicknamed "Little Boy" – inflicted instant devastation on the city, causing 70-80,000 deaths. On August 9, a second atomic weapon (a plutonium fission device, nicknamed "Fat Man") was detonated over Nagasaki, a shipbuilding center on the island of Kyushu. Although less effective than the first weapon in terms of material and personal damage, some 35-40,000 people were killed. Six days later, Japanese Emperor Hirohito announced that his government had accepted the Potsdam Declaration, an ultimatum issued by the Allied powers on July 26, 1945, which called for Japan's unconditional surrender. Japan's war in Asia and the Pacific had ended.

THE JAPANESE WARRIOR CODE

The Pacific War had illustrated to the Allied powers the tenacity of the Japanese fighting soldier. From the earliest combat engagements in the war, it had been made readily apparent that the "warrior-code" ethic ingrained within the Japanese military prohibited any consideration of surrender. By the middle of 1945, Japanese resistance still remained firm in the face of

---

KEY FACTS

● In early August 1945, America dropped two atomic bombs on the Japanese cities of Hiroshima and Nagasaki.

● The prospect of continued fanatical resistance to an Allied invasion of the Japanese mainland persuaded the Americans to use the ultimate terror weapon, the atom bomb, to compel Japan to accept unconditional surrender.

● These two bombs clearly demonstrated the awesome destructive power of the atom bomb.

---

the overwhelming offensive power of the Allies, particularly the forces of the United States. American aerial bombers based on the tiny islands of Saipan and Tinian in the Pacific Ocean had already inflicted devastating saturation attacks against economic, military, and civilian targets in an attempt to induce Japan to surrender. Many of Japan's leading cities were in ruins. A single raid on Tokyo during the night of March 9-10, 1945, burned out 40 percent of the Japanese capital and killed an estimated 87,000 civilians.

NO SURRENDER

In addition to these highly destructive raids against urban areas, Japanese merchant shipping had been reduced to a mere 12 percent of its pre-war strength by continuous U.S. air and naval attacks. For a country dependent on sea communications, the American blockade effectively strangled the Japanese economy. By 1945, Japan's munitions output had fallen to less than half its wartime peak. The Japanese population also suffered through lack of food. The daily rations fell below 1,500 calories per person, about half of today's recommended daily intake for an adult male.

On the surface, Japan appeared to be on the verge of collapse. Yet Japanese policy continued to be one of resistance. As late as April 1945, the Japanese defense of Okinawa island, situated south of Japan's "Home Islands," produced some of the bloodiest fighting of the war, resulting in considerable U.S. casualties.

Despite the destruction being inflicted upon the Home Islands, the Japanese policy of "no surrender" continued because of the complex nature of Japan's political system. The political world was dominated by a military high command that would not permit surrender, even when faced with certain annihilation.

As long as Japan had soldiers to fight and inflict injury on the enemy, the Japanese armed forces did not consider themselves defeated. Furthermore, the military exerted a substantial influence over the Japanese emperor. He, in turn, commanded the loyal

TRH Pictures

The charred remains of a young boy, about half a mile from the center of the atomic explosion at Nagasaki, Japan, on August 9, 1945.

support of his subjects, who regarded the emperor as a divine being.

For the Allies, unable to bomb the Japanese into submission, the alternative seemed to be to mount a seaborne invasion of the Japanese mainland. Given that the Japanese forces would probably fight to the last person, such an operation promised to be bloody. Allied staffs estimated that a million Allied servicemen would die in such an invasion plus a far greater number of Japanese military personnel and civilians.

Unknown to most Allied planners, however, there was another possibility. Since late 1941, at a vast cost of $2 billion, an international group of scientists led by U.S. nuclear physicist J. Robert Oppenheimer had worked toward creating an atomic explosion. The destructive power and force of an atomic weapon would be unparalleled in the history of warfare. The prototype atomic bomb, a plutonium weapon, produced the effects of an explosion of 20,000 tons of

TNT when successfully detonated on July 16, 1945. A terrible weapon was waiting in the wings if the leaders of the Allied powers had the courage to use it. But there had to be overwhelming reasons to visit such devastation on what would be a mainly civilian target.

STRATEGIC AIR POWER DOCTRINE

Bombing Japanese civilians to frighten them into submission was not a new strategy, but it was not a successful one either. For General Curtis LeMay, commander of XXI Bomber Command, America's bomber force in the Pacific, the previous application of terror bombing against highly populated areas, in combination with attacks against Japanese war production, had not provided the anticipated psychological dislocation of Japanese morale. General LeMay could not understand how a civilian population could take such punishment and not surrender. He was a disciple of the Italian Giulio Douhet, who claimed that populations would eventually rise up in the face of repeated aerial attacks and force their governments to demand peace. Using the atom bomb did not conflict with such ideas but instead represented a further stage in their development.

THE DECISION TO DROP THE BOMB

Various agencies within the Japanese government were putting out tentative diplomatic feelers, which implied a willingness to surrender. But these feelers were not on a scale that the Allies believed should be taken seriously. Equally quickly disregarded were suggestions made by some of the atom-bomb scientists that a demonstration atomic explosion should be arranged to show the Japanese what awaited them if they continued to fight rather than surrender.

Instead, President Truman and his advisers, with the agreement of the British who had contributed their own atomic research to the bomb project, decided that it was essential to drop the bomb in order to achieve the final defeat of Japan with the fewest possible casualties. American strategists hoped to convince the Japanese that the United States now held the power to bring about the total destruction of the Japanese nation. Faced with this possibility, the Japanese government would surely surrender unconditionally, as the Potsdam Declaration demanded.

"A BOILING BLACK MASS"

The first atom bombs were accordingly dropped on Hiroshima on August 6 and over Nagasaki on August 9, 1945. Colonel Paul Tibbets, commander of the B-29 bomber "Enola Gay," which dropped the Hiroshima bomb, starkly recalled the visual effect of the first atomic bomb: "I couldn't see any city down there, but what I saw was a tremendous area covered by – the only way I could describe it is – a boiling black mass." For the Japanese civilians on the ground, Hiroshima brought terror that could not have been surpassed if "the sun had crashed and exploded." The scene was one of utter devastation: "Yellow fireballs were splashing down...people's clothes had been blown off and their bodies burned by the heat rays." One solitary bomber had successfully reduced an entire Japanese city to rubble. The terror impact on the surviving civilian population was enormous.

DID THE ATOM BOMB WIN THE WAR?

At the same time, on August 8, 1945, the Soviet Union declared war on Japan and the next day the Red Army attacked Japanese forces in the occupied Chinese province of Manchuria (now Dongbei). The Japanese army in Manchuria collapsed almost immediately under the Soviet attack, illustrating to Japan's military leaders the hopelessness of their position.

The initial reactions by Japanese military leaders to the first atomic bomb were indifferent, even dismissive – probably because they failed to appreciate the full horror of what had happened since it was so far beyond their experience. However, after the dropping of the second bomb, and the Soviet entry into the conflict, only a small minority within the Japanese hierarchy was prepared to fight on, but they were overruled by the emperor. It is not clear whether the atom bombs or the Soviet attacks were the decisive factors in finally causing Japan's surrender.

The dropping of atomic bombs on Hiroshima and Nagasaki was a necessary evil as far as the Allies were concerned. The terror it produced and the slaughter it inflicted on the Japanese civilian population were offset by the Allied lives saved. Along with concern about casualties from the fighting, the Allied leaders and populations were already angered by the ample evidence of barbaric Japanese treatment of prisoners of war, many of whom were still in Japanese hands, and they feared what would happen to them if the war were prolonged.

With two opposing sides, one committed to a policy of no surrender and the other to total victory, enormous destruction was inevitable. The atomic bomb's capacity for utter devastation made it the ultimate weapon in a conflict that had entered the rarely explored realms of "total war." This blurring between civilian and military targets, which had been a dominant feature of the aerial war, not only over Japan but also over Europe, would now become an even greater feature in future military thinking.

Christopher J. Baxter
Andrew Douglas Stewart

SEE ALSO:

JAPANESE TERROR IN THE FAR EAST; JAPANESE TERRORIZATION OF PRISONERS; WORLD WAR II WAR CRIMES TRIALS; THE DEBATE OVER AERIAL BOMBING; NUCLEAR TERRORISM.

FURTHER READING

- Costello, John. *The Pacific War*. New York: Quill,1982.
- Feis, H. *The Atomic Bomb and the End of World War II*. Princeton, NJ: Princeton University Press, 1966.
- Spector, Ronald. *Eagle against the Sun: The American War with Japan*. New York: The Free Press, 1984.

THE BACKGROUND TO MODERN TERRORIST CAMPAIGNS

Popperfoto

George Grivas returns to Athens on March 19, 1959, after leading the EOKA campaign in Cyprus.

THE BACKGROUND TO MODERN TERRORIST CAMPAIGNS:
Introduction

The terrible experiences of World War II set the scene for modern terrorism in two major ways. First, during this bitterly-fought conflict the notion emerged that civilians could be legitimate targets of violence and terror. Second, the war also set the scene in the way that it opened up much of Asia for nationalist and often communist, revolution. The example of revolution in Asia, particularly the example of China, then became very important for the rest of the world, as the old colonial empires of the Europeans crumbled and what became known as the developing world came into being.

In the 1950s and 1960s, there were many nationalist struggles to rid countries of their despised European regimes. The French, for example, faced bloody anti-colonial conflict in Algeria and Indochina, while the British faced the Mau Mau revolt in Kenya and communist insurrection in Malaya. Other European nations also faced such revolts: the Dutch fought a war in what is now Indonesia, for example.

These wars of national liberation threw up a variety of theories and justifications for the use of what we would describe as terror tactics within the context of a more general armed struggle. Terrorism, therefore, was usually one method used in a wider insurgency movement. Some of the theories justifying terror tactics came from the nineteenth century, and were part of the more general revolutionary theories, often connected to Marxism. Such theories did influence to some degree the behavior and strategies used by insurgent movements during the struggles of decolonization.

As these anti-colonial campaigns progressed, however, contemporary theorists added to the mixture, showing how the use of violence could be justified and how it could be used most effectively. Some of the leaders of these anti-colonial struggles produced theories based on their experiences. Now, therefore, practice was feeding back into the theory of terrorism. This two-way dynamic between terrorist theory and its practice would remain a prominent feature of the modern phenomenon of terrorism.

The struggles of decolonization also influenced later terrorism in the sense that they provided the ground for ideas, strategies, tactics, and weapons to be tested. The terrorist campaigns that sprung up in the 1960s and 1970s, many of which are still claiming lives today, learned a great deal from these earlier anticolonial struggles. In many ways these later terrorist campaigns were both more sophisticated and more deadly due to the knowledge and expertise on terror tactics inherited from the era of decolonization. ■

Theories of Insurgency and Terrorism

When a bomb explodes and hundreds die, people start asking why some groups turn to terrorism and how it has become so widespread that it affects everyone's lives. Behind most terrorist groups there is a political influence and often a figure of inspiration, whether a thinker such as Karl Marx or a man of action like Che Guevara. Some terrorists want sweeping change on the scale of the French Revolution, while others such as the colonists in the American Revolution wage wars against a colonial power. Sometimes the government terrorizes its own people, as in many South American countries.

THEORIES OF INSURGENCY AND TERRORISM:
Introduction

The first modern political theorist was the Italian Niccolò Machiavelli. In his book *The Prince*, he wrote: "Since some men love as they please but fear when the prince pleases, a wise prince should rely on that which he controls, not on what he cannot control." The twentieth century has seen the systematic use of secret police to control societies by instilling fear in their citizens, as the Shah did in Iran. Governments have also used methods in their relations with foreign states that they would find unacceptable or unconstitutional at home. Bulgaria's secret service assisted a Turkish right-winger in his attempt to assassinate Pope John Paul II in 1981. State terrorism is used by governments to achieve their own national objectives – for instance, Iraq's savage treatment of its Kurdish minority.

Terrorism can be defined as the selective or indiscriminate use of violence in order to bring about political change by inducing fear. Terrorism is one of the methods frequently used by the would-be revolutionary. This form is called agitational terror. A form called enforcement terror is adopted by governments prepared to use any means to protect themselves from their political opponents. These two examples show that terrorism can be described and even classified.

The term *terror* was first used to indicate a general state of fear deliberately created for political purposes during the French Revolution (1789-94). It particularly referred to the Reign of Terror of 1793-94. Governments like to apply the term to any violent methods used by a political opposition. In all societies, there is a close relationship between government and opposition. The nature of government helps determine the nature of opposition. Where there are no elections, and freedom of speech is limited, opposition groups sometimes resort to violence. However, violence is also used by minorities who feel excluded by society.

Terrorism is not an option chosen by large groups, but rather a strategy adopted by small groups, meeting secretly to organize violent acts. An *insurgency* occurs when an opposition movement combines violence with a political strategy to defeat and replace a government. Terrorism is, however, inextricably linked with insurgencies. There are at least six different goals of insurgent movements: reform, secession, revolution, restoration, reaction, or maintenance of the status quo. Most terrorists are rebels and an understanding of why they use terror requires knowledge of insurgent strategies.

Insurgent strategy can range from political assassination to all-out revolutionary civil war. Terrorism may be used as part of any of these strategies. Being a tool of small groups, terrorism presents governments with a dilemma. It may be possible to defeat a terrorist group if the government is prepared to accept the cost in money and lives, but it usually proves very difficult to eliminate the movement altogether. Terrorist goals can often only be satisfied by a range of concessions the government had previously refused to make.

Three categories of terrorism can be identified: revolutionary, sub-revolutionary, and repressive terrorism. The second and third categories relate to the opposition and government respectively. The first is more complex and embraces both sides. It is difficult to draw a boundary between these categories – the same conflict may have features of more than one category.

Several writers have constructed theories of insurgency involving one or more of these forms of action. Many of these theories are part of a fascist or communist strategy for comprehensive social change using violence. Some theories are part of a program of less far-reaching changes, such as a war of national liberation. Others are from the viewpoint of the government forces whose duty it is to put a stop to insurgency.

Since World War II, a body of writing has developed on the subject, examining insurgency from the "legitimate" government's point of view. The term *low-intensity conflict* has been applied to terrorism, but it is more generally described as counterinsurgency. However, it is often very difficult to make hard and fast distinctions between an insurgency that includes terrorism and one that does not. ■

THEORIES OF TERROR IN URBAN INSURRECTIONS

Revolutionary terrorism has been defined as the use of "systematic tactics of terrorist violence with the objective of bringing about political revolution." This form of terrorism has four major characteristics. First, it is carried out by groups, rather than individuals, which have clearly defined leaderships. Second, it is driven by a clear ideology and intends to create new institutional structures. Third, the movement has a definite strategy involving the planned use of violence against victims who have been selected for their symbolic value for a wider audience. Fourth, the purpose of this violence is to change permanently people's attitudes and behavior.

REVOLUTION

The modern notion of revolution originated at the end of the eighteenth century. Thirteen of the British colonies of North America successfully waged a war of national liberation against the government in London. The independence of the United States was finally secured by the Treaty of Paris in 1783. The French Revolution, which began in 1789, dominated radical political thinking for over 100 years. Both revolutions challenged the notion of a divinely appointed monarch as the head of a hierarchical society. But where the Americans simply transferred political authority from London, ultimately, to Washington, DC, the French tried to transform the social order completely.

A new revolutionary era began in which constitutional republics became the goals for radical political movements. It also set the stage for the nineteenth century as an age of nationalism. Combining the political state and the people's nation into a single entity soon became the ideal of the Serbs, the Greeks, the Poles, the Hungarians, and the Irish, among others.

Revolution was seen by many as the best way to achieve this objective. However, the differences between the American and French revolutions took on great significance. America's revolution had been carefully controlled by its leaders. The French experience involved mass urban insurrections in Paris, such as the storming of the Bastille fortress on July 14, 1789, and the Tuileries palace on August 17, 1792.

For radical revolutionaries of the nineteenth century, the aim was mass urban insurrection. All modern insurgent movements seeking a revolutionary change have been influenced by the popular idea of urban insurrection.

URBAN INSURRECTIONS

Theorists working since the French Revolution have identified three distinct elements of urban insurrections. First, there is a state of dual power as the government changes. At this stage, the opposition has gained sufficient strength to make a bid for power but the government has not yet been forced to give it up. Second, the government is already shaken by economic crisis and industrial strikes make its position impossible. Third, the opposition is temporarily united behind a leadership that has widespread popular support.

KEY FACTS

● The first use of terror as a deliberate political tool occurred during the French Revolution.

● Ideas of revolution developed in different ways during the nineteenth century by radical political theorists like Karl Marx and Mikhail Bakunin.

● Radical theorists differed in the degree to which they planned to use violence to cause and consolidate a revolution.

● Terrorist methods are sometimes used by established governments against their opponents at home or abroad.

Karl Marx believed that governments would use violence to prevent the workers from organizing a socialist economy. He felt therefore that terror was a necessary part of a revolutionary strategy.

Hulton Getty Picture Collection

Terror is a standard tactic in urban insurrection. The assassination of political opponents may mark the start of an insurrection and bombings may be an integral part of its strategy. Further, the government may use terror in an attempt to suppress insurrection. Most of the great social revolutions have been characterized by the use of terror in their later stages. At this point, terror can enforce the authority of the new government to carry through its program of reform. Occasionally, as in Iran after 1979, terror has been used to establish a more traditional regime.

MARX, ENGELS, TROTSKY, AND LENIN

The first important theorist of mass insurrection was Karl Marx. The objective of Marx and his associate Friedrich Engels was to create a mass movement capable of directing revolution to social ends. Other important contributors to the Marxist theory of insurrection have been Vladimir Lenin and Leon Trotsky.

INSURRECTION BRINGS CHANGE

Early examples of insurrection seem to suggest that enthusiasm is the main ingredient necessary for their success. In 1830, an operatic performance in Brussels triggered a mass insurrection for Belgian independence. In 1848, the revolt that overthrew King Louis-Philippe in France apparently also broke out spontaneously. In the same year, some 50 insurrections in the Italian states brought about varying degrees of constitutional government and the proclamation of a Roman Republic.

Such dramatic events caused great excitement throughout Europe. They also gave rise to some well-justified fears among those in power. Government ministers remembered the savagery of the French Revolution, even if now they confronted insurrectionists who avoided widespread terrorism.

NEW SOCIAL ORDERS FROM TERROR

The Terror is the name given to the period in 1793-94 during the French Revolution when the most extreme faction among the revolutionaries, the Jacobins, were in power. The Jacobins deliberately used state power in an attempt to create a new social order. The Terror was used in particular to reduce the authority of local government in France. The revolutionary zealots sent from Paris to purge provincial society of aristocrats also created a more centralized state. Terror was seen as a method of eliminating the regime's opponents. The Jacobins tried to intimidate political neutrals and potential opponents through terror so that they would wholeheartedly support the new government.

The Terror's most spectacular feature was the execution of aristocrats. The nobles were not indicted for any crimes, not even conspiracy against the state (although that was alleged in some cases). Instead, they were charged simply because they had been born into the aristocracy. Those executed, and the many more who fled abroad, were merely incidental victims of a process that was really aimed at other revolutionaries. Opposition to aristocracy, and zeal in rooting it out, became the test of loyalty to a regime based on shaky popular support.

The Terror of the French Revolution, however, came at the end and not at the beginning of a great social revolution. Scholars have described a combination of factors causing the development of terror out of traditional violence like rioting. Such factors include civilian militarism – the desire of some civilians for a government with military overtones; the tendency of extremist governments to value loyalty over competence in their personnel; an acute economic crisis complicated by antagonism between rich and poor; and religious hysteria.

Overturning the old order in the 1917 Russian Revolution, as in the French Revolution and in a number of other great revolutions, was actually a slow process. The immediate aftermath of the urban uprising in each case was a period of provisional government marked by martial law, revolutionary tribunals, and the establishment of a secret police. In each case, the new government was supposed to be more representative than its predecessor.

But each provisional regime turned to terror when its leaders became aware that the old social order was stronger than they thought. Above all, these regimes resorted to terror when they found themselves faced with a combination of internal opposition and external attack or foreign threat. In the case of the Russian Revolution, terror began after the attempted assassination of Lenin in August 1918. In the case of the French Revolution, this change can be dated to the assassination of Jean Paul Marat, one of the radical leaders, in July 1793.

Historians writing 100 years after the French Revolution identified a sequence of events that indicated the point at which terror was likely to occur in a revolution. First, the new regime concentrates on taking control of public administration. Second, the new rulers attack their political enemies. Initially, they target individual opponents, then they conduct a wholesale purge to terrorize potential opponents. Persecution is then relaxed, perhaps accompanied by the execution of the terror's most extreme leaders. Finally, the new regime adopts a form of government strongly resembling that of the old order.

COMMUNISM AND TERRORISM

Karl Marx and Friedrich Engels, writing 70 years after the French Revolution, were utterly convinced that large-scale social transformation could only be achieved by revolution. However, generally they ridiculed those who believed in terror as a means to start one. In Western Europe, Marx thought, revolution would be the product of the gradual development of

Louis Auguste Blanqui, the nineteenth-century French revolutionary agitator and theorist, believed that a successful revolutionary insurrection would occur spontaneously.

class awareness among the urban working class (the proletariat). In other parts of the world, particularly in Russia, Marx was more tolerant of those who used terror against tyranny. In praising the assassins of Czar Alexander II in 1881 for their heroism, Marx stated that their action was historically inevitable in the backward political society in which they lived.

Marx therefore rejected the notion of spontaneity, associated with Louis Auguste Blanqui, the French revolutionary theorist and agitator. Blanqui had been involved with many revolutionary movements in France during the nineteenth century. His study and experience of the 1848 insurrection in Paris helped him form the idea that revolutionary uprisings could occur spontaneously in the right political conditions.

Mikhail Bakunin, Russian anarchist and opponent of Marx, regarded individual terrorist acts as a crucial element in a revolutionary strategy.

Marx argued instead for revolution as the end-product of patient organization by workers' movements.

PARIS UPRISING OF 1871

An example of an unprising in Marx's own time were the events in France following its defeat in the war with Prussia in 1871. In Paris, working-class radicals won an election to the city government after the old regime had fallen but before a new one was properly organized. Members of this Paris government rejected the authority of a more conservative regime based in Versailles. They began to organize the city themselves. The conservatives could hardly tolerate the independence of the national capital. The army at Versailles shot some radicals, the radicals in Paris arrested some conservatives, and a civil war broke out. Although the Versailles army savagely repressed the Paris Commune, Marx hailed it as evidence that a mass political movement could achieve a revolution.

In his writings, Marx focused on the way in which government acts encouraged demand for change. State repression after the defeat of any attempt at radical reform was a step towards a revolutionary situation. In France, nine years after the Paris Commune's fall, the workers organized a revolutionary political party.

Following the failure of the Commune, Engels wrote: "Does this mean that in future street fighting will no longer play any role? Certainly not! It only means that conditions since 1848 have become far more unfavorable for civilian fighters and far more favorable for the military. Accordingly, it will...have to be undertaken with greater forces."

Engels' most important contribution to the theory of insurgency, however, was probably inadvertent. In rebutting others, he emphasized the need to destroy the state's tendency to repress its citizens. This could only be done, he argued, through what Marx had described as a period of economic and political control by the workers – "the dictatorship of the proletariat." Marx himself had believed that once this phase had ended, the state would wither away.

When Vladimir Lenin found himself at the head of the revolutionary government in Russia, he did believe that the control of the state by the workers was essential to create a communist society. Furthermore, Lenin was also convinced that the media, the political process, and education all had to work for the transformation of a capitalist society into a socialist one. But Lenin dismissed Marx's hopes of an end to repression as impractical in the circumstances facing the Russian socialist republic in 1918. In short, for Lenin, the expression "dictatorship of the proletariat," never carefully defined by Marx, required a repressive state apparatus wielded by a working-class party.

THE ANARCHISTS AND TERRORISM

Meanwhile, the anarchists had drawn very different conclusions from the failure of the Paris Commune. They now rejected both the legitimacy of any government, even a working-class one, and the idea of revolutionary insurrection. Anarchists turned to terrorist methods such as political assassination. Since they did not seek to replace one government by another, but merely to destroy the existing order, they did not require leadership or organization. Hence, many of their actions seem to have been the work either of individuals or of very small conspiratorial groups.

Directed terror was employed in Russia between 1878 and 1881 by the People's Will (Narodnaya Volya) group to destroy the czarist regime. It was justified by

Hulton Getty Picture Collection

Vladimir Ilyich Lenin, leader of the October 1917 Russian Revolution, turned to terrorist measures after the attempt on his life in August 1918.

Nikolai Morozov, one of their leading theorists, as costing fewer lives and therefore being ethically more acceptable: "All that the terroristic struggle really needs is a small number of people and large material means." Terrorism's advantage, Morozov continued, was that assassination often hit the intended target. During insurrections, however, the fighting was liable to kill workers and destroy their homes.

Although anarchists killed a small number of prominent political figures, including Presidents Sadi Carnot of France in 1894, and William McKinley of the United States in 1901, their movement seldom achieved much impact outside of Spain and soon dwindled.

Meanwhile, the main trend in socialism was to try to make use of the potentially vast power of the votes of the workers. In France and Germany, most socialists cooperated with capitalist governments to gain social reforms. By the end of the century, socialist ministers were being appointed. In Italy in 1907, the first general strike took place. This event successfully demonstrated the power of the organized workers to bring the economic system to a standstill. One theorist, the French social philosopher Georges Sorel, argued that it would be possible to overthrow the state and to replace it by a workers' government solely by the means of a general strike by the working class.

In Russia, this route was closed off by the government's policy of repression after the assassination of Czar Alexander II. Lenin followed Marx's teaching: He did not see terrorism as having a role in the promotion of revolution. In 1902, Lenin attacked the Socialist Revolutionaries, (another Russian radical political group), for their enthusiasm for terrorist methods. Lenin argued that their use of terrorism was the result of their close political connections with the peasants.

However, as a Russian, he saw terror as having a role in carrying out the revolution once open resistance had begun. As he wrote in 1906, "The party must regard the fighting guerrilla operations of the squads affiliated to or associated with it as being, in principle, permissible and advisable in the present period." But Lenin was specific about the objective of all such guerrilla operations, which was "to destroy the government, police, and military machinery." Furthermore, Lenin maintained that terrorism should always be under the control of the party to prevent effort from being dissipated uselessly.

Lenin's main contribution to the theory of successful insurrection was that it should be led by a relatively small and disciplined party in the name of the working class. The main purpose of the party was to prepare for urban insurrection. In the towns, where the working class was concentrated, the party could exercise the greatest influence on events. But the preparation of an urban insurrection under the eyes of a watchful secret police was not easy. Lenin solved this problem by basing his organization, the Bolsheviks, outside Russia and communicating with his followers through a secret newspaper. This was probably the only way in which the revolution could have been staged.

TROTSKY AND THE RED GUARD

With the outbreak of World War I, Lenin emphasized the importance of two tasks: the subversion of the armed forces, and the preparation of a revolutionary military force, the Red Guard. The latter, he argued,

could be set up under the cover of being an ex-servicemen's organization. The Red Guard could come out into the open only when the government was already on the point of collapse. Yet it was vital that the Red Guard be ready, which presented a problem of both training and supply. Lenin wrote that the insurgents "must arm themselves as best they can….Under no circumstances should they wait for help from other sources…they must procure everything themselves."

TROTSKY'S RUSSIAN REVOLUTION

Despite Lenin's enthusiasm for insurrection, in 1917 it was Leon Trotsky who directed the Bolshevik's seizure of power in Petrograd (now St. Petersburg). The term Bolshevik, meaning majority, dated from a split in the Russian Social Democratic Labor Party in 1903. Trotsky, as people's commissar for war from 1918 to 1925, consolidated the Russian Revolution.

Trotsky thought that only a global revolution could assure the Russian Revolution's success. Trotsky's

Leon Trotsky (foreground), the founder of the Red Army, used terrorist measures to enforce discipline in the ranks.

original contribution to the theory of insurgency was the notion of dual power, the first element required by an urban insurrection. Trotsky arugued that dual power was the key to understanding not only the Russian Revolution of 1917, but to any successful socialist revolution. Dual power referred to the situation in March-November 1917 when there were two centers of power in Russia.

One source of authority was the weak provisional government in Petrograd, which had yet to seek popular endorsement through elections. The other source was the Workers' and Peasants' Soviets, or councils, which had been set up in Petrograd and all over the country. The Bolsheviks, therefore, had made their slogan "All power to the Soviets!" This strategy not only gave the Soviets legitimacy but ensured that the main strength of the alternative government would be provided by the armed workers of the Red Guard.

Trotsky argued pointedly that in taking power and enacting land reform, the Bolsheviks were in fact only legalizing what was already going on in the countryside. Both the czar's regime and the provisional government had been unable to resist the illegal land seizures by the peasants. Trotsky derived from this idea his argument that mass mobilization was the only possible route to a workers' government. Anything less, including the use of terrorist methods, would be unacceptable, since at best it could only lead to a military counter-coup.

Trotsky rejected terrorism in setting the stage for revolution. However, the assumption that the Bolsheviks were the true representatives of the working class led Trotsky to support the use of state terror against those who opposed the revolution: "A victorious war, generally speaking, destroys only an insignificant part of the conquered army, intimidating the remainder and breaking their will. The revolution works in the same way: it kills individuals, and intimidates thousands. In this sense, the Red Terror is not distinguishable from the armed insurrection, the direct continuation of which it represents."

In 1919, the new Soviet Government established the Third International, or Comintern, to promote worldwide revolution. In 1928, Mikhail Tukhachevsky, a former czarist officer turned leading Bolshevik general, wrote about insurrection in the Comintern manual. He took a Leninist line, but went to a lot of trouble to argue that the use of terrorist methods also had a proper part to play. The forces of the government could be disorientated by picking off the leaders and killing them as quickly as possible. The essence of the insurrectionist strategy, too, was surprise. The action had to be carefully planned. The insurgents must not rely on an initial single, physical signal, in case failures of communication put the whole plan at risk.

In the 1920s, there were a number of unsuccessful attempts to carry out insurrections in other major cities in Europe and Asia. But there has been no clear example of a communist government coming to power by insurrection. Romania in 1989, however, is one example of a communist government being overthrown by popular unrest.

After World War II, the traditional Marxist process of slowly building popular support through mass organization demanded too much patience from some revolutionary socialists. Terrorism allied with Marxist ideology was adopted by such groups as the Italian Red Brigades (Brigate Rossi) and the Baader-Meinhof Gang in West Germany.

1968 PARIS STUDENT UPRISING

Both groups advocated the use of armed struggle to overthrow the capitalist state and bring about a socialist revolution. But armed insurrection remained an ideal for many on the Left. In *les évenements* ("the events") of 1968 in Paris, radical students tried to link hands with workers in order to overthrow capitalism and establish in its place a form of socialism.

In some ways closer to anarchism than to Marxism, the French student movement rejected concepts of leadership and political organization. Instead they preferred spontaneously uprising groups, which could neither be penetrated nor co-opted by the regime.

The French government, led by Charles de Gaulle, was not unduly alarmed, and rightly so as it turned out. The workers did not take the students seriously, either. In the end, everyone went back to work, and de Gaulle only lost power in the following year when he resigned after a referendum did not go the way he wanted. There was no revolution in France in 1968.

REVOLUTION IN TEHRAN

Successful urban insurrections, however, did occur in other parts of the world. In 1979, mass demonstrations in the streets precipitated the fall of Mohammad Reza Pahlavi, the shah of Iran. In the weeks that followed, Islamic fundamentalists used demonstrating crowds to bring to power in Iran a clerical regime led by Ayatollah Ruhollah Khomeini.

The Iranian Revolution was significant in the history of insurgency for two reasons. First, a religious belief, Islam, that made no distinction between the sacred and the secular dominated the insurgency.

Second, the objective of the insurgents was not merely to topple the shah. They were also united in a desire to remove the foreign influences that the shah had promoted. The shah had sought to make Iran a modern nation-state. Not only did he bring in bitterly resented foreign capital and multinational corporations, but he also imported the liberal ideas dominant in Western political thought since the French Revolution.

The hostility of the insurgents focused above all on the United States, whose government had helped

Hulton Getty Picture Collection

restore the shah to his throne following an uprising in 1953. Soon after the success of the revolution, armed revolutionary guards broke into the United States' Embassy in Tehran. The guards seized the diplomatic personnel and held them hostage for 444 days.

Terrorism has served as an element of revolutionary urban insurrections since the nineteenth century. Terrorist acts served as a signal for action, and terrorist methods were used in the aftermath of a successful insurrection to intimidate any likely oppostion. But terrorism has always been far less significant than political organization and ideological motivation, as theorists of urban insurrection have come to realize.

Peter Calvert

SEE ALSO:

TERROR IN THE FRENCH REVOLUTION 1789-1815; THE PARIS COMMUNE: STATE TERROR; FRENCH ANARCHIST TERROR; RUSSIAN ANARCHIST TERROR; NATIONALIST TERRORISM; REVOLUTIONARY TERRORISM; DOMESTIC VERSUS INTERNATIONAL TERRORISM; URBAN VERSUS RURAL TERRORISM; TERRORISM AND REVOLUTION IN IRAN; RED BRIGADES.

Mass demonstration in Tehran in favor of Ayatollah Ruhollah Khomeini during the Iranian revolution of 1979. Under the Khomeini regime religous terrorism became an deliberate instrument of Iranian foreign policy.

FURTHER READING

- Hutton, P. H. *The Cult of the Revolutionary Tradition: The Blanquists in French Politics, 1864-1893*. Berkeley, CA: University of California Press, 1981.
- Mayer, T. F. *Analytical Marxism*. Thousand Oaks, CA: Sage Publications, 1994.
- Melograni, P. *Lenin and the Myth of World Evolution: Ideology and Reasons of State*. Atlantic Highlands, NJ: Humanities Press International, 1984.
- O'Neill, B. E., W. R. Heaton, and D. J. Alberts. *Insurgency in the Modern World*. Boulder, CO: Westview Press, 1980.
- Wright, R. *Sacred Rage: The Crusade of Modern Islam*. New York: Simon & Schuster, 1985.

NATIONAL LIBERATION WARS AND TERROR

The American Revolution, though scarcely a revolution in the sense of a complete transformation of society, was one of the first modern wars of national liberation. At its beginning, one of the principal patriots, Benjamin Franklin, put the main requirement for the insurgents succinctly: "Depend upon it, we must hang together, for if we do not, assuredly we shall all hang separately."

The Declaration of Independence, the manifesto of the American Revolution, was designed to serve two purposes. First, it claimed legitimacy for the new government by asserting the right of citizens to "alter or to abolish" the form of government under which they lived. Second, the intent of the Declaration was to persuade other powers that America's cause was just. This would be done by making it clear that the insurrectionists were responsible people driven to rebellion by the unjust treatment suffered at the hands of the British government of King George III. The author of the Declaration was Thomas Jefferson.

As with more recent revolutions, overseas support was forthcoming. The main support came from the French government of King Louis XVI, but supposedly neutral powers supplied aid tacitly. The fact that Jefferson had placed the rebels' case in a broad philosophical context that could be recognized by educated Europeans was, therefore, of key importance. Almost all later insurgent movements have issued a manifesto to the world, setting out their aims and appealing for support and understanding.

COLONIAL RESISTANCE

The Americans created the idea of a citizen militia army. Where a militia could be set up before the colonial power could stop it, insurrection became possible, as demonstrated much later in Vietnam and

Hulton Getty Picture Collection

Thomas Jefferson, author of the Declaration of Independence, which has been a model for later proclamations justifying rebellion against foreign rule.

K E Y   F A C T S

● British collectors of the stamp tax in the American colonies in the 1760s were tarred and feathered in acts of terror to scare them into leaving the taxes uncollected.

● The Cypriot nationalist George Grivas wrote extensively in his memoirs about the decision-making process required of the leader of a national liberation struggle.

Hulton Getty Picture Collection

Indonesia. These two countries had been French and Dutch colonies respectively before World War II, when they were occupied by Japan. After Japan surrendered, it took the colonial powers some time to reestablish control, since both territories were situated far away. This distance was also a disadvantage for the insurgents, since they were unable to strike at the heart of the colonial state, but were themselves open to constant attack. The nearer the colony was to its ruling state, the more effective terrorist acts became.

SECESSIONIST MOVEMENTS

Secessionist movements, groups whose territory is located within a state, have made full use of their ability to strike at the center of power. This has been done for its own sake and for its value as "revolutionary theater." Movements of this type are often able to appropriate generally recognized symbols of national identity to their own causes. This ability was displayed

French philosopher Jean-Paul Sartre (left) had a great influence on the Parisian students who took to the streets in 1968. He also helped popularize the work of Frantz Fanon, the theorist of colonial resistance.

by the Basque nationalist movement, Fatherland and Liberty (ETA), in Spain. ETA drew on a distinctive language, region, and set of cultural traditions, including the ancient tradition of Basque autonomy, to consolidate support for violence against the dictatorship of General Francisco Franco. It gained strength from the trials of some of its supporters in 1970. There was even admiration for ETA when it assassinated the Spanish prime minister Admiral Carrero Blanco in 1973. The murder was carried out in the most spectacular manner, by planting a mine in the road which blew the admiral and his car over a five-story building into the courtyard of the building he had just left.

Rohan Gunaratna

Tamil Tigers. Their campaign against the Sinhalese majority on the island of Sri Lanka has been prolonged and violent.

However, with the restoration of democracy after Franco's death in 1975, the tacit French support on which the Basques had relied was reduced. Moreover, the Spanish government's decision to grant the Basques a degree of autonomy removed much of the justification for the movement. ETA split in 1977, the majority choosing to pursue the electoral road to autonomy.

One of the most distinctive features of nationalist movements that has emerged is the fact that they operate on two levels. On the surface, there is a legal organization, which can raise funds and publicize the cause. Underneath, there is an illegal organization, made up of individuals whose identity as members is not a matter of public record (though it is often known to security forces). Thus Sinn Fein, a legal political party in Northern Ireland, has been closely linked with the illegal Provisional Irish Republican Army.

Algeria's war of independence from France began in 1954 and resulted in Algerian independence in 1962. Here the sense of Islamic identity and the linguistic difference from their French rulers were important in generating resistance to the harsh regime of the French

settlers. It was in this context that Frantz Fanon developed his belief in the cleansing quality of violence.

VIOLENCE – A CLEANSING FORCE

Born in Martinique and educated in the French West Indies, Frantz Fanon trained as a psychologist. He argued that violence could and should be used to free black-skinned peoples of the sense of inferiority instilled by centuries of slavery. Otherwise, true independence would not be attained, since citizens continued to carry around inside themselves the marks of their colonial status. Of killing, Fanon observed that "at the level of individuals, violence is a cleansing force. It frees the native from his inferiority complex and from his despair and inaction; it makes him fearless and restores his self-respect. Even if the armed struggle has been symbolic and the nation is demobilized through a rapid movement of decolonization, the people have time to see that the liberation has been the business of each and all and that the leader has no special merit."

In his introduction to Fanon's work, the French philosopher Jean-Paul Sartre commended it to his countrymen. They will not like it, he said, but they must read it. For colonialism had not only bred violence in the colonized, it had also damaged the European psyche irreparably. Sartre argued that all Europeans, especially in "that super-European monstrosity, North America," had implicitly supported the inherently oppressive colonial system. "We in Europe too are being decolonized; that is to say...the settler which is in every one of us is being rooted out."

Fanon's argument in some respects carries to an extreme conclusion the idea of placing a positive emphasis on a person's African origins. This was first termed *négritude* in 1939 in a poem by Aimé Césaire, who also came from Martinique. The concept was elaborated after World War II by Léopold S. Senghor, a former deputy in the French National Assembly who became president of Senegal.

However, Senegal, like the majority of French territories in Africa, gained independence without an armed struggle. Yet, Fanon's predictions that even a merely symbolic struggle would create a shared experience of liberation have not been fulfilled. Many African countries seem trapped in a cycle of military coups and unstable civilian regimes. This political turmoil has only worsened the economic difficulties they face. On the other hand, the radical wing of the Black Power movement in the 1960s confirmed the predictions of

Associated Press

The corpse of Indian prime minister Rajiv Gandhi (foreground) lies in the street after he was assassinated by Tamil Tigers in May 1991.

becoming a major campaign issue. However, even during the Cold War era (1946-87), guerrilla action did not necessarily involve either of the superpowers.

SECRECY AND COMMITMENT

The Tamil Tigers of Sri Lanka came into existence after attacks by members of the Sinhalese majority on the Tamil quarter of Colombo in 1983. The Tigers' aim is the creation of a Tamil homeland on Sri Lanka. They received Indian support, official and unofficial, and established control of the island's Jaffna Peninsula. The movement is marked by great secrecy. Members carry cyanide capsules to ensure they are not taken alive. Spectacular terrorist acts carried out by the Tigers include the assassinations by suicide bombers of the Indian prime minister, Rajiv Gandhi, President Premadasa of Sri Lanka, and his would-be successor.

The other successful movement of the 1980s was the Shining Path in Peru. Its founder, Abimael Guzmán, was a philosophy professor well acquainted with the theories of insurrection. Like the Tamil Tigers, the group was characterized by two features: extreme secrecy and a key role played by women. The early movement conducted small-scale, low-risk terrorist acts designed to attract maximum publicity to the cause. The very secretive nature of the organization meant, however, that it has had relatively little impact outside Peru.

Peter Calvert

SEE ALSO:

TERRORISM IN FRENCH ALGERIA; TERROR AGAINST THE FRENCH IN INDOCHINA; TERRORISM IN PERU; TAMIL TIGER TERROR IN SRI LANKA; TERROR IN AFGHANISTAN; BASQUE NATIONALIST TERROR: ETA; NATIONALIST TERROR IN NORTHERN IRELAND 1976-1996.

Fanon and Sartre of the potential impact of African nationalism on American society.

Ethnic and linguistic differences were crucial to the majority of the successful guerrilla movements of the 1980s. Soviet intervention in Afghanistan in 1979 resulted in a long-running guerrilla campaign against the occupying forces. In time, the campaign was to wear down the structure of the Soviet state and help precipitate its collapse. Ethnic nationalism continues to fuel civil war, even within the Russian Federation. The campaign against the Chechen insurgents begun in 1995 discredited President Boris Yeltsin's government. During the 1996 presidential election, Yeltsin reached a truce with the Chechens to reduce the risk of the war

FURTHER READING

- Brown, Richard Maxwell. "Violence and the American Revolution." In *Essays on the American Revolution*, edited by Stephen G. Kurtz and James H. Hutson. Chapel Hill, NC: University of North Carolina Press, 1973.
- O'Neill, B. E., W. R. Heaton, and D. J. Alberts. *Insurgency in the Modern World*. Boulder, CO: Westview Press, 1980.
- Palmer, David Scott. *The Shining Path of Peru*. New York: St. Martin's Press, 1994.

GUERRILLAS AND TERROR

Incidents of violence can be used, not to defeat an opponent, but merely to call attention to a cause and dramatize its importance. Political movements that lack the strength to overthrow the established order, or which are denied the right to protest peacefully, may adopt terrorist strategies. While revolutionaries use political assassinations as a signal for a larger insurgency or revolt, terrorist assassinations can also be independent of any strategic revolutionary plan.

Resistance can take the form of a campaign of intimidation of the regime's supporters. It can also take the form of absenteeism, sabotage, crop destruction, or land occupations, which in themselves do not amount to a campaign of violence.

A systematic and prolonged campaign of terrorism with the aim of defeating a foreign enemy (or one seen to be supported by foreigners), is called partisan or guerrilla warfare.

GUERRILLA WARFARE

Guerrilla warfare is first described during the fifth century B.C., when the Chinese general Sun Tzu, wrote about tactics to be used in support of conventional war in *The Art of War*. However, he neglected to give the phenomenon a name.

Until recent times, irregular war was hard to distinguish from ordinary warfare. The Prussian soldier and military theorist Karl von Clausewitz wrote *On War* in the nineteenth century. This book drew on his experiences as a soldier in campaigns against the French emperor Napoleon Bonaparte. Clausewitz observed the value of bands of armed civilians making hit-and-run raids on supply lines or communications centers in order to make the enemy divert forces from the main army. *On War* had a powerful influence on military theory throughout the nineteenth century.

Although guerrilla warfare is often thought of as being alien to the European tradition, the term *guerrilla* originated in Spain. The Spanish word *guerrilla*, strictly speaking, means "little war"; the word for a guerrilla (the person participating in a little war) is *guerrillero* or *guerrillera*. The term was coined in the Spanish War of Independence following Napoleon's invasion of Spain in 1808.

Like those first Spanish guerrillas, today's guerrillas often fight outside the rules of war, sometimes without uniform, and use surprise as a main weapon. Governments and security forces usually treat guerrillas as terrorists or bandits and employ terror tactics against them.

Since 1808, guerrilla warfare has been used in a wide variety of situations. Nineteenth-century references to it, however, were sparse. Most writers seem to have regarded the rural guerrilla as the Marxists did, as a useful addition to urban insurrection, pinning down troops and making the real revolutionaries' task easier.

WARS OF INDEPENDENCE

The Spanish War of Independence (1808-1814) was a partisan war – a war of resistance against foreign occupiers by armed civilians organized on military lines. The Spanish army had largely been defeated by the French, who had captured the capital, Madrid. Some Spanish continued to resist, but not in the traditional way as an organized army. Spain's allies, the British and Portuguese armies under the Duke of Wellington, supported the Spanish partisans. Wellington started out from Portugal and advanced into Spain, supported by the *guerrilla* (little war) of the Spanish partisans, defeating the French in a series of decisive battles.

The success of the guerrillas was directly related to the efforts of Spanish nationalistic political leaders to

---

SUMMARY

● In the twentieth century, Mao Zedong and others developed theories of how to use terror in a revolutionary guerrilla war.

● Ernesto "Che" Guevara wrote his theories of guerrilla warfare after his role as Fidel Castro's second-in-command in the Cuban revolution.

---

organize resistance. The Spanish peasants hated the French, and eagerly joined the nationalists' fighting force. Spain was powerless without the Portuguese and British, but Wellington could not have won without the diversions carried out by the Spanish guerrillas. As a modern historian has written: "It was this continuous resistance, feeble as it often was, which broke Napoleon's doctrine of maximum concentration in the attempt to solve contradictory demands of operation and occupation in the hostile countryside."

The guerrilla element in the Spanish War of Independence converted the enemy's strength into weakness. It wore down the French and it destroyed what should have been their advantage, their superior numbers. When the French tried to concentrate their troops for battle, they found the vulnerability of their supply lines increased as their dependence on them increased. A large army assembled in one place could not live off the country for any prolonged period.

The guerrillas used terrorism to force Spaniards into joining the war against the invader. When they reoccupied areas evacuated by the French, they would punish anyone who had collaborated with the occupying forces. It was much less likely that the victims of terror would cooperate with the next French search for supplies.

The guerrillas' national pride and militaristic organization became part of Spanish progressive political movements. As historian Raymond Carr says in his *Spain, 1808-1939*, the war "gave liberalism its program and its technique of revolution. It defines Spanish patriotism and endows it with an enduring myth. It saddled liberalism with the problems of generals in politics and the mystique of the guerrilla."

TERROR IN THE SPANISH EMPIRE

Three broad geographic areas once part of the Spanish empire have undergone periods of insurgency in modern times. The cultural links between them and Spain are clear. However, it may not be that guerrilla warfare was exported from Spain. It may have been that conditions in the colonies were similar and so the same methods evolved independently.

First, there were the Central and South American countries that became independent in the nineteenth century. Guerrilla warfare in fact went on in various South American countries throughout the nineteenth century. It was responsible to a considerable extent for the ultimate defeat in 1824 of the Spaniards in Peru. Spanish rule had enjoyed considerable support in Peru, but this was eroded by the irregular forces. Guerrilla warfare toppled regimes in many countries, as in Guatemala in 1871. Used to resist foreign intervention, it was very successful in wearing down the French occupation of Mexico in 1862-67.

Cuba represents the second area of sub-revolutionary terrorism in the Spanish colonial empire. It had not gained its independence at the same time as the mainland states. Cuba's wars of independence began in earnest in 1868, but the first phase, the so-called Ten Years' War (1868-78), was unsuccessful. The struggle was resumed in February 1895, when a small invasion force led by the writer and patriot José Martí landed in Cuba. Martí fell into the hands of the Spanish authorities and was put to death. But his movement survived because his efforts inspired two experienced military leaders who had both fought in the Ten Years' War.

Máximo Gómez and Antonio Maceo recruited their forces from the blacks and poor whites of the rural areas. They also received arms shipments from the United States, which the Spanish fleet was unable to intercept. To prevent this traffic, the Spanish commander herded the civilian population into *campos de reconcentración*, or concentration camps. Such camps were also used in 1900-1902 in a similar way by the British in their war with the Boers of South Africa. Both there and in Cuba the death rate of camp prisoners from disease was high. Reports of the conditions in Cuba were a major factor in causing the U.S. to intervene, and led to the Spanish-American War in 1898. (It should be noted that a concentration camp was a place in which the civilian population was concentrated. Only since 1944 has the term become a euphemism for extermination camp.)

The third area affected by the Spanish experience is that of the Philippines in Southeast Asia. Defeated in the Spanish-American War, Spain ceded possession of the Philippines to the United States. However, many Filipinos who wanted nothing less than independence waged an unsuccessful guerrilla war against the American authorities between 1899 and 1902.

THE POLITICAL GUERRILLA

Guerrilla warfare has been used extensively in the twentieth century. This tradition began with T. E. Lawrence, better known as Lawrence of Arabia. He was the first Western military thinker to regard partisan or guerrilla warfare as a strategy in itself.

Lawrence's theory of guerrilla warfare, as set out in his book *The Seven Pillars of Wisdom*, emphasizes two points. First, Lawrence argued that guerrilla forces must avoid engaging the enemy. Guerrillas must be capable of protecting themselves against enemy attacks, but they must not attempt battlefield assaults. Nor did Lawrence consider a guerrilla band to have the potential to be converted into a conventional army. Lawrence instead regarded the Arab guerrillas as a political force. Their existence in itself denied legitimacy to Turkish rule over the Arabian states.

Second, he argued that the best way for guerrillas to attack the enemy was to destroy its supplies and lines of communication. He believed that to destroy the enemy's military infrastructure was to destroy the enemy itself.

Lawrence's small forces, drifting around "like a gas," were entirely at home in the Arabian territory since they could disappear into the civilian population. Lawrence's theory, in fact, described the kind of desert warfare traditional in Arabia. In the first decades of the twentieth century, open areas could be treated as a military asset. The Turks had few aircraft and limited capabilities to transport troops, so forces could hide in the desert and strike at bases and communications with the full advantage of surprise.

It is worth pointing out that if guerrillas wish to blend into a civilian population, they must have a civilian population to disappear into. In South Vietnam during the Vietnam War, all men of fighting age served in the military. This left the old, women, and children as the only people who could sink into the background. Consequently, Vietnamese insurgents frequently used children to carry out bombing attacks.

Lawrence of Arabia allowed his Arab guerrillas to massacre Turkish soldiers.

Hulton Getty Picture Collection

MAO'S GUERRILLA WAR MODEL

During the interwar period Mao Zedong developed a new model for guerrilla warfare, creating a political framework for military strategy. Mao profited from native Chinese experience, and his extensive knowledge of Chinese history and writing since Sun Tzu. The heroes whom he followed were specifically those Chinese who had fought against foreigners.

The theory was developed in Mao's tract *Guerrilla Warfare*, in 1937, and is based on a three-stage model. The first stage is the organization, consolidation, and preservation of base areas. Training programs and village meetings are used to create a network of sympathizers in the countryside around the base area, who eventually form the basis for a militia as well as the party organization. In Peru, the Shining Path closely followed the teaching of Mao Zedong. Their organizational groundwork in the highlands of Peru was well laid before the armed struggle started in 1980.

The second stage of guerrilla war involves the expansion of the base areas. The military campaign features acts of sabotage and the killing of those either collaborating with the enemy or opposed to the guerrillas' politics. Attacks aim at capturing medical supplies and military equipment from outlying police posts and weak groups of troops in the field. For Mao, the expansion of the base areas takes place by recruiting large numbers of defensive militia rather than full-time guerrillas. The militia, being part-time soldiers, can be based in their own homes, which could be behind enemy lines or in the main combat zone. People who collaborate with the enemy in places where there are militia forces can be assassinated, thus eliminating important enemy organizers. Killing collaborators hampers the enemy's efforts to supply its own troops and to gather intelligence about guerrilla operations. Mao referred to this as the "oilspot technique."

The third stage of guerrilla warfare is the destruction of the enemy. This is achieved by turning guerrilla forces into a conventional army capable of defeating the government in pitched battles. The needed retraining of the guerrillas in this phase can be conducted while guerrilla leaders negotiate with the government. Mao emphasized that negotiations would be for purely military purposes, to wear down the opponent's morale, and to allow the guerrillas time to regroup and resupply.

MAO'S ASSUMPTIONS OF GUERRILLA WAR

Mao's work is based on three basic assumptions. The first is the doctrine of strength and weakness. If, for example, the enemy outnumbers the guerrillas, it means their forces require a lot of supplies. The guerrillas should therefore turn the strength of numbers into a weakness by attacking the enemy's supply lines.

The second assumption is the relationship between time, space, and will. Guerrillas should be willing to surrender areas in their control if it will gain time to spread propaganda among the people.

The third, and most dubious, preconception is that guerrillas will have full intelligence and the government will have none. This belief assumes that the guerrillas will succeed in denying all information about themselves to the government. It also assumes that the insurgents, through their network of sympathizers, will discover the strategic and tactical state of the government. This may have been possible when Mao was writing in 1937, but advances in technology since then have strengthened the government's resources. Major powers now have earth satellites, infrared detectors, guided missiles, and smart bombs. Psychological warfare and torture methods have also been developed as ways of gaining information.

The chance of a guerrilla movement being able to deny all knowledge of its activities to the government is now much less likely than it was in Mao's time. Thus, anyone following his advice will be in trouble, unless they remember that the main purpose of guerrilla warfare is not to defeat the enemy's army, but to turn the people into a revolutionary force. This is the difference between Mao and other theorists, with the possible exception of Lawrence, who regarded Arab partic-

Mao Zedong, creator of the People's Republic of China and its ruler from 1949 until his death in 1976.

Hulton Getty Picture Collection

ipation in the fight against the Turks as being essential to fueling Arab nationalism.

MAO'S SIMPLE RULES OF INSURGENCY

Although there is little practical detail in Mao's thought, there are the Three Rules and the Eight Remarks. The Three Rules were general points, while the Eight Remarks were specific ones, relating to how insurgents should conduct themselves. The central aspect of Mao's thought was the close relationship it encouraged between the guerrilla and the people: "It is only undisciplined troops who make the people their enemies and who, like the fish out of its native element, cannot live." Elsewhere he says that the guerrilla moves among the people and is sustained by them like the fish in water.

Hence Mao's forces had to be supported by an organization of agents and informants living legal lives but keeping them provided with food, ammunition, and information about government forces. For this purpose, Mao and his guerrillas had the added advantage of being able to make use of the existing structure of the Triad secret societies, which had emerged as early as the seventeenth century as a reaction to the Manchurian conquest of China. Their nationalist origins made them a natural ally in the Chinese struggle against the Japanese invaders during World War II. This resistance gained Mao many supporters.

In 1949, after four more years of warfare against the Chinese nationalist government, Mao's troops finally entered Beijing, and the Chinese communists took power. It is doubtful, however, if they could have done so by guerrilla warfare had the corrupt nationalist government not already been weakened by a generation of war against the Japanese.

GUERRILLAS IN WORLD WAR II

The Chinese were not the only people to use guerrilla tactics in World War II. In the mobile phases of the war, countries collapsed very quickly. This left a great deal of their social structures intact, with many people opposed to the new occupiers and ready to take up arms against them. However, terrorism in occupied Europe brought massive retaliation from the German secret police. In Warsaw, the Polish capital, both the 1943 Jewish Warsaw Ghetto revolt and the 1944 Home Army uprising were ruthlessly crushed.

However, it was possible to keep guerrilla forces on the edge of the main theaters of conflict to perform an important role in holding down regular troops. The British and American governments encouraged the activities of partisan forces in this way in both Europe and Asia. The Red Army supported similar bands operating behind the German lines on the Eastern Front. One important practitioner was Orde Wingate, who became best-known for his leadership of the Chindits, a behind-the-lines force fighting the Japanese in Burma in 1943 and 1944. Wingate's forces used hit-and-run raids to disrupt Japanese supply lines.

SOUTHEAST ASIA, 1945-60

There are four major postwar examples of insurgency in southeast Asia. After the United States granted the Philippines independence in 1946, a nationalist guerrilla movement began fighting the new, American-backed government. In Indonesia, nationalists waged a war of independence against the Dutch from 1945 to 1948. The Vietnamese fought for their independence from France from 1945 to 1954, and in Malaya, a communist insurgency against the British produced the Malayan Emergency, from 1948 to 1960.

In each case, Western powers had supported guerrilla insurgencies against the Japanese during World War II. By 1945, a great many local inhabitants had been issued guns by the Allies, trained in military techniques, and had four years' experience in fighting the Japanese. The communists, natural opponents of fascism and militarism, had readily joined these resistance movements. But when the war ended, the communists saw no justification in handing back their weapons and submitting to rule by colonial regimes that they opposed just as much as they opposed Japanese militarists.

Malaya supplies one example of how this process worked in practice. In World War II, the Allies had supported the Malayan People's Anti-Japanese Army under the leadership of Chin Peng. In 1945, this force, already well armed and trained, renamed itself the Malayan Races Liberation Army (MRLA). In 1948, it commenced a 12-year campaign to drive the British out of Malaya, in succession to the campaign against the Japanese. The MRLA used surprise tactics to strike at economic targets such as rubber plantations and mines. They ambushed military and police patrols, and used explosives to blow up roads and railroad lines. In 1951, the British High Commissioner, Sir Henry Gurney, was assassinated in the mistaken belief that he was a senior military commander rather than a politician.

Guerrillas do not always resist the temptation to strike too soon or in the wrong place to avoid alerting the government to the urgency and the necessity of combating the insurgency. In this way, Gurney's death forced the British to turn their weakness into strength by developing a systematic anti-guerrilla campaign strategy called the Briggs Plan.

The Malayan guerrillas' selective assassination of key figures in outlying villages was initially successful in making villagers cooperate. However, this terror was countered by the creation of the New Villages, the grouping together of villagers behind fortified stockades defended by militia forces. The mobility of the guerrillas was restricted by a rigorous food rationing system and strict limits on the transportation of food. In addition, the Commonwealth forces enjoyed two great advantages. First, the British had command of sea and air. Second, they had the support of the Malay majority (most terrorists were ethnic Chinese) that came to power when Malaya was granted its independence in 1957.

MAO'S INFLUENCE ON HO CHI MINH

The French in Vietnam were not so fortunate. With the Japanese collapse, the communists under Ho Chi Minh declared Vietnam independent and established a national government. France had the problem of reconquering land from a group who, at least in theory, had been allied with them against the Japanese.

Ho had been a founding member of the French Communist Party in 1920 and of the Indochinese Communist Party in 1930. In 1941, he had a leading role in establishing the League for the Independence of Vietnam. This group, better known as the Vietminh, was formed to fight the Japanese. Ho and the Vietminh received American assistance during the war.

Ho's objective was a Vietnam free of the French colonial system, an aim that enabled him to present his movement in terms that won it broad-based nationalist support. Ho was able to illustrate his arguments with examples of cruelties practiced against the Vietnamese by the colonial settlers. Even now, his descriptions have not lost their capacity to shock.

Ho and his chief military theorist, Vo Nguyen Giap, made intensive use of guerrilla tactics to make the position of the French government impossible. In 1954, after advice from Mao and backed by Chinese supplies, the Vietminh successfully entrapped General de Castries and a large French army at Dien Bien Phu. After this defeat, the French government hastily abandoned Vietnam along with Laos and Cambodia, the other two provinces of French Indochina.

Ho had spent much of World War II in China, which gave him the great advantage of close links with the Chinese communist leadership after it came to power in 1949. It is clear from Ho's work that he shared another aspect of Mao's thought that is often misunderstood: the use of negotiations as a military tactic. Mao is quite clear that nothing less than victory is acceptable to his cause. Negotiations, therefore, are only one further strategy in seeking to achieve that ultimate objective.

Events during the second phase of the Vietnam War provide an example of this strategy. The United States had supported the French in their struggle with the Vietminh. The U.S. continued to support the state of South Vietnam, established on the division of Vietnam after the French withdrawal. Conflict continued with North Vietnamese-backed Vietcong guerrillas fighting against the South Vietnamese government.

In the mid-1960s, the U.S became entangled in a second major campaign in Vietnam. The Americans

Ho Chi Minh prepares for a mission against the French in 1945, shortly after the end of World War II.

Hulton Getty Picture Collection

drew on massive air power and other weaponry, and by the end of 1967 claimed the war was almost won. Then, in January 1968, the Vietnamese launched the Tet offensive. This was a propaganda success but a military failure, and terror featured in the campaign. In accordance with Mao's ideas, the Vietcong shot any prisoner who was identified with the South Vietnamese government. The Vietnamese were no doubt sincere in their desire to negotiate after Tet ended. They also reorganized the Vietcong in South Vietnam (who had lost heavily during Tet) under cover of the negotiations.

FIDEL CASTRO AND CHE GUEVARA

The idea that guerrilla warfare can be used to overthrow a non-colonial government was produced by Fidel Castro and Che Guevara in Cuba. This idea owes more to the native Cuban tradition of insurgency than it does to any foreign theoretical model.

Fidel Castro Ruz had been active in radical politics before attempting unsuccessfully to overthrow the government of General Fulgencio Batista in 1953.

The Vietminh's military theorist Vo Nguyen Giap (right foreground).

Castro seized the military barracks in Cuba's second city, Santiago. Several days later, he fell into the hands of a military patrol in the nearby mountains. He was tried and sentenced to 15 years' imprisonment, but was soon released. He took refuge in Mexico, from where he set sail for Cuba in late 1956 to launch another coup attempt. On landing, he and his companions were ambushed by Cuban forces. The 15 survivors took refuge in the mountains of the Sierra Maestra where, largely by trial and error, they formed the nucleus of a guerrilla force. The ultimate success of the Cuban Revolution created a myth of the intrepid guerrilla, which Castro himself certainly did nothing to restrain.

Those wanting to learn about Cuban methods found them in the writings of Castro's second-in-command, Che Guevara. Ernesto Guevara de la Serna was an Argentine by birth ("Che" is a common nickname for Argentines in Latin America). Guevara had studied medicine before traveling into exile in Mexico, where he met Cubans planning to return to their homeland. In combat he became a leader, directing the crucial battle of Santa Clara in 1958. This proved to be the decisive psychological stroke in the campaign against Batista.

Soon after victory, Guevara wrote his account of the campaign and a handbook for the guerrilla fighter, *Guerrilla Warfare*. Both stress the practical approach he brought to the subject, but the latter work also enunciated three principles which had greater theoretical appeal. The first was that popular forces could win a war against the army. Second, Guevara argued that it was not necessary to wait until all conditions for revolution existed, since the insurrection itself would create them. Last, he suggested that in underdeveloped Latin America, the countryside was the key area.

This was a heady message for his admirers. It was not necessary, they believed, to create a party or even a trained army. All that was needed was a group of guerrillas. This was the theory of the *foco* (focus). The idea of a small group of guerrillas as the starting point for social revolution, *Foquismo*, was elevated to a theory by a French-born professor at the university of Havana, Régis Debray. The *Foquismo* theory had a profound

Hulton Getty Picture Collection

The guerrilla leader Che Guevara, second-in-command to Cuban revolutionary Fidel Castro.

influence on insurgents in Latin America and the rest of the Third World well into the 1970s.

Much of what Guevara wrote was very down-to-earth. As one historian commented, *Guerrilla Warfare* is "a strange mixture of traditional precepts, an elementary exposé of the principles of military training…nostalgic descriptions of life in the open air among men, and the kind of enthusiasm engendered by ex-servicemen looking back."

The book's practical approach disguised the fact that its basic theory was unsound. It was true that in Cuba the party had hardly existed before the guerrillas started their campaign. Before 1959, many Cubans had not realized that they were fighting for any political party, far less a communist one. At this stage even Castro was not a Marxist-Leninist, despite his claim to the contrary in December 1961. This claim reflected a desire to obtain Soviet support after the U.S.-backed Bay of Pigs invasion in 1961 had tried to depose him.

NO CUBAN GUERRILLA VICTORY

A more serious shortcoming of the theory was that the Cuban revolution was not a victory for guerrilla warfare, for the guerrillas' contribution was minimal. What eventually defeated Batista was the mass withdrawal of support by workers in the cities. This proved fatal to the regime when coupled with its inability to control the plantation workers. Moreover, the Cuban situation had no real parallel in Latin America. Even in the 1960s, many Latin Americans did not live in the countryside waiting to be mobilized by Guevara's guerrillas. Instead, it was only by the conquest of the cities that power could be achieved.

Guevara also believed that revolution would not be possible until all other methods of changing the social system had failed. He even thought that in democratic societies where a route to power by peaceful means lay open, neither guerrilla war nor terrorist action could ultimately be successful.

Guevara served in Castro's government, but later left Cuba in an attempt to spread revolution to other South American countries. He was eventually killed by government troops in Bolivia. It is hard to say whether his theories of guerrilla warfare failed in Bolivia because of deficiencies in the theory or in its implementation. Evidence suggests that almost every mistake that could have been made was made.

CHE'S MISTAKES

On the strategic level, the decision to pick Bolivia was a mistake. The decision took no account of the rigors of the climate and the mountains. The peasants in Bolivia had benefited from a political revolution in 1952 and did not wish to risk the gains made then. Besides, they were suspicious of white-skinned bearded people, who reminded them too strongly of the Conquistadors, the sixteenth-century Spanish invaders who had taken their lands in the first place. The guerrillas wisely made no attempt to use terrorist acts to bully the peasants into supporting them. Even if the *foco* had been successful, Bolivia offered too weak a base from which to create revolutions in the rest of South America, as Guevara had hoped.

On the tactical level, errors were legion. Guevara's Cubans had learned Quechua, so that they could talk to the Bolivians in their own language. However, they picked Ñancuahuazu in the southeast of the country as the site for their operations, where the peasants spoke Guaraní. They attacked a government force before they were ready to defend themselves. They took countless photographs of each other, which, with much of their supplies and vital evidence that linked them to Cuba, fell into the hands of government forces.

Even the most trivial mistakes turned out to be fatal. "Tania la guerrillera," apparently both a KGB and an East German agent in her spare time, was killed because she wore a white shirt in the middle of the green jungle, presenting an easy target to her pursuers.

SANDINISTAS VERSUS CONTRAS

The death of Guevara and the destruction of his *foco* did not immediately end guerrilla warfare in Latin America, but by the beginning of the 1970s, government responses had reduced the surviving groups to insignificant levels. The one major exception, the Sandinista movement in Nicaragua, attained power in 1979 as a result of quite exceptional circumstances. The group's success was due to the fact that the Nicaraguan president Anastasio Somoza had concentrated so much power and wealth in his own hands that he had totally alienated all the major groups that might otherwise have helped him.

The Sandinistas were divided initially into three factions. One, the insurrectionist faction, favored the Marxist-Leninist viewpoint, emphasizing the support of organized labor. The second, the Prolonged Popular War (Guerra Popular Prolongada, GPP) followed a Maoist line. This faction relied on a guerrilla campaign in the countryside. It was the third faction, the Terceristas, led by Daniel Ortega Saavedra, who won out. The Terceristas favored an alliance with non-Marxist opponents of the regime that would ensure broad support for strikes in the cities and guerrilla warfare in the countryside.

Helped by the fact that the corrupt Somoza regime had grafted the aid money for the victims of the Managua earthquake of 1972, the Terceristas were able to form a coalition. This included on the one hand the insurrectionary Sandinistas and on the other the church and the Conservative party. The coalition fought their way into what was left of the capital in a two-pronged military campaign that enjoyed support from both socialist Cuba and democratic Costa Rica. In this campaign, terrorism played little or no part.

The Sandinista government of Nicaragua was in turn challenged by an insurgent movement called the Nicaraguan Democratic Force (FDN), but usually known by the Sandinista nickname of Contras (for counterrevolutionaries). The Contras were set up by the Central Intelligence Agency (CIA) under National Security Decision Directive 17, signed by President Ronald Reagan in 1981. Though primarily a guerrilla force, the Contras sought to drive Nicaragua into bankruptcy by attacking economic targets such as coffee mills and warehouses. The force was also implicated in the attempted assassination of the rival insurgent leader Edén Pastora ("Commander Zero"). It was not successful and its activities were wound down in the mid-1980s, after the U.S. Congress refused to go on providing the funds after the Iran-Contra connection was exposed.

MARIGHELLA'S URBAN GUERRILLA

An attempt was made to transfer rural guerrilla principles to the city to create a form of insurgency called urban guerrilla warfare. Carlos Marighella was a Brazilian politician who had served in the Federal Congress as a deputy. Later, he had been editor of the Brazilian communist party journal *Problemas* and visited the People's Republic of China in 1953-54. After Brazil's military coup in 1964, Marighella and others became opposed to the party's strategy of collaboration. In August 1967, they traveled to Cuba against party instructions to attend the conference of the Latin American Solidarity Organization (OLAS) in defiance of the party line. Subsequently, Marighella wrote to Castro to declare that he had chosen the path of guerrilla warfare. Marighella stated that he believed this to be the only course that would unite the different revolutionary groups in Brazil.

In practice, however, Marighella meant something very different from the Cuban model. In his *Minimanual of the Urban Guerrilla*, he argued that in a vast country like Brazil, actions in the large cities would have a much more striking effect those carried out in the countryside. He published his manifesto on September 25, 1968, in a leading newspaper. His aim was to create a crisis that would force the regime to adopt a military response. This in turn, he explained, would lead to a mass uprising, through which "power would pass to the armed people." His approach follows the Marxist strategy known as "the intensification of contradictions." This assumes that revolutionary fervor will be intensified by political repression.

The problem of urban guerrilla warfare is threefold. First of all, urban guerrillas generally lack a safe base to which they can retreat. In principle, every house is safe since the occupants can control entry and exit. Yet

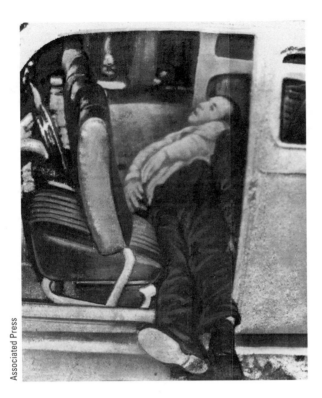

Associated Press

Security forces shot the terrorist Carlos Marighella in São Paolo, Brazil, on November 6, 1969.

at the same time, every house is dangerous, since the occupants are isolated from their comrades in other houses. There is no front line. Second, the urban guerrilla is wholly dependent on terrorist methods, which generate an all-pervading sense of insecurity that the government may manipulate to turn public opinion against the insurgents. Third, the urban terrorist has to rely on absolute secrecy. On the other hand, if secrecy fails, as it did under the repressive regime in Brazil, no organization member is safe. If complete secrecy is maintained, an urban guerrilla movement is almost entirely inhibited from recruiting from its natural sources of support.

Police killed Carlos Marighella, urban terrorism's chief figure, in an ambush in 1969. Urban terrorism in Latin America proved to be a considerable nuisance to governments, but at no time did it threaten to overthrow any of them. Its theory was only sketchily formed. Equally, urban terrorism created a powerful reaction in favor of repression. In Argentina, for example, many citizens were afraid that the urban guerrillas would start a civil war, and so welcomed the army's takeover in 1976.

TERRORISTS, GUERRILLAS, POLITICIANS

Some insurgents practice guerrilla warfare and terrorism without reference to any theoretical framework, and certainly not a Marxist one. One example of this type was George Grivas in Cyprus in 1955-59. Grivas shunned any association with the communists. In his view, communist theory had nothing to do with any war of national liberation.

Grivas is a rare example of a successful guerrilla leader who used terror tactics. But he kept a low political profile after Cyprus gained its independence in 1959. It is hard to think of any major terrorist who has become a successful politician. Those who have took little or no part in terrorist acts. Mao, probably the most successful guerrilla leader of all time, emphasized his talents as a military and ideological thinker. Terrorism may be a fundamental element of guerrilla warfare, but it is apparently not a respectable one.

Peter Calvert

SEE ALSO:

NATIONALIST TERRORISM; REVOLUTIONARY TERRORISM; DOMESTIC VERSUS INTERNATIONAL TERRORISM; URBAN VERSUS RURAL TERRORISM; TERRORISM IN NICARAGUA; TERRORISM IN PERU; TERROR IN THE PHILIPPINES; TERROR IN THE VIETNAM WAR; NICARAGUAN GOVERNMENT'S RESPONSES TO TERRORISM.

F U R T H E R   R E A D I N G

- Daniels, Robert Vincent. *Year of the Heroic Guerrilla: World Revolution and Counterrevolution in 1968.* Cambridge, MA: MIT Press, 1974.
- Guevara, Ernesto. *Guerrilla Warfare.* Lincoln, NE: University of Nebraska Press, 1985.
- Kohl, John, and James Litt, eds. *Urban Guerrilla Warfare in Latin America.* Cambridge, MA: MIT Press, 1974.
- Marighella, Carlos. *Manual of the Urban Guerrilla.* Chapel Hill, NC: Documentary Publications, 1985.
- Moreno, José Antonio. *Che Guevara on Guerrilla Warfare: Doctrine, Practice, and Evolution.* Pittsburgh: University of Pittsburgh, Center for Latin American Studies, 1990.

THEORIES OF STATE TERROR

Terror can be used as a repressive force by a government against its own citizens. Some commentators, such as Noam Chomsky, take the view that national authorities commit most terrorist acts. The aim is to undermine society and subject it to totalitarian rule. The Soviet Union experienced just such state terror on a grand scale during the 1930s. First, in 1930-32, the security police arrested and executed or sent to labor camps large numbers of peasant farmers. Then, in 1936-40, the police arrested millions of members of the Communist Party and their families and subjected them to the same fate as the peasants. These purges crushed any organized opposition to Stalin's personal control of the party, and therefore of the state. Before the 1930s communists discussed and voted on alternative policies. Afterwards, there was only dictatorial rule by Stalin and his inner circle.

Some of the most striking examples of repressive terrorism have occurred in Latin America. During the 1920s, the revolutionary government of Mexico arrested and executed Catholic priests throughout the country. During the 1930s, any priest captured by the authorities in the Mexican state of Tabasco was shot. These policies aimed at wiping out religious institutions, which provided an alternative political power base for conservatives opposed to the revolution.

Repressive terrorism on the part of conservatives dominated Latin American politics during the later 1970s. The excuse for repression during the late 1960s and early 1970s was provided by urban terrorism in Argentina and Uruguay, and the success of leftists in elections in Bolivia, Peru, and Chile. The threat of nationalization of businesses, land reforms, and other social changes provoked a new wave of coups that were followed by repressive military governments.

THE DIRTY WAR

There was, however, a substantial difference between the ideas of the new 1970s Latin American military governments and those of the traditional style of rule by generals. The new military regimes did not even pay lip service to the idea that military rule was a temporary expedient. These new regimes believed that the purpose of military rule was to stay in power as long as necessary to obtain a range of objectives. Their aim was not just to put right inconvenient election results or to reverse a military coup. Rather it was to eradicate the entire basis for left-wing power. This set of ideas was known as the national security ideology. The term refers to the belief that national security was threatened by the spread of revolutionary ideas that ran contrary to the values of western Christian civilization.

When the military seized power in Argentina in 1976, it began the Process of National Reorganization (usually known simply as the Process). This drive was to penetrate the whole of Argentine society, beginning in the schools and universities. Teachers were purged, books burned, political channels closed down, and artists proscribed and driven into exile. A wholesale counterterrror was unleashed on all those thought to be left-wing sympathizers.

Estimates of the number of people who perished in what became known as the "Dirty War" (*la guerra sucia*) fluctuated at the time. However, the figure is now known to be at least 15,000 and almost certainly much more. Many of "the Disappeared," who were rounded up, tortured, and never seen again, were not left-wingers. Friends and relations of subversives were seized merely on suspicion and were also killed. Some children were murdered on the argument that, since

---

KEY FACTS

● Conservative regimes in Latin America in the 1970s employed U.S. military instructors who spread the doctrine that any means of repression was justified to halt the spread of communism.

● It is widely believed that the actual number of people "disappeared" by the Argentine military regime during the Dirty War was more than 15,000.

Workers exhume bodies from unmarked graves in a suburb of Buenos Aires, the Argentine capital, in 1983. The government that succeeded the military regime investigated the disappearance of thousands of people during the military's "Dirty War."

their brothers and sisters were suspects, they in turn would grow up into subversives. The babies of some of "the Disappeared" were taken away from their mothers at birth to be brought up by military families. Other Latin American states whose regimes acted in a similar way at this time included Bolivia, Brazil, Chile, El Salvador, and Guatemala. Amnesty International also has cases from many other countries.

Moreover, these military regimes claimed that any means were justified in countering this left-wing threat. Many Argentine officers who seized power from a democratic government in 1976 believed that World War III had already begun. As General Leopoldo Galtieri, the Argentine president from 1981 to 1983, said: "The First World War was one of armies against armies, the Second World War was one of weapons against weapons, the Third World War is one of ideology against ideology."

RIGHTS AND REPRESSION

The question that now seems most important is why is repressive terrorism used at all. As Frantz Fanon, the French West Indian writer on colonial liberation struggles, recognized, the sustained use of violence, brutality, and torture causes severe psychological damage to the torturer.

The postwar wave of insurgent movements gave rise to extensive literature on counterinsurgency that will influence insurgents of the future. Most counterinsurgency writers stress the importance of civilian control of military operations. They also emphasize the necessity of good intelligence, effective command, appropriate tactics, and the use of advanced technology where available. Ironically, many of these points are equally applicable to the insurgents.

There is a special problem that governments face which insurgents do not. Public support for counterinsurgency is more important to a government than it is to insurgents. Democratic states engaged in counter-insurgency operations have found themselves particularly vulnerable to charges of human rights violations. On the other hand, such states may be equally vulnerable to the gradual withdrawal of public confidence when facing an apparently endless insurgency campaign.

Peter Calvert

SEE ALSO:
STALIN'S GREAT TERROR; URBAN VERSUS RURAL TERRORISM; TERRORISM IN ARGENTINA; TERRORISM IN GUATEMALA; TERRORISM IN PERU; RESPONSES TO TERRORISM IN LATIN AMERICA.

F U R T H E R   R E A D I N G

- Ames, B. *Rhetoric and Reality in a Militarized Regime: Brazil since 1964*. Beverley Hills, CA: Sage Professional, 1973.
- Lopez, George A. "Terrorism in Latin America." In *The Politics of Terrorism*, 3d ed., edited by Michael Stohl. New York: Marcel Dekker, Inc., 1988.
- Tucker, Robert C. *Stalin in Power: The Revolution from Above, 1928-1941*. New York: Norton, 1992.

Campaigns of Decolonization

Few causes make people feel so desperate as the quest to rule themselves in their own country. The 1900s have seen many nationalists who felt passionate enough to turn to terrorism in their desire to be rid of a colonial power. Quite often, the violence has worked and the country has gained its independence, but only after ferocious battles of terrorism and counterterrorism. Africa had a particularly bitter struggle against its various European rulers, but there were vicious campaigns in India, southeast Asia, and parts of Europe, too.

CAMPAIGNS OF DECOLONIZATION:
Introduction

In the aftermath of World War II, a series of bitter wars erupted across the globe. Most were fought between indigenous nationalists and the European colonial powers that had conquered large parts of the world in the nineteenth century. The nationalists strove to rid their countries of European rule. These wars saw the widespread use of terror by both sides. The experiences of these colonies during World War II was the catalyst that triggered these wars of decolonization. In some conflicts, as in Malaya and Indochina, the colonial powers had previously armed the guerrilla terrorists to fight the Japanese who were occupying the two countries during World War II. While many of these conflicts had common features, each had their own distinctive characteristics.

In one exceptional case, however, that of India, terror had been used by nationalists long before World War II. Many Indian soldiers had served with the British army in World War I. The experiences of these indian soldiers dispelled the myth that the European powers were invincible and superior. This realization gave same Indians the strength to challenge British colonial rule. In the 1920s and 1930s, some Indian nationalists, wishing to oust the British colonialists and rule themselves, were prepared to use terror to achieve their aims. Eventually, the burden of governing a huge country like India, when most of the people there wanted independence and the army might mutiny, was too much for Britain to bear.

In other European colonies, it took the events of World War II to make indigenous peoples see that the European empires were shaky. The latter's weakness persuaded many nationalists to make a bid for independence. These nationalists were prepared to use terror since they believed that victory would justify any means they used to attain their end.

The colonial experience itself had also put pressure on some societies. In Kenya, for example, problems of land ownership among the Kikuyu fostered the explosive social conditions that led to Mau Mau terrorism. However, the racism of the white troops maintaining order led to reprisals that fueled the spiral of atrocities.

The most brutal terrorism occurred in countries where the colonial power was determined not to withdraw. Resistance to the nationalists' onslaught was stronger in possessions that had been heavily settled by people from the colonial power. In Algeria, for example, the existence of the *colons*, a large population of white settlers, made a simple French withdrawal impossible. The war in Algeria saw widespread terror used by both sides, and culminated in a bombing campaign by right-wing extremists determined to prevent French withdrawal.

The decolonization struggles were lengthy and vicious. France took eight years to crush the nationalists in Algeria, by which time France was close to civil war. The struggle in Zimbabwe, then called Rhodesia, was prolonged because the country had become an independent state run by white settlers. In Zimbabwe, terrorists led their campaign against a white government that considered itself indigenous, rather than against a foreign European power.

In many decolonization campaigns, the nationalists did not direct terrorism solely at Europeans. Rather, the nationalists also targeted people of the same race as themselves who they suspected of collaborating with the colonial regime. In Malaya and in Portugal's African colonies, the campaigns were rural, targeted at planters and white settlers living in isolated areas.

In Namibia, the terrorism was both urban and rural-based. Although Namibia was not ruled by a European power, South Africa was governing the country as a League of Nations mandate. South Africa defied UN instructions to leave Namibia, leading to a vicious guerrilla war.

The success differed in the various campaigns of decolonization. In Cyprus, terrorism had much impact, but was less influential in Malaya. But all the colonies achieved their independence eventually.

The price of victory, however, was often the sewing of seeds of future conflict, as was the case in 1980s Algeria. Above all, the terrorists that emerged in the 1970s learned much about the practice of terrorism from these struggles. ■

TERRORISM IN FRENCH ALGERIA

The Algerian war of independence, fought by Algerian nationalists of the National Liberation Front (FLN) against the French authorities between 1954 and 1962, saw terrorism employed on a variety of levels. Indeed, it may well be accurate to say that this conflict was dominated by sheer terrorism to a greater degree than any other modern war.

The first major signs of trouble occurred just after World War II. The French had always encouraged their citizens to settle in Algeria. By 1945, ten percent of the population of Algeria were of European descent – the so-called *colons*. The *colons* had a privileged position and would not give it up without a struggle. However, Muslim nationalism, divided into fundamentalist and liberal wings, was also a powerful force.

World War II victory parades in May 1945 brought violence. In the town of Sétif, an Arab crowd overwhelmed and killed 20 French police officers. They went on to kill 103 Europeans, brutalizing their victims. Men's genitals were hacked off and sewn into their mouths; women were raped and their breasts were cut off. Order was swiftly restored. Security forces killed thousands of Muslims while *colons* lynched others. But such acts could not deflect Muslim nationalism.

In the early 1950s, anti-colonial campaigns were taking place worldwide. The French were embroiled in a losing war in Indochina that ended with the spectacular defeat on May 1954 at Dien Bien Phu. In North Africa, there was nationalist discontent in two of

Algeria's neighbors, Morocco and Tunisia (also ruled by France), while in Egypt, the strident nationalist Colonel Gamal Abdel Nasser was proclaiming a new start for the Arab world. In this context, the creation of the FLN in Algeria in October was probably inevitable.

The FLN nationalists planned a series of raids on army installations for November 1, 1954, but these had little effect on French forces who had been expecting an uprising. In order to maintain its control in rural areas, the FLN began using terror on a wide scale. They routinely cut off the lips and nose of anyone suspected of minor crimes and slit the throats of those believed to be collaborating with the French.

SPIRALING VIOLENCE

In April 1955, the nationalists provoked an uprising in the town of Philippeville. Rioters killed and mutilated Europeans, including children. French troops responded by slaughtering Muslims, and a spiral of terror and counterterror began. The nationalist leadership considered the Philippeville massacre a success. In 1956, they decided to launch a terror campaign in Algiers.

The bombing in Algiers was run by Ben M'Hidi and controlled by Saadi Yacef, who used a team of women operatives to plant bombs. Then, in December 1956, FLN terrorists assassinated a well-known conservative politician, Amédée Froger. The discovery of a bomb at the cemetery where his funeral was to take place infuriated Europeans, who rioted against Muslims.

The nationalists were confident early in 1957. With the enforced withdrawal of French and British troops from Egypt after the invasion of the Suez Canal Zone in October, international events seemed to be going their way. Moreover, the United Nations had agreed to debate the situation in Algeria. Ben M'Hidi called a general strike by Muslims in Algiers in January 1957 to show their strength and serious intent.

The French, however, now had their 10th Colonial Parachute Division, under General Jacques Massu, in Algiers. Using the muscle of the paratroopers, the French broke the strike and destroyed the nationalist

---

KEY FACTS

● In 1961-62, the Secret Army Organization (OAS), made up of army deserters, mercenaries, students, and schoolchildren, went on a spree of anti-Muslim attacks in Algeria. They murdered about 1,200 Muslims, French soldiers, and civilians.

● As independence neared, most European settlers left Algeria – of 900,000 settlers in Algeria in 1954, only 30,000 remained by the summer of 1962.

Hulton Getty Picture Collection

network in the casbah, the crowded old quarter of Algiers. The French needed good intelligence to achieve this. A major means of gaining it was through terror and torture, particularly by using electrical equipment and half drowning suspects. Once captives talked, their torturers often threw them from helicopters into the sea. The French captured Ben M'Hidi in February and then announced that he had hanged himself. Whether or not their claim was true, it further cowed the nationalists. By October 1957, there was little terrorist activity in Algiers. The ruthless French methods had secured a key victory.

The French military victory within Algiers was soon mirrored by successful campaigns elsewhere in Algeria. Extensive frontier defenses cut nationalist infiltration from Tunisia and Morocco, while attacks on rural guerrillas showed impressive results.

The Algerian conflict was a source of anxiety in France. Politicians agonized about the morality of the war, especially over the tactics used against the terrorists in the battle of Algiers in 1957. For their part, the

Female Algerian rebels undergo weapons training in a camp in Tunisia in the late 1950s.

Algerian nationalists were often divided, but they knew how to influence world opinion.

The French politicians soon had another problem. In 1958, the Europeans in Algeria feared that politicians in Paris were seriously considering Algerian independence. The constitution of the Fourth Republic was overthrown, bringing an end to short and unstable governments. In its place, war hero Charles de Gaulle was installed as president with sweeping powers.

DE GAULLE AND ALGERIAN INDEPENDENCE

De Gaulle was seen as a strong leader who would prosecute the war against the nationalists with vigor. But within two years it was clear that his vision of the future did not include Algeria as a French province. He believed that France's world role lay in leading a loose federation of former colonies, and that old-style

Hulton Getty Picture Collection

imperialism was finished in the modern world. He announced Algeria's right to self-determination in September 1959. The Algerian *colons* attempted a coup in January 1960. French commander-in-chief General Challe's lukewarm response to putting down this insurrection lost him the confidence of the president. De Gaulle recalled him from his post in Algiers.

De Gaulle's policy was unpopular with others besides the Europeans in Algeria. It also angered many soldiers who had given their all in the fight against the nationalists. Four generals – Challe, Salan, Jouhaud, and Zeller – attempted another coup in April 1961. When it failed, the opponents of de Gaulle's policy were left with few options. Some of them chose terrorism. The Secret Army Organization (OAS) took up arms, planting bombs in Algiers and in France, killing Muslims, and attempting to assassinate de Gaulle.

A timetable for independence was agreed at Evian, eastern France, in March 1962, and a cease-fire was proclaimed. Independence was, for many Algerians, merely the start of terror, however. The nationalists had been split into many factions during the long war. There were two major divisions: first between those who had stayed in Algeria (the internals) and those who had gone abroad (the externals); and second between the political and the army leaderships. Old scores could be settled in the aftermath of victory, often disguised as punishment for traitorous behavior.

French paratroopers, carrying submachine guns, challenge Islamic demonstrators in Algiers in 1960.

There was an immediate and savage backlash against those who had helped the French. Individuals were tortured and killed. In many cases their families also suffered, as did whole villages. The lingering unease afflicting the country led to the Islamic fundamentalist uprising in the 1990s, which was in many ways a continuation of this earlier struggle.

Ashley Brown

SEE ALSO:
TERROR AGAINST THE FRENCH IN INDOCHINA; ISLAMIC FUNDAMENTALISM AND TERRORISM IN ALGERIA; THE FRENCH RESPONSE TO TERRORISM.

F U R T H E R   R E A D I N G

- Crenshaw, Martha. *Revolutionary Terrorism: The FLN in Algeria, 1954-62.* Stanford, CA: Hoover Institution Press, 1978.
- Horne, Alistair. *Savage War of Peace: Algeria, 1954-1962.* New York: Viking, 1978.
- Lacouture, Jean. *De Gaulle: The Ruler, 1945-1970.* New York: W. W. Norton, 1991.

TERRORISM IN CYPRUS

On April 1, 1955, pamphlets proclaimed the existence of the National Organization of Cypriot Fighters, usually known by the acronym EOKA. The pamphlets were written by a Greek Cypriot nationalist, George Grivas, a retired colonel in the Greek army. Along with many Greek Cypriots, Grivas wanted *enosis*, or union with Greece, for Cyprus. He formed EOKA with the aim of bringing about the end of British rule of the island so that such a union would be possible. He was prepared to use terrorism to get his way.

Greek Cypriots made up about four-fifths of the population of Cyprus, and Turkish Cypriots accounted for most of the remainder. This Turkish minority, whose relations with the Greek Cypriots were shaky, was alarmed by the calls for union with Greece. Britain, which had administered the island since 1878, refused to give up control because it wanted to retain Cyprus as a strategic asset in the Mediterranean. The British also wanted to protect the Turkish Cypriots from the wave of Greek Cypriot nationalism.

In 1954, Greece had tried and failed to persuade the UN to take up the case for Cyprus's self-determination. The Greek Cypriots responded by demonstrating in the Cypriot capital, Nicosia, in December. Then, on April 1, 1955, the same day it issued its pamphlets, EOKA

Principal towns in Cyprus, and the locations of major EOKA terrorist attacks.

began its terrorist campaign. Using explosives stolen from the British army and weapons smuggled from Greece, EOKA bombed British government offices in Cyprus and murdered British subjects and Cypriots. Attacks often took place in broad daylight, killing women, children, and members of the clergy.

EOKA'S CAMPAIGN OF VIOLENCE

On May 24, Empire Day, EOKA tried to kill the governor of Cyprus, Sir Robert Armitage, by bombing a movie house he was attending. The explosives, stuffed into a soft drink bottle, blew up, wrecking several rows of seats, but not until after Sir Robert had left.

By November, the situation was so serious that the British declared a state of emergency on Cyprus. Firm retaliatory measures were taken against the Greek Cypriot community, such as levying collective fines on villages, imposing curfews, and introducing the death penalty. The armed forces imposed a blockade to prevent further arms shipments. Remarkably, though, sympathizers could still get weapons to the island in the mail, which was not searched.

On November 26, the day the emergency was declared, EOKA terrorists hurled a grenade into the ballroom of the Ledra Palace Hotel in Nicosia, where a

KEY FACTS

● In its terrorist campaign from 1954 to 1958, EOKA exploded 1,782 bombs, causing damage in the millions of dollars.

● The EOKA campaign cost the lives of at least 104 soldiers, 50 police, 238 civilians, and 90 EOKA operatives.

● Colonel George Grivas, the EOKA leader, used the *nom de guerre* Dighenis during the Cyprus campaign. On his return to Greece afterward, Grivas was rewarded for his efforts with promotion to lieutenant general.

Popperfoto

Colonel George Grivas (third from right), also known as Dighenis, with a band of EOKA gunmen.

large party of Scottish people were celebrating St. Andrew's Day. Four British were wounded, including the wife of the British police commissioner.

No fewer than 21 terrorist shootings and bombings took place in Nicosia from November 1955 to March 1956. On March 3, 1956, 68 air passengers – serving soldiers and their families – had a narrow escape when terrorists planted a timebomb on a Hermes aircraft. The bomb destroyed the plane before the passengers were aboard, the flight having been delayed.

Also in March 1956, the British authorities deported Archbishop Makarios III, the political head of the Greek Cypriot movement for union with Greece. Makarios refused to condemn EOKA's use of violence, and the authorities suspected him of having close links

with the terrorists. However, his exile to the Seychelles Islands, in the Indian Ocean, was a cue for rioting among the Greek Cypriots, with much of the violence directed against Turkish Cypriots. A third major incident in March 1956 was an attempt on the life of the new governor of the island, Sir John Harding. On the 22nd, an EOKA terrorist placed a bomb in the governor's bed. He set the device to go off in the early morning at a temperature of 67 degrees Fahrenheit. However, it failed to go off, since the bomber had not taken into account the drop in nighttime temperature and the habit of many people, Sir John apparently among them, of sleeping with the windows open.

EOKA divided its military campaign into rural and urban theaters. EOKA's fighting force was small – a few hundred activists against a British garrison of 25,000. Mountain groups of five to fifteen men engaged in guerrilla warfare in the Troodos mountains, ambushing military patrols and raiding remote police posts.

Popperfoto

Greek Cypriot Nikos Sampson (right) at the Nicosia courthouse on 25 April, 1957, where he was accused in connection with murders of Britons in Nicosia.

Meanwhile, five-man groups carried out urban terrorist attacks, including street shootings, arson attacks, and bombings. For example, in April 1956, terrorists killed a senior policeman visiting his wife and newborn son at a maternity clinic. On June 16, EOKA bombed a restaurant, mistakenly killing the U.S. vice consul.

During so-called Black November, in 1956, there were 416 terrorist incidents in which more than 35 people died. Even British civilians who had been living in Cyprus for many years were not safe. That month, terrorists killed a certain Dr. Bevan in the sick bay of the Amiandos Mining Company. As the doctor examined a patient, the latter's "escort" shot him dead.

By now, though, the British army had curtailed EOKA's mountain activities, and Greek Cypriots loyal to the authorities had infiltrated the organization. Being a British agent was a risky business, since EOKA dealt ruthlessly with anyone considered a traitor. The usual penalty was death, often at the hands of shotgun squads of village sympathizers. As a result, Grivas was forced temporarily to suspend terrorist activities.

The terror was far from over, however. In the first ten days of April 1957, EOKA exploded 50 bombs, and on May 4, terrorists assassinated two British soldiers. Then, on November 26, 1957, EOKA destroyed a Royal Air Force Canberra bomber on the ground at Akrotiri airbase. Ten months later, the organization attempted to assassinate Major-General D. A. Kendrew, military commander of the Cyprus district. Other less spectacular but no less appalling attacks also took place. In October 1958, EOKA murdered the wife of a British serviceman while she was shopping in Varosha. This incident so outraged army personnel that in the following round-up, hundreds of Cypriots were badly beaten and two died, although one British soldier also died.

PARTITION OR DEATH

Much of the violence after 1957 was intercommunal, and the situation approached civil war. However, a political solution was in sight. The Greek Cypriots, at the start of the campaign, would settle for nothing less than union with Greece. As has been mentioned, this was unacceptable to Turkish Cypriots, and to Turkey. When Britain released Archbishop Makarios from detention in the Seychelles in March 1957, Turkey interpreted it as a step toward *enosis* and called for Cyprus to be partitioned into Greek and Turkish zones under the slogan "Partition or Death." Eventually, though, all parties eased their demands and agreed to independence for Cyprus without either union with Greece or partition. EOKA halted operations on December 31, 1958, and Makarios became president of the republic of Cyprus on December 14, 1959.

Chris Marshall

SEE ALSO:

TERRORISM IN FRENCH ALGERIA; TERRORISM IN COLONIAL INDIA 1900-1947; TERROR AGAINST THE FRENCH IN INDOCHINA; TERRORISM IN MALAYA; TERRORISM IN KENYA; NATIONALIST TERRORISM; BRITISH COUNTERTERROR IN THE ERA OF DECOLONIZATION.

FURTHER READING

- Dewar, Michael. *Brush Fire Wars: Minor Campaigns of the British Army since 1945.* New York: St. Martin's Press, 1984.
- Foley, Charles, and W. I. Scobie. *The Struggle for Cyprus.* Stanford, CA: Hoover Institution Press, 1976.
- Markides, K. *The Rise and Fall of the Cyprus Republic.* New Haven, CT: Yale University Press, 1977.

TERRORISM IN GREECE

Before World War II most members of the Greek Communist Party (KKE) had been exiled or imprisoned by the Metaxas dictatorship. However, from the 1941 German invasion of Greece until 1949, the KKE used terrorism in attempts first to control the resistance to German occupation and then forcibly to seize power.

During the 1941-44 German occupation of Greece, the KKE developed a guerrilla front organization, the People's National Army of Liberation (ELAS). The KKE used ELAS to control the population and destroy other resistance movements, while avoiding direct fighting with the Germans. The KKE launched another attempt to take power in 1946. Its armed wing, now renamed the Democratic Army (DA), fought a terrorist campaign against the Greek state until 1949.

THE PATH OF TERRORISM

The KKE first employed terrorism during 1942-44 to subdue the countryside and secure local support for ELAS. This terrorism involved executions, imprisonment, and torture under the pretext of punishing collaboration with the German forces. In 1944, ELAS undertook widespread terrorism in the Peloponnese, in southern Greece. However, these KKE/ELAS atrocities merely drove many locals to join German-armed security battalions to combat ELAS, thus creating a state of virtual civil war.

From mid-1944, with liberation approaching, the KKE launched a terrorist campaign in occupied Athens to eliminate the non-communist resistance. The party also tried to subvert the power of the police so that it would be able to occupy Athens as soon as the Germans left. The Athens police had managed, despite the occupation, not to collaborate with the Germans, and was an organized, disciplined, armed force that the communists could not infiltrate.

The KKE terrorist organizations in the Athens area were the Organization for the Protection of the People's Struggle (OPLA), the People's National Guard (EP), and the Guardforce. In late 1944, these three organizations eliminated many political opponents. OPLA maintained its grip on large parts of Athens after the German withdrawal. When the KKE attempted to take power in December 1944, OPLA conducted a purge in which at least 5,000 people perished.

However, the defeat of the KKE/ELAS in Athens in early January 1945 forced ELAS to retreat to central Greece. As ELAS retreated, it took several thousand hostages with it, many of whom died during forced marches. The hostages became bargaining chips for the KKE in the subsequent peace negotiations.

Despite the January 1945 Varkiza agreement, which ended the fighting, communist terrorism continued. Until March 1946 this terrorism was aimed mainly at countering retaliation by anti-communist armed groups. In the Peloponnese, for example, right-wing groups attacked ELAS bands.

UNDERGROUND FORCE

During 1945, the KKE created Aftoamyna (Self-defense), an underground communist network of small cells. Its task was to organize intelligence collection against the Greek government, to harass the state with terrorism, and to provide the KKE with an escape and recruitment network. Aftoamyna terrorism took the form of kidnapping, assassinations, bombing of urban centers, and the destruction of communications.

After the resumption of full-scale civil war in March 1946, there were increased numbers of communist terrorist attacks on prominent community figures, such as mayors, teachers, and local administrators. In

---

KEY FACTS

● At their peak, the communists had 25,000 fighters in the field and 50,000 active supporters.

● Troops attacked a major communist base on Mount Grammos in 1948-49, and killed 9,000 terrorists. After this action rural terrorism declined dramatically across Greece.

Associated Press

Some of the 50 civilians and 40 troops killed by 600 ELAS terrrorists near Mount Paikon, Macedonia.

this way Aftoamyna imposed a climate of fear that helped the KKE to control the rural population. In many areas Aftoamyna destroyed the structures of traditional Greek society by the intensive use of terror.

FOREIGN ASSISTANCE

After 1947, the Greek army was able to deal with communist forces by using American aid. The major communist weakness was their reliance on aid from the communist regimes of Yugoslavia, Bulgaria, and Albania. This support made many Greeks suspicious of the KKE's motives, and it led to a disaster when the regimes withdrew support in 1948-9 for reasons connected with relations within the communist bloc.

In the Peloponnese, Aftoamyna proved very resistant. However, in late 1948, the Greek army isolated the area from the mainland and destroyed Aftoamyna by arresting 4,300 suspects in one night.

The police had dismantled the Aftoamyna apparatus in Athens in 1946-47. The remaining Aftoamyna cells were captured during 1950-53. About 8,000 terrorists escaped to Albania, and the army caught any that tried to return to Greece near the border. Many captured terrorists informed on the few remaining cells.

Ashley Brown

SEE ALSO:

WWII RESISTANCE IN YUGOSLAVIA AND TERRORISM; GUERRILLAS AND TERROR.

F U R T H E R   R E A D I N G

- Averoff-Tossizza, E. *By Fire and Axe: The Communist Party and the Civil War in Greece, 1944-49.* New Rochelle, NY: Caratzas Brothers, 1978.
- O'Ballance, Edgar. *The Greek Civil War, 1944-1949.* New York: Praeger, 1966.
- Stavrakis, Peter J. *Moscow and Greek Communism, 1944-1949.* Ithaca, NY: Cornell University Press, 1989.

TERROR IN COLONIAL INDIA 1900-1947

The use of political violence was a distinctive feature of politics in Bengal in British colonial India during the first half of the twentieth century. The intermittent terrorist campaign in Bengal, northeast India, which periodically spilled over into other provinces, posed a serious threat to the British regime, known as the Raj.

In the early 1900s, the local British administration in Bengal was challenged by the growth of a politically motivated extremist revolutionary movement. Its objective was the establishment of Indian self-government, or *swaraj*. Brothers Barin and Aurobindo Ghose were the two principal advocates of violence. They filled newspaper columns with calls for revolutionary action and distributed pamphlets that glorified revolution as a religious duty.

THE RISE OF SECRET SOCIETIES

The propaganda aroused an enthusiastic response from the more prosperous and intellectual sections of the population. Terrorist activity gathered strength after the partition of Bengal in 1907, which was unpopular with the educationally and politically westernized Hindu elite, or *bhadlarok*. Terrorist secret societies, or *samitis*, were founded. These societies were composed of young, idealistic *bhadlarok* students, eager to redress their perceived grievances

KEY FACTS

● From 1905 to 1915, Indian nationalism was expressed through violence and boycotts of British goods.

● In 1942, violent riots and protests spread across India as nationalist leaders were arrested by the British authorities.

● Terrorism continued after India was granted independence. Pacifist nationalist leader Mohandas Gandhi was assassinated in 1948 and thousands killed in sectarian violence.

by force of arms. The two main groups were the Jugantar and Anushilan *samitis*.

Both of these groups resorted to terrorist tactics such as beatings and killings, together with armed robberies known as *dacoities*. The objective was to publicize the existence of the *samitis* and their aims and to collect funds to buy arms and ammunition. Terror was achieved by inflicting casualties on British police, civil officials, and Indian staff in the government. The societies encouraged mass riots, such as those that occurred throughout 1908 and early 1909. The riots were intended to gain public support and lead to nationwide armed rebellion against British rule.

Indian revolutionary groups were even active in north London, U.K. In 1908, for example, the Free India Society acquired a Russian handbook on bomb manufacturing that had been translated for them by a Russian student. The handbook was then sent to India.

BRITISH COUNTERTERRORISM

The initial British response to Bengali terrorism was hesitant, but the amateurish nature of the terror campaign meant that the police were able to seize the leaders of the *samitis* with ease.

Later British action was more decisive. In 1907-08, the British authorities imposed strict censorship of the local press, banned secret societies, and extended the activities of the secret police. The government also authorized imprisonment without trial for certain political offenses. The measures were needed because it was proving difficult to convict terrorists since witnesses and juries were often intimidated. During these security operations by the British security forces, 205 people were convicted.

A brief lull in terrorist activities occurred after the leaders of the *samitis* were arrested in 1908 and 1909. However, on December 23, 1912, *samitis* members tried to assassinate British Viceroy Lord Hardinge in the capital Delhi. Although the attempt failed, it encouraged further attacks on officials and more *dacoities* as public support for the nationalists gradually increased.

The bodies of several policemen who died when terrorists burned down their station and threw them into the fire at Chauri Chaura in 1921.

British opinion was divided on how best to counter this round of terrorism in Bengal. Governor Lord Carmichael favored a conciliatory approach that would secure *bhadlarok* support against the violence. But the Raj took a far firmer line: it pursued a policy of vigorous repression. By 1914, the terrorist violence in Bengal was regarded by the British authorities as "a well-developed criminal conspiracy aimed at the destruction of British rule."

THE GOVERNMENT TAKES A HARSH LINE

During World War I, the British administration took even stronger measures to maintain law and order. However, this did not stop a renewed outbreak of terrorism in Bengal during 1915-16. In addition,

evidence was uncovered that Indian terrorists were attempting to secure German support.

Improved police intelligence was highly effective and, by 1917, the terrorist campaign had almost completely broken down. The introduction of preventive arrest meant that all of the main terrorists were in prison. Those still at large were so demoralized and disorganized that their activity ceased almost entirely.

PEACEFUL NONCOOPERATION

One outcome of the unrest and terrorism was a promise from the British authorities to set in place constitutional reforms. But instead, the British government extended the emergency repression powers into peacetime. As a result, Bengali opposition to the Raj grew widespread in India.

Opposition to British rule immediately after World War I came mainly from the moderate noncooperation movement. The call for independence was led by the Indian National Congress (Congress), a legal political

Sir John Anderson, a counterinsurgency expert, was appointed Governor of Bengal in 1932.

party. This was inspired by the Indian lawyer Mohandas Gandhi and was committed to nonviolent protest and civil disobedience. As most leaders of the *samitis* were still in prison, terrorist activity in Bengal was suspended. In the meantime, this allowed the effectiveness of Gandhi's strategy to be tested, while the shattered *samitis* recovered their strength.

But the rate of progress of this policy of noncooperation was far too slow for an Indian population impatient for change. So when the detainees were released by a royal pardon in 1920, new terrorist groups modeled on the *samitis* of the prewar period sprang up. There were riots in Madras, Bombay, and Chauri Chaura, where 22 police officers were burnt and killed in February, 1921. Exactly a year later, the Congress suspended the noncooperation campaign.

A second terrorist campaign in Bengal began. Jugantar gangs carried out a series of assassinations and *dacoities* in the name of the Congress, demonstrating that radical factions within the party remained firmly committed to violence. At the same time, under the leadership of the 26-year-old socialist Subhas Chandra Bose, the Bengal branch of Congress was influenced by supporters of political violence.

In 1924, there were further attacks on European administrators and police officers. In response, the authorities introduced new emergency legislation in October 1925. The laws allowed them to arrest suspected terrorists and to try them before special tribunals without right of appeal. The prompt arrest of all prominent terrorist leaders achieved immediate results. Over 180 suspects were imprisoned by 1927, quashing the movement before it became widespread.

Order was quickly restored once again and, at the end of 1927, the imperial authorities released all detainees. During their time in prison, however, Jugantar and Anushilan terrorists had discussed new methods of terrorism. More importantly, a logical justification for the use of force had been developed. These ideas were based on those which had been used by the Irish Republican Army (IRA) in Ireland.

Terrorism in Bengal resumed dramatically on April 18, 1930, when 100 terrorists, calling themselves the Indian Republican Army, raided the Police and Auxiliary Force armories in Chittagong, today in Bangladesh. They killed several soldiers, seized 60 rifles and 22 revolvers, and destroyed the telephone exchange, telegraph office, and rail lines. The terrorists then attacked the local European club, but it was empty and they were unable to massacre its members. The size and military organization of the raid, along with the discipline and training of the raiders, shook the British community. On April 22, a brief engagement occurred between troops and the gang in the Jalalabad hills, after which the terrorists returned to forms of violence familiar from the *samitis* activities.

Terrorist activity mounted steadily during the early 1930s. Actions included the assassination of several British and Indian police, and government officials and staff. Female terrorists took an active part in the campaign for the first time and were involved in several attacks, including the attempted assassination of Governor Sir Stanley Jackson in February 1932.

EMERGENCY LEGISLATION

The existing penal code and emergency provisions proved to be insufficient as the violence spread and became more organized. In response, the government introduced a number of new laws. The colonial police were given sweeping powers to stop and search all suspects, impose dawn-to-dusk curfews, and intercept mail. In areas of unrest, district magistrates could confiscate personal property, regulate travel and the movement of goods, and restrict access to certain areas. Heavy fines were imposed on anyone who flouted these new regulations. At the same time, police punishment squads were deployed in villages to prevent the spread of disorder.

Anyone with the slightest suspicion of links to terrorists was rounded up and taken into custody. The authorities hoped that these measures would curtail terrorist activity, but they only produced further political difficulties as the Indian public resented the restrictions put on daily life. In addition, the detention camps became a focus of anti-government feeling and a breeding ground for discontent.

Despite these sweeping measures, fear of insurrection was rife in the British community in Bengal. In 1932, military intelligence officers and seven battalions of regular troops were deployed as backup to the civilian police. Perhaps of greater significance was the appointment of Sir John Anderson as the new governor of Bengal. He was a civil servant with extensive experience of counterinsurgency tactics in Ireland, and his appointment restored police morale.

It was Anderson who recognized that a political solution, hand in hand with repressive measures, was the only way forward. He told the local legislative council: "It is not enough to meet force by force or to answer lawlessness by asserting the majesty and power of the law. An atmosphere must be created in which the seeds of disorder will not germinate."

THE DEFEAT OF INSURGENCY

Following several defeats by government forces in the Jalalabad hills, terrorist groups were forced to revert to isolated robberies and assassinations. In addition, improved police intelligence on terrorist activity and better targeting of searches gradually produced results for the authorities. All known or suspected revolutionaries were detained or watched and all sources of new recruitment were blocked.

Terrorist actions declined by 90 percent during 1932-34. By 1936, the imperial authorities declared the insurgency defeated. The cost was estimated at millions of pounds, and the credibility of the British government had been seriously challenged.

The 1930-36 terrorist campaign made it clear to the Indian revolutionaries in Bengal that isolated acts of violence, while seizing the headlines, would not dislodge the Raj. When the terrorist detainees were released from captivity in 1937-38, both the Jugantar and Anushilan groups disbanded. Terrorism in Bengal never again assumed the same dimensions.

During World War II, the Indian National Congress and the noncooperation movements posed a far more serious threat to the Raj than terrorism, which was conspicuous by its absence. In 1942, Congress began the Quit India movement, which absorbed the few remaining Bengali terrorists into the general resistance to British rule. The movement disrupted rail communications and made the United Provinces, Bihar, Bengal, and elsewhere virtually ungovernable.

At the height of the Quit India movement, the British position in India was endangered seriously enough for the British government to deploy 57 infantry battalions to maintain a semblance of order. This was despite the Japanese threat in neighboring Burma, where manpower was most urgently needed.

Terrorist activity against the Raj finally ended when independence was granted to India by the British government in August 1947. But the struggle to achieve independence left the new state with a legacy of political violence in Bengal. Terrorism between the Hindu and Muslim communities cost tens of thousands of lives in the following decade.

Tim Moreman

SEE ALSO:

TERROR IN COLONIAL CONQUESTS; THE AMRITSAR MASSACRE; TERRORISM IN MALAYA; TERRORISM IN KENYA.

FURTHER READING

- Broomfield, J. H. *Elite Conflict in a Plural Society: Twentieth-Century Bengal.* Berkeley, CA: University of California Press, 1968.
- Brown, Judith M. *Gandhi: Prisoner of Hope.* New Haven, NJ: Yale University Press, 1989.
- Pandey, B. N. *The Break-Up of British India.* New York: St. Martin's Press, 1969.
- Parekh, B. "Gandhi's Theory of Non-Violence: His Reply to the Terrorists." In *Terrorism, Ideology, and Revolution*, edited by Noel O'Sullivan. Boulder, CO: Westview Press, 1986.

TERROR AGAINST THE FRENCH IN INDOCHINA

Indochina is the former name of the region containing the three modern states of Vietnam, Cambodia, and Laos. During the 1940s and 1950s, communists in the area that is now Vietnam fought a long war against the region's French colonial regime. Terror was an important part of the communists' strategy in this war. They used it to extend their control over the local population. Terrorism also kept the French security forces fully occupied while the communists prepared for a decisive military victory. The strategy paid off, and victory came in 1954, when the Vietnamese communists defeated the French at Dien Bien Phu.

Vietnam had been under French rule since the late nineteenth century. But when Germany defeated France in 1940 the Japanese seized control. The takeover was a blow to France's prestige in Southeast Asia and gave Vietnamese nationalist activists a chance to make their mark. The Chinese and the U.S.-armed nationalist groups in north Vietnam acted as guerrillas against the Japanese. One leader, Ho Chi Minh, set up an efficient guerrilla network, with Vo Nguyen Giap as military commander. By mid-1945, there were more than 1,000 fighters under Giap's command. This force was called the Vietminh and had its stronghold in the mountainous Viet Bac provinces.

When the Japanese surrendered in September 1945, the guerrillas in northern Vietnam were able to come out into the open. Nationalist Chinese troops moved down to occupy the northern capital, Hanoi, and the guerrillas set up a provisional government. They also extended their influence into all aspects of village life. More than 80 percent of Vietnamese lived in villages, and the Vietminh set up committees, together with other nationalist groups, run by what was ostensibly a multiparty League for National Salvation.

In the south of Vietnam, French administration was reestablished with British help, after a short struggle with the nationalists. There were negotiations between the Vietminh and the French. But Vietminh operations continued. Under the strain of such activities, the talks eventually broke down, and the French made a successful assault that took them into Hanoi.

TAKING OVER THE COUNTRYSIDE

Although the French controlled the cities, the Vietminh had established themselves thoroughly in the countryside and were almost impossible to root out. To gain control of the villages, the Vietminh not only appealed to inhabitants' sense of nationalism but also spread terror. The Vietminh murdered many village elders and officials of the French administration. In this way the Vietminh broke down the already weak links between the villages and the French administration in the cities.

The Vietminh severely punished villages that failed to cooperate fully – they killed village elders and randomly selected peasants for torture and death. Occasionally the terrorists burned down entire villages. Through this terror, the Vietminh compelled each village in their power to provide five people to prepare for operations against the French, while another 12 were to be ready for armed action.

Within a relatively short period, the Vietminh had made much of the countryside a hostile area for the French. At the lowest level was a peasant militia. Although poorly armed, it is estimated that by the early

KEY FACTS

● The Vietminh created a climate of fear to force the people of the countryside into submission.

● They executed villagers, left their mutilated bodies for all to see, and burned their houses.

● To intimidate the populace, the Vietminh blew up Saigon's pyrotechnics factory in April 1946, killing its 40 Vietnamese workers.

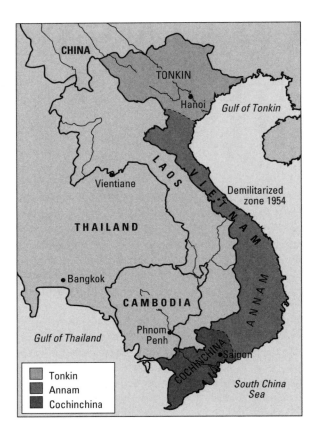

Tonkin and Cochinchina in what is now Vietnam bore the brunt of terrorism in the 1940s and 1950s.

1950s there may have been up to 75,000 Vietnamese organized into what Giap called his "Regional Forces." These troops were capable of setting booby traps, taking pot shots at French forces at night in fortified buildings called blockhouses, or planting a bomb in a restaurant in Hanoi or Saigon.

The French struggled to combat the Vietminh rural takeover partly because their forces were not committed to the kind of "hearts and minds" operations that would have won back villagers' allegiance.

The French failed to offer a clear vision to the Vietnamese of what to expect if the Vietminh were defeated and were unwilling to allow other nationalist groups to present themselves as a credible alternative. The leaders of such groups were, in any case, the target of a successful Vietminh assassination campaign, which effectively neutralized all other nationalist opposition.

In Cochinchina, the Vietminh were organized by Nguyen Binh. He undertook a terror campaign around Saigon that extended to bombs in factories and French enterprises in the city. When the French established a national Vietnamese government of Cochinchina in Saigon in 1949, Binh immediately reacted. He sent terrorists into Saigon, to undertake assassinations and bombings, while the Vietminh radio issued lists of "traitors" to be eliminated. The French security police managed to block this offensive, but were forced to adopt terror methods. They used informers and ruthless interrogation to strike terrorists. They also left the mutilated bodies of Vietminh activists in the streets to serve as a warning to other members.

The French had some success in more regular warfare against the Vietminh, inflicting heavy casualties on the nationalists in the Red River Delta in 1951. However, the French authorities could not offer security to the terrorized rural population in the delta. The only sections of Vietnamese society that could resist Vietminh incursion were certain religious sects (one, for example, worshiped both Karl Marx and Victor Hugo as saints). These sects were strong enough to be impervious to Vietminh terror tactics.

Vietminh control of the countryside was so effective that the French forces were spread very thinly. By 1953, they maintained only a vestige of power, while the communists created a large, well-equipped military force. The French's increasing failure to control the countryside led them to take on regular Vietminh forces at Dien Bien Phu, an attack which ended with a crushing French defeat. Thus, terror played a critical part in the downfall of a colonial regime.

Ashley Brown

SEE ALSO:

NATIONAL LIBERATION WARS AND TERROR; TERRORISM IN FRENCH ALGERIA; TERROR IN THE VIETNAM WAR.

FURTHER READING

- Andrade, D. *Ashes to Ashes: The Phoenix Program and the Vietnam War.* Lexington, MA: Lexington Books, 1990.
- Fall, Bernard. *Street Without Joy: Indochina at War 1946-54.* Harrisburg, PA: Stackpole, 1961.
- Maclear, Michael. *The Ten Thousand Day War.* New York: St. Martin's Press, 1981.

TERRORISM IN MALAYA

In response to a rising wave of terrorism by guerrillas of the Malayan Communist Party (MCP), the British colonial government in Malaya declared a state of emergency in June 1948. It lasted until 1960. Emergency regulations allowed for detention, deportation, and even death for insurgency-related offenses.

The communist guerrillas, organzied after the Japanese invasion of 1941, were drawn largely from Malaya's Chinese community. The British encouraged the MCP during the war, sending in arms, supplies, and advisors until it fielded some 7,000 guerrillas. Led by the tactician Chin Peng, the MCP scored some successes over the invaders.

SETTING UP A TERRORIST WING

After the war, however, the MCP aimed to overthrow the colonial government and set up a communist regime in Malaya. The organization infiltrated labor unions and attempted a Soviet-style revolution through strikes and protests, some violent. In 1948, it accepted that the tactic had failed and launched an armed revolt.

The MCP's military wing was originally called the Malayan People's Anti-British Army. It was renamed the Malayan Races' Liberation Army (MRLA) in 1949 in order to appeal to the non-Chinese majority populace.

In May 1948, Chin Peng mobilized eight regiments using weapons saved from the war. Guerrillas ambushed civilian and military buses, trains, and trucks. They murdered government supporters and informers, abducted businessmen, and extorted bribes. On June 29, terrorists shot up Jerantut township, 20 miles from Kuala Krau, burned down the police station and took Chinese and Malay prisoners.

In the meantime, communist cells on British-owned rubber plantations and in tin mines orchestrated strikes and takeovers. On July 12, communist terrorists attacked the police post at Batu Arang, Malaya's only coal mine, overwhelming the occupants and cutting the telephone wires. The terrorists managed to sabotage machinery before colonial police reinforcements could get to the mine. In response to the agitation and violence, the government banned the MCP.

Although there was substantial support for the insurgency among the Chinese community in Malaya, there was nothing like the general popular uprising that had been predicted by the communist leadership. This disappointment, coupled with the strong response of the colonial police and army, forced the MRLA into the jungle, where they established bases near weapons stashes. The bases were often located near Chinese settlements so that the MRLA could obtain supplies and information from a network of supporters known as Min Yuen.

NEW TERRORIST ATTACKS

Malaya was comparatively calm during the guerrilla reorganization, but by the end of 1949, the terrorists were back in business. The terrorists mostly attacked village police posts, but towns and farming estates were also raided. Attacks were often large-scale. On September 11, a force of 300 communist terrorists raided the town of Kuala Krau, killing four police officers, two British railway engineers, and two Malayan women. The following month, 200 terrorists struck at an isolated rubber plantation in Pahang, setting fire to several buildings.

By early 1950, the MRLA communists had built an organization capable of protracted warfare. They had a hierarchy of military-type units that ranged from terror and sabotage sections in populated areas to village

---

KEY FACTS

● The insurgency resulted in the deaths of 11,000 people, of whom 2,500 were civilians.

● In 1948, about 3,000 full-time and 7,000 part-time communist MRLA guerrillas began making terror attacks against targets throughout Malaya.

● The number of terrorist incidents per month was about 200 in 1948. It dropped to 100 a month in 1949, while the MRLA regrouped.

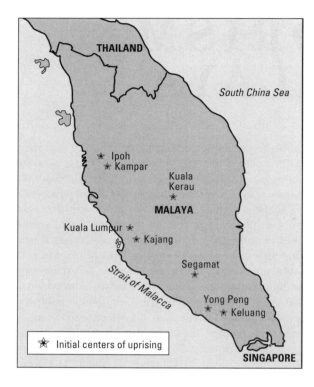

Malaya, scene of a 12-year insurgency campaign.

THAILAND

South China Sea

★ Ipoh
★ Kampar

Kuala Kerau
★

MALAYA

Kuala Lumpur ★
★ Kajang

Strait of Malacca

Segamat
★

Yong Peng
★ ★ Keluang

SINGAPORE

★ Initial centers of uprising

guerrilla units, up to regular units. Food supplies and intelligence were provided by the political organization and the Min Yuen, so military camps in the jungle had to be within a few hours' walking distance of populated areas. Communication between the settlements and the jungle camps was a weak link.

The guerrillas increased their activity until incidents were occurring at the rate of 400 a month – twice their 1948 rate. The terrorists singled out the British planters and their families for particular attention. One family had to withstand no less than 25 terrorist attacks on their plantation in a two-week period in 1951, including three in one night.

The terrorists also took to machine-gunning the "New Villages," set up by Lieutenant General Sir Harold Briggs, the British director of operations in Malaya. Briggs's plan was to separate the MRLA from its supporters in the community, so he resettled the Chinese into newly constructed villages away from the old settlements. Here, housing and sanitary conditions were far superior than in the old shanties and many Chinese welcomed the change. Briggs also imposed

strict allocations of rice. There was little left over to pass to the MRLA, so the terrorists were forced into the open to find food. At the same time, the British army, including the Special Air Service, was getting used to finding and dealing with the terrorists.

By late 1951, the terrorists had been forced to come up with a new strategy. They split their large military units into smaller groups and withdrew deeper into the jungle to rest and retrain.

AMBUSH AND ASSASSINATION

Nonetheless, terrorist incidents continued to take place. In fact, on October 6, 1951, the terrorists pulled off their most notorious operation of the campaign – the assassination of the British high commissioner, Sir Henry Gurney. The terrorists ambushed Sir Henry on the road to Fraser's Hill, a rest station where British officers and officials could get away from the heat and humidity of the Malayan plains. The road was steep and winding for the last 20 miles to the station and was bordered by thick jungle and, in some places, high cliffs. The heavily armed terrorist force chose a 200-yard section of this part of the road as their killing zone and settled down to wait.

At about lunchtime, some 27 hours after the ambush was set, Sir Henry's motorcade came in sight. When it left the capital, Kuala Lumpur, the convoy had consisted of an armored car, a radio vehicle, an unarmored Landrover, and the high commissioner's Rolls-Royce. Unfortunately, the radio truck had broken down en route and the armored car had stopped to help, leaving the limousine only lightly guarded.

As the convoy reached the ambush site, the terrorists opened fire, making short work of the escort before turning their attention to the official car. Trapped in the vehicle in a hail of gunfire, Sir Henry opened the door, possibly to try to make cover. He was killed instantly. Only the arrival of the armored car, machine guns blazing, saved his wife and his private secretary from the same fate. The high commissioner's assassination stunned Malaya.

Soon, the terrorists again struck in spectacular fashion. On October 8, the mail train from Johore to Kuala Lumpur struck a terrorist mine near Johore Bharu. The explosion derailed the train, killing the driver and wounding two railwaymen and three passengers. That same autumn, the terrorists chalked up their first British female fatality, ambushing a British tin miner's wife on the Taiping to Selama road.

Derailing trains was a tactic of the terror campaign of the Malayan Races' Liberation Army (MRLA).

Some attacks were particularly brutal. On November 25, with her parents away in Kuala Lumpur, a plantation owner's daughter was out for a ride in the family Landrover with the estate cook. Terrorists sprang an ambush, shooting the girl through the head. She was only two years old.

Although the insurgency continued for a further nine years, the end of 1951 marked a turning point. Until then the terrorists had been effective. Now, with the guerrillas starved of food and support from the population and suffering high numbers of casualties, the government went on the attack. Using a combination of conventional military force and psychological warfare, including leaflet drops and broadcasting propaganda from aircraft, the British closed in. Many guerrillas turned their backs on communism and accepted British bribes to turn in their fellow terrorists. Malaya was granted independence from Britain on August 31, 1957, and it was only the tenacity of the few remaining hardline guerrillas that kept the emergency in place until 1960.

Chris Marshall

SEE ALSO:

TERRORISM IN FRENCH ALGERIA; TERRORISM IN CYPRUS; TERROR AGAINST THE FRENCH IN INDOCHINA; TERROR IN NAMIBIA; TERROR CAMPAIGNS IN PORTUGUESE AFRICA.

FURTHER READING

- Clutterbuck, Richard. *The Long, Long War: Counterinsurgency in Malaya and Vietnam*. New York: Praeger, 1966.
- Dewar, Michael. *Brush Fire Wars: Minor Campaigns of the British Army since 1945*. New York: St. Martin's Press, 1984.
- Stubbs, Richard. *Hearts and Minds in Guerrilla Warfare: The Malayan Emergency 1948-1960*. New York: Oxford University Press, 1989.

TRH Pictures

TERRORISM IN KENYA

The Mau Mau was a secret society that led a terrorist campaign against colonial rule in the British African colony of Kenya. Like many secret societies in Africa, the Mau Mau was based on a single tribe and evoked supernatural powers.

It is unclear how ancient the Mau Mau was or what its name actually meant. However, by the late 1940s, the society had a political message. It taught that the white farmers who had grown prosperous through raising cash crops had built their success on the backs of the Kikuyu tribesmen. Many unemployed men, able to see the wealth of the whites, joined the movement.

MAGICAL OATHS

The main increase in Mau Mau numbers came in 1949, as the society carried out an aggressive recruitment campaign. Kikuyu were persuaded, or forced, to take an oath, or *thenge*, in a ceremony that often included ritual self-scarring with knives. The recruits swore to carry out Mau Mau instructions on pain of death at the hands of supernatural beasts. The violent deaths of a few recruits served to convince any uncertain tribesmen.

The rising number of initiation ceremonies led the Kenyan colonial government to ban the Mau Mau in 1950. However, by 1952, the society had organized a guerrilla army and begun a campaign of violence. The aim was to overthrow the colonial regime and replace it with Kikuyu supremacy over neighboring tribes.

The forests and mountains north of Nairobi were home to around 12,000 Mau Mau guerrillas, mostly armed with traditional spears and clubs. About 30,000 tribesmen in villages formed the "passive wing," which sent supplies to the guerrillas. Most of the other Kikuyu were bound by magical oath to support the movement. In Nairobi, a central committee gathered information, coordinated activity, and issued orders to the guerrillas. The command structure was loose and relied on obedience to the oath for its efficiency.

During 1951 and 1952, the Mau Mau carried out attacks on isolated white-owned farms and murdered several Kikuyu who opposed the movement. These attacks became so frequent that the government declared a state of emergency in October 1952. At first the authorities could do little because of the lack of troops and poor intelligence work. In January 1953, the Ruck family (husband, wife, and six-year-old son) were hacked to death, an act which outraged the settlers.

In response, the colonial regime imprisoned the leaders of the Kenya African Union, the legal political party representing the Kikuyu. It also increased the British military strength in Kenya, called up native home defense forces, and strengthened the police. In 1953, a conventional military campaign against the Mau Mau began but achieved little. The Mau Mau, which now numbered up to 15,000 fighters, proved an elusive enemy and suffered few losses. Mau Mau guerrilla attacks on villages continued, and the bodies of victims were often mutilated in ritual fashion.

In early 1954, the new British commander, Sir George Erskine, introduced counterinsurgency tactics used in Malaya. He set up propaganda and psychological warfare staffs, improved intelligence gathering, and ensured cooperation between the military and police.

The first major mission under this new initiative was Operation Anvil in April 1954. The Kikuyu population of Nairobi, some 30,000 people, were rounded up and interrogated. Hooded informants were used to identify Mau Mau activists, who were placed in detention camps. Operation Anvil effectively broke the central committee and ended coordinated activity between the different groups of Mau Mau guerrillas.

KEY FACTS

● The sudden intensification of Mau Mau violence in October 1952 caused the British to declare a state of emergency.

● In four years, the Mau Mau suffered 11,500 casualties. The security forces lost 63 Europeans, 3 Asians, and 524 Africans. Some 8,000 indigenous Kenyans were killed in the terror campaigns.

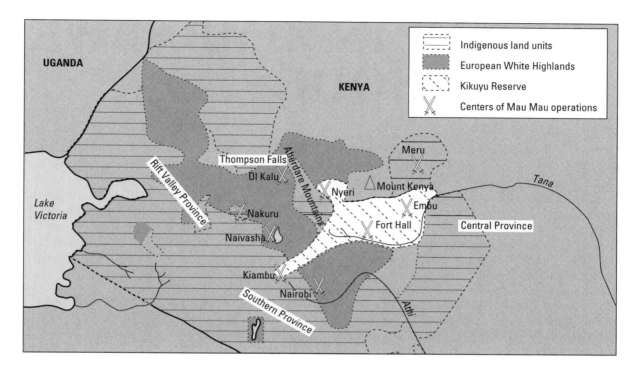

Kikuyu reservations and areas of Mau Mau activity.

Meanwhile, the British declared the denser forests of Kenya to be war zones in which the security forces could shoot on sight, and they often did. The Kikuyu villages were searched for Mau Mau supporters and surrounded by stockades. These measures seriously reduced the Mau Mau's ability to continue its terrorist campaign. Another effective tool was the introduction of cleansing oaths to counter the Mau Mau oath of obedience. Once the British hired witch doctors to cleanse large numbers of Kikuyu in this way, the Mau Mau lost its base of unwilling support.

CLEARING THE FORESTS

In 1955, British military raids forced the guerrillas to split into small groups and flee the forest, making them easier to eliminate. Attempts were made to negotiate surrenders. Captured Mau Mau leader, General China, persuaded guerrillas to surrender and 1,200 members of the passive wing were arrested. There were allegations of torture brought against the security forces. A total of 430 detainees were shot "trying to escape," and over 1,000 executions had been carried out by 1956.

The Mau Mau also found itself faced with "counter gangs." These gangs, made up of native soldiers and cleansed Mau Mau fighters, posed as Mau Mau to locate groups of guerrillas. They successfully made

contact with the guerrillas that the large-scale sweeps missed. These tactics had effectively destroyed the Mau Mau by November 1956.

Kenya gained its independence in 1963 under Jomo Kenyatta, who had been arrested as a leading member of the Kenya African Union during the crisis. Kenyatta, a Kikuyu, rapidly established his tribe in power, though without the radical land policies of the Mau Mau.

John Finlayson

SEE ALSO:

TERRORISM IN CYPRUS; TERRORISM IN MALAYA; BRITISH COUNTERTERROR IN THE ERA OF DECOLONIZATION.

F U R T H E R   R E A D I N G

- Barnett, D. *Karari Njama: Mau Mau from Within.* New York: MacGibbon and Kee, 1966.
- Egerton, Robert B. *Mau Mau: An African Crucible.* New York: Ballantine Books, 1991.
- Majdalani, F. *State of Emergency: The Full Story of Mau Mau.* Boston, MA: Houghton Mifflin, 1963.

TERROR IN ZIMBABWE (RHODESIA)

On November 11, 1965, the British colony of Rhodesia (now Zimbabwe) declared itself independent. Prime Minister Ian Smith declared that "never in a thousand years" would he accept black majority rule, although only five percent of Rhodesia's population was white. As a result, African nationalists set up two terrorist groups to oppose white rule. The Zimbabwe People's Revolutionary Army (ZIPRA), based in Zambia, drew strength from the small but powerful Ndebele community. The Zimbabwe African National Liberation Army (ZANLA), based in Mozambique, was based on the larger Shona tribe.

Differences between the two forces soon became apparent, although their targets were initially similar. China armed and influenced ZANLA. The Soviet Union armed and trained ZIPRA. Both groups launched guerrilla attacks on white-owned farms and police bases between 1966 and 1969, but were all but annihilated by the Rhodesian security forces.

After peace talks failed in 1971, ZANLA hit white targets again. They attacked a farm on December 21, 1972, wounding a three-year-old girl. The Rhodesians countered by launching Operation Hurricane and, by September 1975, claimed 651 guerrillas deaths at a cost of 73 fatalities among their own troops. In June 1975, when neighboring Mozambique became independent, ZANLA gained safe bases from which to attack eastern Rhodesia. By 1978, an estimated 4,645 ZANLA and 953 ZIPRA recruits were active in Rhodesia.

Whites were not the only targets of ZANLA. The terrorists also wished to control the Shona population and began a campaign to intimidate villagers. For example, on August 13, 1973, in the Kandeya area, a headman was shot dead in front of his assembled villagers. The terrorists also committed other atrocities including bayonetting, stabbing, or beating villagers to death, shooting parents in front of their children, blowing up country buses, hacking off fingers and lips, severing feet, and inflicting burns.

USING TORTURE TO ENFORCE SUPPORT

ZANLA lectured people on nationalist aims at compulsory rallies called *pungwes*, reinforcing speeches with calculated terror. They tortured or killed suspected pro-government black Africans. In the Mt. Darwin District in 1973, for example, terrorists beat two wives of an alleged informer and shot his third wife. Terrorists shot another headman, killed his cattle – the wealth of the village – and burnt down every hut. On April 18, 1974, in the Madziwa area, terrorists entered a beerhall. They had a "death list" of those sentenced to die for helping the security forces. Two men answered when their names were called out. Their hands were tied and they were beaten to death before the crowd of 150 people.

The terrorists also attacked rival nationalists, passing strangers, and even people using skin-lightening cosmetics. The police registered 2,751 such killings by 1979. Most people executed at *pungwes* were denounced by *mujibas*, local youths who helped the guerrillas. Many *mujibas* abused their authority by raping, stealing, or killing. The terrorists also killed missionaries and teachers and abducted thousands of pupils for guerrilla training. At night the terrorists forced people to demolish bridges, dig up roads, and cut telephone and electricity lines. Through terror, ZANLA came to dominate the countryside.

From their bases, ZANLA guerrillas regularly raided the 6,000 economically crucial white-owned farms that covered nearly half the country. The terrorists ambushed white farming families, attacked their homes,

---

KEY FACTS

● During 1965-79, 1,300 members of the security forces and 9,000 civilians died in the terror campaigns. However, the estimated death toll of guerrillas was far higher – about 10,000.

● One of the worst ZANLA terrorist incidents was the massacre of 27 tea-plantation workers in the Honde Valley on December 20, 1976.

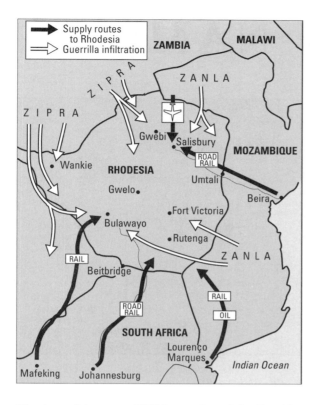

The terrorist group ZIPRA was based in Zambia;
ZANLA operated from Mozambique.

burned their barns, and stole their cattle. They intimidated or killed black farm workers and burned down their huts. As a result, people abandoned hundreds of the most exposed white farms.

The guerrillas ambushed roads and railroads, and mortared Umtali city, but police intelligence made urban terrorism rare. One exception was a bomb that killed 11 black Africans in the capital, Salisbury. The most serious blow to white morale occurred when ZIPRA SAM-7 missiles downed two airliners in September 1978 and February 1979. In the first crash, terrorists shot ten women and children who survived.

HARSH GOVERNMENT COUNTERMEASURES

In May 1973, the Rhodesian security forces declared a no-go zone 190 miles inside the northeastern border and laid widespread minefields. From late 1973, they forcibly removed to protected villages people living in the areas most affected by terrorism in order to deny the guerrillas food, intelligence, and recruits.

In June 1974, the Rhodesians introduced fire forces. A fire force consisted of several helicopters, each carrying four people who would be dropped around a guerrilla sighting. Backed up by helicopter gunships, they would close in on the guerrillas and destroy them.

Rhodesian special forces also resorted to unconventional countermeasures. One unit, the Selous Scouts, instigated clashes between ZANLA and ZIPRA. The Grey's Scouts, a mounted unit, bred killer dogs to hunt down terrorists. Rhodesia's Central Intelligence Organization assassinated nationalist leaders in exile. Rhodesia's Special Air Service laid mines in neighboring countries. By 1976, the conflict was too expensive for any side to maintain. South Africa put pressure on the Rhodesian regime to come to a political settlement, and countries helping the guerrillas began to insist on a compromise.

A conference in Geneva between groups broke down in January 1977. War continued. More guerrillas entered Rhodesia from neighboring states, forcing white farmers to build security fences around their homes and to armor their vehicles. The whites also formed local self-defense militias. But the cost of these measures was immense and prime minister Smith conceded majority rule to moderate Africans in Rhodesia. Neither ZANLA nor ZIPRA leaders accepted this deal and continued their attacks.

In 1979, Britain sponsored a cease-fire, and elections followed in 1980. The new constitution included majority rule and safeguards for the white minority. Most of the black population voted along tribal lines. As the Shona was the largest tribe, ZANLA leader Robert Mugabe became president of Zimbabwe.

Bertrande Roberts

SEE ALSO:

TERRORISM IN NAMIBIA; TERROR CAMPAIGNS IN PORTUGUESE AFRICA.

F U R T H E R   R E A D I N G

- Charlton, Michael. *The Last Colony in Africa.* Cambridge, MA: Blackwell, 1990.
- Cilliers, J. K. *Counterinsurgency in Rhodesia.* Dover, NH: Croom Helm, 1985.
- Godwin, Peter, and Ian Hancock. *"Rhodesians Never Die."* New York: Oxford University Press, 1993.

TERROR IN NAMIBIA

During World War I, South Africa conquered the neighboring German colony of South West Africa on behalf of the Allies. At the war's end, the League of Nations granted South Africa a mandate to govern the territory. In 1946, the League's successor, the United Nations, recommended that South Africa prepare the region for independence.

The South African government in Pretoria, however, continued to govern it as a part of their own country and introduced *apartheid* – the system of legal racial discrimination. This attitude antagonized many and, in October 1966, the United Nations' General Assembly recommended that the mandate be revoked. In June 1968, the assembly renamed the territory Namibia, instructing South Africa to grant independence. Finally, in July 1971, the International Court of Justice declared South Africa's presence there illegal.

Pretoria's control was also challenged by Namibian nationalist movements, most notably the South West Africa People's Organization (SWAPO), founded in April 1960 and drawing most of its members from the Ovambo tribe. The South African authorities soon took repressive measures against SWAPO. Many members fled to Tanzania to organize the People's Liberation Army of Namibia, which led an insurgency combining guerrilla warfare, terrorism, and political activity.

In late 1965, the first trained insurgents set up camps in Ovamboland. These activists attacked security forces and pro-government blacks, and sabotaged installations. In 1966, SWAPO also carried out a number of terrorist attacks on white civilians. In response, Pretoria arrested and convicted 37 Namibians for supporting terrorism. From the first

South African army bases in Namibia and the Ovamboland region where SWAPO was active.

clash with South African forces on August 26, 1966 until 1975, the insurgents made little progress militarily. But their political activities gradually made progress, as SWAPO exploited disquiet over *apartheid*.

SWAPO's prospects improved after 1975 when the Portuguese withdrew from Angola. Independent Angola allowed SWAPO to use that country as a base. By now SWAPO was gaining greater international recognition, including a declaration of support from the United Nations in December 1976. SWAPO gained more recruits, got better weapons from the Soviet Union, and received better training by Cuban and Eastern Bloc personnel in Angola. From 1975, SWAPO tried to extend its campaign beyond Ovamboland.

While SWAPO used traditional guerrilla techniques, they also sometimes resorted to terrorist attacks. According to South African reports, on December 20, 1976, terrorists shot dead a white farmer's wife and her 12-year-old son near Grootfontein, northern Namibia. Moreover, on New Year's Eve, 1976, in Oshandi, Ovamboland in northern Namibia, ten terrorists fired at shoppers, killing two civilians.

KEY FACTS

● In 1966, SWAPO's military strength numbered about 1,000, rising to 10,000 by 1978.

● During the fighting, SWAPO lost 10,000 troops, compared to 700 losses for the security forces.

● In 1980, the Pretoria regime reported 1,175 incidents of what it termed "terrorism" in Namibia.

South African troops in the Caprivi Strip view the corpses of suspected SWAPO guerrillas in August 1978, following a counterinsurgency mission.

South African troops responded with counterinsurgency operations, attacking SWAPO bases in southern Angola. These missions were effective, with SWAPO allegedly suffering ten times as many dead as the security forces. Pretoria also sought to undermine the guerrillas by promising Namibia eventual independence. The insurgents also failed to extend their influence beyond Ovamboland, since ethnic groups other than the Ovambo did not see SWAPO as liberators.

In early 1988, SWAPO again resorted to terrorism as part of their insurgency campaign. On February 19, 1988, the insurgents exploded a bomb in a bank at Oshakati, in Ovamboland, killing 21 civilians.

In 1988, the Soviet Union and the United States sponsored a settlement linking a South African withdrawal from Namibia to a Cuban and Eastern Bloc withdrawal from Angola. In the November 1989 elections, SWAPO's political wing won the most votes, albeit not an absolute majority, and in March 1990 SWAPO formed the first government of the new independent state of Namibia.

Henry Longstreet

SEE ALSO:

TERROR IN COLONIAL CONQUESTS; TERRORISM IN KENYA; TERROR IN ZIMBABWE (RHODESIA); TERROR CAMPAIGNS IN PORTUGUESE AFRICA; STATE-SPONSORED TERRORISM.

FURTHER READING

- Beckett, Ian, and John Pimlott, eds. *Armed Forces and Modern Counterinsurgency*. New York: St. Martin's Press, 1985.
- Herbstein, Denis, and John A. Everson. *The Devils are Among Us: The War for Namibia*. Atlantic Highlands, NJ: Zed Books, 1989.
- Leys, Colin. *Namibia's Liberation Struggle: The Two Edged Sword*. Columbus, OH: Ohio University Press, 1995.

TERROR CAMPAIGNS IN PORTUGUESE AFRICA

Portugal was the first European colonial power to arrive in Africa and, with Spain, the last to withdraw. Portuguese navigators reached each of the three principal colonies of Angola, Portuguese Guinea (now Guinea-Bissau), and Mozambique by the end of the fifteenth century.

The Portuguese claimed that, uniquely, their imperialism was based not upon racial discrimination but upon educating the local people to take their place in Portuguese society. In 1951, they named the three colonies overseas provinces of Portugal but, in reality, the policy was exploitative. Back in 1878, the Portuguese had replaced slavery with a contract labor system. They forced local farmers to grow cash crops for the government rather than food crops for themselves. As an added insult, education was not commonly made available.

ANGOLAN MILITANTS ATTACK PLANTATIONS

Initially, nationalist groups were content to pursue economic or social objectives, but by the late 1950s, meager social progress and the collapse of Belgian authority in the Congo gave rise to a growing militancy. The trigger for violence came in 1961 in Angola. Militants attacked Portuguese cotton plantations in protest over laws forcing farmers to grow cash crops.

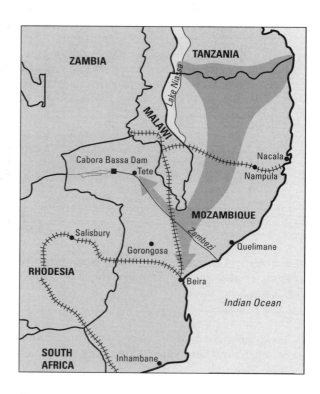

Spurred on by the example of Angolan nationalists, the Mozambique Liberation Front (FRELIMO) advanced from 1964-75.

Meanwhile, an opponent of the then dictator of Portugal, António Salazar, hijacked a Portuguese liner and tried to bring it to Luanda, the Angolan capital. The world press hurried to Angola. On February 4, 1961, three bands of armed Angolans attacked Luanda prison and two police barracks, possibly for the benefit of the press. The militants tried to free African prisoners detained for minor offenses. Security forces beat off the attackers, but there were many deaths.

K E Y   F A C T S

● The liberation movements in the Portuguese African colonies were divided up along tribal lines.

● Five weeks of atrocities started the revolt in Angola in 1961 – 267 civilians, mainly Europeans, were killed. A further 72 were listed as missing.

● Random violence was rare. In general, terrorism toward civilians took the form of outbursts against tribes allied with the Portuguese.

Topham Picturepoint

By 1971, the Angolan FNLA had up to 8,000 troops, ready to fight a guerrilla war for independence.

The next day, at the funeral of the seven policemen killed, shooting broke out. In all, 36 Africans and eight members of the security forces died.

FULL-SCALE REVOLTS IN ANGOLA

A month later, on March 15, terrorists armed with machetes and cutlasses hacked to death 300 farmers, shopkeepers, and their families in the northern cotton plantations. They attacked Portuguese farms, houses, crops, and government property. Refugees shuttled out by aircraft described how the terrorists had butchered the Portuguese without regard to age or sex.

The division was not as simple as native Angolans against the Portuguese. There was much rivalry between nationalist Angolan groups, based on tribal differences. Many refugees reported how the local African population had fought side by side with the Portuguese against the terrorists.

On April 13, 1961, terrorist violence went from bad to worse. Several thousand rebels launched an attack on Ucua village, 100 miles north of Luanda, killing 13 Portuguese. A reporter described how the terrorists were armed with cutlasses inscribed with UPA – standing for the Union of Angolan Peoples – and how they attacked "as if demon-possessed, dancing and singing and shouting."

UPA (later the National Front for the Liberation of Angola, or FNLA) leader Holden Roberto said that the Angolan uprising was "an expression of desperation against Portuguese terrorism over the past 500 years." But he added, "We are deeply sorry that women and children have been killed." Holden Roberto stated that the attacks were the work of laborers rebelling against the Portuguese forced labor system. He admitted that some of his members had taken part but insisted they had done so against orders. The revolt caught the Portuguese army by surprise, but it easily suppressed the rebels. Airpower was used ferociously, killing an estimated 50,000 Africans by September.

The uprising prompted the Portuguese to make concessions. They abolished compulsory cash crop cultivation. They replaced the desire to "civilize" the natives with a declaration that all local people in overseas provinces were equal to Europeans as

Angola, showing the main areas of guerrilla activity.

Portuguese citizens. But insurgency still spread to Portuguese Guinea in 1963 and to Mozambique in 1964.

GUINEA STRUGGLES TO BREAK FREE
The main insurgent group in Portuguese Guinea was the African Party for Independence for Guinea and Cape Verde (PAIGC). The group's targets were primarily the Portuguese military. On January 25, 1963, the terrorists attacked Portuguese barracks in the southeast of the country. They killed 20 army troops. On March 10, PAIGC units killed eight Portuguese troops and, on May 22, they shot down two aircraft. One pilot died in the crash; the terrorists captured the other.

The Portuguese answer to the insurgents was to put more and more troops on the ground. From 1,000 troops in 1961, government forces grew to 30,000 by 1967. The Portuguese intensified counterinsurgency effort centered on concentrating local populations in defended villages. When General Antonio de Spínola took over the military command in Guinea in 1968, he initiated a coordinated "hearts and minds" strategy to win over the local people. Adopting the slogan "Better

Guinea," Spínola based his program on the villages and used the army to build 15,000 houses, 164 schools, 40 hospitals, 163 fire stations, and 86 water points.

MOZAMBIQUE STEPS UP ITS CAMPAIGN
As in Guinea, the Mozambique Liberation Front (FRELIMO) started off in 1964 with military targets, such as a rocket attack on the Cabora Bassa dam in Mozambique. But during late 1973 and early 1974, FRELIMO terrorists shifted emphasis, mounting more than 40 operations against civilian targets. Violent acts included mortar attacks on villages, hostage-taking, and the downing of a private aircraft, killing six. According to the Portuguese, FRELIMO killed more than 300 civilians during 1973, wounded a further 554, and kidnapped 1,768 more. The Portuguese increased troop numbers from 16,000 in 1964 to more than 60,000 in 1974. They took a more active stand against the insurgents after 1968. In 1973, the army was accused of a massacre in which more than 400 African civilians were said to have died. This claim was denied, but some deaths almost certainly occurred.

In the face of an increasingly unpopular campaign at home and in Africa, the Portuguese granted independence to Portuguese Guinea (as Guinea-Bissau) in September 1974, to Mozambique in June 1975, and to Angola in November 1975. In military terms, neither the terrorists nor the authorities had won or lost. It was a military coup in Portugal that destroyed the country's "historic mission" in Africa.

Ian F. W. Beckett

SEE ALSO:
TERROR AGAINST THE FRENCH IN INDOCHINA; TERRORISM IN KENYA; TERRORISM IN ZIMBABWE (RHODESIA).

F U R T H E R   R E A D I N G

• Beckett, Ian and John Pimlott, eds. *Armed Forces and Modern Counter-insurgency.* New York: St. Martin's Press, 1985.

• Bruce, Neil. *The Last Empire.* North Pomfret, VT: David and Charles, 1975.

• Henriksen, Thomas H. *Revolution and Counter-Revolution: Mozambique's War of Independence. 1964-1974,* Westport, CT: Greenwood Press, 1983.

• Porch, Douglas. *The Portuguese Armed Forces and the Revolution.* New York: St. Martin's Press, 1977.

THE GENERAL BACKGROUND TO MODERN TERRORISM

Popperfoto

March 1948: a small Arab boy looks through the bullet-holed window of a bus attacked by Jewish terrorists.

THE GENERAL BACKGROUND
TO MODERN TERRORISM:
Introduction

There are many reasons why individuals or political groups turn to terrorism. Equally, there are many methods that terrorists may use to attack targets or to organize their groups. In order to understand terrorism, it is important to be able to recognize these different aspects - which may, of course, run into each other in various ways. For example, a nationalist may also be a social revolutionary or a religious extremist, as in the case of Hizb'allah in Lebanon.

The most important types of terrorists are those that are fighting for a cause that strikes a chord in many hearts. Thus, nationalists or religious fundamentalists may find themselves representing a cause that has mass appeal, and where recruits are easy to come by. But equally, terrorists that represent a desire for social change, be it of a general revolutionary nature, or a single issue such as a desire to end abortion, may find that they have a ready-made constituency of like-minded supporters. And although terrorists are usually thought of as being left-wing and revolutionary in intent, there have been many examples of terrorists acting from a right-wing position. Sometimes such terrorists aim to destabilize a state, but more frequently – as in Latin America – they act as hit squads against left-wing revolutionaries and terrorists.

The methods that terrorists use are often defined, to a large extent, by how they are set up, and how they identify the audience that they wish to impress or to persuade. One key factor is whether terrorists are sponsored by a state: if they are, this defines and limits their actions, but also gives them access to large amounts of weapons, ready cash and transport to wherever they will be operating. Another key factor is whether they are operating in a rural or an urban environment, for these offer quite different challenges and opportunities. Then there is the target audience – do the terrorists want to make a splash on the international stage, or is this pointless, with only a domestic audience worth influencing?

Many terrorist groups have found it effective to use certain organizational methods, such as independent cells each with a handful of activists. Equally, there are only a certain number of ways of raising funds. And there are also only a limited range of techniques that terrorists can use to gain public attention.

The favourite terrorist technique has always been bombing. It enables the activist to plant a device and then get away before the bomb does its deadly work. There are growing fears that terrorists may use weapons more deadly than a bomb packed with conventional explosive - either some kind of chemical or nuclear device. Either of these could be fired using a rocket or mortar, two means of delivery favored by terrorists.

However, bombs left to explode in a city centre do not necessarily gain the terrorist the exposure that other techniques can. Hijacking an aircraft, something that became a common occurrence in the late 1960s and early 1970s, automatically gave terrorists the ear of the world's media. Hostage-taking, too, sets off a running story that can stay as a headline for weeks. Last, assassination of key political figures also guarantees extensive media coverage. Some terrorists are so committed to their cause that they are prepared to die as suicide bombers. Such attacks can also have wide effects, and are undeniably effective.

The final aspect to terrorism considered as a phenomenon of the modern world is the mind both of the terrorist and of the victim. It is hard to find abnormal psychological traits that link all terrorists – many of them are level-headed operatives who believe that terrorism is the best way to achieve their goals. Nevertheless, the stress of operating in an enclosed world, often lacking contacts outside the terrorist cell, does tend to impose a certain pattern of behavior. Studying these patterns can give those combating terrorism a vital edge in the struggle.

Victims tend to behave in certain patterns too, mainly because they are shocked and bewildered by the train of events in which they have been unwittingly trapped. They are not the real targets of the terrorist - they are often merely the route by which the terrorist intends to influence the real target. The fate of the innocent victims of terror attack is often deeply shocking, and they or their families may never recover from it.

Types of Terrorism

Terrorism has become such an inescapable fact of life that it now falls into clear categories. Some terrorists are committed to a single cause such as anti-abortion, but far right political views or religious zeal motivates others. Terrorism crosses borders, too, with groups carrying out acts of violence on people and property in countries other than their own. Governments are known to sponsor some terrorists, although many groups operate alone. Terrorists organize themselves differently, depending on whether their base is urban or rural, just as the presence of terrorist violence affects citydwellers and countryfolk in dissimilar ways.

CATEGORIES OF TERROR

Many analysts have attempted to classify terrorism. There are four common types or categories into which terrorism and terrorists can be divided: first, by ideological type; second, by the nature of the terrorist's goals; third, by the setting of terrorist violence – by the nature of their targets, and the terrain over which they operate; and last, by the historical origins of terrorist groups.

IDEOLOGY OF TERRORISM

Ideology, the body of ideas that a political group adopts, is a basic method of categorizing terrorists. However, ideology can prove highly misleading as an analytical tool. For example, the early 1970s Red Army Faction terrorist group in Germany could be categorized as Marxist in ideology. They used the language of class analysis, arguing that society is divided by its economic system into classes, a key element of Marxism. However, the Red Army Faction did not attempt to organize the workers into a mass political movement, which Karl Marx would have regarded as the main point of being a Marxist. It is, therefore, not particularly useful to categorize the Red Army Faction as Marxist in anything except rhetoric.

KEY FACTS

● The linguistic theorist Noam Chomsky, writing with Edward S. Herman, identified two categories of terrorism – *wholesale* by fascist regimes and *retail* by insurgents.

● The first attempts to identify terrorism by type were made by Thomas P. Thornton in 1964. He distinguished between enforcement terror and agitational terror.

● The example of the Irish nationalist Michael Collins illustrates the difficulty intrying to categorize terrorism. He fought against the British in Ireland, then fought for the Irish Free State against his former terrorist comrades.

However, the Red Army Faction was clearly a revolutionary political movement, since it aimed to overthrow the existing social order and replace it with something else. But this kind of thinking is not the sole property of left-wingers. The Militia movement in the United States has a revolutionary intent. It objects to the secular tradition of American politics, in which a person's religious and moral views are a matter for their own conscience, and not for government legislation. The Militias, in that respect, are alien intruders on the American political landscape.

Categorizing by ideology is also a complicated task. An ideology can be a political one, such as Marxism-Leninism, or a religious one, such as the fundamentalist Christianity that motivates members of the Militias. Religious dogma is highly political. Apart from such well-known cases as Islamic Jihad in the Middle East, Catholic Irish nationalists established the breakaway Provisional Irish Republican Army (IRA) after a Marxist-influenced leadership took control of the original movement's governing Army Council.

The tangles caused by attempts to categorize terrorism by ideology reach their most extreme form in dealing with the Middle East. Two strands have always coexisted, often uneasily, in Arab nationalism. There have been secular Arab nationalists, such as Gamal Abdel Nasser of Egypt or Hafez Assad of Syria, for whom Arab identity is defined by geography and language. There have also been religious Arab nationalists, such as the Muslim Brotherhood founded in 1928, at one time including the PLO's Yassir Arafat among its members, who regard Islam a vital part of Arab culture. Secular nationalists with Marxist politics from the Popular Front for the Liberation of Palestine planted the bomb in Jerusalem on February 20, 1969, which killed two supermarket shoppers. A devout Muslim convinced that he would awaken in paradise carried out the suicide bombing of the U.S. Marine Corps barracks in Beirut in October 1983. Yet all these terrorists shared a common ideology opposing Western influence in the Middle East.

Hulton Getty Picture Collection

The French Jacobin leader Robespierre operates a guillotine in an anti-revolutionary caricature. The Reign of Terror in France in 1793-94 falls into the goal-oriented category of repressive terror.

GOALS OF TERRORISTS

The goals of a terrorist to an extent overlap with the ideologies he or she may follow. The ideology of a revolutionary terrorist specifically includes the overthrow of the established order. The nationalist terrorist will be working to achieve self-determination for his national group or region. A revolutionary nationalist terrorist, such as a member of Colombia's M-19 movement, will be working to achieve both of these specific aims.

The advantage of categorizing by goals allows a distinction between terror sponsored or conducted by a state and terror against a state. The Reign of Terror during the French Revolution in 1793-94 was the means the Committee of Public Safety used to destroy any possible alternative to the revolutionary regime. It had a repressive effect on the political life of France. Likewise, death squads in El Salvador or Argentina terrorized civil rights groups and labor organizations.

Categorizing terrorism by goals helps identify regimes that are terrorizing their citizens. The links between governments and death squads in Latin America are not always clear. But vigilantes who kill a regime's opponents arouse suspicion that they have been operating with official sanction.

There are drawbacks to categorizing by goals. Both the leftists of the Red Brigades and neo-Nazi racists seek to overthrow the state, a revolutionary aim. But they sit uneasily together in the same bracket, since the Red Brigades profess a rationalist ideology while the neo-Nazis draw inspiration from Nordic myths. The measures needed to deal with groups with such divergent ideologies requires different emphases, since their supporters are very different people.

TARGETS FOR TERRORIST VIOLENCE

Terrorists can also be categorized in terms of the setting in which they operate. The term setting, in the context of terrorism, refers to the types of victims terrorists target and the terrain in which they operate. Grouping terrorists by what they choose as their targets has been examined since the 1970s. Two types of targets emerged: attacks on carefully selected targets, and indiscriminate acts against random targets. An example of the first would be a kidnapping such as that of the CIA's Beirut station chief, William Buckley, in Lebanon in 1984. In this case, a vital member of the U.S. espionage establishment was seized by anti-Western Islamic fundamentalists. He

Despite the complexities of terrorist ideologies, however, ideology does play a role in distinguishing types of terrorism. Some accommodation may be possible with a nationalist terrorist group such as the Basques of ETA (Fatherland and Liberty). The Spanish regime's granting of greater autonomy to the Basque provincial administration appeased all but the most hardline nationalists. A left-wing revolutionary group aiming to overthrow capitalism will be less likely to find common ground with a government.

was no doubt interrogated to gather intelligence information concerning networks of American agents active in Lebanon, and then killed to disrupt American intelligence efforts in the Middle East.

An example of the second type of terrorist targeting would be the Bologna, Italy, railroad station bombing in 1980, believed to be the work of neo-fascists. The bomb devastated the station, disrupting rail traffic, and causing more than 325 casualties. It created a climate of fear among Italians, and encouraged law-abiding citizens to press for more action to be taken in defense of social order. But the people who were its victims included a cross-section of the Italian people, and for all the terrorists knew, some could have sympathized with their ideology or goals.

It was thought, at one time, that leftist groups were more likely to be selective, while right-wing ones would be indiscriminate. However, research revealed that a terrorist group's politics made little difference in target selection.

Linked to categorizing by target is categorizing by the terrain in which terrorists operate. For example, Brazil's National Liberation Action group led by Carlos Marighela operated in an exclusively urban environment, while Peru's Shining Path guerrillas apply terror tactics in the countryside. This method of categorization could be extended to include whether a terrorist organization operates exclusively within its own country, like the Zapatistas in Mexico, or attacks targets internationally, as did the Japanese Red Army.

HISTORICAL ORIGINS OF TERRORISM

A final method of categorizing terrorism has been by the historical origins of the group. There is some overlap between this method and the attempt to categorize by ideology. Revolutionaries such as the Red Army Faction or the Weathermen emerged during the 1960s' student unrest.

Categorization by origin may prove useful in analysing terrorism in post-colonial struggles. The Tamil Tigers, Sikh nationalist terrorism, and terrorists in Kashmir each have their origin in post-colonial political boundaries cutting across ethnic groups. They have more in common with the Moro terrorists of the Philippines than the Moros have with their allies in the social revolutionary New Peoples' Army.

No system of categorization has proven ideal for makers of anti-terrorist policy. Those combating terrorism are devising increasingly complex methods of classification. In these models, terrorist groups are categorized by combinations of numerous variables. Hence, counterterrorist officials have classified the American Militia movement as a Religious-Indigenous-Nongovernment-Anarchist group. However, one problem may be that classification categories are conceived by people who are trying to put a stop to terrorism, rather than by those actually carrying out terrorism. Hence, while categorizing terrorist groups is an essential part of the fight against terrorism, it is difficult for such categorization to be definitive.

Michael Brewer

SEE ALSO:
THE PROBLEMS OF DEFINING TERRORISM; TERROR IN THE FRENCH REVOLUTION 1789-1815; TYPES OF TERRORISM; BOMBING OPERATIONS; HIJACKING AND KIDNAPPING; ASSASSINATION; THE MINDSET OF THE TERRORIST; SUICIDE BOMBING; ARAB NATIONALISM AND THE RISE OF FATAH; TERROR IN LEBANON 1980-1987; TERRORISM IN BRAZIL; TERRORISM IN PERU; TERROR IN THE PHILIPPINES; TAMIL TIGER TERROR IN SRI LANKA; SIKH NATIONALIST TERRORISM IN INDIA; TERROR BY THE HOLY WARRIORS OF KASHMIR; STUDENT TERROR: THE WEATHERMEN; OKLAHOMA CITY BOMBING AND THE MILITIAS; RED ARMY FACTION: THE BAADER-MEINHOF GANG; RED BRIGADES; JAPANESE TERRORISM; BASQUE NATIONALIST TERROR: ETA; IRA: ORIGINS AND TERROR TO 1976; NATIONALIST TERROR IN NORTHERN IRELAND 1976-1996; ARGENTINE GOVERNMENT'S RESPONSES TO TERRORISM; BRAZILIAN GOVERNMENT'S RESPONSES TO TERRORISM; SALVADORAN GOVERNMENT'S RESPONSES TO TERRORISM.

FURTHER READING

- Flemming, Peter A., Michael Stohl, and Alex P. Schmid. "The Theoretical Utility of Typologies of Terrorism: Lessons and Opportunities." In *The Politics of Terrorism*, 3d ed., edited by Michael Stohl. New York: Marcel Dekker, Inc.,1988.
- Laqueur, Walter. *The Terrorism Reader*. New York: New American Library, 1978.
- Livingstone, Marius H. *International Terrorism in the Contemporary World*. Westport, CT: Greenwood Press, 1978.
- Wardlaw, Grant. *Political Terrorism: Theory, Tactics, and Counter-Measures*. 2d ed. New York: Cambridge University Press, 1989.

NATIONALIST TERRORISM

Historically, nationalism is a relatively recent phenomenon, but a powerful one. Some historians argue that nationalism caused the two world wars. It has certainly created some of the most prominent terrorist movements.

The nations of modern Europe took shape during the fourteenth century. States then began to organize themselves along national lines. The English King Edward I (reigned 1272-1307), for example, ruled over a people who spoke a single language, shared the same religion, and had a common legal system. Uniting nations, however, was a slow process. At the same time, Catholic Spain was divided into three separate kingdoms, plus the Muslim enclave of Granada, and only became a united nation in 1512. The Austrian statesman Prince Metternich could legitimately describe Italy as "a geographical expression" in 1849, since it was still divided into seven separate states.

Nationalism only became a powerful political force during the nineteenth century. At this time, certain peoples, who lived in multinational states, identified themselves as a community entitled to choose their own leaders and make their own laws. Between 1820 and 1863, nationalist rebellions occurred in Greece, Poland, and Hungary. Also in the nineteenth century, nationalist political movements emerged in Britain (Irish and Scottish nationalists), Germany (Poles), and Austria (Hungarians, Poles, Italians, Czechs, and

Slovaks), among other countries. This enthusiasm for the nation-state then spread to the European colonial empires in the third world in the twentieth century.

NATIONAL IDENTITY

The nation-state is the physical and political territory of a people who share a culture and live within a defined area. Nation-states are a product of the desire of a people to be self-determined – that is, able to determine their own form of government. Religion, language, economics, ethnicity, and geography are all factors that create a national identity. When a people comes to believe that its rulers are of a different nationality, the pressure for self-determination may propel the people into using any means necessary – including terrorism – to achieve this goal.

TERRORISM FOR POLITICAL CHANGE

Groups that use terrorism to nationalist ends aim to overturn the ruling elite by intimidating, scaring, or panicking the general public. The Provisional Irish Republican Army (IRA), for example, uses terror both in Ireland and Britain. It largely restricts its targets in Ireland to the security services, whom its members see as an army of occupation. The terrorists attack malls and business districts in Britain, however, to influence the people against the government's policy of keeping Northern Ireland a part of the United Kingdom.

Very few individuals are needed to conduct a nationalist terrorist campaign. The important motivator is the depth of their resentment of the ruling power. But the terrorists must achieve a great appeal within the nation they seek to represent in order to have any hope of success. The Algerian nationalists who fought the French in the 1950s numbered fewer than 400 activists in 1954. Thanks to the exploits of prominent nationalists like Ramdane Abane, who became a national hero, their numbers expanded to an army of some 20,000 based in Tunisia in 1956.

The Algerian war was one of national liberation as a colony sought independence from an imperial power.

KEY FACTS

● Nationalist terrorism is often employed by people with a common identity to help achieve independence from a ruling power.

● Terrorist attacks are often dramatic. Two Sikh attacks on Indians took place on the same day, June 23, 1985. A bomb blew up an Air India flight over the Irish Sea killing 329 passengers and crew, and a bomb planted on an Air India plane at Tokyo's Narita airport killed two baggage handlers.

In the aftermath of such wars of independence, nationalists can again turn to terrorism to accomplish their goals. For example, the Sikhs in India have a distinct religion from the Hindu majority. From this, a sense of a distinct national identity emerged among some Sikhs after India gained its independence from Britain in 1947. Sikh extremists turned to terrorism during the 1980s in an attempt to achieve independence.

Political movements of minorities often generate an extremist faction that turns to terror when constitutional politics is perceived to be a dead end. Terrorist groups committed to achieving independence from larger states have emerged in Europe during the postwar era. Basque nationalists in Spain, Corsicans and Bretons in France, and South Tyrolians in Italy have used bombing campaigns to influence the political process. None has yet succeeded in attaining self-determination, but terrorism is seen as the only defense of the nationalists against cultural oblivion.

Terror is also used by nationalist groups to oppose foreign influences in their countries. Many Latin

Palestinian religious and nationalist militants demonstrate against Israeli attacks on bases in southern Lebanon, May 1995.

American terrorist campaigns in the 1960s and 1970s were directed against the United States. While Castro's Communists in Cuba and the Sandinistas in Nicaragua used revolutionary rhetoric, they also identified themselves with anti-American nationalism.

NATIONALISM IN THE MIDDLE EAST

The Middle East has witnessed much nationalist-rooted terrorist activity. Zionism emerged in Europe during the nineteenth century at the same time as other minorities within the multinational empires, such as Habsburg Austria, asserted a right to national self-determination. Menachem Begin, the leader of the Israeli Likud party who was prime minister of Israel during 1977-83, was involved in terrorism. His followers participated in the bombing and shooting of British

TRH Pictures

Masked members of the Provisional IRA patrol the Falls Road area of Belfast during a Sinn Fein march in August 1979. Many Irish see its members as heroes of a national liberation struggle.

soldiers during the late 1940s. Begin's actions helped establish the independent state of Israel in 1948.

Nationalist terrorism was also used by the Palestine Liberation Organization (PLO) against Israel. The PLO organized itself along the lines of a government-in-exile. It had its own army, a system of political representation in the Palestine National Council, and a means of taxing Palestinians. These traditional instruments of state power proved indispensable to giving the PLO the moral authority of a state after signing the Declaration of Principles with Israel in 1993.

Nationalist terrorists direct their actions against the authority that stands in the way of their aspirations. Although government offices, miltary bases, officials, and soldiers are important targets, terrorism differs from guerrilla war in that it is the civilian population rather than the military which is the main target.. The Tamil Tigers, a Sri Lankan group, targeted public utilities, civilians, and government officials. Diplomats are also victims when the government they represent is seen to be opposed to self-determination. For example, because the British monarch, as Canada's head of state, had an interest in Canada's unity, in 1970 Quebec nationalists separatists kidnapped British trade commissioner James Cross.

INNOCENT VICTIMS

Besides attacking individuals directly connected with authority, nationalist terrorists also target businesspeople and even tourists. In Angola, the Front for the Liberation of the Enclave of Cabinda has attacked representatives of foreign corporations that deal with the national government. The United Liberation Front of Assam operates in India mainly by kidnapping and extortion. As long as peoples continue to seek self-determination, the danger remains that they will turn to terrorism to attain their goals.

Noemi Gal-Or

SEE ALSO:

NATIONAL LIBERATION WARS AND TERROR; TERRORISM IN FRENCH ALGERIA; TERRORISM IN CYPRUS; TERROR AGAINST THE FRENCH IN INDOCHINA; TERRORISM IN MALAYA; TERROR CAMPAIGNS IN PORTUGUESE AFRICA; DOMESTIC VERSUS INTERNATIONAL TERROR; HIJACKING AND KIDNAPPING; ASSASSINATION; THE ORIGINS OF ARAB-JEWISH TERRORISM; ARAB NATIONALISM AND THE RISE OF FATAH; THE BIRTH OF THE PLO AND THE 1967 WAR; TERRORISM IN NICARAGUA; NATIONALIST TERRORISM IN POST-COLONIAL ASIA AND AFRICA; NATIONALIST TERRORISTS.

FURTHER READING

- Gilbert, Paul. *Terrorism, Security and Nationality.* New York: Routledge, 1994.
- Harris, Nigel. *National Liberation.* Reno, NV: University of Nevada Press, 1993.
- Moxon-Browne, Edward. *European Terrorism.* New York: G. K. Hall, 1994.
- O'Brien, Conor Cruise. *Passion and Cunning: Essays of Nationalism, Terrorism and Revolution.* New York: Simon and Schuster, 1989.

REVOLUTIONARY TERRORISM

Terrorists seeking to overthrow a constitutional government as part of a program of social transformation can be called revolutionary terrorists. Left-wing political movements are the obvious ones to use revolutionary terrorism, but revolutionary politics are not restricted to the Left. The Nazi party in 1930s Germany was as much a revolutionary party as were the Communists.

Revolutionary terrorism has its roots in a political ideology, from the Marxist-Leninist thinking of the Left, to the fascists found on the Right. Both ideologies emerged in the first decades of the twentieth century. Each was influenced by the revolutionary socialists of the late nineteenth century, who are often numbered among the first revolutionary terrorists.

A COMMON WEAPON

Despite the differences in motivation and intention, terrorism is the common weapon for all these groups, based on the principle that actions speak louder than words. Revolutionary terrorism employs a vast arsenal of violence ranging from discriminate terrorism, such as political assassination, to the use of lethal indiscriminate tactics. Planting bombs in airplanes and market places, and introducing poison into food, the water supply, or the air are examples of methods designed to injure the general population.

Terrorist actions in themselves are revolutionary. They disrupt the social order, for an instant transforming it from an orderly group of people into a chaotic mass of individuals, each striving to escape the panic that surrounds a bomb blast or gunshot.

THE CHARACTER OF THE REVOLUTIONARY

Social hardships like unemployment and related poverty and racial or sexual discrimination cause people to join left-wing revolutionary political movements. The social system itself breeds revolution. The accident of birth can condemn an individual to an inferior education and a lifetime of poor housing and inadequate medical care. Those who benefit from the system live in good neighborhoods, have plenty to eat, and the money to enjoy a fulfilling social life. The revolutionary believes this system can be changed to eliminate or at least reduce the level of injustice. Left-wing revolutionary movements emphasize how new social forms can be created. People will have more influence over social conditions in the post-revolutionary world. The promise of this future motivates the revolutionary terrorist. The system itself is worth destroying by any means necessary.

The ability to see the system as an impersonal force victimizing working people aids the intention of the revolutionary terrorist to commit violent acts. A police officer becomes an individual who opposes any possibility of improving housing for thousands. A building full of government workers becomes a center for administering injustice. Police and government officials condemn themselves by assisting the system.

Right-wing revolutionaries find their motivation from another source. They often feel threatened by the left-wing view that working people all have the same political interests, regardless of nationality. In other cases, they fear the direction of social changes that give equal opportunities to women or people of a different race. A political system seen to support this kind of social agenda becomes a threat. As with the left-wing revolutionary, the people carrying out or aiming at these social changes acquire the characteristics of an impersonal, even non-human, force.

KEY FACTS

● Marxist revolutionaries do not believe in indiscriminate violence. Frederich Engels wrote that they should behave like soldiers and only kill those fighting against them.

● Revolutionary terrorists (such as the Red Brigades in Italy) use violence against constitutional democracies because they believe it is the only way to expose these regimes' repressive nature.

French writer Regis Debray faces trial in 1967 for aiding revolutionary guerrilla groups in Bolivia.

THE OPTION OF TERRORISM

Social revolutionaries have turned to terrorism in many countries. It is frequently a response to specific circumstances, and normally carried out by small groups of conspirators. But an individual's actions against some perceived injustice can be construed as revolutionary terrorism. A prime example of an individual terrorist is Theodore Kaczynski, thought to be the so-called Unabomber. Kaczynski waged a private mail-bomb campaign in his fight against the U.S. establishment.

Nationalist terrorism has a clear purpose, but the aims of revolutionary terrorism are often also present within a movement for national liberation. Radical social change may coexist in the same political movement as the struggle for national self-determination. For example, the Palestinian Liberation Organization (PLO) sought to establish a Palestinian state on land occupied by Israel. But the PLO has many factions, each with its own vision for a post-independence Palestine. These agenda range from the Marxism-Leninism of the Democratic Front for the Liberation of Palestine and the Popular Front for the Liberation of Palestine, to the traditionalist, religiously inspired members of Hamas and the Palestinian Islamic Jihad.

When revolutionary ideology is the only excuse for terrorism, and terrorism is the sole strategy employed in the armed struggle, the terrorist campaign usually

fails. Thus, Nazi terrorism during the Germany's Weimar republic of the late 1920s and early 1930s was able to undermine the constitution specifically because it was coupled with legal political activism. By contrast, the German Red Army Faction in the 1970s used terrorism exclusively in its struggle against the German Federal Republic and failed.

Revolutionary terrorism does not seek to preserve the status quo. The aim is to change the rules of the political game. Left-wingers such as the Red Army Faction used terror to reveal the repressive character of the state they opposed, because the state's position was that civil liberties must be restricted in order to catch the terrorists. In general, gun battles between police and revolutionaries reveal the violence inherent in the system, and law enforcement agencies certainly make mistakes, imprisoning innocent political activists who may be opposed to the state but who do not use terrorism against it.

The Red Army Faction's logic for adopting a terrorist strategy to achieve political change shows how terrorism has appealed to many other revolutionaries. Membership of a political movement opposed to the status quo is a choice made by people angry with the system. Those whose personalities require them to act may find constitutional approaches too limiting. Someone opposed to the established order can fight it more dramatically using a bomb or a gun than by attending political rallies or selling a party journal. The burning government building or the shot police officer is a far more dramatic route for a revolutionary.

REVOLUTIONARY TERROR BY THE RIGHT

Fascist terrorist acts have a slightly different objective. Like the Red Army Faction in Germany, they seek to create a sense of alarm on the part of those in power. But what they wish to achieve is a general crisis that will require an increase in repression.

In August 1980, terrorists blew up a bomb in the Bologna railroad station, killing 75 people. This event occurred at a time of Red Brigade activity. In the same way that investigators at first believed the Oklahoma City bombing in 1995 to be the work of Middle Eastern terrorists, so the Bologna bombing was initially blamed on the Red Brigades. The inability of investigators to link Bologna with the Red Brigades led them to a group of Neo-Fascists called the Armed Revolutionary Nuclei, who had set the bomb. The Bologna bombing was part of a right-wing strategy of

The body of a Red Brigade terrorist lies in a Roman street in February 1986. Security forces killed him during an attempt to assassinate Antonio da Empoli, an aide to the Italian prime minister.

terror to force the authorities to suspend civil liberties, or encourage generals to stage a coup to restore order. In either case, a dictatorial regime would result, which was the Neo-Fascists' aim.

Similarly, the Nazis in Germany engaged in street battles with Communists. The Nazis had a party militia, called the Stormtroopers or Brownshirts. They played on the fears of middle-class people with a small stake in the system, such as their own home or a family business. These people were concerned about damage to their property. The sense of anarchy that emerged whenever a political rally degenerated into a brawl helped make Hitler's message of a leader who would restore order to Germany more appealing. They overlooked other parts of Hitler's platform – his denunciation of the Weimar constitution and of elected parliaments – which should have been things they wished to safeguard.

THE REVOLUTIONARY STATE

Terror is also a strategy for governments committed to social revolutionary programs. Two of the best-known examples of state terror occurred in the aftermath of major revolutions.

In France during 1793, the Jacobin faction faced domestic opposition to their economic program. The Jacobins responded by sending their political enemies to the guillotine while they took over local government by imposing greater control from Paris, the capital. In

1928, the communist regime in the Soviet Union began a program of economic modernization. Part of the program required grain requisitioning to provide the industrial workers with cheap bread, and to force the collectivization of peasant landholdings. Farmers and their families were left to starve to death in the streets of their villages. The police arrested those who protested – and many who didn't – and sent them to forced labor camps. The police shot anyone who took a leading role in organizing protests.

In both these cases, terror was a weapon used against opponents of the revolutionary order. However, at the same time it helped the revolutionaries to accomplish their goals. Local government in France remained centralized until the 1980s, in spite of the collapse of the Jacobin government nearly two centuries before in 1794. Collective farms replaced small peasant farms in the Soviet Union from the 1930s until the 1990s. Society in both these cases had been wholly reshaped by terrorism.

Noemi Gal-Or

SEE ALSO:

TERROR IN THE FRENCH REVOLUTION 1793-1815; RUSSIAN ANARCHIST TERROR; FRENCH ANARCHIST TERROR; THEORIES OF TERROR IN URBAN INSURRECTIONS; FAR-RIGHT EXTREMISM; RELIGIOUS EXTREMISM; THE BEGINNING OF INTERNATIONAL TERRORISM; THE POPULAR FRONT FOR THE LIBERATION OF PALESTINE; TERRORISM IN LATIN AMERICA; BLACK PANTHERS AND TERROR; STUDENT TERROR: THE WEATHERMEN; URBAN TERROR: THE SYMBIONESE LIBERATION ARMY; THE OKLAHOMA CITY BOMBING AND THE MILITIAS; RED ARMY FACTION: THE BAADER-MEINHOF GANG; ACTION DIRECTE; FRENCH RIGHT-WING TERRORISM; RED BRIGADES; MODERN GREEK TERRORISM; JAPANESE TERRORISM; TERROR IN CAMBODIA.

F U R T H E R   R E A D I N G

• Ellis, John. *From the Barrel of a Gun: A History of Revolutionary and Counter Insurgency Warfare,* Mechanicsburg, PA: Stackpole Books, 1995.
• Rubenstein, R. E. *Alchemist of Revolution: Terrorism in the Modern World.* New York: Basic Books, 1987.
• Rubin, Barry, ed. *The Politics of Terrorism: Terror as a State and Revolutionary Strategy.* Washington, DC: Foreign Policy Institute, 1989.

FAR-RIGHT EXTREMISM

In several parts of the world, including Europe, acts of terrorism increasingly come from the extreme right. The forces of racism and militant nationalism have adopted slogans such as "ethnic cleansing" and "race war." This resembles the situation between the world wars, when fascism was a major force.

Since the late 1980s, nationalist movements and rebellious youth cultures have turned to notions of "people, blood, and soil." These ideas emphasize the race or nationality of people, and how they are linked to historic territories. Such ideas are often associated with right-wing and fascist ideologies. The trend is being expressed through electoral support for radical right-wing parties, through the growth of neo-Nazi organizations, and through youth cultures that despise foreigners. At the same time religious militancy and millenarian movements, which believe the world will soon end, are growing. Some of their beliefs fit well with far-right politics and violence.

There are five common explanations for this shift in youth ideology. First, the collapse of Soviet domination in the late 1980s meant that communism was no longer a credible model for radical change. Second, modern youth rebels want to go against their parents, who were influenced by the leftist youth rebellion movements during the 1960s and 1970s. Third, in times of social and economic crisis, young people may look for security by being part of a group, and characteristics of race and nationality are easy to define. Fourth, increasing immigration has raised racial tension. Fifth, loss of confidence in established political parties has given far-right groups a chance to present themselves as a fresh alternative to a corrupt old guard.

EXTREMIST IDEOLOGY

The far right can be difficult to define. What is considered rightist changes from country to country and over time. Many groups and individuals who carry out acts of violence for far-right or racist motives may turn out to have no connections with political organizations.

However, the basic elements of right-wing extremism can be sketched out. There is usually the idea that certain groups of people are inferior or superior as an innate principle. This is combined with an acceptance of violence as a legitimate form of action.

There are other issues and values often promoted by groups described as extreme right-wingers. Authoritarianism, the belief that human society needs a strong leader, is common, as is a hatred of communism or socialism. Militant nationalism can involve racism or anti-Semitism and intolerance toward minorities. The most extreme groups, such as the Nazis and modern Italian neo-fascists, see violence as a creative, cleansing force. Some groups like the Militias create "Golden Age myths," beliefs that there was a time when conditions were perfect for that group. "Golden Age myths" are often important components in the millenarian belief systems, which hold that some gigantic disaster will occur soon to transform the world. Right-wing millenarianists like the American Christian Identity movement usually believe that they will survive this event and emerge to rule the world.

Some modern reactionary groups deliberately link themselves to the past history of the extreme right – to the German Nazi Party and Italian Fascist Party, for example. Other groups deny that they have any connection with this past. Some movements considered as "extreme right" may also promote certain issues that are more often associated with the left, such as socialism or environmentalism.

KEY FACTS

- Many of the beliefs of far-right groups are based on racial or national superiority over others.

- Adverse economic conditions have led to hostility to racial minorities and immigrants.

- Adolf Hitler, the Nazi dictator of Germany from 1933 to 1945, is an inspirational figure for many far-right terrorist groups.

Rex Features

It is not possible to define the essence of right-wing extremism in terms of a core issue. Nor is it true to say that violence and terrorism follow automatically from right-wing extremism. Violent right-wing groups tend to be those who think their opponents are dangerous. They also believe their opponents are less than human. Such is the case in France, where extreme followers of the National Front party attack French Algerians.

FAR-RIGHT GROUPINGS

The types of far-right terrorist groups can be classified by the principles around which they are organized and by their relations with minority and authority enemies. The discussion below is based on a typology originally developed by Ehud Sprinzak

Revolutionary terrorism of the far right is historically represented by Italian fascism and German Nazism. These movements aimed to overthrow the established political regime and take over the state apparatus. Although they used illegal methods to cause unrest, their eventual take-over of power happened in relatively legal ways.

A Turkish guest-worker's home in Germany, bombed in 1992 by Germans resentful of jobs going to foreigners.

Present-day racial revolutionaries have refined the old anti-Semitic idea of a Jewish world conspiracy. They believe in the Zionist Occupation Government (ZOG), said to be a worldwide network of Jews who have gained control of the political establishment. The revolutionaries think these Jews can be overthrown only through a total race war. The war would be against Jews, foreign intruders, and "racial traitors" in the white race.

Reactive terrorism, in contrast, is carried out by those wishing to maintain an established system. They may fear that their privileges are threatened, or are struggling to restore lost political power. Such terrorism has come from Jewish settlers in Israeli-occupied territories. Israeli prime minister Yitzhak Rabin was assassinated in 1995 to undermine the Palestinians peace process. And the Italian masonic organization P2 is thought to be behind the killing of Roberto Calvi,

Popperfoto

German neo-Nazis give the fascist salute at a rally on August 17, 1991, to celebrate the fourth anniversary of the death of Rudolf Hess, Hitler's deputy.

the Vatican's chief banker found hanging from a bridge in London in 1986. He may have been about to expose high-level corruption, so upsetting the status quo.

Those who have lost power may attack the new regime, as in the case of the fascist Ustasha movement in the 1950s in Croatia (then part of Yugoslavia) in southern Europe. The Ustasha ruled Croatia until 1945, but were ousted by the communists. The Ustasha then ran a terrorist campaign against the new regime.

Vigilante terrorism is a variant of reactive terrorism. Initially, such terrorists do not feel they oppose the government or the law. They believe that the authorities have failed in their task of keeping order. Vigilante terrorists use stronger means than the authorities themselves. Prime examples are Latin American death squads, often consisting of off-duty police and military officers, striking against left-wing revolutionaries.

Millenarian terrorism is the hallmark of groups that believe a new age will come out of a disaster, as already mentioned. Most such groups wait for the cataclysm to happen, but a few use violence to try to bring it about. A bizarre variant on this theme are neo-Nazis who have taken up Odinism, the pre-Christian pagan religion of Germany. They believe the gods and demons will gather for a final battle, called Ragnarok. Humans will fight alongside gods and be destroyed, except for one couple who will repopulate the Earth.

Skinheads and similar youth subcultures are often alienated from the mainstream community. Their violence and the texts of their music and fanzines are directed against immigrants, Jews, communists, and homosexuals. Such gangs have carried out much of the racist violence in Europe that has caused public concern in recent years. In Britain, the group Combat 18 (the numbers correspond to A and H in the alphabet, Adolf Hitler's initials) is responsible for many racial attacks. Skinheads in Germany have bombed houses of foreign guest-workers, refugees from former Yugoslavia, and Eastern Europeans.

However, some individuals and groups may adopt more radical ideological notions and ultimately turn into revolutionary terrorists. These subcultures constitute important pools of recruitment for more organized neo-Nazi and racial revolutionary groups.

Tore Bjorgo

SEE ALSO:
THE BIRTH OF JEWISH TERRORISM; JEWISH TERROR IN THE WEST BANK; JEWISH TERRORISM IN THE 1990s; KU KLUX KLAN TERROR; FRENCH RIGHT-WING TERRORISM.

FURTHER READING

- Heitmeyer, W. "Hostility and Violence against Foreigners in Germany." In *Racist Violence in Europe,* edited by Tore Bjorgo and R. Witte. New York: St. Martin's Press, 1993.
- Hoffman, Bruce. *Right-Wing Terrorism in West Germany.* Santa Monica, CA: Rand Corporation, 1986.
- Sprinzak, Ehud. "Right-Wing Terrorism in a Comparative Perspective: The Case of Split Delegitimization." In *Terror from the Extreme Right,* edited by Tore Bjorgo. Portland, OR: Frank Cass, 1995.

SINGLE-ISSUE GROUP TERRORISM

The activists in single-issue groups have chosen to focus on a specific concern that they believe demands immediate attention. It is a concern for "the one issue" above all else that separates them from revolutionary groups with wider aims. Most single-issue groups have their origins in the democratic process. They turn to violent tactics only when they believe that the issues they promote become too urgent for the slow progress of traditional campaigning. Activists' main goals are publicity or changes in the law. Focusing on the one cause, the groups usually ignore the wider effect of their efforts, believing their violent acts are justified because they are morally superior to those who hold a different view.

What constitutes a single-issue group? During his early phase, the Unabomber appeared to be a single-issue terrorist – a violent environmental activist who targeted technocrats and businessmen. However, the publication of his manifesto in 1995 highlighted the Unabomber's aim to overthrow modern society itself. Animal rights activists, on the other hand, pursue an identifiable single issue, as do anti-abortion groups. Single-issue groups are not prevented from being part of larger campaigns – the anti-abortionists can be set within a wider Christian movement pressing for improved public morals, for example, and the animal rights people within a larger movement concerned with environmental issues.

ANTI-ABORTION TERRORISM

The violent anti-abortion groups are the undemocratic face of a movement for law reform. Frustrated by an inability to overturn the Supreme Court's 1973 decision that laws forbidding abortion are an unconstitutional infringement of a citizen's rights, anti-abortionists have formed a number of groups to campaign against abortion providers. Defensive Action, Operation Rescue, the American Family Association, Lambs of Christ, and similar organizations have demonstrated outside clinics, even establishing blockades to prevent people going in or leaving.

Some anti-abortionists have turned to firebombing clinics and murdering medical staff. The Reverend Paul Hill, director of Defensive Action, was charged with the murders of Dr. John Britton and James Barratt, who were shot outside a clinic in Pensacola, Florida. In December 1994, John Salvi went on a shooting spree at clinics in Massachusetts and Virginia, killing two people.

EARTH FIRST!

Earth First! is the foremost militant environmentalist group in America and is another prime example of a single-issue activist organization. It was founded in 1980, with the rallying cry of "No compromise in defense of Mother Earth." The group seeks to save as much of the American wilderness as possible from modern society. Earth First! began by staging a series of theatrical publicity stunts. The campaign escalated into one of fully fledged industrial sabotage, or "monkey wrenching." The sabotage included arson, disabling logging equipment, and strewing metal spikes onto rural roads to make them impassable to

---

KEY FACTS

● Earth First! monkey wrenchers refer to industrialists and developers as "concreteheads."

● In April 1994, a British ALF leader who had escaped from police custody the previous year was recaptured – by a police dog.

● According to National Abortion Federation figures, 161 bombings and arsons took place against abortion clinics between 1977 and 1992.

John Salvi during his arraignment for opening fire on an abortion clinic in Norfolk, Virginia.

Hulton Getty Picture Collection

tree-felling machinery. As a part of their campaign against the cutting down of forests, Earth First! supporters also hammered spikes into trees so that they would be useless for felling as lumber.

Besides the forestry industry, Earth First! monkey wrenchers also targeted the nuclear power industry in their environmental campaign. The group severed power lines and caused domestic blackouts. Members have also been accused of sabotaging a ski lift and an atomic-weapons factory.

ANIMAL LIBERATION FRONT

On the extreme fringe of the animal rights movement is the Animal Liberation Front (ALF). In Britain, the ALF has not hesitated to use terrorism against those who, in its opinion, maltreat animals. In January 1981, the homes of several Oxford University scientists were attacked by ALF activists. The activists daubed slogans on walls, and damaged a garage and cars. In March 1984, the group issued a warning that it had contaminated bottles of shampoo in stores in London, Leeds, and Southampton, claiming the manufacturers

tested the product on animals. Bottles spiked with bleach were discovered in Leeds and Southampton.

On October 24, 1984, a group of ALF activists attacked a dog kennel in southern England, assaulting three people. Simultaneously, other ALF supporters attacked buildings at two research laboratories with sledgehammers. A fourth group visited the home of a laboratory research director, who was beaten with an iron bar. In December 1987, the ALF targeted the fur trade, firebombing stores selling furs in Manchester, Liverpool, and Cardiff.

America also has a group called the Animal Liberation Front. It is one of the U.S.'s most publicized illegal activist organizations. In April 1985, 16 members of the group raided the Riverside Life Sciences Building of the University of California, taking hundreds of animals. ALF spokespeople claimed that the institution caused the animals to suffer in isolation and sight-deprivation experiments. Sabotage makes research more expensive, so the movement hopes its actions will encourage animal friendly methods – the attack at Riverside caused hundreds of thousands of dollars' worth of damage. The U.S. version of the Animal Liberation Front has a policy of avoiding injuries to people.

In terms of a group being able to realize its goals, though, the shift from democratic campaigning to direct violent action may prove counterproductive. Single-issue groups that move outside the democratic process automatically lose the moral high ground, and with it may go any public support they have.

Toby Dodge

SEE ALSO:

NUCLEAR TERRORISM; THE MINDSET OF THE TERRORIST; ANTI-ABORTION ACTIVISTS' TERROR CAMPAIGN.

FURTHER READING

- Finsen, L., and S. Finsen. *The Animal Rights Movement in America: From Compassion to Respect.* New York: Twayne Publishers,1994.
- Lee, M. F. "Violence and the Environment: The Case of Earth First!" *Terrorism and Political Violence* 7, No. 3 (Autumn 1995): 109-127.
- National Abortion Federation. *Incidents of Violence & Disruption against Abortion Providers.* Washington, DC: National Abortion Federation, 1993.

DOMESTIC VERSUS INTERNATIONAL TERRORISM

Some terrorist groups are exclusively concerned with affecting politics within a single state. Such groups include pro-life (anti-abortion) terrorists, some animal rights activists, and the individuals who planted the bomb in Oklahoma City in 1995. However, most terrorism has some kind of international tinge. It is the international aspect that makes cooperation between states essential in combating terrorist activity, and which makes terrorism so difficult to root out.

Since 1945, there have been three aspects of the relations between states that have fostered the internationalization of terrorism. The first is the collapse of European colonial empires. Many states have aided the campaigns of terrorists seeking to end colonial dominance. In the 1950s, for example, Morocco and Tunisia helped Algerian National Liberation Front terrorists against the French. The second aspect is the Cold War. Both the West and communist states aided groups that they described as freedom fighters but which their opponents described as terrorists. The final aspect in international relations that made terrorism an international activity is the situation of Israel, a state created within an Arab bloc. Many of these Arab states have, at some point, assisted terrorist groups.

Within this general climate, there are a number of levels at which terrorists operate internationally. The first level of international terrorism is one in which some of one country's population actively help terrorists from another country. The examples of the Basques of ETA, operating in Spain, and the Provisional IRA, operating in Northern Ireland, are instructive. Although there was no state aid to either group in neighboring France or the Irish Republic respectively, there was certainly a sizable group of sympathizers who were prepared to give help, or at least turn a blind eye, to would-be terrorists.

In the case of ETA, there was a large expatriate Basque community in southern France, and many French people were inclined to be sympathetic to ETA while the dictator General Franco ruled Spain. In the Republic of Ireland, the wish of the IRA to unite the whole of Ireland struck a chord in many hearts. Events such as "Bloody Sunday" in 1972, when British paratroopers killed 13 Catholic demonstrators, reinforced such feelings of nationalism.

SYMPATHY IN ANOTHER COUNTRY

Support and help from elements within states takes many forms. At one level, there is covert protection. At another, there is fundraising, lobbying of government, and enthusiastic propagandizing. The Provisional IRA provides a good example of popularity abroad. In the Republic of Ireland and especially in the U.S., large groups of people are prepared to do much to help the Provisional IRA, and have raised millions of dollars that sustain terrorist activity. The attempt to mobilize U.S. public opinion and to gain support from within the U.S. government achieved great success in 1995, when Sinn Fein president Gerry Adams was invited to the White House.

Another good example of this kind of international help from sympathetic communities has occurred in the case of the Tamil Tigers, fighting for a Tamil state

---

KEY FACTS

● In 1944, Jewish terrorists of the Stern Gang assassinated British minister Lord Moyne in Egypt, carrying out an operation outside Palestine in order to sway world opinion to their cause.

● In 1985, Middle Eastern groups carried out 75 terrorist attacks in Western Europe, killing 65 people. Twenty of these attacks were aimed at Western people or property, rather than at Arab and Palestinian or Israeli and Jewish targets.

Spanish repression, including death sentences on these Basque separatists at Burgos in 1970, encouraged French sympathies for the Basque cause.

within what is now Sri Lanka. They have an effective fundraising organization within Tamil communities worldwide that gives them the resources to buy whatever weapons and equipment they feel they need. For a long period they were also able to smuggle such arms into Sri Lanka with the active help of the Tamil population of southern India, even though there was no help given them by the Indian authorities.

When a nation state, rather than individuals within that state, aids a terror group, then potentially there is a great benefit to the terrorists. In many struggles since 1945 which have involved terrorism, such aid has been available across borders. The communist Chinese gave aid to the Vietminh nationalists in Vietnam in the 1950s. In the 1980s, the South Africans helped guerrillas in neighboring Mozambique to destabilize the government there.

State aid to terrorists is not only confined to obvious movement across a border. In the modern world, aid from state governments is often sent to terrorists from long distances. For example, in Central America during the 1980s, the U.S. government aided the Contras in their fight against the Sandinista regime by secretly funneling weapons and money to them. During the Cold War, states in the Soviet Eastern Bloc also aided terrorists if they considered communism's interests best served by such terror groups. Since the fall of communist regimes in Europe in 1989, information has emerged detailing many links between Eastern bloc countries and terrorists. The communist East German regime, for example, gave support to the Baader-Meinhof terrorists operating in West Germany.

STATE SPONSORSHIP

The most notorious examples of state sponsoring of terrorism have come from the Middle East. Since the 1960s, both Syria and Colonel Muammar al-Qaddafi's Libya have provided arms, funding, and training for a variety of guerrillas and terrorists. The fighters were mainly Palestinian, or linked to Palestinian organizations, but Qaddafi, for example, also sent large quantities of arms and explosives to the Provisional IRA in Northern Ireland. Even after air strikes against Libya in the 1980s and the alignment of Syria with Western powers during the Gulf War of 1990-91, it is still suspected that Libya and Syria have many terrorist connections. The planting of a bomb on Pan Am Flight 103, which exploded over Lockerbie, Scotland, in 1988, has been generally laid at the door of agents working with Libyan backing. But many commentators believe that Syrian terrorists, not the Libyans, were involved.

In the 1980s, Syria and Libya were joined by Iran in sponsoring terrorism. Under the fundamentalist regime of Ayatollah Khomeini, Iran funded many organizations involved in terrorist activities, such as the Palestinian Hizb'allah group based in Lebanon.

Many states have concluded that sponsoring terrorism is a successful way of achieving foreign policy objectives. States where foreign policy involves an ideological struggle are most likely to lean toward sponsoring international terrorism. Examples are found in the Cold War struggle between countries espousing capitalist and communist ideologies or in the Middle East, where religion and nationalism are intertwined.

Given that so much modern terrorism has an international dimension, it is not surprising that terrorist

Reuters

This memorial at Arlington, Virginia, honors the 270 victims of the Lockerbie Pan Am Flight 103 bombing in 1988. Libyan or Syrian terrorists are thought to have been behind the explosion over Scotland.

acts themselves often take on an international form. Terrorists may direct their violence against people or property having only a loose connection with the main aims of the terrorist group. The intention is to gain worldwide publicity that is considered an end in itself. The terrorists may also plot actions to make the whole international community feel unsafe while the group's objectives remain unfulfilled. There is the additional attraction that targets in countries not directly involved in a terrorist campaign may be easy to attack.

In this context, Palestinian groups or their supporters have carried out the most notorious acts of international terrorism. The Palestinians' view of the late 1960s was that there was an American-Zionist plot to stop them from attaining a Palestinian homeland. Palestinian groups then considered that any attacks on property belonging to America or its allies were justified. They also wanted publicity for their cause. From

Popperfoto

In October 1985, Arab terrorists hijacked the Italian cruise liner Achille Lauro *in the Mediterranean Sea.*

1968, there were attacks on Israeli targets in Europe, which evolved into a wave of airline hijackings by Palestinian groups such as Black September and the Popular Front for the Liberation of Palestine (PFLP).

The most spectacular single hijacking incident was in 1970, when the PFLP blew up three airliners it had had flown to Dawson's Field in Jordan. But the attack that made the most impact was in 1972, when Black September terrorists took Israeli athletes hostage at the Munich Olympic Games. The event ended tragically when the hostages were killed in a furious gun battle between terrorists and security forces.

Since the mid-1970s, such international acts have been rarer, partly because of better security by national and international police forces. But they still occur. One example was the hijacking of the cruise ship *Achille Lauro* in 1985 by Palestinians. One justification terrorists use for attacks on innocent victims is the belief that there is an international conspiracy to prevent the achievement of Palestinian aims. This

leads naturally to treating the leading Western power, the U.S., as an enemy. On the *Achille Lauro*, the terrorists killed Leon Klinghoffer, a disabled U.S. citizen. Americans have also been singled out in other attacks.

Similarly, European terrorists sympathetic to the Palestinians have often targeted U.S. officials. In 1981 in Italy, the Red Brigades kidnapped U.S. general James Dozier. Before then, the Red Brigades had been a purely Italian problem. In the Middle East, distrust of the U.S. received a boost in the 1980s after the Islamic revolution in Iran. Militant fundamentalists described America as the "Great Satan." The most notable terrorist act expressing this hatred was the bomb planted by Islamic militants in the World Trade Center in 1993.

Effectively, then, terrorism in the modern world has been pushed into an international position because certain states use it and encourage it, and individual terrorists feel justified in attacking foreign states that they consider to be ideologically hostile to them.

Noemi Gal-Or

SEE ALSO:

TERRORISM IN FRENCH ALGERIA; TERROR AGAINST THE FRENCH IN INDOCHINA; SINGLE-ISSUE GROUP TERRORISM; BOMBING OPERATIONS; HIJACKING AND KIDNAPPING; COLLABORATION BETWEEN TERRORISTS; THE BEGINNING OF INTERNATIONAL TERRORISM; THE BLACK SEPTEMBER ORGANIZATION; TERRORISM AND REVOLUTION IN IRAN; HIZB'ALLAH; TERRORISM IN NICARAGUA; TAMIL TIGER TERROR IN SRI LANKA; THE OKLAHOMA CITY BOMBING AND THE MILITIAS; RED ARMY FACTION: THE BAADER-MEINHOF GANG; RED BRIGADES; BASQUE NATIONALIST TERROR: ETA; IRA: ORIGINS AND TERROR TO 1976; NATIONALIST TERROR IN NORTHERN IRELAND 1976-1996; STATE-SPONSORED TERRORISM.

FURTHER READING

- Chomsky, Noam. *Pirates and Emperors: International Terrorism in the Real World.* New York: Black Rose Books, 1991.
- Guelke, Adrian. *The Age of Terrorism and the International Political System.* New York: St. Martin's Press, 1995.
- Heitmeyer, W. "Hostility and Violence against Foreigners in Germany." In *Racist Violence in Europe,* edited by Tore Bjorgo and R. Witte. New York: St. Martin's Press, 1993.

STATE VERSUS NON-STATE TERRORISM

The term *terrorism* has been used to describe violent political acts carried out by informal, illegal, and basically private groups. In recent years a number of analysts have criticized this approach. They argue that acts carried out by governments, or security forces, should also be included.

Some claim that governments have all too often used terrorism, employing the same fear-inducing methods as illegal, revolutionary groups. In reality, both government and non-government violence has intimidated and terrorized civilian populations.

It is not always easy to distinguish between state and non-state terrorism since the strategies and tactics may be identical. But terrorism carried out in the service of a government is classed as state terrorism. Sometimes the government carries out the actions itself; sometimes it uses agents to do its dirty work.

WHAT IS STATE TERRORISM?

Most analysts distinguish between three types of state terrorist activity. The first, state terror, is the use of terrorism by a government turning against its own citizens to enforce its rule. The second is usually termed state-sponsored terrorism, in which the government controls a terrorist group abroad. Finally, state-supported terrorism occurs when a government provides funds or supplies to an independent terrorist group. Both of the latter forms of state terrorism are usually directed against foreign governments or critics abroad.

State terror by the authorities is a means of oppression and intimidation. The government may direct it against the whole population or just particular groups. Often laws are passed that legalize torture, beatings, and killing by police or the army under certain conditions. Alternatively, terror practices may be carried out in violation of the legal code. The state may justify these illegal acts as necessary for the defense of law and order or for the survival of the regime. Those who act illegally in this way are rarely punished.

State terror can suppress resistance and subdue populations. Dictators or governments that cannot be charged by judicial investigators use it. Stalin's purges or Saddam Hussein's gas attacks on Iraqi Kurds are typical of such acts. In Central and South America, right-wing regimes that do not wish to be directly connected to state terror have formed unofficial death squads to strike at their opponents. Members of the police or armed forces often staff the squads.

STATE SPONSORSHIP AND SUPPORT

Whereas repressive state terror is designed to maintain a country's internal status quo, state-sponsored and state-supported terrorism are intended to destabilize a hostile foreign government. The support of guerrilla insurgents in Mozambique and Angola by the South African government in the 1980s is a classic example.

State-sponsored terrorism occurs when a government plans, directs, and controls terrorist operations in another country. The activities may be carried out by individuals or by government officials. State-supported terrorism has less involvement, providing a

---

KEY FACTS

● In an example of state-supported terrorism in 1991, Gulbuddin Hekmatyar became the most powerful guerrilla in Afghanistan because of Pakistani government funding.

● During 1975-79 the Cambodian government employed state terror, killing a million of its own citizens to stay in power.

● The Iranian government has sponsored uprisings in Bahrain, Iraq, and Lebanon.

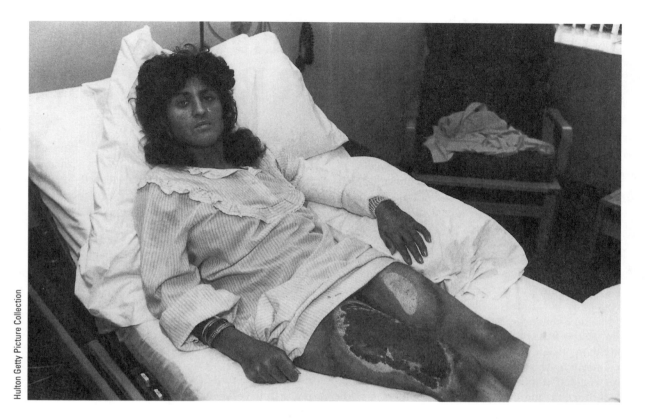

Hulton Getty Picture Collection

A Kurdish victim of a 1988 Iraqi gassing. Saddam Hussein instigated the attacks on his own people.

revolutionary group with transport, training sites, money, propaganda, and diplomatic protection.

Iran is a notorious example of a state practicing all three forms. It has a record of terrorizing members of ethnic and religious minorities within Iran, and has assassinated exiled members of the opposition. Iran has also provided funds, weapons, training, and protection to terrorists from Islamic organizations. It has a special relationship with the Lebanese group Hizb'allah, which it gives nearly $5 million a year.

Although associated with authoritarian regimes, terror has also been supported by democracies. The U.S. has participated in running countries in Central America, supporting right-wing regimes in Nicaragua and El Salvador. In Guatemala in 1954, the U.S. supported a regime that massacred 100,000 peasants.

States have the advantage over terrorist groups, in terms of means at their disposal. But the non-state terrorist can at least make some claim to be at war with the enemy, whereas the state hides behind the terrorist smokescreen, blurring the boundaries between peace and war.

Noemi Gal-Or

SEE ALSO:

STALIN'S GREAT TERROR; THEORIES OF STATE TERROR; TERRORISM AND REVOLUTION IN IRAN; HIZB'ALLAH; TERROR BY THE HOLY WARRIORS OF KASHMIR; THE ISRAELI RESPONSE TO TERRORISM; STATE SPONSORSHIP OF TERRORISM; SADDAM HUSSEIN'S TERROR IN KURDISTAN; TERROR IN CAMBODIA.

FURTHER READING

- Agger, I. and S. B. Jensen. *Trauma and Healing Under State Terrorism.* Atlantic Highlands, NJ: Zed Books, 1996.
- Bushnell, P. T., ed. *State Organized Terror: The Case of Violent Internal Repression.* Boulder, CO: Westview Press, 1991.
- Murphy, J. F. *State Support for International Terrorism.* Boulder, CO: Westview Press, 1989.

URBAN VERSUS RURAL TERRORISM

Terrorism in the countryside is totally unlike terrorism in urban areas, and this divide is important in understanding modern terrorism. The same groups may operate in both areas but use different methods. The key differences arise from the physical environments in city and country. In a city, there are usually crowds and security forces are rarely far away. Urban terrorists must move secretly, strike quickly, and then hide again. If properly handled, a single dramatic act by an urban terrorist group in a major city can attract headlines worldwide.

In the countryside, there is more space and freedom for the terrorists or guerrillas to operate. Rural groups are more able to control large areas. They can openly take over a village, murder a headman or government representative in front of the villagers, propose a political program, and promise to return – a promise the population knows they probably will keep.

RURAL THEORIES

Another distinction between urban and rural terrorism derives from their histories. Terrorists and guerrillas operating in rural areas in the two decades after 1945 owed a great debt to the ideas of Mao Zedong. He devised a plan for rural guerrilla warfare after his successful campaign for communism in China. He argued that safe base areas should be established from which a more conventional military campaign could be launched. Later, in the 1960s, the success of the Cuban

revolutionaries meant that the theories of Che Guevara took precedence. Guevara followed Mao in advocating that insurgents establish bases, but believed the group could form a *foco*, or ideological focus, which would inspire a widespread revolutionary uprising.

URBAN STRUGGLES FOR VICTORY

By contrast, urban terrorism has never had a strong theoretical base. Sometimes urban terror has been added to a campaign of rural terrorism, as in Vietnam during the 1950s and 1960s, or has been used simply because enemy targets are concentrated in urban areas, as in Cyprus during the 1950s.

There were some attempts to create theories of urban action against the state in the 1960s, notably by the Brazilian Carlos Marighella. However, all these theorists have failed to solve a central problem: how to progress from small-scale action to takeover of the state. Mao's theories showed how rural guerrillas could develop into large conventional forces that could confront the government army, and Guevara's theories combined guerrilla forces with civilian revolution. However, urban guerrillas have never known how to translate the first stages of their action – bombs or assassinations – into a final victory.

SEEKING A GOVERNMENT RESPONSE

Unable to achieve military victory, urban terrorist action has three underlying aims. First, it may show up the weakness of the state to the population. Second, it may cause the government to retaliate and so alienate the population. Third, the terrorist attacks may impose so high a price that the government may decide to concede to terrorist demands.

This latter aim has not been achieved in modern times. Urban guerrillas have rarely been able to present more than a short-term threat. The Irish Republican Army (IRA), for example, has not been able to impose an unacceptable cost on the British government to drive them out of Northern Ireland. Perhaps the largest urban terrorist operation in

KEY FACTS

● In rural areas, small squads conduct a slow war of attrition on isolated security forces units.

● Urban campaigns focus on mass action and single acts of violence. Their aim is to win over their own community, maintain social pressure on their nation, and manipulate world opinion.

● Rural terror involves tactical planning; urban organizations are more managerial and financial.

Hulton Getty Picture Collection

The London department store Harrods was bombed in 1993 by the Provisional Irish Republican Army.

modern times was that of the Algerian nationalists who set up an urban terrorist network in Algiers in 1957, but they were rounded up in a matter of months.

These differences between rural and urban tactics affect operating methods and structures. Rural guerrillas tend to have a military structure, which can deploy large units. When government or enemy forces attack, the rural guerrillas aim to resist by ambushes, delaying tactics, and booby traps. If the forces involved are too large, they retreat and regroup elsewhere.

URBAN ADVANTAGES

Urban terrorists, on the other hand, rarely assemble in large military groups. Typically, they will be organized in cells of four or so activists, only one of whom will have other contacts within the organization. They may do little or nothing for long periods of time; and even when they do get the opportunity to act, this action may involve nothing more than taking a package from one place to another. Confrontation with government forces is usually avoided at all costs.

Virtually the only occasion when urban terrorists are prepared to confront government forces is during mass crowd action, when the overwhelming military force available to the government is almost useless. When the government does make use of such force, there is the possibility of adverse publicity. For example, on "Bloody Sunday," January 30, 1972, British

paratroopers killed 13 Catholic protesters during a mass demonstration in Northern Ireland. Worldwide condemnation followed, and the army lost the respect of the Catholic population.

Urban terrorists benefit from the fact that they are operating in a vulnerable environment. A firebomb in a store or a hand grenade in a crowded street can have a great impact on a society. Few single actions by rural guerrillas will ever have the same effect.

The final comparison between rural and urban terrorists lies in their vulnerability to security forces. In general, the two forms of terrorism are met in different ways. Classically, rural counterinsurgency begins by guarding potential targets, then cutting the guerrillas off from the rural population, and only later progresses to fighting the guerrillas themselves. In Mao's terms, the fish cannot be caught until the sea in which they are swimming is hostile to them.

To protect every vulnerable point of a modern city from urban terrorists would impose terrible constraints on the population as a whole, which might prove to be unacceptable politically. Consequently, the general method of combating urban terrorists is to penetrate their networks and groups of possible sympathizers, using informers and undercover police. This is usually a long-term process. Arrests and discoveries of caches of arms punctuate prolonged periods of painstaking detective work – mirroring the urban group's careful planning before a terrorist act.

Heinz Tittmar

SEE ALSO:

TERROR'S USE BY THE FRENCH RESISTANCE; THEORIES OF TERROR IN URBAN INSURRECTIONS; GUERRILLAS AND TERROR; TERRORISM IN FRENCH ALGERIA; TERRORISM IN CYPRUS; TERRORISM IN KENYA; TERRORISM IN ZIMBABWE (RHODESIA); TERRORISM IN BRAZIL; TERROR IN AFGHANISTAN.

FURTHER READING

- Black, I. and B. Morris. *Israel's Secret Wars: A History of Israel's Intelligence Services.* New York: Grove Weidenfeld, 1992.
- Spencer, M. *Foundations of Modern Sociology.* Englewood Cliffs, NJ: Prentice-Hall, 1979.
- Toolis, Kevin. *Journeys within the IRA's Soul.* New York: St. Martin's Press, 1996.

RELIGIOUS EXTREMISM

"I have no regrets. I acted alone and on orders from God," was the explanation offered by Yigal Amir, the young Jewish extremist who assassinated Israeli prime minister Yitzhak Rabin in November 1995. His words were not the rantings of a madman, but expressed the views of a religious zealot and terrorist. His violent act was not only calculated to achieve a political end – to destroy the Arab-Israeli peace process – but was also motivated by the desire to fulfil, in his own mind, a divine command. If terrorism is in essence the use of violence, or the threat of it, for political purposes, then Rabin's assassination was undoubtedly a terrorist act. But it was one with a distinct, profoundly significant, religious background.

This mix of political and religious motivations is found in many extremist groups that emerge from mostly peaceful, mainstream religious movements. The divinely inspired explanation offered by Amir could as easily have come from the lips of other religious terrorists. The Islamic Hamas terrorists, responsible for the wave of suicide bombings that convulsed Israel in the 1990s, could have spoken Amir's lines. So could the Muslim Algerian terrorists who, in 1995, bombed commuter trains, tourist spots, schools, and markets in France. The Japanese followers of the Aum Shinri-kyu sect who allegedly perpetrated the March 1995 gas attack on the Tokyo subway were similarly motivated.

In all these cases, the perpetrators were driven by the belief that their acts were not only fulfilling God's will, but were also hastening the redemption of mankind. The aims of religious terrorists go beyond the fundamental political, social, or territorial changes that most non-religious terrorists seek. Religious terrorists often pursue a quirky combination of mystical, transcendental, and divinely inspired objectives. In most cases, they are vehemently anti-government on religious, racial, and political grounds.

TRADITIONS OF DIVINE INSPIRATION

Religion has increasingly become a rallying point for terrorism in the post–Cold War era because communist ideologies have been discredited by the collapse of the Soviet Union, and the promises of well-being prophesied by capitalist states have not been fulfilled.

But the link between religion and terrorism is not new. More than 2,000 years ago, the first acts of what is now termed "terrorism" were perpetrated by religious fanatics. Some of the words that describe terrorists and their actions come from the Jewish, Hindi, and Muslim terrorist groups active long ago.

The word *zealot*, for example, now meaning a fanatic, comes from the name of a Jewish sect which opposed the Roman empire's conquest of what is now Israel. The Zealots waged a ruthless campaign of assassination. A Zealot would emerge from the anonymity of a crowded market and draw out the *sica* (dagger) concealed beneath his robes. In full view, he would slit the throat of a Roman legionnaire or Jewish citizen judged guilty of betrayal or religious heresy.

The Zealots' public acts of violence – like those of terrorists today – were designed to have repercussions far beyond killing the victim of the attack. Murders were supposed to send a powerful message to a wider "target audience" – in this case, the Romans and the members of the Jewish community who collaborated with the invaders.

Similarly, the word *thug*, now meaning a rough or brutal hoodlum, comes from a religious cult that

---

KEY FACTS

● In 1968, none of the 11 identifiable active terrorist groups were religious. Today, there are about 50 known groups, and about a quarter of them are religious in motivation.

● Religious terrorists want sweeping change and are prepared to inflict a high death toll to achieve it.

● Since 1982, Shiite Muslim terrorists have committed eight percent of terrorist acts, but are responsible for 30 percent of deaths.

Rex Features

A Palestinian suicide bomber blew up five other people with him on a bus in Tel Aviv, Israel, in 1995.

terrorized India until its suppression in the mid-nineteenth century. On holy days throughout the year, members would lie in wait for innocent travelers and ritualistically strangle them as sacrifices to Kali, the Hindu goddess of terror and destruction. According to some accounts, the Thugs killed a million people during their 1,200-year existence, an average of more than 800 victims a year. Such an assassination rate is rarely achieved by the Thugs' modern counterparts, even with their advantage of more lethal weaponry. The word *assassin* itself literally means "hashish-eater" – a reference to the ritual drug-taking of an eleventh-century Muslim sect before they went on their divinely inspired murder missions.

RELIGIOUS TO SECULAR AND BACK

Religion and terrorism share a long history. But for most of the twentieth century, ethnic, nationalist, or ideological issues have motivated terrorist groups. The end of the divine right of monarchs to rule, Marxist ideology, and movements such as anarchism completed terrorism's shift to the secular. Now the pendulum of terrorism is swinging back toward religion.

While religious terrorism has been growing steadily in recent years, fewer than 15 of the known terrorist groups active worldwide today have a predominantly religious motivation. Many contemporary terrorist groups also have a religious background – such as the Catholic-dominated Provisional IRA and the Protestant paramilitary groups in Northern Ireland – but it is the nationalist or separatist aspects of these groups that predominate.

Motives are different for the religious terrorist. Violence is an inspired duty carried out in response to some specific theological belief. So this extremism has a god-driven aspect absent from secular terrorism. Religious and secular terrorists also differ in the "audience" toward which their acts are directed. Secular terrorists attempt to appeal to sympathizers, members of the communities that they claim to defend, or the aggrieved people they say they speak for. But some religious terrorists are engaged in what they regard as a "total war." This sanctions almost limitless depths of violence, and anyone who is not a member of the terrorists' religion may be seen as a legitimate target.

Popperfoto

Shoko Asahara, leader of Japan's Aum Shinri-kyu sect, alleged to have unleashed gas on Tokyo's subway.

Religious terrorists usually want the greatest benefits for members of their faith only. They are not interested in the greater good. Secular terrorists see violence primarily as a means to an end. But religious extremists, because of the divine element of their motivation, often view violence as an end in itself. Clerical authorities – be they ayatollahs or mullahs, priests or rabbis, pastors or reverends – may interpret sacred texts so that religion justifies violence.

Religious and secular terrorists can have very different perceptions of themselves and their acts. Whereas secular terrorists may regard violence as a way of improving an existing system, religious terrorists often see themselves as outside a system not worth preserving. They seek vast changes. This sense of alienation lets religious extremists contemplate far more destructive violence against far more people than do secular terrorists. Religious extremists also view people outside their community as inferior. They describe them in deliberately dehumanizing and denigrating terms, calling them names such as nonbelievers, dogs, children of Satan, and mud people.

Contrary to popular belief, terrorism motivated by religion is not restricted to Islamic groups in the Middle East. The Tokyo subway gas attack, the Oklahoma City bombing, and the assassination of Yitzak Rabin all demonstrate this fact. Just since 1985 there has been a string of international attempts at mass slaughter. An unnamed group of 14 white supremacists plotted to dump cyanide into reservoirs in Washington, DC, and Chicago, Illinois. The Rajneesh cult, followers of an Indian mystic living in a rural Oregon religious commune, contaminated the salad bars of restaurants with salmonella bacteria to influence the outcome of local elections. In Israel, the Lifta Gang, a group of Jewish fanatics, plotted to blow up Jerusalem's Dome of the Rock, Islam's third holiest shrine. They hoped to provoke a massive "holy war" that would obliterate the Muslim world.

Extremist religious groups can represent a different and potentially far more deadly threat than traditional terrorists. These groups are unpredictable. No one is sure why many fringe movements or hitherto peaceful religious sects suddenly turn to violence and embark on lethal campaigns of indiscriminate terrorism. Traditional policies designed to counter terrorism, such as political concessions, financial rewards, and amnesties, are wasted on religious zealots. Instead, new approaches are needed to bridge the chasm between these extremist religious organizations and mainstream society.

Bruce Hoffman

SEE ALSO:

THE ASSASSINS: A TERROR CULT; TERRORISTS' USE OF CHEMICAL WEAPONS; TERRORISM AND REVOLUTION IN IRAN; HIZB'ALLAH; HAMAS; THE WORLD TRADE CENTER BOMBING; ANTI-ABORTION ACTIVISTS' TERROR CAMPAIGN; THE OKLAHOMA CITY BOMBING AND THE MILITIAS.

FURTHER READING

- Brackett, D. W. *Holy Terror: Armageddon in Tokyo.* New York: Weather Hill, 1996.
- Hoffman, Bruce. "Holy Terror: The Implications of Terrorism Motivated by a Religious Imperative." *Studies in Conflict and Terrorism*, Vol.18, No.4 (Winter 1995): 271-84.
- Rapoport, D. C. "Fear and Trembling: Terrorism in Three Religious Traditions." *American Political Science Review,* Vol. 78, No. 3 (Sept. 1984): 668-72.
- Wright, Robin B. *Sacred Rage: The Wrath of Militant Islam.* New York: Simon and Schuster, 1986.

Terrorist Techniques and Methods

Today's terrorists have the full battery of modern weaponry at their disposal, from surface-to-air missiles to chemicals, as well as more traditional bombs and mortars. There's even the horrific specter of a nuclear weapon getting into the hands of terrorists. But first, any terrorist group needs some kind of structure so that their campaigns run efficiently – just like a legal political party. They have to plan whether they are going to plant bombs, carry out hijackings and kidnappings, or assassinate a prominent figure, or whether to use a combination of methods. Whatever tactics they use, they need to raise funds to finance their operations.

TERROR GROUP ORGANIZATION

There are three critical issues to consider in a discussion of the organization of terrorismand terrorist groups. The first is the different ways in which rural and urban terrorists construct and organize their movements; the second is the role of leadership and control; and, finally, the relationship between such movements and more or less legitimate political groups.

Rural terrorism is almost always associated with guerrilla warfare, in which terror is part of a larger campaign. The single most influential advocate of terror was Mao Zedong. He stated that the ultimate military aim of the guerrilla army was to create a force capable of operating in open battle, and that this force should be built up in a safe base area while enemy forces were kept occupied by small guerrilla groups. The key to this organization was the establishment of core units within villages. The Vietminh in Vietnam in the 1940s, for example, applied Mao's theories. In areas where the Vietminh had some influence, each village was expected to provide a "self-defense" core unit of 12 guerrillas, in addition to a further five who could be used on operations outside the village's immediate area. These core units gave the Vietminh a strong base and made it difficult to root out their organization, even when French forces moved into an area with force.

Although this Maoist model has been most important in rural terrorism, in South America, Che Guevara's *foco* theory was very influential. The *foco* was a group of guerrillas who would establish themselves locally and then grow to take on the forces of the state. Various unsuccessful attempts were made to establish such groups in Latin America during the 1960s and 1970s.

Urban terrorism demands different structures. It requires great secrecy, and the terrorists often move in an environment physically dominated by their opponents. The problem for the leadership is how to maintain control and pass on orders without leaving the organization open to being broken up by a few arrests or even a single informer. The answer to this is a cellular structure, in which each cell, consisting of maybe four individuals, contains only one member who has any contact with others in the organization. Whereas rural terrorists are engaged in propaganda and broadening the organization's base as well as in guerrilla warfare, urban terrorists who launch attacks are usually isolated from other aspects of a campaign.

A typical example of cellular organization was that of the Algerian urban terrorists of the National Liberation Front (FLN) who carried out a bombing campaign in Algiers during the late 1950s. The French authorities eventually broke the campaign by using massive force and by constructing a huge organization chart on which they gradually filled in, and eliminated, names in all the cells. To extract detailed information, they routinely tortured suspects.

In Northern Ireland, the Provisional IRA was set up using an essentially rural structure inherited from earlier in the century. British security services had penetrated the terrorist group by the mid-1970s. In response, the IRA established a cell network and drastically reduced the number of activists. Today, it is estimated that there are just a few dozen IRA terrorists active at any one time.

Another terrorist organization that set up a successful cellular network was the Italian Red Brigades. It

---

KEY FACTS

● Rural and urban terrorists adopt different structures. Urban terrorists generally use a cellular structure; rural terrorists build up large structured groups out of small assault groups.

● The Provisional IRA reorganized itself into cells in the late 1970s to evade British security services.

● Many terrorist groups have a close but informal relationship with a political group, which acts as their mouthpiece and provides helpers and recruits.

Italian Red Brigades Organization

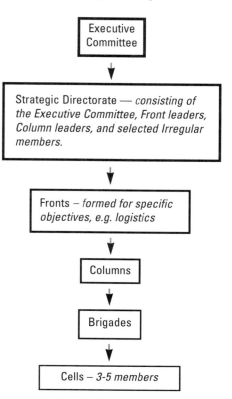

Like many terrorist groups, the Red Brigades had a clear hierarchical structure. Brigades and cells consist of regular members (illegal activists) and irregulars (activists involved in legal activities).

was only late in the group's operational life that the Italian government was able to get near its leadership.

The problem with this cellular organization is that leaders are not able to communicate very quickly with operatives. Good communication is crucial, partly because terrorist groups are often based on charismatic leaders. For example, Menachem Begin commanded the Jewish terrorist group Irgun like an older brother guiding the younger members of his family. George Grivas ran the Cypriot EOKA group like a Greek patriarch, and George Habash dominated the Popular Front for the Liberation of Palestine by strength of character and mastery of ideology.

But in a more general sense, the central leadership must be able to allot certain tasks (operational direction, intelligence, and acquiring, storing, and deploying

arms, for example) and maintain contact with the direct operatives. This is normally done through a network of individuals who are sympathetic to the cause, but who are not full-time terrorists. Like the cell members, they have little contact with other members of the formal organization and are given occasional tasks – delivering a package here, making a telephone call there. They are, however, the sinews that bind the organization together. Without them the active cells could quickly become isolated.

These sympathetic individuals are often members of some kind of political organization. Some groups – such as the Italian Red Brigades – did not have a legitimate mouthpiece so they publish their own manifestos. The Provisional IRA, however, has an informal relationship with Sinn Féin, a legal political party.

The Palestine Liberation Organization (PLO) is often described as terrorist. Its leadership regularly denies knowledge of terrorist activities. However, it is now widely accepted in political and academic circles that Yasser Arafat, head of the PLO and of its major component, the party Fatah, set up Black September as a terrorist unit in the early 1970s to retain the allegiance of disaffected activists. Again, PLO involvement was strenuously denied, but there was a tight, if informal, relationship.

John Bowyer Bell

SEE ALSO:

TERRORISM IN FRENCH ALGERIA; TERRORISM IN CYPRUS; TERROR AGAINST THE FRENCH IN INDOCHINA; COLLABORATION BETWEEN TERRORISTS; THE BLACK SEPTEMBER ORGANIZATION; RED BRIGADES; NATIONALIST TERROR IN NORTHERN IRELAND 1976-1996.

F U R T H E R   R E A D I N G

- Becker, J. *Hitler's Children: The Story of the Baader-Meinhof Terrorist Gang.* Philadelphia and New York: J. B. Lippincott, 1977.
- Bell, John Bowyer. *The Secret Army: The IRA 1916-1996.* New Brunswick, NJ: Transaction Publishers, 1996.
- Collin, R. O., and G. L. Freedman. *Winter of Fire: The Abduction of General Dozier and the Downfall of the Red Brigades.* New York: Dutton, 1990.
- Livingstone, N. C. and D. Halevy. *Inside the PLO.* New York: William Morrow, 1990.

BOMBING OPERATIONS

Most terrorist groups find that bombs are convenient and effective weapons. Bombs can be used in small but lethal booby traps or in massive, headline-grabbing acts. Repeated attacks can traumatize a society, eventually producing precisely the sort of disruption the terrorists want.

Most terrorist groups have few active members and operate by means of still smaller cells. Bombs enable terrorists to be economical in their use of limited numbers and still kill many of their enemies. In addition, a bomb exploded by a small cell of terrorists can gain worldwide publicity while offering the terrorists a fair chance of escaping unharmed; even in suicide attacks only one terrorist is sacrificed.

Governments and other victims routinely describe bomb attacks as "cowardly," but such name-calling is unlikely to stop terrorists from planting bombs. Terrorists usually see themselves as engaged in a war. Successful war strategies are about achieving political ends by violent means with minimal losses on one's own side. Bombs work well for terrorists for exactly these reasons.

WHAT TERRORISTS USE TO MAKE BOMBS

Bombs are composed of three elements: explosives, detonators, and fuses. Most terrorists have two problems: first, getting hold of the relevant materials,

and second, developing the knowledge to assemble these into reliable and effective weapons.

Governments that carry out terrorist-type attacks generally do not share these difficulties and can prepare sophisticated devices such as the booby-trapped cellular phone used by Israel to kill a Hamas bombmaker in January 1996. Other terrorist groups receive training and supplies of explosives and related items from foreign governments. Libya, for example, maintains training camps for a number of Middle East terrorist groups and has made large shipments of arms and explosives to the Irish Republican Army (IRA). During the 1980s, the U.S. did the same for the Mujahidin fighting the Soviets in Afghanistan.

In addition to clandestine shipments and purchases, terrorists can obtain explosives by thefts or armed raids on their military opponents or from civilian users, such as quarries. Armies use explosives so powerful that bombs can be small and easily hidden or carried, but still greatly effective. Plastic explosives used by terrorists, including the exceptionally powerful Semtex type, are often stuffed into confined spaces or molded to resemble an innocent object.

However, when powerful explosives are not available, terrorists have used common materials. Gasoline, fertilizers, and weed-killers have been combined to make bombs. The truck bomb that exploded in April 1995 in front of the Alfred P. Murrah federal building in Oklahoma City, killing 168, contained a mixture of gasoline and ammonium nitrate.

Having obtained or made the explosive, the terrorist provides it with a detonator and a fuse or timing device to ensure that the bomb explodes, and does so where and when intended. Military explosives, designed to be stored and handled safely in difficult conditions, need a correctly placed, powerful detonator. Home-made compounds must be stable enough not to explode prematurely (possibly killing the bomber) but sufficiently explosive to cause damage.

Simple fuses and timing devices are often used by terrorists, such as the burning cord used at Oklahoma

KEY FACTS

● On July 22, 1946, a bomb placed by the Zionist guerrillas Irgun in Jerusalem's King David Hotel killed 91 people. The hotel was being used as headquarters for the British authorities.

● A right-wing Italian terrorist group killed 75 and wounded 186 in a bomb attack on a station in Bologna, Italy, in 1980.

● On June 23, 1985, 329 people died when a bomb attributed to Sikh extremists exploded on an Air India flight from Toronto while over the Atlantic.

TRH Pictures

City; but they can also be sophisticated. The timer bomb placed in the Grand Hotel in Brighton, England, by the IRA in 1984, claimed a number of victims and nearly succeeded in killing Prime Minister Margaret Thatcher. The items to make such devices can be as cheap and readily available as the batteries that are often used to provide the power.

This encyclopedia has no intention of providing anyone with instructions on how to make explosives or timing devices. But terrorists easily manage to find the information they need, in addition to whatever training they may receive from their organization and its sympathizers.

Skilled bombmakers are rare in most terrorist organizations. They have invariably had to learn from experience, and many have been killed by their own mistakes. Within a terrorist organization, a distinction is often made between the bombmaker, who never goes near a target and whose skills are carefully preserved, and the other operatives who risk arrest and premature detonations while planting the devices.

TYPES OF TERRORIST BOMBS

Letter and package bombs are probably the smallest terrorist devices used. They seldom fully achieve the terrorists' aims, however. Even if they actually reach their destination, their victims are as likely to be office

An American killed by a suicide truck bomb attack on the U.S. embassy in Beirut, Lebanon, on April 18, 1983. At least 40, including the bomber, were killed.

staff as the prominent individuals targeted. Those likely to receive such items quickly learn to take effective precautions. Research scientists have been targets for letter-bomb attacks by animal rights activists in a number of countries, and the Unabomber also used this method.

Various types of suspect packages, booby traps, and incendiary devices have been used by almost every terrorist group. They have been carried by hand and left in a phone booth or garbage can, or introduced as luggage or freight on aircraft or buses. In one incident in October 1994, a Hamas suicide bomber blew up a bus in Tel Aviv killing 21 people and wounding 45. Just one of many notorious aircraft bombings was the downing of PanAm Flight 103 on December 21, 1988, over Lockerbie, Scotland. Police investigating the wreckage revealed that a bomb in a luggage rack had caused the explosion. It killed all 259 people aboard and 11 on the ground.

Car and truck bombs are used by most terrorists. Some of these bombs have been huge and have caused great destruction. In February 1993, a large car-bomb

Central Press Photos

British politician Airey Neave died when his car was bombed by an Irish group in 1979. The terrorists gained extra publicity because the bomb placed in the car exploded outside the British parliament.

exploded in a parking garage below the World Trade Center in New York. Six were killed, and 1,000 injured. In an incident in 1991, a massive IRA truck bomb exploded in London's financial district, killing three. The loss of life, however, was surprisingly small considering the widespread damage to the area, totaling more than $1 billion. Bombs can also be placed in houses or vehicles used by specific targets. Pakistan's General Zia and Mozambique's Samora Machel are

only two of the national leaders assassinated in this way, both being killed when their aircraft blew up. Sometimes terrorists place the bomb to intercept a victim – for instance, under a street or in a culvert – and then explode the device when the relevant vehicle passes over it.

TRANSPORT OF BOMBS

Letter and package bombs reach their targets with the unwitting assistance of the postal service, and terrorists are seldom concerned if a postal worker is injured. Even more cynical are the terrorists who trick friends into carrying their bombs. In 1986, Nezar Hindawi, a Jordanian associated with the hard-line Palestinian Abu Nidal Organization, persuaded his pregnant girlfriend to carry a package onto an airliner at London's Heathrow Airport. Both were arrested before the bomb could explode.

Suspect packages and car bombs are placed by terrorists who then escape, or they are detonated by suicide bombers. Suicide bombers drive their vehicles through protective barriers to carry a bomb nearer its target. This method was used in Islamic Jihad's bombing of two barracks in Beirut that killed 241 U.S. Marines and 58 French soldiers in October 1983.

TARGETS

By definition, terrorist attacks are designed to produce terror or, in other words, to defeat the enemy, not by the killing or destruction they cause, but by the threat of killing and destruction yet to be carried out. Some bomb attacks, especially the attempts to assassinate prominent individuals, are very precisely targeted. Others seek to cause clear economic or military damage to the terrorists' enemies. But many terrorists are ruthless and indiscriminate.

Assassinations of national leaders are difficult for terrorists to achieve because of heightened security, but they still occur. Zia and Machel have been mentioned. Others include Spanish prime minister Carrero Blanco, killed by a bomb in his car by the Basque separatist group ETA in 1973, and Lebanese president-elect Bashir Gemayel, blown up in his office in Beirut in 1982. Such assassinations are in fact one of the oldest forms of terrorism. Czar Alexander II of Russia was killed by a bomb in 1881, and the British still celebrate Guy Fawkes Day (November 5), the anniversary of a thwarted attempt to blow up their king and parliament in 1605.

Terrorist groups often claim to attack military targets, but their definition of the term *military* is a broad one. Soldiers carrying out security work are often hit by land mines. Even more common are terrorist attempts against those off duty, such as the attack on the U.S. and French troops in Beirut in 1983. Soldiers engaged in ceremonial functions are also targeted. In 1982, the IRA attacked a military band playing in a London park and a Household Cavalry detachment on ceremonial duties. Pubs frequented by off-duty British soldiers have also been IRA targets on a number of occasions. The terrorists claim that any civilians injured or killed are legitimate targets because their presence was in indirect support of the military. The IRA has also attacked civilian contractors who carry out work on police stations.

For the committed terrorist, the end clearly justifies the means, but terrorists occasionally react to public opinion. In December 1983, an IRA bomb killed six and wounded 94 people doing their Christmas shopping at London's most famous store, Harrods. The IRA leadership responded to worldwide condemnation by declaring that the bombers had acted without permission.

Many bomb attacks make no concession to such considerations, working instead on the belief that the higher profile the target and the more casualties inflicted, the more publicity and terror caused. Crowds offer terrorists anonymity when placing a bomb and are easy targets when it goes off. On July 27, 1996, during the Olympic Games, one woman was killed and 111 people were injured by a bomb at Atlanta's Centennial Olympic Park. The device used was a pipe bomb, an explosive-filled length of pipe that burst into shrapnel on detonation.

DOES BOMBING WORK?

Terrorist bombings have occasionally influenced wider events in the way that the terrorists planned. There is no doubt, for example, that the American and French forces left Beirut far more quickly after the massive bombings of October 1983 than they otherwise would have done. Bombings have also been effective as part of a longer struggle, as in the case of the successful campaign for independence waged by the Algerian National Liberation Army against France in the 1950s.

In other cases, the verdict has not been so clear-cut, but even if a terrorist group never achieves its ultimate aim, bombings most certainly hurt their targets. Governments often claim that they never give in to terrorist threats and hence never allow the terrorists to "win." However, the British government has for years tried to silence Sinn Fein, the political wing of the IRA. Most recently, the group was barred from talks on the future of Northern Ireland in July 1996. Yet the talks would not have taken place without the impetus of the IRA's bombing campaign.

Even when bombing has an effect, it may not be the one the terrorists desire. Hamas' suicide bombing campaign in Israel in 1993-96 put in jeopardy the developing peace between the Palestine Liberation Organization (PLO) and the Israelis, as Hamas undoubtedly wished. But it may also have helped to bring about the election of a new Israeli government, which has more hard-line views than those of its predecessors.

Terrorists view events from an entirely different perspective from that of the societies they try to change. They do not necessarily judge their actions by the same standards of success and failure used by politicians. Asking if terrorist bombings are effective may not be a useful question. Terrorists are ultimately distinguished by the violence with which they are prepared to support their views, and bombs are among the methods used. Whether they work or not, we can expect bombings to continue as long as there are terrorists – or until the terrorists find something worse.

Donald Sommerville

SEE ALSO:

SUICIDE BOMBING; TERRORISM IN THE 1948-1949 ARAB-ISRAELI WAR; HAMAS; TAMIL TIGER TERROR IN SRI LANKA; SIKH NATIONALIST TERRORISM IN INDIA; TERROR BY THE HOLY WARRIORS OF KASHMIR; THE WORLD TRADE CENTER BOMBING; BASQUE NATIONALIST TERROR: ETA; NATIONALIST TERROR IN NORTHERN IRELAND 1976-1996; TERRORISM IN THE CITY OF LONDON.

FURTHER READING

- Bell, John Bowyer. *The Irish Troubles: A Generation of Political Violence, 1967-1992*. New York: St. Martin's Press, 1993.
- Emerson, Steven, and Brian Duffy. *The Fall of Pan Am 103: Inside the Lockerbie Investigation*. New York: G. P. Putnam's & Sons, 1990.
- Hammel, Eric. *The Root: The Marines in Beirut, August 1982-February 1984*. New York: Harcourt, Brace, Jovanovich, 1985.

HIJACKING AND KIDNAPPING

Hijacking and kidnapping have been important components of the terrorist's arsenal since the start of modern international terrorism in the late 1960s. The international nature of these terrorist methods is closely associated with worldwide advances in communications, which terrorists have exploited to publicize their causes, and with technologies that have provided them with new modes of mobility and anonymity. The frequency of hijacking and kidnapping has increased with the advent of state sponsorship of terrorism.

However, hijacking and kidnapping or hostage-taking are not new inventions. They have been used frequently throughout history as effective means to achieve strategic or tactical objectives. Political kidnapping was well known in antiquity. Roman emperors took hostages from tribes subject to Rome as a guarantee of good behavior. The emperors brought the hostages to Rome and assimilated them into the wealthiest, most educated families. If the hostages returned to their provinces, such friendships would encourage them to spread the pro-Roman word.

Also in antiquity, the Roman general Julius Caesar (102-44 B.C.) was captured by pirates who then held him for ransom. The practice of holding prisoners for ransom has continued from ancient to modern times. It is especially commonplace in the various cultures of the Middle East, where it has long been customary to abduct and conceal hostages and then to trade them for political purposes, or to kill them to exact revenge.

Similarly, long before the invention of the first aircraft, hijacking of ships was common throughout history. In 1789, Barbary pirates captured 11 American ships and 98 sailors. They were taken to North Africa and held for ransom. U.S. president George Washington was forced to negotiate and eventually handed over money and arms to secure the release of the seized ships and sailors.

Since the late 1960s, terrorists have refined the techniques of hijacking aircraft or ships and have come to rely on this activity as a source of funds and publicity. Extensive campaigns of kidnapping have also been launched to achieve an array of strategic and tactical aims. These goals have included pressuring governments into implementing policy changes and releasing other terrorists held in jail. Other objectives involved raising the terrorists' cause from obscurity through publicity and obtaining substantial sums of money to be used to fund further political goals.

Hijacking and kidnapping incidents have tended to fluctuate in scale and frequency because of changes in the terrorists' own objectives and in response to improved countermeasures by targeted states.

SEIZURE AND DETENTION

Hijacking, kidnapping, and hostage-taking share a number of common elements. First, they all involve the seizure and detention of a single person or a group of individuals such as diplomats, government officials, tourists, or businesspeople. The victims may be held in either a known siege site – such as an embassy, a private house, or public building; a passenger airliner, train, or ship – or in a concealed place that is known only to the terrorists.

In a siege situation, the terrorists and their victims are besieged in a location that is known to and

S U M M A R Y

● Kidnapping and holding people as hostages is an activity that has been used by criminals and terrorists for centuries.

● The number of hijackings declined after 1985 as security measures improved.

● Many countries now have specialist hostage-rescue teams to deal with hijackings and kidnappings if negotiations break down.

● Probably the foremost objective of hijackings and kidnappings is to enable terrorists to manipulate the news media and spread their message.

Popperfoto

A British SAS man enters a window of the Iranian embassy in London, ending a six-day siege in 1980.

controlled by the authorities. This is a serious disadvantage to the terrorists, because their mobility is severely restricted and they are unable to escape. They are vulnerable to hostage-rescue operations launched by the authorities.

The 1980 Iranian embassy episode in London illustrates the vulnerability of the terrorist in a siege situation. After six days of unsuccessful negotiation, 12 Special Air Service (SAS) commandos blew their way into the embassy. They killed five of the six militants holding the building and rescued the 19 hostages.

In a kidnapping, the perpetrators hold hostages at a location unknown to the authorities. These incidents usually last longer because they provide the terrorists with anonymity, security, and mobility, while rendering the security forces almost powerless to intervene.

Latin American terrorist groups have long favored this technique. The left-wing Tupamaros in Uruguay held British ambassador Sir Geoffrey Jackson hostage

for nine months in 1971, then released him in return for the freedom of 106 prisoners and for a large sum of money in ransom.

Muslim terrorist groups have also frequently used kidnapping. Notable examples are the Hizb'allah (Party of God) in Lebanon – which held a total of over 130 foreigners hostage in secret locations between 1982 and 1991 – and the Iranian militants who seized the U.S. embassy in Tehran in 1979, holding 52 American diplomats hostage for 444 days.

The continuous mobility of the terrorists in some hijackings has been as effective as having a hideout. During the 17-day hijacking of TWA flight 847 in June 1985, the Lebanese hijackers – who denied belonging to any organized group – forced the flight to make several trips between Beirut and Algiers. After finally halting in Beirut, they removed 39 passengers from the plane and hid them in different places in the city. The hijackers eventually released the passengers in return for the freedom of 766 prisoners held in Israel.

THE THREAT TO KILL

The second shared element of hijacking and kidnapping is that both involve the threat to kill, to injure, or to continue the detention of a hostage in order to compel a third party to perform or abstain from specific acts.

In the bargaining process between a hostage-taker and a third party, the hostage-taker has two options to achieve concessions if the first threat is not successful. Either the level of the threat may be raised to force submission or inducements may be offered to reward compliance. The credibility of threats depends on the willingness of the terrorists to kill some of their hostages after a deadline has passed to raise the cost of noncompliance. Noncompliance is often punished by the sequential killing of additional hostages.

A prime example was the 1985 hijacking of an EgyptAir Boeing 737 by three members of the radical Palestinian Abu Nidal Organization. While the Maltese authorities refused to refuel the aircraft during the first 12 hours of the hijacking, the terrorists methodically shot five passengers – two Israelis and three Americans. Similarly, when the hijackers of TWA flight 847 needed to put pressure on the U.S. and Israeli authorities to comply with their demands, they severely beat U.S. Navy diver Robert Stetham before they killed him and dumped his body on the tarmac. The TWA flight hijackers also offered inducements, releasing hostages in batches in response to concessions and to show good faith.

Events have shown that terrorists are usually not interested in killing most or all of their captives in major incidents. Such action would probably be counterproductive. This is especially the case in siege situations because it is in the terrorists' own interest to keep hostages alive as an insurance against armed assault and their own possible deaths.

Many terrorists feel that their best insurance against potential hostage-rescue operations is to seize highly prominent officials or businesspeople. This increases the publicity for their cause as well as the bargaining value of the hostage.

In one of the most famous hostage-taking incidents of the 1970s, the terrorist known as "Carlos the Jackal" and five members of the Popular Front for the Liberation of Palestine (PFLP) raided a meeting of the Organization of Petroleum Exporting Countries (OPEC) in Vienna, Austria, in December 1975. After a one-day standoff, the terrorists were granted free passage to Algeria where they released the 11 Arab oil ministers in exchange for a $25 million ransom.

HOSTAGE MURDER

However, hostage-taking incidents have on occasion ended in the murder of the hostage when the authorities failed to comply with the terrorists' demands. In practice this seems to be most often the case with the abduction of a single prominent captive. Under such high-profile pressure, many governments feel unable to give in to demands and attempt to maintain a policy of not negotiating with terrorists.

Among the most notorious cases were the kidnap and murder of prominent West German businessman Hanns-Martin Schleyer by the Baader-Meinhof gang (also known as the Red Army Faction, or RAF) in late 1977 and the kidnap and murder of former Italian prime minister Aldo Moro by the Red Brigades in the spring of 1978.

The terrorists' decision to use the techniques of hijacking and kidnapping is usually influenced by their particular strategic and tactical objectives at any given time. Their choice of tactics is also influenced by the reactions of the targeted states and the employment of effective countermeasures, such as improved X-ray machines at airports, or the states' willingness to use hostage-rescue teams. Often the decision to switch between hijacking and kidnapping is inspired by

successful acts by other groups, assisted by the media's intense coverage of major terrorist events.

HIJACKING HEYDAY

Since 1968-69, an array of different terrorist groups have targeted civil airline passengers and their crews for hijacking. The trend began with a spate of more than 120 hijackings by Cuban criminals and refugees in 1969-70, diverting the aircraft between the U.S. and Cuba. The practice was reduced by the U.S.-Cuba Hijack Pact of 1973, which extradited hijackers to their country of origin and severely punished them.

Various Palestinian terrorist groups quickly emulated this tactic. By hijacking an El Al airliner to Algeria in August 1969, the Fatah organization was the first to employ the headline-grabbing tactic of holding airline passengers hostage in an attempt to exchange them for the release of imprisoned Palestinians. After two months of negotiations, Israel yielded and released 16 imprisoned terrorists in exchange for the the passengers being held hostage.

This success led to more than a dozen hijackings by Palestinian terrorists between 1968 and 1972. The most spectacular of these was the PFLP's simultaneous seizures of five airliners on September 6-9, 1970. For four days, PFLP terrorists kept more than 300 passengers in three of the airliners at Dawson's Field in the Jordanian desert. The hostages were released only after the British, Swiss, and West German governments agreed to free seven Palestinian terrorists from prison. These concessions did not, however, get the airliners back intact. Before television cameras, the terrorists blew up all three aircraft at Dawson's Field.

In May 1972, a Sabena Boeing 707 airliner at Lod airport in Tel Aviv was hijacked by four Palestinian members of the Black September terrorist group. The Israeli authorities pretended to be willing to grant the hijackers' demands for the release of 317 Palestinians being held in Israel. But the elite Israeli counterterrorist unit, Sayaret Matkal, managed to board the plane. They killed or arrested the terrorists and rescued the 89 passengers. This was the first time a hostage-rescue unit had managed to storm a hijacked airliner successfully.

Governments were alarmed by the wave of 286 hijackings worldwide between 1969-72 and began to take significant steps to improve airline security. In 1973, it became obligatory for all U.S. airports to process every passenger through metal detectors. The

The body of Italian politician Aldo Moro is found in Rome, May 1978, after his kidnappers shot him.

effectiveness of this procedure was rapidly demonstrated the following year when 25 potential hijackings were averted and more than 2,400 firearms were confiscated at various airports in the United States. The spate of hijackings also led to the 1970 Hague Convention, which required contracting states either to extradite apprehended hijackers to their country of origin or to prosecute them.

However, this convention and other legislation did not provide a complete barrier against aircraft hijackings or attacks, especially because some states remained non-signatories and provided safe havens to which the terrorists could direct hijacked aircraft. Equally, while improved airport and airline security measures deterred some attacks, as shown by the reduction of annual incidents from 80 to 30 between 1973 to 1981, terrorists could simply switch to less protected airports. They also supplemented hijacking with other methods, such as hostage-taking and

seizing embassies or other public locations. At the 1972 Munich Olympic Games, the Palestinian Black September group seized and killed Israeli athletes, and in December 1972 the Israeli embassy in Bangkok was seized and held for 19 hours. A series of hijackings then followed to gain the release of imprisoned terrorists held in Israel and West European countries, in revenge for successful hostage-rescue missions and once again to publicize the terrorists' causes.

THE DECLINE OF HIJACKING
The PFLP was responsible for two of the most dramatic hijackings during the 1970s. In 1976, six PFLP members hijacked an Air France airliner and diverted it to Uganda's Entebbe airport. There they demanded the release of 53 terrorists, most of whom were held in Israel. The hijacking was foiled by the dramatic hostage-rescue operation by Israeli units in which 100 passengers were rescued, although three were killed along with one Israeli commando, Jonathan Netanyahu, brother of Israeli politician and later prime minister, Benjamin Netanyahu. The second spectacular incident was the hijacking of a Lufthansa plane in

1977, by the PFLP in conjunction with four West German Baader-Meinhof terrorists. The hijackers diverted the plane to Mogadishu, Somalia. They demanded the release of imprisoned Baader-Meinhof terrorists and killed the airline captain. Using "flash-bang" grenades – which stun people into temporary insensibility with a mixture of noise and light – 28 West German GSG-9 commandos stormed the plane and rescued the remaining 91 passengers and crew, while killing the hijackers.

While scores of hijackings of airliners occurred in the mid- to late 1970s, these were mainly perpetrated by splinter groups of the Palestine Liberation Organization (PLO). The PLO itself tried to distance itself from terrorism in foreign countries and concentrated on attacks against Israeli targets. Airliners were not the only targets for hijacking. The PFLP was involved in a joint operation with the Japanese Red Army to hijack a ferry in Singapore in 1974.

The decrease in the number of incidents toward the end of the 1970s was due mainly to internal Palestinian feuds. These were brought forcibly to world attention in November 1974 with the hijacking at Dubai of a British Airways jet, later flown to Tunis. The four terrorists called themselves followers of Abou Mahmoud, a Palestinian executed two months earlier by the PLO leadership. The terrorists demanded the release of extremist Palestinians held by Egypt and the Netherlands. These men were released, and the hijackers surrendered on a promise of asylum. Despite this promise, Tunisian authorities arrested the terrorists and sent them to the PLO for trial and imprisonment.

HIJACKING TRENDS

Since 1982, the average number of hijackings has reduced to fewer than 20 per year. Terrorists have switched to other methods, such as bombing, shooting, and kidnapping.

However, a few major Palestinian hijackings have occurred in this period. In two cases, unsuccessful military rescue operations resulted in massive casualties. In the autumn of 1985 three Abu Nidal terrorists hijacked an EgyptAir plane. The event ended in disaster, with the deaths of more than 60 passengers after Egyptian commandos made a failed rescue attempt. Similarly, Abu Nidal's 1986 hijacking of a New York-bound PanAm Boeing 747 ended in tragedy at Pakistan's Karachi airport when the terrorists began firing with Kalashnikov AK-47 assault rifles at the passengers. In all there were 21 deaths and more than 100 people wounded.

STORMING SHIPS AND AIRCRAFT

In 1985, four members of the Palestine Liberation Front (PLF) hijacked the cruise ship *Achille Lauro*. During the hijack, they killed an American wheelchair-bound passenger before receiving free passage out of Egypt on board an airliner. In a dramatic interception of the EgyptAir jet carrying the hijackers, U.S. fighter jets forced it to land in Sicily. Italy, however, failed to detain all the members of the terrorist group for political reasons. The resulting confrontation between Italian and U.S. authorities constituted a major setback in dealing with terrorists through international legal cooperation. While the four hijackers were eventually tried, convicted, and imprisoned in Italy, the Italian government collapsed as a result of its lenient action toward the other members of the terrorist group.

During the 1980s, there were two spectacular hijackings by the Muslim terrorist group Hizb'allah, who took elaborate precautions against any hostage-rescue attempts. Mention has already been made of the 1985 TWA flight 847 hijacking. During this flight the Hizb'allah hijackers flew back and forth between Beirut and Algiers to avoid a commando assault. They used statements to the international mass media to strengthen their bargaining positions. After the release of prisoners held in Israel, the hostages were released but the hijackers went free via Algeria.

In their next hijacking, of Kuwait Airlines flight 422 in 1988, Hizb'allah showed that they had learned from earlier mistakes. The type of aircraft chosen, a 747 jumbo jet, made rescue attempts hard because of its internal layout. One hijacker was reportedly capable of flying the aircraft. The terrorists took the precaution of wiring the doors with explosives and maintaining tight control over the passengers. They also made shrewd use of the media to gain publicity and by indicating their willingness to die for their cause.

The selection of Algeria, a consistent supporter of the PLO and Palestinian causes, as the final destination indicated careful planning. When Algeria granted them free passage back to Lebanon, the ineffectiveness of international agreements to suppress hijackings was revealed. Despite these apparent successes, however, the hijackers failed to achieve their principal objective, which was gaining the release of imprisoned members held in Kuwait.

The trends of hijackings in the 1980s differed greatly from those of the 1970s. The hijackings of the early 1970s were occasionally carried out by a few armed terrorists. These prompted the development of tighter aviation security procedures, international agreements, and the establishment of hostage-rescue units which were successfully deployed in the Mogadishu and Entebbe incidents.

In the mid-1980s, however, hijackers became increasingly operationally sophisticated as well as more willing to kill their hostages. This led to several failed rescue attempts resulting in many deaths. At the same time, terrorists increasingly switched to sabotaging and bombing airliners as the continuously improved aviation security measures made hijacking more difficult. In the 1990s, the majority of hijackings have been carried out by individuals seeking asylum in the West from the former Soviet Union and other countries with repressive regimes.

HOSTAGE-TAKING

The wave of Palestinian hijackings during the early 1970s was complemented by the takeover of several embassies around the world by the Black September organization. In 1972, four terrorists seized the Israeli embassy in Thailand and made a demand for the release of 36 comrades imprisoned in Israel, which was refused. This was followed by Black September's seizure of the Saudi Arabian embassy in Khartoum, Sudan, when they demanded the release of imprisoned comrades in Israel and of members of the Baader-Meinhof gang in West Germany. This incident revealed the emergence of extensive cooperation and solidarity between terrorist organizations. This proved to be especially true of links between Palestinian groups, Baader-Meinhof, and the Japanese Red Army.

But the most famous hostage-taking incident of all was staged by the Black September group. It occurred at the 1972 Olympic Games in Munich. Eight terrorists managed to seize 11 Israeli athletes at the Olympic village. The terrorists demanded the release of more than 200 of their comrades held in Israeli prisons. While Israel refused to grant the demands, West German police attempted a rescue by force. It ended in tragedy when the hostages were killed in a fire fight, which also cost the lives of a policeman and four of the terrorists.

The Munich incident prompted extensive improvement in the training of existing hostage–rescue teams

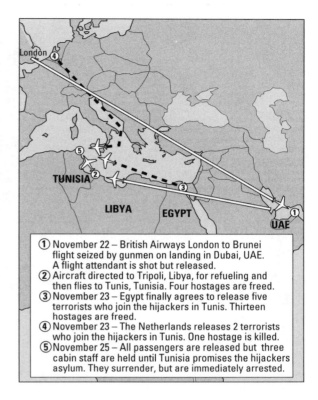

① November 22 – British Airways London to Brunei flight seized by gunmen on landing in Dubai, UAE. A flight attendant is shot but released.
② Aircraft directed to Tripoli, Libya, for refueling and then flies to Tunis, Tunisia. Four hostages are freed.
③ November 23 – Egypt finally agrees to release five terrorists who join the hijackers in Tunis. Thirteen hostages are freed.
④ November 23 – The Netherlands releases 2 terrorists who join the hijackers in Tunis. One hostage is killed.
⑤ November 25 – All passengers are released but three cabin staff are held until Tunisia promises the hijackers asylum. They surrender, but are immediately arrested.

A Palestinian group calling itself the Martyr Abou Mahmoud Squad carried out the 1974 Dubai hijack.

in those countries that had them, and to the establishment of similar elite units in several other countries. At the same time, the publicity surrounding the Munich incident, coupled with the increase in the number of joint operations between terrorist groups, led to a wave of further siege situations. In many cases, the terrorists hoped to strike before hostage–rescue teams improved their tactics.

In 1974, the Democratic Front for the Liberation of Palestine (DFLP) infiltrated the Israeli town of Ma'alot and seized a school with more than 90 teenage students. The terrorists demanded the release of 20 Palestinian comrades held in Israel. They threatened to blow up the building with wired charges unless their demands were met. The incident ended in tragedy when Israeli elite units stormed the building, but failed to kill one of the terrorists outright. Although wounded, he turned his guns and grenades toward the teenagers. Before Israeli commandos killed him, the terrorist had slain 21 teenagers and wounded 65 others.

American hostages arrive at Frankfurt in 1981 after being released from their 444-day ordeal in Iran.

There were also a number of hostage-taking incidents in Europe. For example, in 1974, the Japanese Red Army seized the French embassy in The Hague, Netherlands. In 1975, the Baader-Meinhof gang took the West German embassy in Sweden, demanding the release of their jailed leaders. Apart from free passage out of the country in some instances, these hostage-taking incidents generally failed to achieve their objectives. However, South Moluccan terrorists did achieve their aim of obtaining publicity for their problems in Indonesia when they seized the Indonesian embassy and a train in Holland in 1975, and then a second train and a school six months later.

EMBASSY CRISES

Between 1971 and 1980, there were more than 50 terrorist embassy seizures. In 1979 alone, terrorists occupied no less than 26 embassies worldwide. However, events showed that the terrorists had only a

50 percent chance of avoiding capture or death because more countries had formed elite hostage-rescue units and showed a willingness to use them.

However, the elite U.S. Delta Force was unsuccessful in its attempt to rescue the 52 American diplomats held in Tehran after 400 Iranian students stormed the U.S. embassy on November 4, 1979. The students demanded the extradition of the shah of Iran, then in exile and receiving medical treatment in New York. The Iranian government sanctioned the embassy siege, grossly violating international laws of diplomacy. The Iranians used the hostage crisis to inflict maximum embarrassment on the United States and President Jimmy Carter. Carter made the release of the American hostages a central issue in his unsuccessful campaign for re-election. The Iranians were keen to humiliate Carter after he gave sanctuary to the shah. The hostages were not released until after he handed over office to Ronald Reagan in 1981.

This incident marked a watershed since it revealed the West's vulnerability, and it led to a rapid increase in state-sponsored terrorism. Hizb'allah, actively encouraged by Iran, later exploited this weakness through the kidnappings of Westerners in Lebanon during the 1980s. Embassy sieges, on the other hand, declined during the 1980s.

Other spectacular terrorist incidents occurred in the developing world, including the taking of 300 hostages in the Palace of Justice in Colombia in 1985. As in the case of hijackings, the overall incidence of siege-hostage situations declined as security improved and hostage-rescue operations increased in number, raising the risk of capture and death for the terrorists.

Instead, most terrorist groups relied more and more on kidnappings and bombings as more effective and less risky means to achieve their objectives. And an added advantage was that there was less danger of capture and interrogation by the authorities. This became particularly important with the increase of state sponsorship of terrorism as the states involved wished to conceal their part in the terrorist activities.

KIDNAPPING

The kidnapping and holding of individuals at secret locations has often been used by a variety of Middle Eastern and Latin American terrorist groups. They frequently demand money, changes in government policy, and the release of prisoners in return for the safe release of kidnap victims.

Latin American terrorists particularly have resorted to politically motivated kidnappings of foreign businessmen and diplomats. Colombia's kidnapping rates, which ran at an annual 600 cases in both 1988 and 1989, clearly demonstrate the popularity of the tactic. The Armed Forces of National Resistance (FARN) abducted multinational executives in El Salvador between 1978 and 1980. And mention has already been made of the Sir Geoffrey Jackson case, which took place in Uruguay in 1972 during the first wave of Latin American kidnappings.

Kidnapping is popular because it is a relatively low-risk and high-yield method. Between 1971 and 1975 in Latin America, kidnappers managed to extort more than $80 million in ransom. In most cases of kidnappings, the terrorists have an 80 percent chance of escaping capture or death. At the same time, the hostages themselves are relatively safe since only four percent of all kidnap victims are killed by terrorists. Ransom is paid in over 50 percent of all kidnappings.

Governments face two problems in responding to kidnapping: first, it is difficult to locate hostages; second, most governments have publicly declared policies of no concessions to terrorists. However, refusal to accede to terrorist demands has resulted in instances in which the terrorists have killed their hostages: the murder of business leader Hanns-Martin Schleyer by the German Red Army Faction in 1977 is one example.

By kidnapping a number of individuals at the same time, terrorists have continued to raise the pressure on the authorities by sequentially killing hostages, as hijackers also have done.

Hizb'allah used this strategy in Lebanon. Hizb'allah's kidnappings of more than 100 foreigners were a prolonged and effective campaign. Although the terrorists killed only a handful of these hostages, they managed to exact huge ransom payments and the release of prisoners, and induced a number of Western governments to modify or change their policies in various ways. One of the most dramatic changes of government policy was the U.S.-Iranian arms-for-hostages deal in the mid-1980s. Although it had previously refused to trade in arms with Iran, the U.S. secretly now did so in order to secure the release of hostages held in Lebanon. When this deal was exposed, it caused one of the most serious crises of the Reagan administration during its two terms in office.

Magnus Ranstorp

SEE ALSO:

TERROR IN ANCIENT GREECE AND THE ROMAN REPUBLIC; HOSTAGE NEGOTIATIONS; MIDDLE EASTERN TERRORISM 1948-1969; MIDDLE EASTERN TERRORISM 1970-1987; MIDDLE EASTERN TERRORISM 1988-1996; TERRORISM AND REVOLUTION IN IRAN; HIZB'ALLAH; TERRORISM IN LATIN AMERICA; RED ARMY FACTION: THE BAADER-MEINHOF GANG; RED BRIGADES; JAPANESE TERRORISM.

FURTHER READING

- Arey, J. *The Sky Pirates*. New York: Scribners, 1972.
- Aston, C. *Governments to Ransom: The Emergence of Political Hostage-Taking as a Form of Crisis*. Westport, CT: Greenwood Press, 1982.
- McClintock, M. C. "Skyjacking: Its Domestic, Civil, and Criminal Ramifications." *Journal of Air Law and Commerce* (Winter 1973).
- Middendorff, W. *New Developments in the Taking of Hostages and Kidnapping*. Washington, DC: National Criminal Justice Reference Service, 1975.

ASSASSINATION

Assassination is the murder of a prominent person for political reasons. It is illegal but not always irrational – the act is usually carefully planned and long premeditated. There have been many famous victims od assassination in recent history – the Kennedys and Martin Luther King, and the Gandhis in India among others. Targets of unsuccessful assassination attempts include Ronald Reagan, Margaret Thatcher, Benito Mussolini, Adolf Hitler, and Pope John Paul II. But assassination is by no means a recent development. Several Roman statesmen, notably Julius Caesar in 44 B.C., met sudden death at the hands of opponents. Emperors Caligula, Nero, Domitian, and Elagabalus were all victims of assassination. Even the word *assassin* has ancient origins, deriving from an eleventh-century Islamic sect that specialized in political murder.

The typical assassination may seem to be an isolated, arbitrary act of violence. But this is rarely the case. Assassination can be part of a wider terrorist campaign or one tactic of a guerrilla war. It may be a stunt that a group tries once and then abandons, or it may be used regularly.

Most assassinations are part of a conspiracy. However, there are examples of lone assassins – Israeli prime minister Yitzhak Rabin was killed on November 4, 1995, by Yigal Amir, a lone gunman discontented with the Israeli-Palestinian peace process.

Whatever the motive and background to a murder, it is easy to define a killing as an assassination if both the perpetrator and the victim are engaged in politics. It is less clear-cut if the act is part of a broader pattern of violence such as war. Some ideological murders are carried out on a vast scale, for example, those of the Holocaust in World War II or Pol Pot's killing fields in Cambodia. Many experts prefer to treat these mass killings as genocide, while reserving the term *assassination* for the violent death of specific individuals.

THE ENVIRONMENT OF POLITICAL MURDER

Some societies are plagued by acts of political murder. There can be many reasons for this – the government may be tyrannical, or have been put in place by foreign invaders, or the society may be divided on ethnic, religious, or political lines.

In Western society, assassination is generally not the first choice of groups intent on political violence. Western groups that do turn to assassination almost always lack the means to wage a more conventional terrorist campaign or guerrilla war. Cultures with traditions of religious fanaticism, however, opt for assassination more readily. The Palestinians have made extensive use of political murder, as have the Tamil Tigers in Sri Lanka.

Assassinations are easiest to carry out in societies where the government authority is weak, as in Sri Lanka today and Russia during the period 1917-23. Brutal authoritarian states – such as Stalin's Soviet Union or Mao's China – have such powerful state security forces that political killers tend to be those secretly sponsored by the state against internal opposition.

THE PURPOSE OF KILLING

Assassins are usually proponents of a political theory that gives legitimacy to their actions. The few who target prominent figures for personal reasons may be compelled to do so because of psychological disorders. In 1981, in his assassination attempt on U.S. president Ronald Reagan, John Hinckley appeared to have been influenced by the film *Taxi Driver*. He was acquitted and committed to a mental institution.

Killers often believe that a single murder will change the future. They may believe that one spectac-

---

KEY FACTS

● Rumors of conspiracy still surround the assassination of U.S. president John F. Kennedy in 1963. He was shot dead in his motorcade in Dealey Plaza, Dallas, by Lee Harvey Oswald, himself later shot dead as he was taken out of a police station.

● In 1968, civil rights leader Martin Luther King's assassination by James Earl Ray in Memphis, Tennessee, led to widespread rioting.

● In 1984, Indian prime minister Indira Gandhi was assassinated; her son Rajiv took over the premiership but was himself killed by a bomb in 1991.

Secret service agents arrest John Hinckley. He fired six shots, wounding President Reagan, who was leaving the Hilton hotel in Washington D.C. in 1981.

ular event will help publicize their political ideas and make the authorities more aware of them. More directly, they may hope that eliminating a major figure will be enough to topple a government or rival cause.

The sudden killing of a powerful individual will undoubtedly have a significant political impact, whatever the original motive. For example, the assassinations of American presidents have had dramatic repercussions, although they were not all politically motivated. They were generally the acts of weak individuals who believed that they would gain personal prestige by killing an important person. The widespread political fallout was incidental.

Famous politicians are most often singled out for assassination. But other targets include state officials, such as judges or police officers. If the state itself practices assassination, terrorists themselves may become targets. Assassins may choose the victim because of his or her political actions and beliefs or because he or she holds a particular office of state or somehow symbolizes the rival cause. Earl Louis Mountbatten was chosen as an assassination victim by the Provisional Irish Republican Army (IRA) in 1979 for symbolic reasons. He had little power, but as a member of the royal family and a retired senior naval officer he epitomized the British establishment.

Although most assassins working to preserve the status quo are authorized or encouraged by the government, some illegal groups kill to defend the existing order. In Northern Ireland, Protestant paramilitaries have targeted Catholic political leaders who oppose

their desire to maintain union with Great Britain. Such paramilitary defenders of a status quo are more likely to kill vulnerable targets than powerful, usually protected, individuals.

Each assassination has not only a victim but also a target audience. The audience is the wider public, which the assassin wishes to influence, either by striking fear or by gaining support. The attack may intimidate or horrify an audience. Equally, an assassination may reassure or reward it. The more important the target, the greater the audience, and the wider the impact. Even if the attempt fails, it may serve to highlight a grievance.

The victim may be not only a symbol, as was Mountbatten, but also irreplaceable. In 1944, a group of German army officers attempted to assassinate Adolf Hitler in what became known as the July Bomb Plot. If they had succeeded, it is likely Germany would have surrendered sooner than it did.

In any effective assassination, the greater the symbolic value of the target, the greater the impact. Some targets are high-profile leaders while others have a key, if invisible, role – for example, the head of counterintelligence or a propaganda chief. A long campaign will target all of these. Rebels with limited capabilities or a greater sense of urgency will choose more prominent targets.

ACCESS TO THE VICTIM

Assassins have used the full range of weapons: explosive devices, pistols, knives, firing squads, and even poison. The reasons behind a murder do not often have any impact on the method of assassination chosen. Usually, the assassin chooses the method that is most likely to achieve success. The crucial, and often trickiest, part has always been gaining access to the victim. In the fifteenth century, John the Bold, duke of Burgundy, was lured to a bridge ostensibly to discuss peace negotiations with the king of France. There, he was stabbed to death by assassins.

If the chosen weapon is a revolver or knife, the killers have to determine how to get close enough to touch the target. To poison, the assassins need access only to the victim's food. To plant a time-bomb, they need to know the victim's intended route or location.

In 1984, the IRA terrorists knew British prime minister Margaret Thatcher's schedule during the Conservative party conference in Brighton in October. The terrorist group was able to plant a bomb in her hotel weeks before her arrival. An electronic timer detonated the device when the prime minister was present in the hotel. She had just emerged from the bathroom of her hotel suite when the bomb went off. Although she was shaken, she escaped physically unscathed. But other politicians and members of their families were seriously injured, and five people died.

More successful was the attack on the Spanish premier Carrero Blanco in December 1973. Basque separatists (ETA) planted a massive mine under a road along which it was known that Blanco would travel. The mine was detonated as the car passed over it, killing Blanco and his entire entourage.

Another requirement for most assassins is a reliable escape route. The team who planted the Brighton bomb had made their getaway weeks before the explosion took place, while the Basque terrorist squad who killed Blanco set off the mine from a distance and fled the area.

However, those who kill at close range have more difficulty in escaping the security team surrounding a target. The squad of al-Jihad Islamic fundamentalists who machine-gunned Egypt's President Anwar Sadat in 1981 were immediately attacked by loyal army units. The few who survived were later sentenced to death.

A few assassins have no escape route at all. Palestinian groups, for example, have made use of suicide bombers. Driving vehicles packed with explosives to a target and then detonating the bomb, these religious fanatics know that their death is certain. But so too is that of their victims.

AUTHORIZED ASSASSINS

Assassination may be used as a tactic in conventional war. Modern wars are generally fought between massive organized forces, but sometimes a key individual presents a target. In April 1943, with World War II at its height, the Americans shot down the aircraft carrying Japanese naval commander-in-chief Admiral Yamamoto, having discovered its flight plans. Earlier in the same conflict, the Germans bombed Buckingham Palace and the House of Commons, hoping to kill important members of the British royalty or government. Such assassinations and attempts are generally reckoned to be legitimate acts of war – murder carried out under government orders.

More conventional assassinations are also authorized by governments. Many nations have used assassination because it is sometimes convenient, often cheap, and easily denied. Most often this tactic is used by totalitarian governments against internal dissidents. It is a convenient way to quell dissent at home and to terrorize opponents into silence. For example, Mussolini had his greatest domestic critic, Giacomo Matteoti, murdered in June 1924. The interests of national security can be invoked to legitimize assassination by the government.

THE IMPACT OF ASSASSINATION

Assessing the impact of an assassination is tricky. Governments tend to deny that the assassination achieved anything at all (unless they sanctioned or engineered it). In contrast, the assassins usually suggest that they have gained far more advantage from the deed than they actually have. The killing of President Sadat of Egypt, for instance, did little to harden that country's attitude to Israel, which was the goal of the assassins.

At the very least, an assassin wants to draw attention to a grievance. Far more preferable is to force a change in the political situation. The degree of change anticipated gives some indication of how realistic the assassins are. The German conspirators of July 1944 expected too much when they thought the death of Hitler would lead to a negotiated peace with the Allies rather than unconditional surrender. However, the Basque terrorists who killed Spanish premier Blanco were correct in thinking that the assassination would make the government believe ETA a formidable force.

Another obstacle to judging the impact of a successful assassination is that it is, of course, impossible to know what would have happened without the attack. Some political analysts believe that major historical trends are unlikely to be shifted by a single murder. For instance, they argue that Egyptian policy would have differed little had President Sadat lived from the course the government took without him. Others believe that the contribution of individual leaders to the political landscape of their times is so fundamental that their removal alters history.

But whatever the impact of assassinations on mainstream politics, such killings can have profound effects on the organizations that carry them out. In March 1978, the Italian left-wing Red Brigades murdered Aldo Moro, one of the most important politicians in Italy. The terrorist group believed that the Italian government had been corrupted by what they called the State of Imperialist Multinationals (SIM), a sinister group of large companies based in America. Despite the death of Moro, the government did not

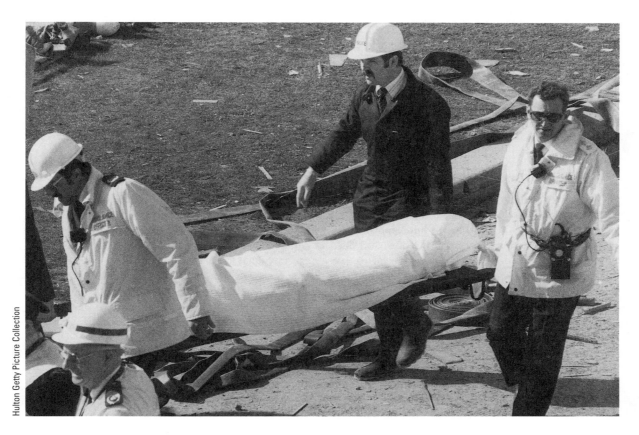

Hulton Getty Picture Collection

In 1984, the Provisional IRA bombed a hotel in Brighton, England, in an unsuccessful attempt to assassinate British premier Margaret Thatcher. There were, however, several other victims.

collapse because there was no such thing as the SIM group. The operation allowed the security forces to gain invaluable intelligence about the terrorists. Many of the Red Brigades' volunteers were swiftly arrested and the organization was weakened. Although the attack on Moro was effective as a murder and had an immediate destabilizing impact on Italy, it was ultimately unsuccessful because it marked the beginning of the end of the terrorist group.

Despite the general distaste of the public, assassination has long been an acceptable revolutionary method. It appears to offer a low-cost means of changing public opinion. It has been so attractive that even established states have used authorized assassins. Active most often during times of turmoil in divided societies and uncertain governments, the assassin finds it difficult to

act against leaders of authoritarian states. Events may not always change as anticipated, but assassination remains a terrible but compelling way to alter history.

John Bowyer Bell

SEE ALSO:
THE ASSASSINS: A TERROR CULT; ASSASSINATION AT SARAJEVO 1914; BOMBING OPERATIONS; SUICIDE BOMBING; TAMIL TIGER TERROR IN SRI LANKA.

FURTHER READING

- Bell, John Bowyer. *Assassin. The Theory and Practice of Political Murder.* New York: St. Martin's Press, 1979.
- Clarke, J. W. *American Assassins: The Darker Side of Politics.* Princeton, NJ: Princeton University Press, 1982.
- Ford, F. L. *Political Murder, From Tyrannicide to Terrorism.* Cambridge, MA: Harvard University Press, 1985.

ROCKETS, MORTARS, AND MISSILES

By a combination of theft, improvisation, and knowing the right people, terrorists can lay their hands on destructive but sophisticated mortars, rockets, and surface-to-air missiles, or SAMs.

Mortars are muzzle-loading weapons used to fire shells at low-velocity and at short range. The mortars terrorists use fall into two categories. First, there are conventional, factory-made mortars, which can be fired at some distance from the target, granting the terrorists a good chance of escaping. They can also do significant damage, even against fortified targets. Terrorists have managed to get hold of mortars by robbing armories or through arms shipments from sympathetic states, and they are not afraid to use them. The Islamic fundamentalist group Hizb'allah has regularly used mortars to bombard villages in northern Israel from just over the border in southern Lebanon.

The second category of mortars favored by terrorists is the homemade type. This is the preferred weapon of the Irish Republican Army (IRA). Homemade mortars are easy to make. The IRA, for example, used tubes mounted on trucks to bombard police and army posts in Northern Ireland. They have also used portable homemade mortars. From the terrorists' point of view, the drawback of such crude devices is their lack of accuracy and unpredictability. Many bombs fall wide of the target, and accidents are common. But when the bomb is on target, the damage can be high. On the morning of February 7, 1991, the IRA mortared the British prime minister's London house at No. 10 Downing Street. The projectile missed the house and landed in the garden. The damage was slight, but it was a close call that shook the nation.

FROM SIMPLE TO SOPHISTICATED

Terrorists also use various types of rockets. There are comparatively simple, unguided, rocket-propelled grenade launchers, such as the Soviet-made RPG-7. Terrorist organizations, such as the IRA, Palestinian groups, and Zimbabwean nationalist guerrillas, have had the RPG-7 in their armories. The weapon is basically an anti-tank rocket, but terrorists have found other uses for it. In September 1991 in Germany, terrorists fired an RPG-7 at the armored limousine of U.S. General Frederick Kroesen while the car was stopped at a traffic light. Although the projectile found its mark, it caused only superficial injuries.

The second category of rockets used by terrorists includes the sophisticated guided anti-tank missiles, such as the American M72.750 LAW (light anti-tank weapon). This highly portable weapons weighs a mere seven pounds, yet its projectile can penetrate one and a half inches of armor. More powerful weapons include the wireguided Russian Spigot and NATO's MILAN anti-tank missiles. MILAN's missile weighs 25 pounds and the launching and guidance system weighs a further 37 pounds. The extra weight makes it less portable than the M72. But MILAN fits in the trunk of a car and is very accurate at distances between 250 and 2,000 yards. However, throughout the missile's flight, the operator must keep the target in view in the crosshairs of the launcher's sight to be sure of a hit.

KEY FACTS

● Terrorists believed to be Muslim extremists mortared Maganoy in the Philippines in May 1995, killing three people during a referendum on the first three years of President Fidel Ramos's rule.

● On January 13, 1975, the international terrorist Carlos the Jackal and associates from the Popular Front for the Liberation of Palestine opened fire on an El Al airliner with RPG-7 grenade launchers at Orly airport, Paris, France. They missed the target but hit a Yugoslav aircraft and a building.

TRH Pictures

The IRA has used homemade mortars such as this captured weapon in attacks in Northern Ireland.

The third type of rocket that terrorists use are the "Katyushas." These are Russian-made weapons whose multi-barreled launchers are usually vehicle-mounted. In the 1990s, Hizb'allah have made great use of Katyushas, along with mortars, to bombard northern Israel. While the Russian army carries its Katyushas on specially-built trucks, Hizb'allah mounts its rockets onto pickup trucks. The terrorists can launch a salvo from close to the Israeli-Lebanese border, then dash for cover before the Israeli security forces locate them.

Some terrorist organizations have acquired handheld guided surface-to-air missiles, or SAMs. SAMs can be carried and operated by one person, making them suitable for terrorist acts. But SAMs are expensive and require extensive training to be operated successfully. This means that terrorist groups require state sponsorship both to obtain the SAMs and

to operate them effectively. That terrorists had surface-to-air missiles first became clear on September 5, 1973, when Italian police in Rome arrested five members of the Palestinian Black September organization. The Arabs were armed with two Soviet-made SAM-7s and were occupying an apartment beneath the flight path into Rome airport. Their intention was to shoot down an aircraft belonging to El Al the Israeli airline. Since then, terrorists have successfully used SAMs. In 1978, guerrillas in Zimbabwe (then Rhodesia) shot down a civil airliner, killing 48 people. The next year, the terrorists downed another airliner, killing 59.

SAMs are also used by terrorists to deny free use of the skies to government forces. During the war in Afghanistan in the 1980s, Mujahedin used U.S. Stinger missiles with great success to shoot down Soviet helicopter gunships. This made it increasingly difficult for the Soviets to prosecute the war. These attacks both hampered Soviet re-supply to remote bases from the air and also limited the Russians' ability to provide close air support to soldiers on the ground. It has been argued that the Mujahedin Stinger campaign accelerated the Soviet decision to withdraw from Afghanistan, which was reached in 1988.

In Northern Ireland, the opposite may be the case. Some experts maintain that the IRA's failure to deploy SAMs was a factor in the group's inability to force the British government to look for a solution to the conflict. In some border areas, the casualties caused by IRA bomb attacks on army vehicles forced the British to re-supply isolated bases from the air. But the IRA has been unable to impede the army because it cannot shoot down the British helicopters.

Nadine J. Gurr

SEE ALSO:

TERROR IN ZIMBABWE (RHODESIA); THE BLACK SEPTEMBER ORGANIZATION; CARLOS THE JACKAL; HIZB'ALLAH; TERROR IN THE PHILIPPINES; NATIONALIST TERROR IN NORTHERN IRELAND 1976-1996.

FURTHER READING

- Clutterbuck, Richard. *Terrorism in an Unstable World.* New York: Routledge, 1994.
- Gander, Terry. *Guerrilla Warfare Weapons: The Modern Underground Fighters' Armory.* New York: Stirling Publishing Co., 1990.

TERRORISTS' USE OF CHEMICAL WEAPONS

On March 20, 1995, several small gas dispensers were smuggled onto three subway trains in Tokyo, the Japanese capital. The dispensers released a nerve gas called Sarin, which killed 12 people, including two U.S. citizens. The attack was carried out by the Aum Shrinri-kyu sect, a religious cult led by Shoko Asahara. Although the attack was the first successful use of chemical weapons by terrorists, the death toll would have been much higher if Asahara's chemists had made the concoction stronger.

In its purest form, Sarin is colorless and odorless. But the low-quality Sarin used in Tokyo smelled of rotting vegetables. Nevertheless, over 5,500 people were injured, many seriously. Nerve gases such as Sarin attack the central and peripheral nervous system. Symptoms are progressive and include breathing difficulties, sweating, vomiting, cramps, involuntary bowel movements, fainting, and confusion, usually leading to coma and death.

The significance of the Tokyo incident was that it showed how easily terrorists could deploy chemical and biological weapons in an open society. When police finally broke into the sect's headquarters, they found over 500 drums of phosphorus trichloride, an essential ingredient in Sarin. It became clear that Asahara's doomsday cult had the facilities to produce

other nerve agents, including Tabun, Soman, and the highly dangerous chemical known by the symbol VX.

The use, or threatened use, of chemical and biological weapons is one of the most frightening forms of terrorism. The advantages to the terrorist are that nerve agents are cheap and easy to obtain, no training is required in their use, and production of the crude agents is straightforward. Terrorists can steal chemical and biological weapons from laboratories or manufacturing plants. They may even use commercially available insecticides such as parathion.

TARGETS OF CHEMICAL ATTACKS

Mounting a direct attack on a military or civilian target, as in Tokyo, is the most straightforward way in which terrorists can use chemical or biological agents. It is also a way for a government to launch a low-cost terror campaign as an alternative to conventional war. In the 1980s, President Saddam Hussein of Iraq used chemical weapons against the Kurds of northern Iraq. In one infamous incident, in March 1988, Iraqi aircraft bombed the town of Halabja with chemical weapons, killing more than 6,000 Kurdish civilians in two days.

Terrorists might choose slightly more indirect methods of turning chemical and biological agents to their advantage. By bombing a chemical plant, for example, a terrorist organization could cause toxic material to leak into a city's water supply or into the atmosphere. The accident at Bhopal in India in 1984, in which thousands died when gas leaked from a factory, showed the potential for disaster if a terrorist attack on a chemical plant should ever take place.

Besides the Aum Shrinri-kyu sect, a number of terrorist groups have been linked to chemical and biological weapons. In 1978, a group of Palestinians injected Jaffa oranges with cyanide to damage Israeli citrus fruit exports. In the same year, the British police

---

KEY FACTS

● About 1,800 pounds of Sarin can inflict heavy casualties over a square mile. A quarter ounce of anthrax spores can do the same job. Anthrax is a disease harnessed as a biological weapon.

● In 1995, a U.S. court found two people guilty of possessing ricin in breach of the Chemical and Biological Weapons Anti-Terrorism Act. Ricin is a poison derived from beans of the castor-oil plant.

Popperfoto/Reuters

Japanese troops clean a Tokyo subway car contaminated by the nerve agent Sarin on March 20, 1995.

uncovered a plot to detonate cans of dioxin all over Cyprus unless the Cypriot government paid out a $15 million ransom. Dioxin is the toxic by-product of pesticide production and an ingredient of Agent Orange, a defoliant used by the U.S. in Vietnam. In 1984, police in Paris found a culture of the bacterium that forms botulin in a safe house of the German Baader-Meinhof gang. Botulin is the toxin that causes botulism, an often fatal disease of the nervous system. In 1991, the German authorities foiled a neo-Nazi plot to pump hydrogen cyanide into a synagogue.

There have been other examples, but chemical and biological terrorism is still relatively rare. One reason is that terrorists prefer the immediate, dramatic effect produced by a hijacking or a bombing. Chemical weapons can also be dangerous to handle. An attack generally requires vast amounts of chemicals to have

any significant effect. Chemical weapons are hard to control and might cause massive loss of life and lingering illness – possibly a counterproductive result on the terrorists. Still, events in Tokyo show that some groups regard chemical warfare as a justifiable tactic.

Nadine J. Gurr

SEE ALSO :

RELIGIOUS EXTREMISM; NUCLEAR TERRORISM; SADDAM HUSSEIN'S TERROR IN KURDISTAN.

FURTHER READING

- Douglass, J. E., and N. C. Livingstone. *America the Vulnerable: The Threat of Chemical and Biological Weapons*. Lexington, MA: Lexington Books, 1987.
- Spiers, Edward M. *Chemical and Biological Weapons*. New York: St. Martin's Press, 1994.
- Spiers, Edward M. *Chemical Weaponry*. New York: St. Martin's Press, 1989.

NUCLEAR TERRORISM

The threat of nuclear terrorism covers a broad spectrum, from low-level threats or hoaxes involving radioactive material, through attacks on reactors, to a terrorist nuclear bomb. The most likely of all scenarios is sabotage or a siege-and-hostage situation at a nuclear facility, staged in all likelihood by an antinuclear group. In most cases, these terrorist tactics aim to highlight failures in security and safety at facilities. Another scenario would be an attack on the missiles used to carry nuclear warheads. In the past, antinuclear protesters have concentrated on trespassing at military sites, but there have also been a few attacks on factories that make nuclear missiles. However, where the objective is to embarrass the government or to gain leverage for a terrorist group, other types of nuclear terrorism are becoming increasingly likely. Acquiring fissile material (an essential ingredient for making a nuclear bomb) is becoming easier and thus a more attractive proposition for terrorists.

GROWTH IN NUCLEAR TRAFFICKING

That fissile material is now easier to access, is largely thanks to the collapse of the former Soviet Union and the growth in nuclear trafficking that has stemmed from it. Even though Russian nuclear weapons are under tight military supervision, there is a huge quantity of nuclear material dispersed throughout Russia is far less secure, and which is, therefore, difficult to keep track of. In addition, poor security at nuclear sites – often

situated in secret cities not on the map due to the sensitive research carried out there, and at research institutes heightens the danger. Much of the theft is by "insiders" – staff who have access to nuclear material.

There is much debate about the extent of this secretive market. Some say that the traffic is almost exclusively in non-weapons-grade material, and that it is a situation artificially created by journalists and the security services. But there is evidence that at least some weapons-grade material is being trafficked.

On November 29, 1993, Lieutenant-Colonel Tikhomirov of the Russian navy, and Alyak Beranov, deputy administrator of the Polyarnyy submarine base, entered a naval fuel store through a hole in the perimeter fence and stole three fuel rods of uranium 235, intending to sell it for $50,000. The fuel was kept in Beranov's garage for seven months, until Tikhomirov got drunk and boasted of the theft to fellow officers. Both were arrested.

In 1994, German police intercepted four separate radioactive shipments, three of which were of plutonium 239 – an essential component in nuclear weapons. The shipments probably came from Russia.

Most of the smuggling so far has been by amateurs trying to make quick money. Increasingly, though, it appears that entrepreneurs are treating smuggling as an extension of their legitimate activities. In 1994, German police discovered a vial containing a fifth of an ounce of plutonium 239 in the garage of businessman Adolf Jaekle. Its origins are still unknown.

BUYERS OF NUCLEAR MATERIAL

The main buyers of nuclear material are almost certainly those states eager to take a shortcut towards nuclear programs of their own. Some people doubt whether there really is a demand for stolen or illegally bought nuclear material. However, in view of the expense and time needed to develop a nuclear capability legally, it seems unlikely that states would miss out on such an opportunity. Whether this will equate with an increased likelihood of state-sponsored nuclear

---

KEY FACTS

● Many states have tried to acquire nuclear weapons by various means since World War II.

● Mafia involvement in nuclear trafficking is unclear: the latter has few incentives and is high risk compared to the Mafia's other, safer activities.

● In March 1993, Japanese police seized nuclear information from the doomsday cult Aum Shinri-kyu, which staged the Tokyo subway gas attack in 1995.

TRH Pictures

Members of the U.S. Nuclear Emergency Search Team (NEST) remove radioactive debris from a Russian satellite that fell over Canada in 1978.

terrorism has yet to be seen. It makes sense to suggest that, having obtained such material, a state would exploit the situation. As yet, there is little evidence that independent terrorists are capable of buying nuclear material. But if the flow of nuclear goods out of Russia continues, it probably will happen eventually.

The amount of fissile material required to build a bomb, and the difficulty of doing so, is also a matter of debate. The International Atomic Energy Agency assumes that 18 pounds of weapons-grade plutonium is enough for a bomb, but other sources put the figure at much less. However, the sort of efficiency required with a small amount requires computer-modeling and components testing. Without these techniques, it is

still possible to make a device, but it would require more material. Still, if a terrorist group is contemplating buying a nuclear device, it would be unwise to suppose that it cannot acquire enough fissile material. The technical knowledge needed depends on the weapon desired: an advanced plutonium device requires precision engineering, specialists, and the facilities for testing; but the design for a crude "gun-barrel" uranium bomb has been in the public domain for many years. But whether nuclear terrorism is made more likely because of this is far from clear.

HIGH-LEVEL NUCLEAR TERRORISM

One problem with high-level acts of nuclear terrorism is credibility. Terrorists have to prove to governments that they can carry out the acts they threaten. But both sides know that low-level threats can give almost as much leverage. For example, shortly after the World Trade Center bomb in February 1993, the FBI investigated allegations that Iranian terrorists were planning to release radioactive material in Manhattan. A successful attack would have been an ecological and human disaster. New York would have become a no-go zone, even without the use of a nuclear bomb. The FBI was also worried that the availability of fissile material from the former Soviet Union would result, not in a nuclear bomb, but in a nuclear-rich conventional explosion.

However, it is less likely that terrorists will opt for nuclear weapons. A disadvantage in using high-level nonconventional weapons such as nuclear, biological, or chemical ones, is that the effects are unpredictable and continue over a long period. This could bring the group involved bad publicity long after the event. The devastation caused by fertilizer bombs at the World Trade Center and at Oklahoma suggests that, for most groups, conventional weaponry is still the primary option. Furthermore, conventional weapons are cheaper, easier to access, harder for the authorities to detect and, given most terrorists' unfamiliarity with nonconventional weapons, probably safer to use. All of these factors militate very strongly against high-level nuclear terrorism, and to a lesser extent against any terrorist use of other weapons of mass destruction. However, the availability of fissile material has meant that the authorities have to take all threats seriously, giving the terrorist much leverage.

MOTIVATIONS FOR NUCLEAR TERRORISM

Terrorists have never used nuclear weapons for mass murder, one important reason being that they have yet to reach their killing potential using conventional weapons, and so do not need to be innovative. But terrorism is becoming increasingly lethal. In the 1980s, terrorist incidents rose by a third compared with the 1970s, but there was a twofold increase in fatalities.

One possible motivation for nuclear terrorism is if a group decides it has nothing to lose. If the group feels that it is in decline, dissolving into factions, or being usurped by another group, it might launch an act of nuclear terrorism to justify and call attention to its existence. Ideology erodes the moral constraints against terrorism, causing a gulf between "them" and "us." If an act, no matter how terrible, furthers the cause, then, by definition, it must be good.

Religious terrorists seem more likely to resort to nuclear weapons than other terrorist groups. Religion is a legitimizing force that can inspire total loyalty and commitment. Morally, it can justify, and even require,

indiscriminate violence. A religious group may want to remove sections of society unconstrained by the political, practical, or moral factors that limit others' actions. But other groups may also feel less constrained if it is a matter of carrying out a nuclear hoax or seizing a nuclear weapon rather detonating it.

Democratic governments are limited in their ability to deal with the problem of nuclear terrorism, but they have to take preventive measures. Soft targets, such as reactors or convoys carrying nuclear material, have been hardened against attacks. Some nations have emergency response plans, including, in the U.S., a highly skilled Nuclear Emergency Search Team (NEST), which gives technical and scientific support to the FBI. The team deals with all potential nuclear emergencies, and is equipped to search and recover lost or stolen materials and to deactivate any homemade devices.

However, since no target can ever be completely secure, the best means of countering nuclear terrorism lies with effective intelligence. Intelligence also has a role in promoting nonproliferation by ensuring compliance with agreements such as the Non Proliferation Treaty, between major nuclear powers.

The biggest problem with antinuclear terrorist policies in former Eastern-bloc states is a shortage of money, but the West is not able to make up this shortfall. Any such policy, therefore, must apply resources and influence wherever it is needed most. It is a far from ideal solution to this escalating problem.

Gavin Cameron

SEE ALSO:

THE DEBATE OVER THE ATOM BOMB; THE WORLD TRADE CENTER BOMBING; THE OKLAHOMA CITY BOMBING AND THE MILITIAS.

FURTHER READING

- Allison, G. *Avoiding Nuclear Anarchy.* Cambridge, MA: MIT Press, 1995.
- Leventhal, P. and Y. Alexander, eds. *Nuclear Terrorism: Defining the Threat.* Lexington, MA: Lexington Books, 1985.
- Leventhal, P. and Y. Alexander, eds. *Preventing Nuclear Terrorism.* Lexington, MA: Lexington Books, 1987.
- Norton, A. R. and M. H. Greenberg, eds. *Studies in Nuclear Terrorism.* Boston, MA: G. K. Hall, 1979.

TERRORIST FUNDRAISING

Every armed struggle and terror campaign, especially urban campaigns, needs money – to pay volunteers, to support families of activists taken prisoner, to buy guns and other weapons, to buy safe houses, to pay for international travel, and to fund propaganda. There are a number of methods that terrorist groups use to raise money – and if they are successful, vast amounts may be at their disposal.

At the beginning of campaigns, terrorists may raise income by legal means, such as contributions from supporters and fundraising at rallies. Until 1971, for example, the Provisional IRA in Northern Ireland existed on the charity of sympathizers and modest contributions. The few salaries given were tiny and bills were seldom paid on time. Volunteers spent much of their time looking not so much for more money as for any money. Even so, it was rare for the IRA to resort to illegal means during this very early period.

A few terrorist groups make enough money from their groups of supporters without having to resort to other methods. The Palestinians, with a relatively high level of education, prospered economically throughout the Middle East in the years after the 1948 Arab-Israeli War that established the state of Israel, and have invested wisely in the West. Legal Palestinian organizations can collect official grants and contributions from Palestinians worldwide, much of which may filter down to terrorist organizations. Similarly, the Tamil Tigers in Sri Lanka command large financial reserves,

freely given by the prosperous Tamil community throughout the world. Another valuable source of income for terrorists is money from a sympathetic state. It is estimated, for example, that Colonel Qaddafi of Libya gave $30 million to the Palestinian group Black September in the 1970s.

But although payments from sympathizers or sympathetic states are important sources of terrorist funding, they have their drawbacks. Paymasters usually demand some say in the activities of their clients, while funds may be cut off by a change of government or a change in public perceptions. Sooner or later, most organizations wish to control their own cash.

THE POWER OF THE GUN

Each movement undertakes the kind of crime that appeals to its membership. Rural insurgents seize foreigners and resort to banditry, or they hold up cars and take money from the passengers. Urban terrorists rely more on theft, fraud, and extortion.

Terrorist groups usually rationalize their illegal fundraising, explaining away extortion as "revolutionary taxes." In the 1970s, the military cells of the People's Revolutionary Army of Argentina (ERP) concentrated on bank robberies and kidnapping for ransom, crimes they euphemistically described as "expropriation." The group built up a central fund of $30 million from these activities. Ulrike Meinhof of the Baader-Meinhof Gang also justified bank robbery: "No one claims that bank robbery of itself changes anything. It is logistically correct, since otherwise the financial problem could not be solved at all. It is tactically correct, because it is a proletarian action. It is strategically correct because it serves the financing of the guerrilla."

Many terrorist organizations have dealt in drugs to gain money for operations. Latin American rebels such as Peru's Shining Path and some Palestinian factions – operating in regions rich in the crops needed for drugs such as cocaine and marijuana – are known for drug dealing. The terrorists explain, in ideological terms, their production, refinement, packaging, and shipment

KEY FACTS

● The German Baader-Meinhof terrorist group raised $185,000 from a two-month spate of six bank robberies in 1972.

● After "Carlos the Jackal," leader of international terrorism in 1970s Europe, kidnapped the Organization of Petroleum Exporting Countries (OPEC) oil ministers in Vienna in 1975, the Libyan head of state Colonel Qaddafi gave him $1.5 million.

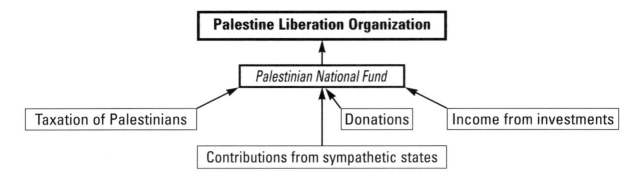

```
            Palestine Liberation Organization

              Palestinian National Fund

  Taxation of Palestinians      Donations      Income from investments

          Contributions from sympathetic states
```

The PLO gathers funds from a variety of sources, and some of this money finds its way to terrorists.

of drugs as a way of corrupting the enemy state, normally the market for their goods.

There is, of course, a danger that involvement in criminal activities involving large amounts of money may in some way corrupt a movement. Criticism of the Baader-Meinhof terror group in West Germany often focused on the lavish life-style that huge amounts of money gained from successful bank robberies gave its leaders. Indeed, one of its most important leaders, Gudrun Ensslin, was arrested while out shopping.

Other methods of using armed force to extort money include kidnapping and hijacking. These have the advantage that they are political acts as well as being effective for fundraising. Huge sums have been raised by kidnapping. In 1975, the Argentinian terrorist group the Montoneros claimed to have exchanged the lives of businessmen Jorge and Juan Born for $60 million in cash and $1.2 million in food and clothing for the poor. Hijacking too has raised enormous amounts. However, terrorists may well find that their need to find a safe haven means that they have to share the money with others. In 1972, the Lufthansa airline paid $5 million for the release of passengers from a hijacking carried out by the Popular Liberation Front of Palestine. However, the government of Yemen, in which the hijackers had landed the plane, demanded $1 million as their share of the booty.

In the long run, a movement may even set up its own "black economy," or illegal trading where no tax passes to the government. In Northern Ireland, both loyalist paramilitaries, such as the Ulster Defence Volunteers and the Ulster Freedom Fighters, and the Provisional IRA have "taxed" private enterprise and directly controlled commerce and manufacture. The fact that these illegal practices bleed the state legitimizes them in the terrorists' eyes. Smuggling, fraudulent welfare claims, pirate video cassettes, and tax-free liquor became common in Northern Ireland.

Once they get their hands on money, terrorist groups may then wish to invest it. Again, there may be a "virtuous circle" in which well-placed sympathizers advise on investments and help find ways to "launder" the money, or channel it into legal ventures to conceal its illegal origins. For its fifth revolt in India, the United Liberation Front of Assam collected hundreds of millions of dollars in local currency by "taxing" tea plantations, companies, and individuals. It spent money on arms and any money left over was legitimately invested in Calcutta. The insurrection continued until 1991 and only ended when the Indian government responded by clamping down on fund sources.

John Bowyer Bell

SEE ALSO:

HIJACKING AND KIDNAPPING; COLLABORATION BETWEEN TERRORISTS; THE BLACK SEPTEMBER ORGANIZATION, THE POPULAR FRONT FOR THE LIBERATION OF PALESTINE; RED ARMY FACTION: THE BAADER-MEINHOF GANG; NATIONALIST TERROR IN NORTHERN IRELAND 1976-1996.

FURTHER READING

- Adams, James. *The Financing of Terror.* New York: Simon and Schuster, 1980.
- Bell, John Bowyer. *The Secret Army: The IRA, 1916-1996.* New Brunswick, NJ: Transaction Publishers, 1996.
- Dobson, Christopher and Ronald Payne. *The Terrorists, Their Weapons, Leaders, and Tactics.* New York: Facts on File, 1979.

COLLABORATION BETWEEN TERRORISTS

During the 1940s and 1950s, the opportunities for collaboration between terrorist groups were limited. At this time, terrorism was mainly carried out by nationalist guerrillas in colonial wars. Nationalist terrorists were concerned with gaining independence for their own countries and tended not to have links with organizations fighting similar campaigns elsewhere. In the late 1960s, though, new types of terrorist groups began to emerge, and by the 1970s there was wide-scale collaboration between terrorists. It took many forms: moral support or help with propaganda; help in training or getting weapons; provision of safe havens or giving shelter; and, at the most extreme level, joint operations by terrorist groups.

The new terrorist groups that came to the fore in the late 1960s were of two main types. In western Europe and in Japan, social revolutionary terrorists appeared. In these places, young people were dissatisfied with traditional institutions and expressed this feeling in mass demonstrations in 1968. When these demonstrations failed to transform society, hard-line activists created small terrorist groups. The Red Army in Japan, the Red Army Faction in Germany, the Red Brigades in Italy, and Action Directe in France all aimed to destroy the fabric of Western society by violent means. In the Middle East, meanwhile, Palestinians were looking for ways to destroy Israel, whose territories they claimed as their own. In the late 1960s, Palestinian groups took their struggle beyond the Middle East, hijacking aircraft and attacking Israeli targets abroad to attract attention to their cause.

JOINT ATTACKS

The European/Japanese social revolutionaries and the Palestinian radicals had common enemies. Both hated Israel, the U.S., and capitalist society in general. Links were soon forged between European/Japanese organizations and the Palestinian groups and their supporters. It is widely believed that various Arab regimes used diplomatic bags to move terrorist money, information, and weapons around the world. In addition, training camps were established in South Yemen, where terrorists mingled to learn how to operate more effectively. Support was also forthcoming from communist regimes, such as East Germany.

During the 1970s, a number of terrorist attacks took place that could be described as joint operations. In March 1971, the Popular Front for the Liberation of Palestine (PFLP), run by George Habash, allied with French left-wing terrorists to blow up oil tanks in Rotterdam in the Netherlands. Habash's group went on to collaborate on several occasions with non-Palestinian organizations.

In November 1971, a new terrorist group shot and killed Jordanian prime minister Wasfi Tal. Called Black September, this mysterious group appeared to have no known base or leadership. But, in later years, it emerged that Black September was merely a front. The funds and recruits for individual missions came from Yasser Arafat's militant Fatah organization. In April

KEY FACTS

● In July 1976, a group of terrorists from the Popular Front for the Liberation of Palestine and the German Red Army Faction hijacked a plane from Paris to Tel Aviv with 246 passengers aboard.

● Libyan leader Colonel Qaddafi was suspected of instigating Black September's 1973 attack on the Saudi Arabian embassy in Khartoum, in which three diplomats were held hostage and later killed.

● At a conference of "anti-NATO" terrorist groups in Lisbon in June 1984, the Red Army Faction, Action Directe, and Belgian and Italian comrades formed the "Political-Military Front."

Hulton Getty Picture Collection

Israeli defense minister Moshe Dayan visits Tel Aviv's Lod airport after the massacre carried out by the Japanese Red Army, working with Palestinians.

1972, Black September sent the "Easter commando" into Israel to carry out attacks during the pilgrimage season. Led by Evelyne Barges, a Frenchwoman who had taken part in the PFLP operation in Rotterdam, the mixed nationality team arrived with toiletries impregnated with incendiary chemicals. But Israeli security forces were alert and arrested all the terrorists.

In May 1972, the PFLP called a meeting for Black September and other allies in an attempt to organize on an international scale. Three weeks later, the PFLP sent the Japanese Red Army on a kamikaze mission. Three Japanese terrorists opened fire in the lounge at Tel Aviv's Lod airport, killing 26 people and wounding 76. The event, which shocked the world, came to be known as the Lod massacre.

In September 1972, Black September gunmen massacred Israeli athletes at the Munich Olympics, but after 1973 the group took a less active part in terrorism. The network of contacts was established, however. The Popular Front (PFLP) and European terrorists carried on their campaign. Ilyich Ramírez Sánchez, known as "Carlos the Jackal," was a central figure, responsible for many acts of terrorism from late 1973 to late 1975. In the most spectacular event, Carlos led a gang of German Red Army Faction and Palestinians in a raid on the Organization of Petroleum Exporting Countries headquarters in Vienna in 1975. The terrorists held 11 oil ministers hostage.

In the 1980s, mutual support was still prevalent. In a coordinated action on July 9, 1986, the German Red Army Faction killed a top business director in Strasslach, near Munich, while the French Action Directe bombed the anti-terrorist base in Paris. Improved international security networks, however, were easing the situation for Western governments. The crisis came in 1977, when PFLP and Red Army Faction terrorists hijacked a Lufthansa airliner. German and British anti-terrorist troops combined to storm the aircraft. Thereafter, the threat ebbed. There is still collaboration among groups, notably those attempting to destroy Israel, such as the PFLP, Hizb'allah, and Hamas; there is also a network of Islamic fundamentalists. However, with the Soviet communist bloc's collapse and the decline in social revolutionary fervor in the West, terrorist links have become less important.

John Bowyer Bell

SEE ALSO:

THE BLACK SEPTEMBER ORGANIZATION; CARLOS THE JACKAL; ENTEBBE; RED ARMY FACTION: THE BAADER-MEINHOF GANG; JAPANESE TERRORISM.

FURTHER READING

- Cline, R. S. and Y. Alexander. *Terrorism: The Soviet Connection.* New York: Taylor & Francis, 1984.
- Ra'anan, U., R. L. Pfaltzgraff Jr., R. H. Shultz, E. Halperin and I. Lukes. *Hydra of Carnage: International Linkages of Terrorism – The Witnesses Speak.* Lexington, MA: Lexington Books, D. C. Heath, 1986.
- Sterling, Claire. *The Terror Network: The Secret War of International Terrorism.* New York: Reader's Digest Press, 1981.

CHAPTER SEVEN

The Psychology of Terrorism

What is it like to be a terrorist and why should anyone want to be one? It is easy to dismiss terrorists as mad fanatics, but in fact they need to be level headed to cope with long periods of meticulous planning in between bouts of violent activity. It is fascinating to gain some insight into the mindset of terrorists, especially those so completely convinced of their cause to act as suicide bombers. And what about those unfortunate enough to be victims of terrorism? Being bombed or held hostage by terrorists is the stuff of nightmares, but the legacy of dread after the ordeal can be even worse.

THE MINDSET OF THE TERRORIST

Blanket psychological explanations of terrorism are difficult to construct, because there are many varieties of terrorism and because all terrorist campaigns are different. The mindset of someone who acts alone to change the nature of society, such as the Unabomber in the U.S., is very different from a religiously inspired suicide bomber who is part of a nationalist movement in the Middle East. However, there are certain aspects of the terrorist mindset that can be examined. These include: the reasons for joining a terrorist movement; the relationship between individuals within a terrorist movement; the strength of terrorists' beliefs; how the developing psychology of a terrorist group affects the way terrorists operate; and how terrorists justify their acts.

These aspects are all important for the security forces who have to deal with terrorists. They try to build up a psychological profile so they can act against groups such as the left-wing Weathermen of the 1960s; they also try to predict where a group is likely to strike next and decide the best way of negotiating with hijackers who are demanding money and the release of imprisoned members of the group.

THE TERRORIST PERSONALITY

Psychological profiles of terrorists are often completely different from popular perceptions or media portrayals. When news of an outrage breaks, there is a tendency to describe the terrorist as being

mentally unbalanced, having broken the rules of "normal" behavior. In fact, the terrorist does follow rules – but not necessarily those followed by most of the population. And although the acts are violent, such extreme violence is common in other contexts – in warfare or self-defense, for example.

The starting point for the psychologist, then, is that the terrorist will usually have a relatively normal psychological profile. There is no common personality that is unique to those who commit acts of political violence; the violence occurs because people have chosen that path for a variety of reasons. The overwhelming majority of terrorists are not mentally ill, abnormal, psychopathic, or even especially predisposed to violence. An individual may be predisposed to terrorism, but it is unlikely that a terrorist group would knowingly choose an unstable individual. Such a person would be a loose cannon – a security threat that could endanger the whole group.

In any case, most terrorism involves long periods of inaction interspersed with short bouts of activity. The terrorist needs to be able to be patient during the long and dull planning stages of preparation for an attack. It is doubtful whether such inactivity would appeal to, or satisfy the needs of, a psychopathic personality.

A common reaction from politicians when a terrorist bomb has been planted is to label the bombers as "cowards." But this label does not aid our understanding any more than does assuming they are all abnormal. Terrorists are committed individuals, prepared to carry out often horrific acts, accepting that such deeds may have severe consequences for them personally. They perform violent actions because they believe in their cause. Terrorists may be unpleasant and they may be scared, but they are rarely cowards. If they were, it is unlikely that they would have become terrorists in the first place.

The reasons a person joins a terrorist group often define how effective they will be as terrorists, and how they will operate. It is difficult to make sweeping generalizations because people become terrorists for

---

SUMMARY

● Social revolutionary terrorists use Lenin as an icon – as leader of a minority group, he manipulated a favorable situation to reach power in 1917.

● "Ethnic cleansing" of Muslims by Serbs is an example of nationalism leading to terror.

● Terrorist groups may make it difficult for members to leave by making them commit some crime as a kind of initiation.

---

very different reasons. However, for many it seems to involve a desire to belong to an organization or to be part of a movement.

NATIONALISM AS A MOTIVATION

Nationalism is perhaps the strongest motivation to take up terrorism. The appeal of being part of a national group fighting for a homeland is very strong. Indeed, many of the most notorious terrorist acts of modern times have been part of nationalist struggles.

For example, the Tamil Tigers in Sri Lanka have proved impossible to control because of the powerful attraction of Tamil nationalism within the Tamil community – not only in Sri Lanka itself, but in southern India and worldwide as well. The appeal of nationalism in the human psyche is rooted in a deep emotional need to bond to a group. It can lead to acts

Popperfoto

The massacre of Palestinians at Sabra and Chatila in 1982 drove many to terrorism for revenge.

of great self-sacrifice, and to acts that have horrible consequences for those who get in the way.

The importance of nationalism is reinforced if it is linked to political or social repression or lack of opportunity. Thus, Palestinian terrorist groups have a ready-made pool of recruits in the refugee camps of Lebanon or the crowded tenements of Gaza. Many young Palestinians growing up in poverty know that their families were forced off their land in 1948, and may even have seen the Israelis launch air raids against refugee camps, or fail to prevent the massacre of Palestinians at the Sabra and Chatila camps in 1982. If someone is convinced that Israel will never permit the existence of a Palestinian state, joining a terrorist group becomes a chance to achieve more status and to strike a blow against the "oppressors." Acts of terrorism do not seem mad or irrational to a young Palestinian. The idea that Western-style democracy could persuade Israel to create a Palestinian homeland or stop the influx of Jewish settlers onto the west bank of the Jordan River may seem far more irrational.

Nationalism as a motive is often reinforced by religion. In Sri Lanka, Hindu Tamils fight against the majority Buddhist Sinhalese; in Northern Ireland, the IRA represents a Catholic nationalism fighting against Protestant loyalists; and in Bosnia, Catholic Croats, Muslim Bosnians, and Orthodox Serbs are the three competing parties.

However, religion may also outweigh nationalism as a motive. The most important examples of this are found in the Middle East. The mix of religion, particularly fundamentalist Islam, with nationalism has led to extravagant terrorist acts. Here, the idealism and intensity that characterize nationalism are mixed with the certainties of faith. This results in patterns of terrorism such as suicide bombings, where the bombers are convinced they will rest in paradise and so are prepared to detonate a bomb, for example, while sitting on a crowded bus in Tel Aviv.

A SENSE OF BELONGING

The certainties of nationalism and religion are not the motivation for all terrorists. Some become terrorists because of their commitment to a political cause or from a desire to revolutionize their society. The cause may be animal rights or a pro-life campaign; it may also be a desire to create a communist society.

It is in groups on the fringe of mainstream society that individuals who have problems adjusting to

TRH Pictures

Rioters form part of the support network for the IRA, stirring up conflict, as here at Bogside, a Catholic area of Londonderry, in the 1970s.

society, or who have an overwhelming need to belong, may find sanctuary. In psychological terms, individuals who are alienated from society or who feel worthless may find purpose and a positive identity within a terrorist group. Such people can abandon their individual responsibilities and embrace the collective identity of the group. Of course, not all terrorists are motivated simply by a need to belong; but there is a tendency within such groups to attract negative individuals. Nationalist or religious terrorist groups may also attract such individuals.

THE IMPORTANCE OF A GROUP NETWORK

It is important to remember that there are many different layers to terrorist organizations. Only a minority of

members plant bombs or take hostages. The majority are involved in setting up the network that enables such acts to be committed. They may be fundraisers, sympathizers providing safe houses, observers providing information, technicians making bombs, or politicians who direct terrorist activity or act as spokespeople. This network sustains the active terrorist who plants the bomb. The different members may have varying motives, and the strength of their commitment may be greater or lesser. Nevertheless, the network is crucial to bolstering morale.

It is useful, in this sense, to compare social revolutionary terrorists, such as the Baader-Meinhof gang (also known as the Red Army Faction) in West Germany, with nationalist terrorists such as the IRA in Northern Ireland. The Baader-Meinhof gang appeared to pose a major threat to West German democracy in the mid-1970s, primarily because its support seemed to be spread throughout German society, especially among young people and at professional levels. This was because there was a strong intellectual and political tide of opinion that Germany's liberal democracy was a failure. Many of the laws passed to limit the activities of the gang were actually aimed at curbing access of the captured terrorists to lawyers: the suicides of three of the gang's leaders in custody in 1977 were partly blamed on lawyers smuggling in guns. But the group lost power rapidly after the suicides. Neither the remaining terrorists nor their sympathizers were sufficiently motivated to sustain the campaign, partly because the broad and diffuse social background that had once seemed so threatening weakened the cohesiveness of the group.

The IRA, by contrast, has managed to sustain a campaign for more than 25 years, because the commitment of its active terrorists is aided by a background of support, both in Northern Ireland and in the Irish Republic, that hardly wavers. There is a widespread social and religious identity in the IRA and its supporters, as well as an intellectual and political common ground. Under these circumstances, the identity and prestige that the terrorist achieves through IRA membership is reinforced at every turn.

JUSTIFICATION OF VIOLENT ACTS

For most terrorists, membership of a group may be the main motive, but usually there is a progression through the ranks before a person can become a full-fledged terrorist. The decision to use violence, though, is not a sudden one. Eventually, the choice will be to participate in violence or to leave the group. This is a difficult choice for an individual who has become emotionally dependent on the group. A powerful need to belong and intellectual agreement with the aims of the group often leads to acceptance of violence.

The first step for an individual is to forget that others are being killed through some small action in which the individual has taken part. Once this step has been taken toward accepting violence, the individual may experience a sense of purpose and control over his or her life, and over the lives of others. Feelings of futility, for example from having been raised in the poverty of a refugee camp or from a disturbed adolescence, may be replaced by the feeling that he or she is an important person whom the authorities must respect.

Once in this position, other emotions such as excitement and stress become important. Some individuals, such as the international terrorist "Carlos the Jackal," are effectively "guns for hire" whose

Rex Features

The international terrorist "Carlos the Jackal" enjoys a night out with his girlfriend in 1994.

motives are emotional and financial not political. Aggression is another important motivation. In some terrorist groups, such as the Quebec Liberation Front, active in Canada during the 1970s, the aggressive instincts of certain individuals seem to have taken over as motivating factors for the group as a whole. However, it is important to recognize that these emotional factors become important only after the individual has become a member of the group.

PSYCHOLOGICAL IMPACT OF THE GROUP

A terrorist group offers members a counterculture, with its own norms and values into which it indoctrinates new recruits. The group tends to demand complete obedience and isolation from society. It strives for uniformity and cohesion, building the group on the political homogeneity of like-minded individuals, whose lives, goals, and futures are identified with the group. Often there are few alternatives to membership, and the main fear of group members is that they will be abandoned.

KEEPING THE GROUP TOGETHER

But this very cohesion and obedience of the group can cause its own problems. The first is that authorities trying to break up terrorist groups can offer the individual a positive route of escape. Once an alternative is shown to the attraction of belonging to a terrorist group, the terrorist may lose all loyalty.

A second problem is that groups tend to be self-perpetuating. The group and its survival become paramount; its aims become less so. Ultimately, violence may become an end in itself. Ironically, the achievement of political aims may actually be unpopular, because their achievement will result in the destruction of the group. The tendency is to reject any "compromise," and for the group to become ever more purist, and to use more absolutist rhetoric.

A third problem is that terrorist groups tend to become very authoritarian, even when their political aims ostensibly may be libertarian, and they clamp down hard on dissent. When members wish to leave, there can be furious internal feuds. If the individuals who leave set up similar but rival organizations, they may compete furiously and violently with the established group, claiming a greater degree of ideological purity for themselves.

The final problem is the way terrorists justify the horror that they inflict on others, especially on those who seem innocent. The sense of exclusiveness explains much of this. The group filters all news of external events that reaches its members, putting an interpretation on such events that emphasizes the evils of the enemy.

Terror group leaders tend to dehumanize any victims, accusing them of crimes and outrages. Alternatively targets are portrayed as being a structure or organization, not individual human beings with personal lives. Every effort is also made to associate the victims of the attack in some way with the enemies the terrorists are fighting.

Even when it is clear that one terrorist must carry out an attack, the cohesion of the group takes away the sense of personal responsibility. Membership of the group may heighten a terrorist's self-worth, but when it comes to deadly action, the terrorist becomes a foot soldier in a much wider movement.

In assessing the mindset of the terrorist, then, two factors stand out. The first is that terrorists usually have a very strong motivation, and the strength of this motivation is the principle key to why they are prepared to kill and maim. The second is that terrorists usually operate in close-knit groups that reinforce this motivation and encourage certain tendencies, particularly ones that enable individual terrorists to escape the intense guilt that they might otherwise feel for the consequences of their actions.

FUTURE HEROES?

The group reinforces belief in the cause by reminding the individual of how previous individuals have risen from being minor terrorists and bandits to great national icons or heroes.

It has become almost a truism of politics in the Third World, for example, that those imprisoned as criminals or accused of terrorism by colonial or other ruling powers have gone on to be regarded as fathers of their country: the most recent examples being Nelson Mandela in South Africa and Yasser Arafat in the Middle East. In the same way, there is no doubt that the success of Fidel Castro and Che Guevara in 1950s Cuba had an enormous effect on Latin America as a whole. For terrorists, a successful insurgency helps them to feel part of an historical process that will eventually condone the violent action.

Gavin Cameron

SEE ALSO:

CATEGORIES OF TERROR; HOSTAGE NEGOTIATIONS; SUICIDE BOMBING; CARLOS THE JACKAL; TERROR IN LEBANON 1980-1987; TAMIL TIGER TERROR IN SRI LANKA; RED ARMY FACTION: THE BAADER-MEINHOF GANG; IRA: ORIGINS AND TERROR TO 1976; NATIONALIST TERROR IN NORTHERN IRELAND, 1976-1996; TERROR BY QUEBEC SEPARATISTS.

F U R T H E R   R E A D I N G

- McKnight, G. *The Terrorist Mind*. Indianapolis, IN: Bobbs-Merrill, 1974.
- Taylor, M. and E. Quayle. *Terrorist Lives*. Washington, DC: Macmillan, 1994.
- Taylor, M. *The Fanatics*. Washington, DC: Brassey's, 1991.

VICTIMS OF TERRORISM

The ultimate target of terrorist activity is a large institution, such as a government or large corporation. The terrorist organization is trying to weaken this entity, either through direct strikes and intimidation or by shifting public opinion on a national or international basis. In the study of terrorism, the focus is generally on the terrorists themselves, their tactics, and the processes required by their opponents to arrest and prosecute them. Little attention is paid to the human victims of this violent process.

There are two types of victims of terrorist activity: selected targets, who are generally high-profile individuals, and random targets, who happen to be in the wrong place at the wrong time. Some people, including politicians, those holding high ranks in the military, and senior business figures, may be aware that they are at risk of terrorist attack or kidnapping; other people may simply be caught by chance, as is the case of victims of skyjacking or of terrorist bombs. But for both kinds of victims, the experience is a horrible ordeal, as the accounts of former hostages and others who have experienced terrorist attacks have shown.

Terrorists often choose as targets for assassination or kidnapping, well-known figures such as diplomats and other government officials, high-ranking military officers, or senior businesspeople. An attack on a

prominent personality invariably attracts a great deal of media attention for the terrorists. If successful, this type of attack can also serve to intimidate the terrorists' enemies – whoever they are. Well-known figures often have substantial personal security, and by outwitting or overpowering their safety measures, the terrorist organization can show its tactical intelligence and strength. By targeting a supposedly well-protected person, the terrorist organization is able to demonstrate the vulnerability of the enemy.

Terrorists carefully plan their attacks on high-profile targets and carry them out with military precision, often putting their human targets under surveillance for long periods. The assault itself may take place somewhere the victim is most comfortable: in his or her home, club, office, or car. Although familiar surroundings may provide victims with a sense of security, they are often easier marks because such places are readily identifiable. And when places are secluded, they are easier to watch without detection.

HIGH-PROFILE VICTIMS

Government officials and military personnel are often considered the most valuable trophies for terrorists. Governments immediately respond to the kidnapping of an official, which suggests a willingness to bargain. There are many examples of this kind of terrorist activity, including the kidnapping of former Italian prime minister Aldo Moro. The capture of Organization of Petroleum Exporting Countries (OPEC) foreign ministers in Vienna in December 1975 by Carlos the Jackal and Palestinian terrorists was a major coup.

Terrorist groups have also considered members of the business community to be legitimate targets. This form of terrorist action was particularly prevalent in the 1970s. In Latin America, the Tupamaros in Uruguay viewed Western businesspeople as representatives of capitalism, social injustice, and exploitation of the poor. Similarly in Europe, left-wing socialist groups such as the Red Army Faction in Germany and Action Directe in France kidnapped high-ranking executives.

KEY FACTS

● An individual who has been taken hostage or injured or killed in a bombing is the victim of terrorist activity, but may not be the principal target.

● When terrorists target public places, such as airports, shopping centers, and large offices, they can cause a great deal of material damage at the same time as endangering many innocent lives.

● The families and friends of victims of terrorist activity can be considered secondary victims, because they may also suffer emotionally and sometimes financially.

national, religious, or political group, rather than because of any individual notoriety. Victims selected for hostage-taking do not necessarily have any intrinsic value as individuals. They are simply a form of leverage – bargaining chips – with authorities.

An example of this kind of targeting is the kidnapping of foreign nationals in Lebanon in the 1980s. With the exception of Terry Waite, the British Anglican Church Envoy who had gone to Lebanon on a high-profile mission to negotiate for the release of other hostages, Hizb'allah and Islamic Jihad targeted their victims simply on the basis of their nationality. For example, Jean-Paul Kaufman and Michel Seurat, the two French citizens captured, were relief workers. The American Thomas Sutherland, kidnapped in 1985, was a professor. Terry Anderson, also American, was a reporter for CNN; he was captured in 1985 and spent more than seven years in captivity. Other hostages held in Lebanon were Irish, Greek, German, and Dutch.

The Palestinian Black September was able to capture world attention by taking Israeli athletes hostage at the 1972 Olympic Games in Munich. None of the athletes were well known as individuals – the terrorists targeted them simply because of their nationality. After 15 hours of grueling negotiations, the nine athletes died in a shootout (two died during the terrorists' assault on the athletes' housing area).

The kidnap and murder in Rome of Aldo Moro, former Italian prime minister, shocked the world in 1978.

The ransoms paid to gain the freedom of kidnapped businesspeople can fund a terrorist organization's other activities. In the 1970s, the Montoneros in Argentina were able to collect as much as $60 million for the release of two industrialists, the Born brothers.

Many organizations, both professional and governmental, have tried to limit the opportunities for terrorist groups. They have adopted rigorous security measures, including securing offices and personal residences, and using armored vehicles and security guards. They have also established survival training programs for employees and their families who are potential targets, particularly for those who travel abroad. This training can increase their chances of survival if they are taken hostage.

People can also be selected as targets for terrorist activity because of their affiliation with a particular

RANDOM ATTACKS

Terrorist groups can also choose their hostages randomly. Rather than targeting individuals, they target a place or a circumstance and select hostages from the pool of people who happen to be there. Terrorist groups often choose crowded public places in which there will be victims of both sexes and all ages, nationalities, races, and social strata. Large numbers of hostages guarantee safe passages for terrorists, and a range of nationalities gives a larger number of host governments to negotiate with.

The victims in situations like these tend to feel that they are totally innocent and not related in any way to the cause of the terrorist attack. However, George Habash, head of the radical Popular Front for the Liberation of Palestine (PFLP), declared that: "There are no innocent victims. All share the responsibility for society's wrongs. No one is innocent."

In the event of such a group hostage-taking, the pool of victims are confused and panicked, while the terrorists, who have generally meticulously planned

U.S. Marines carrying out the body of a victim after terrorists bombed a Marine base in Beirut, Lebanon, in 1983. The blast killed 241 American servicemen.

their attack, are more organized, which allows them to consolidate their control. Because the hostages are in all likelihood strangers to each other, their group dynamics will not threaten the terrorists.

SKYJACKING

Middle Eastern terrorists often turned to hijacking in the 1970s and 1980s, taking hostages on American, French, Greek, German, and other airlines. This kind of attack came to be known as skyjacking. According to the terrorist groups, the air carriers were targets because they were flying to Israel. Because of the threat of skyjacking, El Al, the Israeli national carrier, imposed tight security measures to defend itself against skyjacking and other forms of terrorist activity. It remains one of the safest airlines in this regard.

On a hijacked plane, as in any other public place, an individual passenger is the victim but not the target.

For innocent people taken hostage, this increases the shock. They often cannot understand why they have been caught up in the violence and the terror.

During this period of hijacking and skyjacking, Middle Eastern terrorists ranked Israeli passengers as the most desirable, with American officials and members of the U.S. military ranking second and third. Non-Israeli Jewish passengers were also singled out: for example, after hijacking the Italian ship *Achille Lauro* in October 1985, the Palestinian Liberation Front (PLF) murdered Leon Klinghoffer, a wheelchair-using elderly Jewish American.

Leftist European and Latin American terrorist groups have often selected American victims because of the significant role of the U.S. in world affairs, the likelihood of media coverage, and because of their perceptions of the American government as an evil world force. Terrorists may single out other nationals depending on the political climate. At various times, French, German, Italian, Spanish, and Turkish nationals have been singled out during hostage situations.

Women and children, when they are taken hostage, may be treated with greater leniency than other

Popperfoto

victims, often being released immediately. However, there are exceptions. In the skyjacking of a TWA flight in June 1985, Shiite Muslim terrorists initially mistreated the women and children on board, although they released them after a few days. In November 1985, Palestinian terrorists of the Abu Nidal Organization hijacked an EgyptAir flight from Athens to Cairo. On board they identified three American and two Israeli women. They shot and killed all five.

In general, though, few hostages are killed. They often endure verbal and physical abuse, torture, beatings, starvation, and sleep deprivation, however. Their physical survival is threatened daily. All victims of hostage-taking experience emotional and psychological traumas of the highest degree. They go through extreme feelings of fear, anxiety, disbelief, guilt, shock, and denial. After their release, many ex-hostages suffer post-traumatic stress syndrome, experiencing withdrawal, isolation, fear, and nightmares.

MASS ATTACKS

Many of the highest-profile terrorist actions of the late twentieth century have been attacks on public places. Examples include the bombing of the World Trade Center in New York City in 1992, the Oklahoma City bombing in April 1995, the chemical attack on the Tokyo subway in 1995, the IRA bomb in the town center of Manchester, England, in 1996, and the bombing in Atlanta, Georgia, during the 1996 Olympics. Sometimes such attacks have a high death toll, as in the Oklahoma City bombing. At other times, the terrorists issue an advance warning in order to minimize the deaths and injuries while still demonstrating their ability to cause large-scale destruction.

An attack on a public place guarantees immediate media coverage; in this way, a terrorist group can be assured of achieving publicity if nothing else. These attacks also put the government on the defensive. A successful assault on a public place shows that the authorities have failed in their responsibility to protect the citizenry. Therefore, the terrorists hope they will force the government to negotiate.

The terrorists involved carefully select the sites they attack, and part of the places' attraction is the combination of human and non-human targets. Frequent targets include airplanes and airports, trains, buses, stations or terminals, shopping centers, marketplaces, and large public buildings such as military barracks or government institutions. Terrorists may also choose to target hotels, restaurants, or bars that are frequented by foreigners, in an attempt to include people of several nationalities among the victims. The human victims, who may suffer injury or death in such attacks, are randomly selected, and their individual identities rarely have any significance to the terrorists.

SECONDARY VICTIMS

Family members and close friends of victims of terrorist attack also experience trauma. If the victim was targeted because of an affiliation with the government, the military, or a large business corporation, there is often a great deal of support for the family. This help comes in the form of counseling, financial support, information, and contacts. For example, the U.S. government provided support to the families of the 52 American hostages held in Iran from October 1979 until January 1981. In the 1970s, many corporations whose executives were kidnapped in Latin America paid high ransom to obtain release of their employees.

The families of victims who do not have that sort of professional affiliation rarely receive much support, either from the private or the public sector. Even the information they receive from the authorities may be limited. This was the experience of the families of the American hostages held in Lebanon. They complained about the limited assistance from the Reagan administration, saying that they were left in the dark. Many also suffered financial difficulties, particularly when the hostage was the family's primary wage earner.

R. Reuben Miller

SEE ALSO:

BOMBING OPERATIONS; HIJACKING AND KIDNAPPING; ASSASSINATION; THE WORLD TRADE CENTER BOMBING; THE OKLAHOMA CITY BOMBING AND THE MILITIAS.

F U R T H E R   R E A D I N G

- Carlson, K. *One American Must Die*. New York: Congdon & Weed, 1986.
- Jacobsen, D. and G. Astor. *Hostage: My Nightmare in Beirut*. New York: Donald I. Fine, Inc., 1991.
- Ochberg, F. M. and D. A. Soskis, eds., *Victims of Terrorism*. Boulder, CO: Westview Press, 1982.
- Kleinman, Stuart B. "A Terrorist Hijacking: Victim's Experiences Initially and Nine Years Later." *Journal of Traumatic Stress*, Vol. 2, No. 1, (Jan. 1989): 49–58.

HOSTAGE
NEGOTIATIONS

At the heart of almost all dealings with hostage takers is an impossible equation. The desire to secure the freedom of the hostages must be balanced against reluctance to concede to the terrorists' demands. Even if the demands are met, hostages may still be killed. Worse, surrender to demands may simply encourage the terrorists to strike again.

In practice, the response of most authorities falls between giving in to demands and refusing to talk. Negotiations lower tensions and help gain an understanding of the terrorists. In 1975, the British police commissioner Sir Robert Mark remarked on siege situations that: "Human life is of little importance when balanced against the principle that violence must not be allowed to succeed." But in reality, however, negotiators are sensitive to loss of life among hostages.

DEMANDS OF HOSTAGE TAKERS

Hostage taking has several advantages for the terrorist. It forces governments to negotiate with groups they refuse to recognize. Taking important hostages also gives the impression that the terrorists are a powerful force. In the 1970s, the Organization of Petroleum Exporting Countries (OPEC) enjoyed great power and prestige. Hence, when the terrorist "Carlos the Jackal," in reality Ilich Navas, took 11 OPEC ministers hostage in Austria in 1975, his prestige soared.

Hostage taking is less likely to alienate public support than are other terrorist acts like bombing since its main aim is not to harm its victims. If victims are hurt, the authorities may be partly blamed for not making greater efforts to negotiate a settlement.

Ransoming hostages can be a way for terrorists to raise funds. Japanese Red Army terrorists demanded and were granted a $6 million ransom after hijacking a Japanese Airlines plane in 1976. However, the main object of terrorists is to instill terror, and hostage taking can be very effective. In the 1980s, during a spate of abductions in Lebanon fear spread widely among Westerners in the Middle East. Normal business activity became almost impossible.

THE TECHNIQUES OF NEGOTIATION

Experience has shown that negotiating with hostage takers is a complicated task. The first step is to understand the psychology of the terrorists. Hostage takers' demands and their attitude about their survival and that of the hostages varies greatly. But negotiators find some common ground in different hostage situations.

The first problem is that terrorists may act apparently irrationally. For example, they may be willing to sacrifice their lives. So negotiators need to be aware that a promise of safety is not always a bargaining chip.

Even if shrouded in a ski mask, the hostage taker is an exhibitionist and one prepared to kill. Negotiators must respect, and even appear to give in to this characteristic, while they work on a psychological profile and examine alternative strategies.

During sieges, the authorities have some advantages, chiefly being able to supply or withhold various services. In 1984, British police cornered four Irish Republican Army (IRA) terrorists in a London flat, where the gunmen held hostage an elderly couple. The police withheld food for a week, then supplied some to gain better treatment of the hostages. Later, when the gunmen turned violent, police cut off electricity and other supplies. Eventually the terrorists released the hostages unharmed and surrendered.

Other pressures were used in the 1993 siege of the Branch Davidian religious cult at Waco. Eventually, the FBI played loud music and shined strong lights to deny

---

KEY   FACTS

● In 1974, in return for Patty Hearst's release, her father gave $2 million in free food to the poor.

● In London in 1980, gunmen killed two hostages in the Iranian embassy. The Special Air Service (SAS) stormed the building, saving the other 19.

● American Terry Anderson was held hostage in the Middle East for 2,455 days, from 1985 to 1991.

TRH Pictures/Associated Press

Palestinian terrorists, during their 1985 seizure of the cruise ship Achille Lauro, *executed the disabled American hostage Leon Klinghoffer.*

sleep to the cult members. Here, the pressure failed and the siege ended in heavy loss of life.

Negotiators need both to persuade hostage takers that their demands are being taken seriously, and to drag out negotiations. The longer the negotiations, the better the chance of hostage survival since a lengthy relationship between the terrorists and their hostages makes the captors less prepared to kill their captives.

Although their safety is of prime importance, hostages are rarely involved in negotiations. This assures that the hostage takers get the center stage, and helps avoid complications if the hostages act out of fear or desperation, or even side with their captors.

Negotiators also need to know what deal is politically acceptable to their own authorities. There is greater willingness to concede to armed criminals who take hostages, since they can be pursued by normal legal processes. Terrorists, however, have safe havens and, hence, giving them money increases their ability to undertake further attacks. In 1973, when Carlos

took Jewish emigrants hostage in Austria the authorities gave in to all demands. This ensured the hostages' release, but also encouraged Carlos to take hostage the OPEC ministers in Austria in 1975.

The history of hostage taking suggests that a firm response is best in the long run. But there is always a likelihood of compromise since there are few votes in body bags draped in the national flag.

John Collis

SEE ALSO:

HIJACKING AND KIDNAPPING; TERRORIST FUNDRAISING; THE MINDSET OF THE TERRORIST; JAPANESE TERRORISM.

FURTHER READING

- Antokol, Norman. *No One a Neutral: Political Hostage-Taking in the Modern World.* Medina, OH: Alpha, 1996.
- Howard, Lawrence, ed. *Terrorism: Impact, Response.* New York: Praeger, 1992.
- Livingston, Marius H., ed. *International Terrorism in the Contemporary World.* Westport, CT: Greenwood Press, 1978.

SUICIDE BOMBING

The sheer terror induced by suicide bombers was first experienced in modern times on Allied warships in the Pacific during World War II. It was clear that one aircraft crashing into a ship did more damage than a squadron of bombers. In October 1944, when Takijiro Onishi took command of the outdated Japanese air force in Manila, he made the deliberate crashing of aircraft an official tactic. The advantages of suicide or "kamikaze" attacks was plain: inexperienced pilots could carry out the raids, a kamikaze plane was hard to combat since it had to be destroyed to be stopped, and such heroism would boost Japanese morale and inspire terror in the enemy.

The pilots were assured of national honor. Onishi told them, "You are already gods." There was no shortage of volunteers. Between April 6 and June 22, 1945, 1,465 aircraft were spent in ten kamikaze raids. Before his mission, one pilot wrote: "Please congratulate me, I have been given a splendid opportunity to die."

HIZB'ALLAH AND RELIGIOUS TERROR

Suicide bombings have again emerged as a tactic, particularly by Islamic terror groups in the Middle East. Although there were sporadic Palestinian suicide bomb attacks during the 1970s, the tactic developed specifically in response to Israel's invasion of Lebanon in 1982. A Muslim terrorist group, Hizb'allah, formed a religiously motivated guerrilla army and began using suicide bombings against the Israelis. Iran's spiritual leader, Ayatollah Khomeini, greatly influenced Hizb'allah's ideology. As a leader of the Shiites, one of the two major branches of Islam, he reinterpreted the Shia cult of martyrdom. Islam bans suicide, but death in holy struggle assures the faithful a place in heaven. Muslim cleric Sheikh Fadlallah claimed: "There is no difference between dying with a gun in your hand and exploding yourself."

At the same time, a group called Islamic Jihad began to stage suicide bombings. In November 1983, an Islamic Jihad operative drove a truck full of explosives into the Israeli Border Guard headquarters in Tyre, waving and smiling as he passed a United Nations checkpoint. The bomber negotiated three concrete barriers and machine-gun fire to get his truck to the target. That he accomplished his goal shows the determination of suicide bombers to complete their missions. By the time the truck reached the headquarters, the driver was dead, but the vehicle continued on its course, knocking down the main gate. Troops blew up the truck before it reached the main building, but the damage was severe and 28 Israelis died. Also killed in the blast were 32 Palestinian and Shiite prisoners. Islamic Jihad knew these people were being held prisoner in the base but decided to martyr them.

In Beirut in 1983, suicide bombs at the U.S. embassy, U.S. Marine Headquarters, and French army headquarters caused huge loss of life and cataclysmic political effects. Young men exploding themselves sent shock waves through Lebanon. The multinational peacekeeping troops began to pull out. Israeli forces vacated most of Lebanon's southern territory after two years' occupation. Suicide bombing declined in Lebanon after 1985, but its effectiveness had been noted.

HAMAS TERROR

From the early 1990s, the Palestinian Islamic fundamentalist group Hamas employed its own brand of martyrdom. Hamas rejected the peace accord between Israel and the PLO reached in September 1993. Under

---

K E Y   F A C T S

● On October 23, 1983, suicide bombs struck bases of the U.S. and French marines in Beirut, Lebanon, killing 241 Americans and 58 French troops.

● It is estimated that 30 percent of Palestinians support the suicide bombers.

● The Tamil Tigers of Sri Lanka have used suicide bombs, both in vehicles and on motorcycles. Tamil Tigers carry cyanide capsules with which to commit suicide if captured. The group venerates its martyrs.

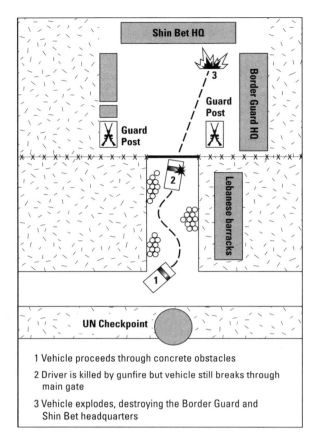

1 Vehicle proceeds through concrete obstacles

2 Driver is killed by gunfire but vehicle still breaks through main gate

3 Vehicle explodes, destroying the Border Guard and Shin Bet headquarters

The suicide attack on the Border Guard headquarters at Tyre, November 4, 1983, which killed 28 Israelis.

from the poorest sections of society, with few opportunities. Extreme Islamists exploit this sense of despair by recruiting them to their cause.

Bombers are usually in their mid-to-late teens. They are regarded by the community as old enough to be responsible for their actions, but too young to have wives and children. According to Hizb'allah, the volunteers are "married to death" and know their families will be supported by the terrorist organizations.

Hamas claims that suicide bombers repeatedly volunteer to be allowed to go to their death. Years of prayer in Hamas mosques lead young men to believe that, as martyrs in the struggle for an Islamic Palestine, they will go to heaven and receive posthumous adulation. One volunteer, a 15-year-old from Gaza City, claimed that, in heaven, "I would enjoy a special place near Allah (God), along with the prophets and saints. This vision so excited me that I could hardly bear the wait for my face-to-face encounter with Allah." Belief in heavenly reward, the ideology of revolutionary Islam, and conviction in the need for a Palestinian state sends young Muslims to their death.

The Israeli government has acknowledged that it has yet to find a way to combat such zealots. When technology confronts radical theology, not much can be done to deter individuals set on destruction.

Toby Dodge

SEE ALSO:

BOMBING OPERATIONS; THE MINDSET OF THE TERRORIST; TERROR IN LEBANON 1980-1987; THE ORIGINS OF PALESTINIAN ISLAMIC JIHAD; THE PALESTINIAN INTIFADA; PALESTINIAN ISLAMIC FUNDAMENTALISM; TERROR IN LEBANON 1987-1996; THE 1996 SAUDI TRUCK BOMB IN DHAHRAN; HIZB'ALLAH; HAMAS; ISLAMIC FUNDAMENTALIST TERRORISM IN EGYPT; TAMIL TIGER TERROR IN SRI LANKA.

the accord, a Palestinian National Authority was granted limited self-government in Gaza and the West Bank, previously defined as integral parts of Israel. In the weeks after Hamas rejected the accord, they staged suicide bombings. Bombs exploded in the Gaza Strip, including one on a bus carrying Israeli troops. In 1994, two bombs killed 13 Israelis in Jerusalem, and a crowded bus exploded in Tel Aviv, killing 21. A Hamas bomber killed himself and injured 13 Israelis in a Christmas Day attack in Jerusalem. Two Muslim suicide bombers killed 32 people in Jerusalem and Tel Aviv on March 3 and 4, 1996.

The suicide bombers of Hizb'allah and Hamas have much in common. They are motivated by a heady mix of nationalism, Islam, rhetoric, and poverty. Lebanese and Palestinian militants have suffered physically and economically under Israeli occupation. They are often

FURTHER READING

• Abraham, A. J. *The Warriors of God: Jihad and the Fundamentalists of Islam.* Bristol, IN: Wyndham Hall Press, 1989.

• Krammer, Martin. "Sacrifice and Fratricide in Shiite Lebanon." *Terrorism and Political Violence* 3, no. 3 (November 1991).

• Reich, Walter. *Origins of Terrorism: Psychologies, Ideologies, Theologies, States of Mind.* New York: Cambridge University Press, 1990.